Dynamics of the Arab–Israel Conflict

Michael Brecher

Dynamics of the Arab–Israel Conflict

Past and Present: Intellectual Odyssey II

Michael Brecher
McGill University
Montreal, Québec, Canada

ISBN 978-3-319-83771-0   ISBN 978-3-319-47575-2 (eBook)
DOI 10.1007/978-3-319-47575-2

© The Editor(s) (if applicable) and The Author(s) 2017
Softcover reprint of the hardcover 1st edition 2017
This book was advertised with a copyright holder in the name of the publisher in error, whereas the author holds the copyright.
This work is subject to copyright. All rights are solely and exclusively licensed by the Publisher, whether the whole or part of the material is concerned, specifically the rights of translation, reprinting, reuse of illustrations, recitation, broadcasting, reproduction on microfilms or in any other physical way, and transmission or information storage and retrieval, electronic adaptation, computer software, or by similar or dissimilar methodology now known or hereafter developed.
The use of general descriptive names, registered names, trademarks, service marks, etc. in this publication does not imply, even in the absence of a specific statement, that such names are exempt from the relevant protective laws and regulations and therefore free for general use.
The publisher, the authors and the editors are safe to assume that the advice and information in this book are believed to be true and accurate at the date of publication. Neither the publisher nor the authors or the editors give a warranty, express or implied, with respect to the material contained herein or for any errors or omissions that may have been made.

Cover image © Nir Alon / Alamy Stock Photo

Printed on acid-free paper

This Palgrave Macmillan imprint is published by Springer Nature
The registered company is Springer International Publishing AG
The registered company address is: Gewerbestrasse 11, 6330 Cham, Switzerland

In loving memory of my wife, Eva Danon, and for our daughters, Leora, Diana, and Seegla, who experienced, from their early years, the Arab–Israel conflict as a compelling part of their lives.

BOOKS BY MICHAEL BRECHER

THE STRUGGLE FOR KASHMIR (1953)
NEHRU: A Political Biography (1959)
THE NEW STATES OF ASIA (1963)
SUCCESSION IN INDIA: A Study in Decision-Making (1966)
INDIA AND WORLD POLITICS: Krishna Menon's View of the World (1968)
POLITICAL LEADERSHIP IN INDIA: An Analysis of Élite Attitudes (1969)
THE FOREIGN POLICY SYSTEM OF ISRAEL: Setting, Images, Process (1972)
ISRAEL, THE KOREAN WAR AND CHINA (1974)
DECISIONS IN ISRAEL'S FOREIGN POLICY (1975)
STUDIES IN CRISIS BEHAVIOR (ed.) (1979)
DECISIONS IN CRISIS: Israel 1967 and 1973 (with Benjamin Geist) (1980)
CRISIS AND CHANGE IN WORLD POLITICS (with Patrick James) (1986)
CRISES IN THE TWENTIETH CENTURY: Vol. I, Handbook of International Crises (with Jonathan Wilkenfeld) (1988)
CRISES IN THE TWENTIETH CENTURY: Vol. II, Handbook of Foreign Policy Crises (with Jonathan Wilkenfeld) (1988)
CRISIS, CONFLICT AND INSTABILITY (Vol. III of CRISES IN THE TWENTIETH CENTURY) (with Jonathan Wilkenfeld) (1989)
CRISES IN WORLD POLITICS (1993)
A STUDY OF CRISIS (with Jonathan Wilkenfeld) (1997)

A STUDY OF CRISIS [CD Rom edition] (with Jonathan Wilkenfeld) (2000)
MILLENNIAL REFLECTIONS ON INTERNATIONAL STUDIES (ed. with Frank P. Harvey) (2002)
REALISM AND INSTITUTIONALISM IN INTERNATIONAL STUDIES (ed. with Frank P. Harvey) (2002)
CONFLICT, SECURITY, FOREIGN POLICY, AND INTERNATIONAL POLITICAL ECONOMY (ed. with Frank Harvey) (2002)
EVALUATING METHODOLOGY IN INTERNATIONAL STUDIES (ed. with Frank P. Harvey) (2002)
CRITICAL PERSPECTIVES IN INTERNATIONAL STUDIES (ed. with Frank P. Harvey) (2002)
INTERNATIONAL POLITICAL EARTHQUAKES (2008)
THE WORLD OF PROTRACTED CONFLICTS (2016)
POLITICAL LEADERSHIP AND CHARISMA: Intellectual Odyssey I (2016)
DYNAMICS OF THE ARAB–ISRAEL CONFLICT: Intellectual Odyssey II (2017)

Preface

The elusive, largely unresolved Arab–Israel conflict, except for the Egypt–Israel and Israel–Jordan segments, is among the longest and most severe enduring interstate conflicts in world politics during the twentieth and early twenty-first centuries. It has generated 30 international crises and 9 wars since 1948, the latest between Israel and the *Hamas*-ruled Gaza Strip in July–August 2014. Moreover, while peace agreements have terminated the formal interstate conflicts between Egypt and Israel (1979) and between Israel and Jordan (1994), the core dispute—between Israel and the Palestinians—remains unresolved. Furthermore, it was reactivated in 2015–16, in an informal, unorganized replica of two earlier Palestinian *Intifadas* (Uprisings) against Israel's occupation of the West Bank and East Jerusalem since 1967.

Like most *interstate* protracted conflicts (PCs), the configuration of this PC is *multilayered, multidimensional,* and *multi-issue.* This will become evident from the analysis of crisis management and the myriad of failed attempts to achieve conflict resolution, from 1949 to 2014, later in this book. I begin with a brief Introduction on "Many Paths to Knowledge" about this PC, followed by an overview of its deep-rooted origins.

Acknowledgments

This book has benefited greatly from the comments of the following readers, who devoted time and care to its contents: two friends and colleagues, Jonathan Wilkenfeld and Patrick James, and Diana Brecher, Eric Robbins, and Steven Finestone. McGill students, Sean Cohen, Cody Levine, and Adam Strychaluk, contributed valuable research assistance. The Editor and Editorial Assistant for International Relations at Palgrave Macmillan USA, Dr. Anca Pusca and Anne Schult, were very generous in their time and attention from the moment the typescript was submitted to them, as were Baghyalakshmi Jagannathan, Rajkumar Sharon, and Rachel Taenzler, the Springer production team.

Contents

1	**Introduction: Many Paths to Knowledge**	1
2	**Historical Roots**	9
	Four Levels of Conflict	9
	Clash of Belief Systems	9
	Competing National Goals	10
	Intercommunal Rivalry	10
	Discordant British Pledges	11
	Political and Military Acts, 1933–1947	12
	Transformative Event—UN Partition Resolution 181	13
3	**Struggle for Jerusalem**	15
	Onset	15
	Decisions	17
	Decision-Makers	20
	Attitudinal Prism-Perceptions	21
	Decision Process	24
	Implementation	31
	International Boycott	32
4	**Arab–Israel Perceptions**	35
	Israel–Palestine	35
	National Identity	35

Attitudinal Prisms	36
Israel–Syria	39
Attitudinal Prisms	39
Arab–Israel Perceptions of the Balance of Military Capability	41

5 Israeli Leaders' Perceptions of the Arabs, the Arab–Israel Conflict, and Peace: Formative Generation, 1948–77   43
Ben-Gurion and Sharett: Two Competing Perceptions   43
Levi Eshkol: Changing Views of the Arabs   47
Golda Meir: Ben-Gurionist Image of the Arabs   48
Yigal Allon and Moshe Dayan: Sabra *Views of the Arabs and Israel's Strategic Goals*   48
Abba Eban: Sharettist Views of the Arabs, the Middle East, and Peace   51
Shimon Peres: Ben-Gurionist Views of the Arabs and the Middle East   51

6 Encounters with Arab Intellectuals and Officials: Views on Israel, Palestine, and Their Conflict (1975)   53
Mohammed Sayeed Ahmad: Commentator, Al-Ahram Center, Cairo   54
Osama Al-Baz: National Security Advisor to Presidents Sadat and Mubarak   66
Boutros Boutros-Ghali: Professor of International Law, Cairo University; Later, Minister of State for Foreign Affairs, Egypt, and UN Secretary-General (1992–1996)   77
Al-Ahram Center for Political and Strategic Studies   100
Disquieting Reaction in Israel   115

7 Conflict-Sustaining Acts in the Arab–Israel Protracted Conflict   117
Violence   117
Political Hostility   121
Economic Discrimination   124
Verbal Hostility   126

8	**Crises Within the Arab–Israel Protracted Conflict: 1948–2014**	**127**
	Evidence on Crisis Triggers and Crisis Management	127
	Violent Crises (Less than Full-Scale War) (15)	127
	Crises That Escalated to Full-Scale War (9)	133
	Nonviolent Crises (6)	141
9	**The Arab–Israel Military Balance: 1967 and 1973**	**145**
	Military Lineup in 1967	145
	Arab Forces	145
	Israel Forces	146
	Forces Committed on 5 June 1967	146
	Qualitative Balance	148
	Military Lineup in 1973	149
	Arab Forces	149
	Israel Forces	152
	Qualitative Balance	152
	Notes	153
10	**Israel's Behavior in the 1967 and 1973 Wars: Overall Findings**	**157**
	Decisions, Decision-Makers, Decision Process: Prewar Crisis Period (17 May–4 June 1967)	157
	Decisions	157
	Decision-Makers	157
	Decision Process	160
	Phase I: Apprehension and Mobilization (17–22 May)	160
	Wednesday, 17 May	161
	Thursday, 18 May	162
	Friday, 19 May	164
	Saturday, 20 May	166
	Sunday, 21 May	167
	Monday, 22 May	168
	Phase II: Delay and Diplomacy (23–28 May)	170
	Tuesday, 23 May	170
	Wednesday, 24 May	176
	Thursday, 25 May	180

Friday, 26 May	183
Saturday, 27 May	188
Sunday, 28 May	192
Phase III: Preemption (29 May–4 June)	197
Monday, 29 May	197
Tuesday, 30 May	198
Wednesday, 31 May	201
Thursday, 1 June	202
Friday, 2 June	204
Saturday, 3 June	208
Sunday, 4 June	210
Decisions, Decision-Makers, Decision Process: Before and During October Yom Kippur Crisis-War (5–26 October 1973)	214
Decisions and Decision-Makers	214
Decision Process	214
Notes	244

11 Evidence on Conflict Resolution: Partial Agreements and Overall Failed Attempts, 1937–2014   277

Peel Commission Report (7 July 1937)	277
UN General Assembly Partiton Resolution (29 November 1947)	278
UN Conciliation Commission for Palestine (UNCCP) (Better Known as the Palestine Conciliation Commission [PCC]), Lausanne Conference (27 April–12 September 1949)	278
UN Security Council Resolution 242 (22 November 1967)	280
Jarring Mediation (23 November 1967–March 1971)	281
Camp David Summit I and Egypt–Israel Peace Agreement (5 September 1978–26 March 1979)	282
Israel–Lebanon Abortive Agreement (17 May 1983)	284
Arafat Statement at Stockholm News Conference and Address to UN General Assembly (8 and 13 December 1988)	285
Madrid Peace Conference (30 October–1 November 1991)	286
Oslo I Accord (20 August and 13 September 1993)	287
Gaza–Jericho Agreement (Also Known as the 1994 Cairo Agreement) (4 May 1994)	288
Oslo II Accord (28 September 1995)	289
Hebron Agreement (17 January 1997)	290

Wye River Memorandum (23 October 1998) 291
Sharm el-Sheikh Memorandum (4 September 1999) 291
Camp David Summit II (11–25 July 2000) 291
    Territory 292
    East Jerusalem 292
    Palestinian Refugees 293
    Security 293
Clinton Parameters (23–27 December 2000) 294
    Territory 294
    Jerusalem 294
    Palestinian Refugees 294
    Security 295
    End of the Conflict 295
Taba Talks (21–27 January 2001) 296
Arab Peace Initiative (27 March 2002) 299
Road Map for Peace (24 June 2002) 301
Olmert Peace Plan (September 2008) 303
Israel–Palestine Peace Talks—Kerry Mediation (29 July 2013–29 April 14) 305
Causes of Israel–Palestine and Overall Arab–Israel Deadlock in Quest of Conflict Resolution 306
Arab–Israel PC: Causes of Conflict Resolution 308
    Exhaustion 309
    Balance of Capability 310
    External Pressures 311
    Domestic Pressures 311
    Reduction of Discordance Among Basic Objectives 312
    Decline in Conflict-Sustaining Acts 313

12 Assessments of the Way Out 315
1972: Brecher, The Foreign Policy System of Israel, pp. 562–565 318
1975: Dialogue in Cairo 319
1975: Israel Council for an Israeli–Palestinian Peace 321
1977: Lessons from the Begin–Sadat Jerusalem Encounter 322
2001, 2016: Principles and Proposals for Negotiating Peace and Conflict Resolution 323

13 Israel at 68: Beneath the Glitter 329
Tributes 329
State of the Economy 331
Poverty 332
Inequality 334
Israel's Senior Citizens 336
Education 337
Other Societal Changes 340
Corruption 341
Censorship 342
Malpractice of Politicians 344
Treatment of Arab Israelis 349
Renewal of Turmoil, 2015–16 355
Disenchantment 358
Notes 359

Bibliography 365

Name Index 387

Subject Index 395

List of Tables

Table 9.1	Arab military forces, early June 1967	146
Table 9.2	Israel armed forces, May 1967	147
Table 9.3	Egypt, Syria, and Jordan air forces, early October 1973	149
Table 9.4	Egypt and Syria naval forces, early October 1973	149
Table 9.5	Arab land forces on Egyptian front, early October 1973	150
Table 9.6	Arab land forces on Syrian front, early October 1973	150
Table 10.1	Israel's decisions: May–June 1967 crisis-war	158
Table 10.2	Israel's decision-makers, 1967 crisis-war	159
Table 10.3	Israel's decisions and decision-makers, 1973 crisis-war	215
Table 10.4	Israel's decisions, decision-makers, and decision process, 6 October 1973	219
Table 10.5	Estimated Arab military losses	243

CHAPTER 1

Introduction: Many Paths to Knowledge

Academe is perceived by many as an ivory tower, a place to which scholars retreat from the real world of stress and strife. To some members of the fraternity, however, it provides a crucial setting in which intellectual resources can be mobilized to attack the great ills that beset the planet—poverty, disease, injustice, and conflict, crisis, and war. To a young Canadian student in the mid-late 1930s and early 1940s, world politics seemed distant yet compelling. The first awareness from afar was the Spanish Civil War (1936–39) and the Munich Crisis (1938), symbols of Western self-delusion and surrender, events that were puzzling and troubling then and long after. The years of death and destruction on a cataclysmic scale that followed, World War II, as evil forces swept through Europe and Asia challenging the foundations of a civilization which, in word if not always in deed, placed a high value on human and national rights, strengthened an emerging conviction that *systematic knowledge of interstate crises, international conflicts,* and *wars* could contribute, however modestly, to the restoration and enhancement of these values.

An initial immersion in South Asia—three intense periods of field research (1951–52, 1955–56, 1964–65) and a dozen shorter visits, from 1951 to 1974—had several intellectual spin-offs for the study of world politics. Perhaps the most notable was an enduring intellectual interest in the concepts and substance of *international systems, subordinate systems,* and *protracted conflicts* (PCs). Yet it was not until a no-less deep encounter with the Arab–Israel conflict in the 1960s, 1970s, and 1980s that the

© The Author(s) 2017
M. Brecher, *Dynamics of the Arab–Israel Conflict*,
DOI 10.1007/978-3-319-47575-2_1

significance of *interstate Protracted conflict* as a profound contextual influence on world politics became a major focus of later research (my article in 1984, and books in 1997 [with Jonathan Wilkenfeld] and 2016).

Another benefit of *field research* was an early recognition that world politics is not synonymous with relations among the major powers. Those who ventured forth from the ivory tower could not but be struck by the existence of another domain of interstate conflict and cooperation which, although on the periphery of the *dominant system* of international politics in terms of geography, military power, and economic development, is an essential component of a comprehensive paradigm of world politics. *Polycentrism* and the dispersion of decisional centers from the early 1960s onward merit recognition in a restructuring of a world politics paradigm. The failure to do so adequately led to grave distortions and lacunae in the dissection of global politics in the late twentieth and early twenty-first centuries (Brecher and Patrick James 1988; Brecher, James, and Wilkenfeld 1990; Brecher 2008).

My first direct contact with *Israel's foreign policy system* and the *Arab–Israel conflict* was on the diplomatic periphery. In the summer of 1948, toward the end of graduate studies at Yale, I served as a research assistant to Abba Eban, then beginning an illustrious career as the "Voice of Israel" at the United Nations and, later, everywhere. A one-year sojourn in Israel's Foreign Ministry (1950–51) provided insight into the making of foreign policy and the intensity of the conflict, with its multiple spillovers to world politics. Twenty-five years later, on the political periphery, I helped to draft the first manifesto of the Israel Council for an Israeli–Palestinian Peace, along with then leaders of the Israeli peace movement; we were among the first to advocate a two-state solution to the PC. Few listened at the time, and a resolution of this conflict remains elusive.

My systematic and systemic research into Israel's foreign policy did not begin until the mid-1960s: the research began after the guiding construct of a *foreign policy system* had been developed. In that quest, the major influences were: David Easton's input–output model (1957); Snyder, Bruck, and Sapin's foreign policy decision-making framework (1962); and the Stanford's perception–action model (Holsti, North, and Brody 1968). Moreover, Harold and Margaret Sprout's distinction between the operational and the psychological environment (1965), along with Kenneth Boulding's (1956) and Ole Holsti's (1965) work on images, seemed to me a necessary corrective to the exclusive focus on objective reality that pervaded the comparative foreign policy literature at the time. My study of Nehru's and Krishna Menon's worldviews (1959, 1968), as well as that of Israel's political decision-makers (1972, 1974–75, and 2016), was an attempt to shed light on the perceptual dimension of foreign policy analysis.

Living in the Middle East for most of each year from 1969 to 2013 made one acutely sensitive to the pervasiveness of *crisis, conflict*, and *war*. Apart from the earlier Arab–Israel upheavals in 1948–49 and 1956–57, a brief span of six years, 1967–73, witnessed three additional outbursts of major violence—the June-Six-Day War in 1967, which transformed the power constellation of the Middle East subordinate system, with Israel at its apex; the War of Attrition in 1969–70; and the October-Yom-Kippur War in 1973–74, with its near-superpower direct confrontation, including the implied threat of resort to nuclear weapons. Ironically, it was the 1973–1974 Egypt-Israel War that created the auspicious condition of accommodation that culminated in the Egypt–Israel peace agreement in 1979.

This PC, in a volatile subordinate international system, now posed an even greater danger to global stability than in the past. Yet, ironically, both the 1967 and 1973 wars facilitated important developments in the quest for peace: the 1967 war catalyzed a major UN effort to resolve the conflict, Security Council Resolution 242, which envisioned a trade of "land for peace"—Israel's withdrawal from the occupied West Bank in exchange for the Palestinians conceding formal peace between Israel and Palestine—as the optimal path to peace in the Arab–Israel domain; and the 1973 war set in motion a process that culminated in two Arab–Israel peace agreements—between Egypt and Israel in 1979, which terminated the most crucial dimension of this multistate PC, and more than a decade later, between Israel and Jordan in 1994.

The first step on the long road to effective crisis management and conflict resolution of the Arab–Israel PC, and one to which systematic research on world politics could contribute, was the accumulation of reliable knowledge about Arab–Israel crises to be managed and their conflict to be resolved in order to prevent runaway turmoil. How to proceed? There was, and is, no simple and straightforward answer, for contending scholars and schools of thought praise their own, and decry other methods and approaches to the generation of knowledge about this or any aspect of world politics. Endless debates have occurred between advocates of *a priori theorizing* versus *empirical data-gathering, quantitative* versus *qualitative* methods, and *aggregate data analysis* versus *comparative case studies*. As a convinced pluralist in the matter of research strategy, there is much wisdom and relevance in the Hindu dictum that there are many paths to truth and that no single faith (school) has a monopoly over truth. Indeed, the debates over method seemed to be sterile, from the Bull–Kaplan exchange (1966) to the more mutually tolerant discussion by Bueno de Mesquita, Krasner, and Jervis (1985).

Returning to the enduring controversial issue of *paths to knowledge about the Arab–Israel conflict*, as for Political Science and International Relations generally, theory clearly occupies a central place, whether deductively or inductively derived. Although the former is accorded higher status in the natural science enterprise, the evidence thus far in the study of world politics is mixed; and, in any event, the choice depends upon a researcher's intellectual disposition. Stated differently, the issue of whether formal theory must precede—and take precedence over—empirical investigation (e.g., espoused by Bueno de Mesquita, Young, Zinnes, and all game theorists) or the reverse (e.g., Russett, Singer, and all Correlates of War Project researchers) remains unresolved. Others, I among them, advocate a *dual path to knowledge, framing a priori models and hypotheses and a framework/taxonomy to guide empirical inquiry, leading to the testing of model-derived hypotheses and their refinement or abandonment as the evidence dictates, further testing, and so on.*

The stimulus is often, if not always, a puzzle. In this book, *core questions* include the following: When did the Arab–Israel PC begin? What conditions triggered its *onset*? What have been the *phases* of this PC, the time frame of its *escalations*? What have been the *causes of* its *persistence* during the past near-seven decades, even longer in the pre-1948 historical experience? Who have been the *principal adversaries*, both states and nonstate actors? What was the *role of violence* and acts of *political hostility* in sustaining this conflict? What have been the *discordant objectives* of the adversaries, and have their objectives changed over time? What *conditions* generated formal resolution of the Egypt–Israel and Israel–Jordan dimensions of this multistate international conflict? What are the *necessary conditions for overall resolution* of the Arab–Israel PC? A quest for credible answers to these and other questions about a complex protracted international conflict will be evident throughout this book.

What *path(s) to knowledge*, that is, *which method(s) of analysis*, should be pursued in an attempt to answer the questions posed above and contribute to an understanding of the Arab–Israel conflict? As indicated above, a *two-track strategy* will be utilized, flowing from a conviction about the *inherent merit of methodological pluralism*. One path is *in-depth case studies* of perceptions and decisions by senior decision-makers of a single state, using a micro-level model designed to guide research on state-level behavior in PCs and to facilitate rigorous comparative analysis of findings about state behavior in the military-security issue-area (Brecher 2016).

In terms of policy relevance to the future of world politics, the aim is to use the findings from this knowledge to enhance the quality and effectiveness of crisis management; that is, at the micro level, to enable decision-makers to cope more effectively with crises, and, at the macro level, to reduce the likelihood of escalation of crises to full-scale war, with potentially grave consequences in a world saturated with nuclear and other weapons of mass destruction. In the largest sense, the objective is to apply the lessons of history to the advancement of international peace and world order.

Have these goals been achieved? Certainly not yet. Can they be attained? Unlikely, because of the enormous divide between the academic world and the foreign policy–national security decision-making élite. The latter, with few exceptions, regard academic research on world politics as irrelevant ("ivory tower"), inaccurate ("scholars don't see the cables"), and unrealistic (systematic, where decision-making is chaotic and personal). Academic research allegedly suffers from all of these shortcomings combined.

I personally encountered this ill-founded view in three states, namely, Canada, India, and Israel, the last two profoundly affected by the stress of a PC. I have been chided for reconstructing decision processes more systematically than they occurred in reality. "Your facts are correct," I would (sometimes) be told by professionals from the Foreign Ministry and the Prime Minister's Office, "but the way the decisions you write about were reached is much sloppier, more haphazard and disorganized than you make out." To my reply that one task of the research scholar is "to make order out of disorder," the rejoinder is invariably, "Michael, you don't understand." Parenthetically, I have always placed a high value on *interviews* with decision-makers (preferably when they are no longer in office) as a vital path to knowledge about the decision-making process and about specific decisions. Treated with care, checked against other primary sources, when available, for consistency, plausibility, and reliability, they are indispensable for decision-making analysis.

Interviews can illuminate in several respects. First, *they add a crucial human dimension* to an outsider's understanding of the decision process. One illustration will suffice. During extended interviews with David Ben-Gurion in 1966, three years after he resigned for the last time as Israel's Prime Minister and Defense Minister, I asked why he had made a provocative speech in the *Knesset* (Israel's parliament) on 7 November 1956, soon after Israel's triumphant Sinai Campaign (Suez War). In that address, the Prime Minister figuratively tore up the 1949 Armistice Agreement with Egypt—it is "dead and buried," he said. He challenged Egypt's sovereignty over the Sinai Peninsula. He implied that Israel would not withdraw its forces from Sinai. And he rejected in advance the stationing of any foreign or international military force in the area. In so doing, he alienated Israel's friends around the world, including the United States, which threatened to terminate all aid to Israel, governmental and private, and to support UN sanctions against Israel. When asked why he spoke so harshly and bluntly that day, he paused for a moment and replied, slowly: "You see, Mr. Brecher, the victory was too quick; I was drunk with victory!" Within a day he was to pay heavily for his "victory" speech: massive pressures from abroad compelled him to agree, earlier than planned, to Israel's withdrawal from Sinai and Gaza.

More generally, interviews with decision-makers help to clarify and elaborate facts and themes, often important pieces in a puzzle, which may be barely mentioned in documents or other written sources. They thereby shed fresh light on the complex process through which politicians and officials cope with a problem for decision. Of course, the danger of distortion, either consciously, to strengthen one's "place in history," or as a result of a lapse in memory, should lead to caution in the use of interview materials. Yet, even to those disposed to formal theory alone, this dimension of research would not undermine the quality of their theorizing or the validity of their theories.

In the context of divergent perspectives by scholars and national security officials on the value of interviews as a *path to knowledge* about perceptions and behavior by foreign policy decision-makers, sometimes with serious consequences, an incident relating to Arab–Israel peace merits attention. In the summer of 1975, I participated in a study mission of North American academics to Egypt, Jordan, Syria, and Israel. While in Cairo, I interviewed members of the Egyptian political, bureaucratic, military, and intellectual elites and was struck by a common theme communicated to a foreign scholar, about to leave for Israel and to meet with political figures, academics, and journalists there: "Egypt wants peace; Egypt needs peace because of its economic, social, and political problems; Egypt can no longer bear the enormous burden of the Palestinian cause; Egypt is prepared to make meaningful concessions for peace." Among my interlocutors were Osama el-Baz, then (and later) the principal national security adviser to President Sadat (and, later, President Mubarak), and Professor Boutros-Ghali, about to become Egypt's Minister of State for Foreign Affairs.

In Israel, I presented my findings in public—an article in *Ha'aretz*, a prominent daily newspaper (14 November 1975) and in private, a lecture at the Foreign Ministry. I pleaded for an understanding of a fundamental change in the attitude of Israel's most powerful adversary. "Michael, what a pity, you have been brain-washed," was the disbelieving response. *Two years later, President Sadat offered peace to Israel from the podium of the Knesset in Jerusalem.* The rest is history. As one scholar, Russell Leng, asked, in an insightful paper on crises, "When Will They Ever Learn?" (1983). Moreover, Neustadt and May (1986), along with Janis (1972, 1989), Janis and Mann (1977), and Vertzberger (1990), recounted episodes demonstrating that decision-makers do not always learn.

What can scholars contribute to the foreign policy process? The most valuable contribution of scholars to the foreign policy–national security process is a twofold educational role. One is a fundamental, enduring penetration of the mind-set of political and bureaucratic decision-makers on how to perceive the world in which choices must be made, often in conditions of severe stress. The other path, open to many academicians, is through an impact on students, who later enter the public service and who bring to the task of decision-making an approach to analysis and choice learned in the academy. This is far from a direct or immediate influence on policy, but it is not insignificant, and it is more enduring than a possible, transient influence on a specific decision.

Scholars have an obligation to make their *paths to knowledge* and *findings* on any aspect of world politics, especially on issues of *conflict, crisis*, and *war*, intelligible for persons authorized to make decisions relating to foreign policy and national security. Decision-makers must disavow their long-assumed monopoly of knowledge and wisdom about world politics. The intellectual gulf remains. Should the efforts be abandoned? No, because too much is at stake—ultimately, human survival—and because the need for improved communication and more soundly based decision-making on PCs, among which the *Arab–Israel conflict* is a classic illustration, remains great. This is the *raison d'être* of scholarship on conflict, crisis, and war: to persist, however difficult the task and however little the likelihood of success, to make persons with power and authority open their minds to the findings from systematic scholarship. If successful, the effort would contribute to a more secure and stable world. If it fails, the cost may be intolerable. All of the themes discussed in this Introduction will be elaborated in the chapters to follow.

CHAPTER 2

Historical Roots

Conflict between the principal adversaries in the modern *intrastate–interstate Arab–Israel* protracted conflict (PC) began long before the post–World War II phase of intense competition, including periodic violence, between the Arab and Muslim worlds, and Israel and world Jewry. As in other PCs, the struggle for control over the Land of Israel/Palestine and the ultimate prize, Jerusalem, operated at several reinforcing levels, sometimes sequentially and at other times simultaneously, one of the sources of its complexity.

The ancient Israelites and their belief system, Judaism, entered the stage of Jerusalem-centered history long before the entry of the predominant Arab belief system, Islam. The *first period* of Jewish rule over the Land of Israel began in the thirteenth century Before the Common Era (B.C.E.) and lasted until the Babylonian conquest of Judea and the enforced lengthy exile of Jewry in 586 B.C.E. Jews regained control of Jerusalem around 164 B.C.E., including a brief revival of the Kingdom of Judea in 64 C.E. Soon after came the era of Roman rule, in 70 C.E., and with it, the end of the Jewish state for two millennia.

FOUR LEVELS OF CONFLICT

Clash of Belief Systems

The initial presence of Islamized Arabs in the contested city of Jerusalem was its conquest by Caliph Omar in 638 C.E., six years after the death

© The Author(s) 2017
M. Brecher, *Dynamics of the Arab–Israel Conflict*,
DOI 10.1007/978-3-319-47575-2_2

of Muhammad. While the Prophet's attitude to Jewish tribes in Medina began on a positive note—Jews, like Christians, were given the special status of *dhimmi* ("People of the Book") and allowed to practice their faith, and the Koran incorporated many rules, attitudes, and practices from Judaism—the unwillingness of Jews to convert to Islam, as early as Muhammad's lifetime, set in motion what was to become a *clash of civilizations*. Initially expressed in terms of *belief systems*, this was the *first and broadest of four levels of Muslim–Jewish*, later *Arab–Israel, conflict*, which persisted for 14 centuries, though with long periods of Muslim toleration, even encouragement, of Jews, Judaism, and their civilization, notably during the period of medieval Muslim rule in parts of Spain and in the nineteenth-century Ottoman Empire. As for Jerusalem, the Arab-Muslim control of the Holy City and Jewry's age-old sense of individual and collective loss continued until the conquest of Jerusalem in 1917 by British General Edmund Allenby and the formal installation of the British Mandate over Palestine by the League of Nations in 1923.

Competing National Goals

The *second, ideological, level of Arab–Israel conflict*, competing *nationalisms*, stemmed from the French Revolution and was carried to the rest of Europe and the Middle East by the Napoleonic wars at the turn of the nineteenth century. The ideas and movement of Arab nationalism were cultivated by intellectuals in the coffeehouses of Beirut and Cairo in the first half of that century, while the idea of Jewish nationalism was developed by Jewish intellectuals in Eastern and Central Europe in the second half of the nineteenth century. The Jewish national movement emerged as "facts on the ground"—from the beginning of the Return of a small number of East European Jews to the historic Land of Israel in 1881. Its ideological rationale, Zionism, was formulated in the writings of several Jewish intellectuals, decisively in Theodore Herzl's *The State of the Jews/The Jewish State* in 1896, and was given institutional form at the founding conference of the World Zionist Organization in 1897. *In sum*, the competing expressions of Arab and Jewish nationalism were slow to crystallize.

Intercommunal Rivalry

The *third, intercommunal, level of Arab–Israel conflict* dates to the beginning of the Jewish Return in 1881. The principal sources of this Jewish–Palestinian tension were the purchase of land by Jewish immigrants in

Palestine from the Ottoman government (until 1918) and Palestinian landholders, and the crisis arising from the exclusivist organization of early Jewish agricultural settlements in Palestine, which excluded Palestinian labor. This led to Palestinian attempts to discourage the sale of land to Jews, which, in turn, exacerbated the tension between the two communities.

Discordant British Pledges

The most important, *fourth level* of conflict among the pre-state historical roots of the Arab–Israel PC was a myriad of *political* acts, some by the two principal adversaries, the Arab and Jewish communities in Palestine, most by the British Mandate authorities. These acts began even before the British Mandate for Palestine was formally implemented in 1923. Among them, two important acts, both initiated by the British government, occurred during World War I and were designed to secure Arab and Jewish support for the British World War I effort.

The first was a written pledge by an authorized British government representative, Sir Henry McMahon, then British High Commissioner in Egypt—a letter in October 1915 to Hussein, Sharif of Mecca, The Guardian of Islam's Holiest Places in the Hejaz, which later became Saudi Arabia—of active support for an independent Arab state in Asian parts of the Arab world after the war (McMahon–Hussein correspondence, 14 July 1915–30 January 1916). There were several qualifications, notably the exclusion from the British commitment to support an independent Arab state of "portions of Syria" west of "the districts of Damascus, Homs, Hama and Aleppo." Palestine lies to the south of these areas and was not explicitly mentioned. However, during a meeting of the British Cabinet Eastern Committee on policy regarding Syria and Palestine, held on 5 December 1918, Lord Curzon, in the presence of Lord Balfour, who did not dissent, stated that "Palestine was included in the areas as to which Great Britain pledged itself that they should be Arab and independent in the future." This correspondence was a continuing source of controversy about the territorial scope of an independent Arab state, especially at the time of the United Nations (UN) General Assembly's *Partition Resolution* in November 1947, which called for the creation of *two independent states in the territory of the British Mandate, an Arab state and a majority Jewish state.*

The second crucial British act during World War I that became a continuing source of discord in the historical setting of the Arab–Israel conflict was the *Balfour Declaration*, issued by British Foreign Secretary Lord Balfour in a letter to Baron Rothschild on 2 November 1917. The key passage in this pledge about the future of Palestine read:

> His Majesty's government view with favor the establishment in Palestine of a national home for the Jewish people, and will use their best endeavors to facilitate the achievement of this object, it being clearly understood that nothing shall be done which may prejudice the civil and religious rights of existing non-Jewish communities in Palestine, or the rights and political status enjoyed by Jews in any other country.

It was noteworthy that the expressed wish by Chaim Weizmann and Nahum Sokolow, the Zionist leaders, to include a reference in the Declaration to the goal of the *reconstitution of Palestine as the Jewish national home* was not accepted; rather, the Declaration referred to the "establishment in Palestine of a national home for the Jewish people." Moreover, Weizmann's proposed wording of a *Jewish state* was replaced by "a national home ..." However, the text of the Balfour Declaration was incorporated into the League of Nations Mandate for Palestine.

POLITICAL AND MILITARY ACTS, 1933–1947

There were many other political and military acts that contributed to the cumulative tension between the contestants for influence throughout the history of the British Mandate, 1923–48, an environment that led to the onset of the Arab–Israel PC in 1948. Among them were:

- The coming to power of the National Socialist German Workers' Party (*Nazi Party*) in Germany in 1933, leading, *inter alia*, to a substantial migration of German Jews to Palestine from 1933 to 1938, before the entry gate from Germany to the "Promised Land" was closed by the United Kingdom;
- The *Peel Commission* (1936–37), whose report advocated the partition of Palestine into Jewish and Palestinian states; it was accepted by the majority of the leadership of the Jewish Agency for Palestine, and rejected by the Palestinian institutional counterparts;

- The *Arab Revolt* (1936–38), advocating a single state of Palestine, with a Palestinian majority;
- The *British White Paper* (1939), which drastically curtailed future quotas of Jewish immigration to Palestine;
- The creation of the *Jewish Brigade* by Palestine Jewry, which fought alongside Allied forces for the duration of World War II and created a reservoir of Jewish officers and soldiers that became a major contributor of trained soldiers in the emerging Israel Defense Forces (IDF) at the time of Israel's independence in May 1948;
- The *escalation of violence* between Jewish and Palestinian militias from 1940 to 1948, especially after the end of World War II, with a shared Jewish and Palestinian anticipation of the termination of the British Mandate and the creation of a military vacuum, which both of the principal adversaries sought to fill; and
- The *UN General Assembly's Partition Resolution* on 29 November 1947, which heralded the termination of the British Mandate and the near-certainty of an Arab–Jewish civil war in Palestine. This UN resolution served as the *transformative event* in the historical setting of this emerging PC, leading to its onset on 14–15 May 1948.

Transformative Event—UN Partition Resolution 181

The most *crucial event* in the historical setting of this *interstate–intrastate* PC was a *transformative verbal act*, the *UN General Assembly's Partition Resolution 181* on 29 November 1947, which called for *the creation of two independent states, one with a majority of Jews, the other, predominantly Palestinian, in the British Mandate territory of Palestine*. This act provided a verbal sanction by the UN for the proclamation of Israel's independence in May 1948, an act rejected by all Arab states and the Palestinian community. This act and the *Jewish–Palestinian reactions in mid-May 1948*—the *proclamation of independence by the State of Israel* and the *Arab states' initiated war against Israel*—transformed an *intercivilizational* and *intercommunal* conflict into an *interstate–intrastate* Arab–Israel PC.

In sum, the unresolved Arab–Israel PC began in *civilizational belief system* terms (Islam vs. Judaism), with the emergence of a proselytizing Islam in the seventh century C.E. Specifically, its historical roots lasted *1310* years—from the conquest of Jerusalem by Caliph Omar in

638 C.E. to 1948. It became manifest in *intercommunal* terms (Jewry vs. Palestinians) in 1881, with the beginning of the Return of the Jews to the Land of Israel. It was *transformed* into an *interstate–intrastate PC* (Arab states and the Palestinians vs. Israel and Jewry) in mid-May 1948.

CHAPTER 3

Struggle for Jerusalem

ONSET

From its onset, one of the most contentious issues among the principal adversaries in the Arab–Israel PC, the Arab states (and later, the Palestine Liberation Organization [PLO]) and Israel, has been the struggle for control of Jerusalem. While the conflict over—and within—Jerusalem long preceded the creation of Israel as an independent state, Jerusalem emerged as a crucial Arab–Israel and Israel–Palestine conflict issue as a result of a cluster of five closely related events in 1947–49:

- The first was *UN General Assembly Resolution 181* in November 1947, recommending the creation of two independent states from the territory about to be vacated by the United Kingdom's announcement of the termination of its League of Nations Mandate over Palestine in May 1948.
- The second event was the inclusion, in the General Assembly's Partition Resolution, of a provision for the *territorial internationalization of Jerusalem*.
- The third and fourth events were the *General Assembly's reaffirmation* of the territorial internationalization of Jerusalem in December 1948 and December 1949.
- The fifth event was the *Israel government's decision* in December 1949 to *proclaim Jerusalem the capital of the new state*.

© The Author(s) 2017
M. Brecher, *Dynamics of the Arab–Israel Conflict*,
DOI 10.1007/978-3-319-47575-2_3

15

The cumulative impact of these events, especially Israel's responsive decision and act, was to generate, for the struggle over Jerusalem, *very high global, regional, and multilateral visibility*—for the principal adversaries, initially the Arab states organized in the League of Arab States (Arab League) since its creation in 1944, and the new state of Israel; for the Palestinian nationalist movement, which became a principal adversary in this conflict soon after the formation of the PLO in 1964, escalating in 1967 with Yasser Arafat's emergence as its long-term leader (1967–2004), and the beginning of varying degrees of support from members of the Arab League; and for non-Arab Muslim states which shared the Arab states' view of the Jerusalem issue and the larger issue of control over the West Bank territory.

The first high-profile world politics episode in the persistent Arab–Israel struggle for control of Jerusalem centered on Israel's *strategic* decision to make Jerusalem its capital, in a context of intense opposition by a rare "unholy alliance" of the Vatican (the global Roman Catholic hierarchy), the Arab states, the community of Muslim states, and the Soviet-led Communist UN members. This alignment of otherwise ideological belief system incompatibilities and the intense competition of claims over a coveted unique territory, in 1947–49, provide an illuminating starting point for an analysis of the dynamics of the long-term Arab–Israel conflict over the entire disputed territory of Palestine. Moreover, the focus on the ongoing struggle over Jerusalem will cast light on the failure to resolve the entire Arab–Israel conflict during the past seven decades, to be analyzed later in this book.

Among the most contentious issues in the Israel–Palestine and Arab–Israel conflicts, the ultimate status of Jerusalem ranks very high as an obstacle to a mutually accepted peace agreement. In essence, Israel has consistently claimed sovereignty over the entire territory of the disputed city—East Jerusalem, West Jerusalem, and the Old City—since its annexation of East Jerusalem and the Old City immediately after its victory in the June-Six-Day War in 1967. The Palestinians have claimed sovereignty over East Jerusalem and all of the Old City, except for an autonomous Jewish Quarter, with equal persistence.

In sum, the Arab–Israel conflict over Jerusalem dates to the beginning of the pre-state ethnic Jewish–Palestinian conflict in the late nineteenth century. It attained high-profile recognition in the chancelleries of the world with UN General Assembly Resolution 181 on 29 November 1947, reaffirmed in December 1948 and December 1949, and the decision of the State of Israel, on 11 December 1949, to make West Jerusalem its capital. (Under the terms of the UN Partition Resolution, Jerusalem was to become an international city, at least for ten years.) Thus, Israel's decision to proclaim Jerusalem its capital marked the beginning of the latest, continuing phase in the unresolved conflict over the ultimate status of a city claimed by both parties to the conflict, Israel and the Palestine nationalist movement, supported by the Arab and other Muslim states, with equal fervor.

The *contested legal status and political fate of Jerusalem* has been and is one of the pivotal issues in the Israel–Palestine and the Arab–Israel conflict, as well as in the Middle East and world politics. The city's role as a uniquely unifying symbol of the Jewish People during the past three millennia is acknowledged in most of the non-Muslim world. Its national, religious, and cultural associations are deeply rooted in the consciousness of Jews everywhere. Thus, it was natural for Jerusalem to be perceived by Zionists and world Jewry as an inseparable part of the revived Jewish state. Throughout, it was also perceived and identified by Muslims everywhere as a fundamental part of their religious heritage, especially the Al-Aqsa Mosque, and by Palestinians as central to their national identity and aspiration for an independent state. Thus, it is essential to illuminate the process leading to this crucial decision-turning point in the enduring Arab–Israel conflict.

DECISIONS

The following reconstruction and analysis of Israel's *strategic decision* on *11 December 1949* to *make Jerusalem the seat of government* is based largely on my interviews in the 1960s and 1970s with 12 Israeli political leaders and many senior officials at the time of this controversial decision 67 years ago, including four who served as Prime Minister from 1948 to 1974: David Ben-Gurion, Head of Government and Defense Minister throughout this crisis and later (1948–53, 1955–63); Moshe Sharett, Foreign Minister during this crisis and beyond (1948–56), and Prime Minister (1953–55); Levi Eshkol, Director of the Settlement Department of the Jewish Agency (1949–63) and molder of economic policy in Israel from 1952 to 1969, and Prime Minister (1963–69); and Golda Meir, Minister of Labor and National Insurance at the time of Israel's Jerusalem strategic decision, and Prime Minister (1969–74).

In the last stage of its struggle for political independence, the Jewish community in Palestine before 1948, the *Yishuv*, made a difficult-to-contemplate concession, namely, *acceptance of the territorial internationalization of Jerusalem*, an integral part of the UN General Assembly Partition Plan of 29 November 1947. Two years later, the most crucial of several early decisions on Jerusalem was taken by the leaders of the new state: *on 11 December 1949, the Government of Israel decided to make Jerusalem the seat of government by proclaiming it the capital.* This was among the most controversial and politically significant decisions by Israel since its proclamation of statehood in May 1948, continuing its role as a major source of this persistent, high-profile interstate–intrastate conflict until the present.

I recall this turning-point decision vividly, from two personal associations with Jerusalem; first, as a research assistant to Israel's Representative to the UN, Abba Eban, and his Legal Advisor, Dr. Jacob Robinson, in the summer of 1948: my main task was to dissect the working of the UN Palestine Commission, which was created soon after the Partition Resolution was approved by the General Assembly, to guide its implementation, including the provision of Jerusalem as a *corpus separatum* (an international city). Moreover, I was living in Jerusalem at the time the crucial 1949 Government of Israel decision was made.

On two earlier occasions, in November 1947 and December 1948, the UN General Assembly had approved resolutions calling for the territorial internationalization of Jerusalem. Few, if any, acts were perceived by Israeli decision-makers and their attentive and mass publics as more inimical to Israel's interests. The second resolution (December 1948) was even more disquieting, for it was proclaimed soon after the Israel Defense Forces (IDF) had broken the Arab siege of the New City of Jerusalem and thereby saved the 100,000 Jerusalem Jews from what Israelis were convinced would have been a fate of genocide.

Soon after the UN General Assembly convened in the autumn of 1949, evidence mounted that another diplomatic assault on Israel's claim to Jerusalem was in the making. Not only did internationalization have the support of the United States and the USSR (Union of Soviet Socialist Republics), notwithstanding their formal recognition of the new state immediately after Israel's proclamation of independence on 14–15 May 1948. More perilous for Israel was the massive pressure being brought to bear on Roman Catholic member-states of the UN, especially the large number in Latin America, by the Vatican: papal diplomacy aimed at forging a victorious (and unusual) coalition of Catholic, Muslim, and Communist states in favor of territorial internationalization once more, planning for a 9 December 1949 UN Resolution.

Within what Israel perceived as an "Unholy Alliance," all Arab states except Jordan actively supported territorial internationalization. However, Jordan's posture amply counterbalanced the rest; it was, in reality, an informal ally of Israel in the struggle against the Vatican–Arab–Communist alliance because, like Israel, it opposed any physical international presence in Jerusalem. Eban, then head of Israel's Delegation to the UN, noted this cooperative Israel–Jordan relationship during the diplomatic battle to negate internationalization in 1949–50 (author's interview with Eban, December 1965).

Within Israel, several interest groups urged the government to take decisive steps to ensure the safety and well-being of Jerusalem Jewry and the effective incorporation of the city into the new state. One such group was that of *Jerusalem residents* led by Jerusalem Cabinet Ministers Dov Joseph (*Mapai*, Israel's Labor Party) and Rabbi Fishman [Maimon] (the moderate–religious party, *Mizrahi*). It was vocally supported by a small group of *parliamentarians*, at first in the Provisional State Council, the pre-Independence Palestinian Jewish legislature, and from February 1949, after Israel's first general elections, in the *Knesset*, Israel's parliament. The Israeli decision of 29 July 1948, two months after Independence, to appoint a Military Governor of Jerusalem (Dov Joseph), was a partial response to those pressures. Once the Arab military siege of West Jerusalem was broken, delegations of prominent Jerusalemites began to lobby for official action to confirm Israeli sovereignty over Jerusalem (author's interview with Dov Joseph, July 1960).

All of the secular Zionist parties, from the Revisionist, Nationalist Right (*Herut* [Freedom], later, the *Likud*) to the Marxist Left (*Mapam*), insisted throughout that Jerusalem be territorially integrated into Israel. The ultra-Orthodox, anti-Zionist *Agudat Yisrael* Party and the Communist Party (*Maki*) opposed Israeli sovereignty over the Holy City. In addition, the moderate–religious Zionist *Mizrahi* was prepared to accept internationalization in the summer of 1948 as preferable to the imminent danger of damage to the holy shrines; by September, it advocated Israeli control and never wavered thereafter (author's interview, April 1966, with Yaacov Herzog, the Foreign Ministry official in charge of the Jerusalem issue and later Israel's Ambassador to Canada and Director-General of Prime Minister Meir's office).

On the related issue of Jerusalem as the capital of Israel, the far-Right *Herut* was relentless in urging the *Mapai* (Social–Democrat)-dominated government to act, from the earliest days of Independence (May 1948) to the eve of the strategic decision in December 1949. In other parties, many persons had doubts, for several reasons—a perceived intolerable security burden for the new state—Jerusalem was physically distant from the concentration of population and economic and military resources along the Sharon Plain close to Tel Aviv, the certain drain on very limited economic resources, and so on. As Israel's first and longest-serving prime minister (1948–53, 1955–63), Ben-Gurion recalled: "In almost all parties—all but *Herut*—there were those who opposed the transfer of the Government to Jerusalem: they were concerned about international repercussions" (author's interview with Ben-Gurion, June 1966). These pressures reinforced each other. Yet their demand for government action was resisted by Israel's government until 18 months after Independence, when the far more dangerous external pressure for territorial internationalization of Jerusalem was bluntly reaffirmed by the UN Security Council.

The decision to proclaim Jerusalem the capital of Israel was taken by its Cabinet on 11 December 1949, less than 36 hours after the UN General Assembly had reaffirmed its 1947 and 1948 recommendation for territorial internationalization of the city.

Decision-Makers

Throughout that early period of Israel's statehood, an informal triumvirate held sway in *Mapai*, the largest party in the governing coalition and the Cabinet from 1948 to 1977—Prime Minister and Defense Minister Ben-Gurion, Foreign Minister Moshe Sharett, and Finance Minister Eliezer Kaplan. On this issue, however, Kaplan did not play an active role. Dov Joseph, an articulate spokesman of Jerusalem residents, filled that void with a forceful advocacy, as did Rabbi Fishman/Maimon, the senior minister from the Religious Front, whose view on an issue like Jerusalem was highly respected by the Prime Minister and the Cabinet.

It was Ben-Gurion who took the initiative leading to the first (December 1949) strategic decision on Jerusalem. (There were other strategic decisions, notably the annexation of East Jerusalem and the Old City after Israel's triumph in the June-Six-Day War in 1967.) He was actively encouraged, and on earlier occasions prodded, by two other ministers, as noted—

Rabbi Fishman/Maimon and Dov Joseph. Ben-Gurion was no less attached to Jerusalem than these active advocates, but he waited for a favorable moment to act; it came the day after the General Assembly's reaffirmation of *corpus separatum* (territorial internationalization). Most of the other ministers supported the Cabinet's decision proclaiming Jerusalem Israel's capital. A few were hesitant (Eliezer Kaplan [Finance, and Commerce and Industry] and David Remez [Communications and Transport]). And one dissented—Sharett, the Foreign Minister. All three were from Ben-Gurion's *Mapai* party! (Based upon author's interviews with many participants in the crucial 11 December 1949 Cabinet meeting—see below.)

The Foreign Minister cabled his resignation from New York immediately after the Cabinet decision: he felt responsible for Israel's setback at the Assembly, which, he acknowledged, he had not anticipated; and his view that Israel should not act directly against a UN General Assembly resolution had been rejected by Ben-Gurion and the Israel Cabinet. "I never showed the [Sharett] cable to my colleagues," recalled Ben-Gurion. Instead, he wrote to Sharett that the UN Assembly vote was not his responsibility and that the Cabinet of ten voted against him, too (author's interview, June 1966).

Attitudinal Prism-Perceptions

How did Israel's central decision-makers at the time perceive the setting for a decision fraught with controversy? What was the nature of the attitudinal prism governing their images? There were, in fact, two early critical decision points on Jerusalem: one, before Independence, related to the UN General Assembly Partition Resolution, calling for territorial internationalization, passed on 29 November 1947; the other was to make Jerusalem the seat of Israel's government, two years later.

Ben-Gurion laid bare the core of his Jerusalem image on 5 December 1949, in the *Knesset*:

> A nation which over 2,500 years has always maintained the pledge vowed by the banished people on the rivers of Babylon, not to forget Jerusalem – this nation will never sanction its separation. [Moreover,] Jewish Jerusalem will never accept foreign rule after thousands of her sons and daughters have freed, for the third time, their historic homeland and delivered Jerusalem from destruction ... [Finally, lest the commitment be undervalued,] Israelis are ready to sacrifice themselves for Jerusalem no less than the English for

London, the Russians for Moscow, and the Americans for Washington. (*Divrei Haknesset* [Parliamentary Proceedings], iii, 1949, p. 221)

By agreeing to the 1947 UN Partition Plan, the Executive of the Jewish Agency, headed by Ben-Gurion, gave the *Yishuv*'s (Palestinian Jewry's) sanction to the proposal of *corpus separatum*, which placed Jerusalem's 100,000 Jews under an international administration, *at least for a period of ten years. Why was Jerusalem "sacrificed"*? Reflections of many Israeli decision-makers after the event illuminate their perceptions at the time and their ensuing decision in accepting territorial internationalization.

Ben-Gurion recalled, a few years after leaving the prime ministership and the government in 1963: "It was *the price to be paid for statehood*. We accepted the UN decision, everything. If the Arabs had accepted it fully, we would have carried it out fully" (author's interview, June 1966). Five years later, he elaborated on this without hesitation, emphasizing the same rationale—"the price of statehood": "In November 1947 I was of the belief that we have the right to the entire Land of Israel. But if the UN passed the [Partition] Resolution by a large majority, and if the Arabs would concede [Israel's independence], the issue would be settled totally, and it shall be so" (author's interview, May 1971).

Sharett, who presented the Jewish case for Jerusalem at the UN, together with American Zionist leader Abba Hillel Silver, recorded 11 years after the diplomatic battle his explanation for the acceptance of internationalization: "As regards Jerusalem ... it became evident that *the requisite majority for the* [UN] *Partition plan could not be mustered if the internationalization of the Holy City was omitted from it*" (author's interview, July 1960). Moreover, the Vatican regarded the latter measure as one which would "vest the Catholic Church with predominant influence ... [and thus] warranting acquiescence in the elevation of the Jewish People to the level of sovereign statehood" (as quoted by Zeev Sharef, long-time Secretary of Israel's government, in *Three Days* [New York: Doubleday, 1962], 111–112).

This perception of a necessary trade-off was articulated by other decision-makers as well. Dov Joseph recalled:

> In particular, the proposal that Jewish Jerusalem should be detached from the Jewish state evoked resentment .... In spite of all [their] misgivings, the partition settlement was accepted by the bulk of the Jewish community as *offering the only practicable way out from the untenable White Paper 1939*

regime ... which had played havoc with Jewish immigration and reconstruction. (Joseph, *The Faithful City*, 1960, 18, emphasis added)

Many years later, he put the issue more bluntly:

We had no alternative; we wanted a Jewish state; we weren't prepared to oppose an independent state without Jerusalem. And so, on a provisional basis, we *acquiesced* in the plan for *a corpus separatum*. But we didn't *accept* it—voluntarily. In a word, we yielded to the facts. But we never ceased to protest against the setting up of an internationalized Jerusalem. (author's interview, June 1971)

David Horowitz, then Director-General of the Finance Ministry, also differentiated between acquiescence and positive acceptance (author's interview, December 1965).

Labor Minister, and later Prime Minister (1969–74), Golda Meir, too, recalled: "We went along with the 1947 UN [Partition] Resolution, as painful as the idea was that Jerusalem would be internationalized. Had the Arabs gone along with the Resolution, Jerusalem would not have been the capital" (author's interview, August 1966).

H.M. Shapiro, then the senior member of the religious Zionist party in the Cabinet and Minister of Immigration, expressed a widespread but rarely acknowledged motivation for acquiescence: "For us, the State of Israel without Jerusalem is an amputated state. True, we agreed to a state without Jerusalem in 1947; but we merely waited until an opportunity arose to rectify the situation" (author's interview, August 1968).

The image of *ein breira* (no alternative), "bitter sacrifice," "the price to be paid," was also noted by Israeli civil servants, UN aides, and scholars, who offered an explanation of the Palestine Jewry's [*Yishuv*'s] response to the 1947 General Assembly Partition Resolution. These included:

- The first, long-serving Director-General of the Foreign Ministry (1948–59), Walter Eytan: "the establishment of an independent Jewish state outweighed the bitter sacrifice" (author's interview, January 1971);
- Yaacov Herzog, the Adviser on Jerusalem Affairs in the Foreign Ministry: "the price of internationalization was worth paying, if necessary, for independence" (author's interview, April 1966);

- A personal consultant to the UN Mediator and, later, Personal Representative to the Acting Mediator, Dr. Ralph Bunche, in Tel Aviv: "[it] was finally accepted as the price to be paid for the coming into being of a Jewish state" (Paul Mohn, "Jerusalem and the United Nations," *International Conciliation*, no. 464 [October 1950]); and
- Scholar B. Halpern, *The Idea of the Jewish State*, 1961, 373–374: "in order to gain the most essential sovereign rights needed to solve the post-war problems of the Jews."

Only one divergent perception was encountered. Eban, then a promising young member of the Jewish Agency's Political Department, headed by Sharett, recalled: "This question has to be seen against the background of the Peel Commission's recommendation for the internationalization of Jerusalem in 1937. Moreover, the *Yishuv* had developed in the Galilee and the coastal plain, with Jerusalem a mixed population center surrounded by Arab areas. I do not recall any discussion among the leadership in that period suggesting Jerusalem as part of a Jewish state. *The best that could be imagined* was internationalization—to prevent it from being incorporated into an Arab state" (author's interview, December 1965).

At first glance, Eban's perception appears to contradict the widespread consensus view of Israeli decision-makers and others, but it does not negate the sense of loss and sacrifice felt by Palestine Jewry. Rather, territorial internationalization of Jerusalem was regarded as a temporary acquiescence, for the attachment of Jewry to Jerusalem was deep. According to Ze'ev Sharef, then, and for many years, Secretary to the Government, the idea of Jerusalem as *a corpus separatum* began to fade among *Yishuv* leaders as early as January–February 1948 (author's interview, March 1966). This was certainly true of Ben-Gurion at the dawn of Independence, May 1948.

Decision Process

Israel's decisions relating to Jerusalem extended over a period of more than 17 years, from November 1949 to June 1967. They may be grouped into two clusters or stages:

(1) From 15 November 1949 (Ben-Gurion's advice to the Israeli Cabinet to act quickly in the matter of Jerusalem as Israel's capital) to 11 December 1949 (the day the decision to make Jerusalem the

seat of government was approved by Israel's government): This core decision was implemented swiftly for all government ministries except Defense and Foreign Affairs, from 11 December 1949 to 23 January 1950—see below. A formal government announcement that the Foreign Ministry would move to Jerusalem was made on 4 May 1952, and the actual transfer of the ministry occurred on 12 July 1953.

(2) From 7 June to 28 June 1967 Israel's annexation of East Jerusalem and the most contested area, the Old City: The primary focus of this inquiry into the Jerusalem decision process is Israel's first and most significant strategic decision on 11 December 1949—to proclaim Jerusalem the capital of Israel. Although the annexation of East Jerusalem and the Old City and their integration into Jerusalem in June 1967 was even more controversial than Decision (1), it was, in essence, the attainment, throughout the Arab–Israel and Israel–Palestine conflicts, of Israel's unconcealed claim to all of the territory of Jerusalem, a goal that merely awaited an opportunity for implementation. This opportunity, 18 years later, was Israel's decisive military triumph in the June-Six-Day War in 1967, which included the conquest of East Jerusalem and the supreme prize, the Old City, along with the entire Palestinian West Bank. Viewed from a historical perspective, Israel's successful political triumph in the struggle for Jerusalem, in June 1967, was the logical extension of the strategic decision in December 1949.

Viewed within the larger Arab–Jewish and Arab–Israel conflicts, the struggle over Jerusalem had deep historical roots, comprising the following events and developments, including some noted above:

- The *claims to Jerusalem* inherent in Jewish nationalism (Zionism) and a decisive Jewish majority in the city for a century, on the one hand, and a *prolonged Arab majority* in, and domination of, the city (during many earlier centuries), on the other;
- The beginning of the *Return of Jewry to its ancestral homeland* from the early 1880s;
- The *Balfour Declaration* 1917;
- The *Arab disturbances* of 1920–21 and 1929 in Jerusalem (and Hebron);

- The *League of Nations Mandate* for Palestine, granted to the United Kingdom, 1923;
- The UK *Peel Commission Report* of 1937, which preceded the UN General Assembly Resolution in 1947, recommending the partition of Palestine into two independent states;
- The *Arab Revolt*, 1936–38, from which its (Israel's struggle over Jerusalem) deliberations and content arose; and
- The presence in Jerusalem's Old City of Al-Aqsa Mosque, the third holiest shrine in Islam.

Viewed as a decision by the Jewish Agency for Palestine, the pre-Independence authorized representative of the Palestinian Jewish community, the November 1947 UN General Assembly Resolution 181 (II) is the most appropriate and relevant point of departure. Under the terms of this Partition Resolution, the City of Jerusalem was to become a *corpus separatum* (international city), administered by the UN Trusteeship Council, acting on behalf of the United Nations as the administering authority. An appointed Governor would serve as the chief administrative official, with the assistance of an administrative staff composed principally of Palestinians (the two communities), a police force composed of non-Palestinian nationals, and an elected Legislative Council. Jerusalem was to be demilitarized and neutralized. It was to form a part of the Economic Union of Palestine, along with the independent Jewish and Arab states called for in this Resolution, and Jerusalem was designated the headquarters of its Economic Board. Representatives of the two states were to be accredited to the Governor of Jerusalem and were to be responsible for the protection of the interests of their states and nationals in the City. There were also provisions concerning the administration of justice, citizenship, local autonomy, freedom of transit, the acceptance of two official languages (Arabic and Hebrew, though other "working languages" [English] could be—and were—adopted), and the special powers of the Governor for the protection of the holy places.

The Trusteeship Council was directed to prepare and approve a detailed Statute within five months. It was to take effect no later than 1 October 1948 and was to remain in force initially for ten years. Thereafter, the Statute was to be subject to reexamination by the Trusteeship Council. Residents of Jerusalem were to be free to express, by means of a referendum, their wishes as to possible modifications in the regime of the City. (The text of the crucial Partition Resolution is in UN General Assembly

Resolution 181 (II), "Future Government of Palestine," 29 November 1947.)

The Jewish Agency for Palestine, the organizational forerunner of the State of Israel, acquiesced in the UN proposal for territorial internationalization on purely pragmatic grounds: it was, as noted above, the perceived *sine qua non* of independence. Among many, too, there was the conviction that the unfolding of events would prove a *corpus separatum* unworkable. Joseph summed up the decision-makers' mood:

> We hoped that Jerusalem would be part of the state eventually. We thought that because we had a clear majority [in the city] this would take place. But we didn't think about what would happen ten years later [referring to the referendum provision of the Partition Resolution]. We were then in the midst of a struggle over *corpus separatum*. The outcome was far from certain. It could have turned out better than it seemed. (author's interview, June 1971)

And, indeed, as the appointed day for the termination of the Mandate (15 May 1948) approached, the battle for, over, and in Jerusalem rendered the UN Plan abortive.

The proclamation of Israel's independence on 14–15 May 1948 did not refer specifically to Jerusalem or to any other town or district in Israel. But within hours, Arab armies invaded the new state, and Jewish Jerusalem (the New City and the Jewish Quarter in the Old City) came under siege. In the midst of this first assault, Ben-Gurion declared before the provisional parliament: "Until peace is proclaimed ... we speak of Jerusalem as within the boundaries of the Jewish State (as of now, to my regret, without the Old City), exactly as Tel Aviv." As Joseph recalled: "From the first day of the state, we behaved as if Jerusalem were part of Israel—with one difference: many ministries were not yet established there" (author's interview, June 1971).

The UN Mediator, Count Folke Bernadotte, startled and angered Israel's leaders on 29 June 1948 by proposing the transfer of Jerusalem—as a whole—to Jordan. This proposal was dismissed out of hand and was formally rejected by Israel's Provisional State Council on 5 July. Yet the mistrustful Israeli élite perceived it as symptomatic of a pro-Arab outlook in the UN establishment.

In mid-July, the IDF, the successor to *Hagana*, the Jewish community's largest pre-state self-defense organization, made an ill-fated attempt to conquer the Old City of Jerusalem: *Operation Kedem* failed, and East Jerusalem remained under Jordan's control for the next 19 years. Nevertheless, the New City (West Jerusalem) came under effective Israeli authority. The New City held fast against the assault of Jordan's Arab Legion during the four-week war (14 May–11 June 1948) and again, after the first truce, during the ten-day war (9–19 July). The prolonged second truce (19 July–22 October) witnessed limited hostilities on every front. One of the victims was Bernadotte. But on 16 September, just a day before his assassination by members of the Israeli right-wing paramilitary underground, *LEHI* (Fighters for the Freedom of Israel), the UN Mediator reverted to the idea of internationalization of Jerusalem.

The UN General Assembly, acting on the late Mediator's suggestion, instructed the newly created Palestine Conciliation Commission (PCC) on 11 December 1948 to "present detailed proposals for a permanent international regime for the Jerusalem area." There was no immediate official Israeli reaction, unlike a year later, "because we weren't sufficiently strong and we wished to enlarge our presence in Jerusalem. We knew that the population division was clearly in our favor. And we wanted, if possible, to avoid an open conflict with the UN," especially when Israel was about to seek admission to the world organization (author's interview with Joseph, June 1971).

In late September 1948, Ben-Gurion suffered a setback when three of his senior fellow *Mapai* party ministers (Sharett, Kaplan, and Remez) aligned themselves with lesser Coalition Cabinet members to reject his proposal for a military operation against Latrun, which was designed to ensure a Jewish Jerusalem. The Prime Minister, in anguish, warned his colleagues that their inaction would cause a tragedy for the generations. Ben-Gurion's rationale was stated by him thus: "It is necessary that Jerusalem will be Jewish, and it will not be Jewish unless Latrun is conquered" (author's interviews with Ben-Gurion, May 1971, and with Pinchas Rosen, a Progressive (centrist) Party leader, February 1971).

As the UN General Assembly convened for its annual autumn session in 1949, pressures for internationalization mounted once more. There were several sources. One was a Vatican-launched massive press campaign, which urged Catholic states around the world, notably the large Latin American group, then constituting 40 percent of the UN membership, to support *corpus separatum*. A special envoy to Jerusalem, recalled Ben-Gurion, "came to see me and told me [in August 1949] that if they [the Vatican] had been aware of the fact that we were going to proclaim

Jerusalem as our Capital, the State of Israel would not have been established at all." He was emphatically rebuffed by the Prime Minister with the theme: "'I don't understand you; Jerusalem was Israel's capital a thousand years before the birth of Christianity.' Monsignor McMahon was not easily moved" (author's interview with Ben-Gurion, June 1966).

A second source of pressure, largely influenced by the first, was Latin America. It had supported the Partition Plan of 1947 on the understanding that Jerusalem would be internationalized—under *de facto* Catholic control. This expectation—and demand—remained undiminished in 1949. A third substantial pressure group at the UN was the Arab states, all of which, except Jordan, reverted to a pro-internationalization stand in the autumn of 1948, when Bernadotte's proposal to give Jerusalem to Jordan's King Abdullah proved abortive. And finally, the Soviet Union and its clients were still committed to a territorially internationalized Jerusalem. It was a formidable alliance—Catholics, Muslims, and Communists—with Australia's External Affairs Secretary, Herbert Evatt, playing the role of savior-advocate.

The first and most decisive stage in Israel's initial decision process on Jerusalem began in mid-November 1949. On the 15th, following Sharett's report to the Cabinet on the imminent UN General Assembly discussion of Jerusalem, the Prime Minister urged his colleagues to act quickly and transfer the seat of government to Israel's historic capital. There was no decision. *Ben-Gurion's statement to the Knesset* on 5 December was a conscious, unequivocal act of defiance. His words were blunt and firm:

> [W]e will not consider any attempt made by the United Nations to forcibly remove Jerusalem from the State of Israel or to interfere with Israel's authority in the eternal capital .... We declare that Israel will never willingly give up Jerusalem, as she has never surrendered her faith in the thousands of years of peoplehood, her national unity, or her right to Jerusalem. (*Divrei Haknesset*, iii, p. 221)

Four days later, on 9 December 1949, the UN General Assembly reaffirmed the plan for *corpus separatum* by a vote of 38 to 14, with 7 abstentions. It was even more decisive than the vote in favor of the 1947 Partition Plan itself. The Trusteeship Council was directed to revive and revise its Statute for Jerusalem, suspended in April 1948, and, further, to implement it immediately. It was also specifically instructed not to "allow any actions taken by any interested Government or Governments to divert it from adopting and implementing the Statute." No coercive sanctions were provided.

It was this *UN act which served as the decisive input into Israel's* first *Strategic decision on Jerusalem*. News of the General Assembly vote reached the Government of Israel in the early hours of Saturday morning, 10 December. The next day, the Cabinet decided to make Jerusalem the seat of government, that is, the capital of Israel. It was an historic decision, 19 months after the proclamation of independence. Ironically, it was in response to a perceived threat from the world organization, which, at the outset, had provided international political sanction to the new Jewish state.

All Israeli decision-makers interviewed during a decade (1960–71), on what induced them to make the 1949 strategic decision on Jerusalem at that time, responded without hesitation—it was the General Assembly Resolution of 9 December 1949, reaffirming the plan for *territorial internationalization* of the contested city. *Ben-Gurion* confirmed this on two occasions: "My decision stemmed from the fact that the UN passed a resolution once more concerning Jerusalem" (author's interview, June 1966; reaffirmed in an interview in May 1971). *Joseph* termed Israel's Strategic decision "a deliberate defiance of the United Nations; there was a direct connection between the two." Indeed, "without the [UN] Assembly resolution on December 9th we would not have made the decision to move to Jerusalem at that time. But of course we would have done it later." It was, he continued, "a deliberate attempt to prevent the implementation of the UN decision – to confront them with a *fait accompli*" (author's interview, July 1960).

Eban reflected that, in one of those quirks of history, Jerusalem became Israel's capital in 1949 primarily because of errors and massive pressures from the UN: "Had the United Nations recognized our deep emotional attachment to Jerusalem, that might well have been sufficient, for many of our leaders thought of Jerusalem as an educational and cultural center, but not necessarily, not even ideally, as the political capital. It was the violation of that intangible bond by the UN, its insensitivity that pushed us to action, by asserting Jerusalem as an integral part of the state, as its capital" (author's interview, December 1965).

Herzog referred to the Cabinet decision of 11 December as "a reflex assertion of Israel's rights" (author's interview, April 1966).

And while *Sharef* emphasized that Israeli leaders perceived Jerusalem as part of Israel from the very outset, "the role of the General Assembly resolution was to catalyze the timing of our decision" (author's interview, March 1966).

Perhaps the most impressive evidence of a direct UN stimulus to Israel's decision to make Jerusalem the capital, a classic *input–output* relationship, is the fact that the idea of Jerusalem as the capital was not discussed by Israel's Cabinet *until a few months before the Strategic decision was made*. Sharef, who, as Secretary to the Government, attended almost all Cabinet meetings, recalled: "I did not meet people who thought Jerusalem would be the capital—all through 1948 and until the last months of 1949. The question was not put to a serious discussion, as far as I know" (author's interview, March 1966). Moreover, Ben-Gurion acknowledged that "the question of Jerusalem didn't reach the Government table until after the Armistice Agreements [the first half of 1949], because the main problem was to win the war. After the United Nations Resolution in December 1949, I called a Government meeting and we decided to transfer it to Jerusalem" (author's interview, June 1966). *Rarely has there been a more illuminating example of a Strategic decision, with long-term consequences for a state's foreign policy and for regional and world politics as the direct output of pressure from the world organization.* That input, as perceived by Israel's decision-makers, was the decisive element in their 1949 decision process on Jerusalem.

Implementation

All Israel government ministries but two moved to the capital, to West Jerusalem, by 1951. One stayed in Tel Aviv by choice—*Defense*: it was universally agreed in Israel that the conditions of prolonged war and Jerusalem's isolation required that the IDF be directed from a relatively secure headquarters in the Tel Aviv area. The other was the *Foreign Ministry*, which remained there until July 1953, because of Foreign Minister Sharett's commitment to avoid alienation of the UN. The Prime Minister and others were annoyed by what they perceived as Sharett's procrastination. As *Yitzhak Navon*, then Political Secretary to the Prime Minister, and later, President of Israel, recalled, he telephoned the Foreign Minister's Political Secretary every other day and said: "Ben Gurion wants to know from Sharett, 'when are you coming to Jerusalem?'" (author's interview, May 1966). Sharett remained unmoved because of his acute sensitivity to adverse international repercussions. Finally, on 13 July 1953, the Foreign Ministry was transferred to Israel's capital. It was the last implementing act concerning Israel's Strategic decision of 11 December 1949 on Jerusalem.

INTERNATIONAL BOYCOTT

The domestic Israeli response to the transfer of the Ministry of Foreign Affairs to Jerusalem was enthusiasm, but reaction abroad was undisguised anger. A boycott of the Foreign Ministry was declared by the United States and the United Kingdom. Other states followed their lead: diplomats from many missions were not permitted to conduct business or to attend official functions in Jerusalem, and all communications continued to be sent to the Ministry's Liaison Office in Tel Aviv. Washington even scolded Israel for the transfer, claiming that it had a solution for the Jerusalem issue, about to be unfolded. The Dean Rusk plan provided for *de jure* territorial internationalization of Jerusalem. Israel and Jordan were to be designated by the UN Trusteeship Council as administering authorities of their respective zones with complete *de facto* control. Their only obligation would be to send an annual report to the Trusteeship Council. It was discussed with Eban in 1950 but never formally proposed (author's interview, December 1965).

The boycott was gradually relaxed, with the turning point in 1955, when US Ambassador Edward B. Lawson conveyed the State Department's willingness to deal with the Israeli Foreign Ministry in Jerusalem. From 1956 onward, almost all new diplomatic missions, with the notable exception of West Germany in 1965, were established in Jerusalem. However, the vast majority of embassies remained in the Tel Aviv area—to the present day.

The Arab–Israel conflict over East Jerusalem and the Old City continues unabated; in fact, it is, by consensus, a grave obstacle to a mutually agreed peace agreement between Israel and Palestine. Nonetheless, a recent carefully researched, and highly informative analysis of the past two decades of Israel–Palestine negotiations, since the initial Oslo Accord (1993), concludes with a cautiously optimistic assessment of the prospect of an agreement on Jerusalem.

> A thorough examination of past rounds of negotiations reveals that gaps narrowed on the four main issues that constitute the question of Jerusalem, and that boundaries of possible compromise were drawn .... On the issue of Arab and Jewish neighborhoods in East Jerusalem, the 'Clinton prin-

ciple' – Jewish neighborhoods under Israeli sovereignty and Arab neighborhoods under Palestinian sovereignty; on the issue of the Old City and Holy Basin, division of sovereignty on the basis of the 'Clinton principle' or the solution of an international regime; on the issue of the Western Wall and Temple Mount/Al-Haram Al-Sharif, Israeli sovereignty over the Western Wall and a solution for Al-Haram Al-Sharif/the Temple Mount that will allow Palestinian control while addressing needs stemming from the Jewish affinity to the place and from security considerations; and finally, on the issue of 'two capitals', two municipalities in Jerusalem with a special mechanism for coordination and cooperation .... Despite the different obstacles to an agreement on Jerusalem and to a peace agreement in general ... the framework of principles that was outlined in previous negotiations ... can serve as a basis for future negotiations on the complex and sensitive issue of Jerusalem. (Lior Lehrs, 2016)

Pesscul thinking"; optimists, however, will welcome the limited achievement thus far and anticipate an ultimate meeting of minds. (A proposed solution to the impasse on Jerusalem is presented later in this book, in a discussion of the broader question, *is there a way out of the Israel–Palestinian impasse?*)

CHAPTER 4

Arab–Israel Perceptions

How did the principal adversaries in this protracted conflict (PC) view themselves—their rights, objectives, and methods to achieve them, along with views of "the other"? Two levels of analysis will be explored in the realm of perceptions: two pairs of adversaries, Israel–Palestine and Israel–Syria, and the articulated views of political leaders and officials conveyed to me in extensive interviews.

ISRAEL–PALESTINE

National Identity

Jewish national identity, known for most of Jewish history as the identity of the Jewish People, was sustained for more than three millennia by a distinctive and unifying belief system, Judaism. Only in the last half of the nineteenth century C.E., did the Jewish communities in Central and Eastern Europe, as did peoples later in all continents, begin to imbibe the ideology of modern *nationalism*, emanating from revolutionary France.

A distinctive national identity emerged among the *Palestinians* much later than among Jews or other Arab nations. *Egypt* was by far the oldest self-conscious national entity in the Middle East, dating to its pre-Arab and pre-Muslim Egyptian antecedents in the ancient world. *Lebanon* and *Egypt*, specifically the small Westernizing intellectual Arab élites in Beirut and Cairo, were the first Arab peoples to be influenced by the modern nationalist ideology, exported by post-Revolutionary France in the first half of the nineteenth century. Palestinians, many of whom migrated to what later became Israel and the West Bank, were viewed by Syria and others as "South Syrians." There were some early national stirrings in the aftermath of World War I, when these Palestinian (and Jewish)-populated areas became part of the UK Mandate for Palestine in September 1923 (see below), but the ideas of self-determination and independence date to the late 1930s, the period of the Arab Revolt (1936–38).

Both *Jewish nationalism*, generally identified then and later as Zionism, and *Palestinian nationalism* created institutions to mobilize support from their own and other communities, and to perform valuable political, economic, and public relations activities to advance their cause. The Zionist Organization was founded in 1897 (and renamed the World Zionist Organization [WZO] in 1960), and the Jewish Agency for Palestine was created in 1929 (and renamed the Jewish Agency for Israel in 1948).

The first significant institutional manifestation of a Palestinian identity, the counterpart of the Jewish Agency for Palestine, was the creation of the Arab Higher Committee in April 1936 as the central organization of the Arab community of Palestine, at the initiative of Haj Amin al-Husseini, one of the most controversial Palestinian leaders of the twentieth century. Interestingly, the word "Palestine" was conspicuously absent from the name of the Arab Higher Committee, designed to represent the Palestinian nation in the Arab Revolt (1936–38) and all negotiations with the British Mandatory government until 1948. Only much later (1964) did the Palestinian community create an organization dedicated to the attainment of Palestinian statehood, the Palestine Liberation Organization (PLO); it was the Palestinian counterpart of Jewry's independence-striving institution, the Zionist Organization—created 67 years later, and 16 years after the proclamation of Israel's independence. The dominant party within the PLO since the late 1960s, *Al-Fatah*, was compelled by domestic Palestinian pressures and civil war to share the mantle of Palestinian leadership since 2006 with the Islamist organization, *Hamas* (Palestine Resistance Movement), the governing party in the Gaza Strip since 2007.

Attitudinal Prisms

Attitudinal prisms of interstate PC decision-makers, the lens through which perceptions of reality are filtered—rarely change, for they reflect deep-rooted societal and personality factors, and historical experiences.

The core elements of *Israel's* attitudinal prism relating to the Arab world have been essentially the same for all Arab states. One is a belief in *pervasive Arab hostility* to the idea of a Jewish state in the self-designated Arab spatial domain, the Middle East. Closely related is Arab *unwillingness to recognize Israel as a legitimate state.* The two exceptions, Egypt in 1979 and Jordan in 1994, are treated, in Israel's prism, as *pro forma* recognition of reality, namely, "the State of Israel exists," and especially in the case of Egypt, the necessary price to achieve its most crucial goal, the restoration of Israel-occupied Sinai to its rightful owner (1979–82).

Another autonomous, but closely related, component of Israel's attitudinal prism is a perceived *continuing threat to Israel's security/survival* arising from the *long-term imbalance in key indicators of military capability* between Israel and a realistic Arab anti-Israel coalition—size of territory, size of military-age population, vast oil reserves, and consequent financial resources for a military buildup. Another prismatic component is *the Jewish People's memory of catastrophes in their history*, the latest trauma being the *Holocaust*, which ended only three years before the proclamation of Israel's independence.

While these elements were common to Israel's attitudinal prism relating to all of the frontline Arab states—Egypt, Iraq, Jordan, Lebanon, and Syria—the *intensity* of these components varied greatly. Lebanon was, in fact, and was perceived by Israel as, the least hostile Arab enemy of Israel during most the Arab–Israel PC. It was also the weakest member of the Arab anti-Israel coalition, militarily, and was not an active threat to Israel's security until the emergence of *Hezbollah*, as evident in the 2006 Hezbollah–Israel (Second Lebanon) War. Jordan was the second least hostile Arab state during most of this PC; in fact, its ruler at the onset of this PC, King Abdullah, tried and almost succeeded in making peace with Israel in 1947–48, before Israel achieved statehood. At the other extreme was Israel's perception of Syria's relentless hostility to Israel throughout the Arab–Israel PC, to be elaborated below.

The essence of this Israel prism regarding the Arabs and Arab states was summarized by me in an earlier book as follows:

> For Israel's High Policy Élite, as for the entire society, there is a primordial and pre-eminent aspect of the political culture—its *Jewishness*: this pervades thought, feeling, belief, and behavior in the political realm ....

> The consciousness of being Jewish creates a unique Attitudinal Prism for members of the High Policy Élite, as for most Israelis. They perceive Jewry as a world people of which Israelis are an integral part ...
> They emphasize Israel's link with Jewish antiquity and refer to the rebirth of Jewish sovereignty as the "Third Commonwealth" after two millennia of dispersion ...
> They have a searing consciousness of the Holocaust ... and they perceive the State of Israel as the logical, necessary, and rightful successor to the collective interests and rights of the few who survived. Israel as the voice, the representative, and the defender of Jews in distress anywhere—that is a role which flows naturally from the "Jewish prism." Through this lens, too, there is created an expectation that world Jewry will reciprocate with massive and continuous support for that segment of the People resettled in the Homeland. In its extreme form ... on many occasions [Ben-Gurion] declared that world Jewry is the only certain and reliable ally of Israel ...
> Many of these themes are part of the Israeli élite image. At the same time, they are inexorable 'spill-overs' from the Attitudinal Prism ... [To cite one example], "that unparalleled tragedy [the Holocaust] was the catalyst to his [Ben-Gurion's] policy of reconciliation with Germany from the late 1950s onward." (Brecher, 1972, 229–231)

While some elements of Israel's policy have changed, this core attitudinal prism remains unchanged.

The attitudinal prism of the *Palestinians* reveals several similar elements to those of Israelis. One of the most important is the widely shared *national identity* that matured during the near-seven decades of mostly intense conflict with Israel. Although Palestinians do not have the collective experience of independent statehood in their past history, they have experienced a deep sense of "national" loss and dispossession, in the form of two-thirds of the territory of Mandated Palestine (1923–48), which now belongs to its primordial enemy, Israel, or remains under Israeli occupation. A large part of this near-universal awareness of dispossession and loss is the result of the trauma of 1948–49, identified with the initial large-scale problem of Palestinian refugees and their accompanying loss of land and property, which remain a constant source of deprivation, material and emotional.

The dominant element of the prism, which has shaped Palestinian perceptions among the élite, the attentive public, and the mass public, has been captured most powerfully among Palestinians by the emotive Arabic word, *al-Naqba*, that is, *the catastrophe*, identified with Israel's proclamation of independence on 14 May 1948 and what for Palestinians is the ultimate iniquity of Israel's occupation of most of the territory perceived as morally and historically part of Palestine's patrimony. Despite the substantial differences in policy and tactical behavior between the two most influential and, more often than not, mutually hostile political organizations within the Palestinian national movement, *Fatah* and *Hamas* share the core elements of the Palestinian attitudinal prism, as do most of the competing Israeli parties in the essence of the Israeli prism with regard to the Palestinians.

The existence of sharply conflicting attitudinal prisms, in which the two principal adversaries share, project, and are driven by competing and often incompatible attitudes toward rights in general and the ultimate test, the *right to self-determination and national independence*, explains much about the adversaries' behavior on most contested issues. The substantive and symbolic perception of *Independence* and *al-Naqba* in 1948 dominates the essence of the attitudinal prism that shapes specific objectives, and perceptions of "the other" point to the extraordinary intensity of collective hostility, fear, and mistrust that have characterized this conflict for most of its history—notwithstanding a considerable number of agreements between pairs of adversaries, for example, the Egypt–Israel peace agreement (1979), the Israel–Jordan peace agreement (1994), and several Israel–PLO agreements, notably the Oslo Accord (1993) and follow-up limited issue agreements.

The writings and speeches of the two most influential Israeli and Palestinian political leaders during most of the conflict—Ben-Gurion, during the formative period of Israel's attitudinal prism and the framing of core policy decisions toward the Palestinians (1948–63), and Arafat, who articulated Palestinian attitudes during most of the conflict and was crucial in shaping decisions toward Israel (1967–2004)—provide a plethora of illustrations of the dominant attitudinal prisms of the adversaries and the impact on their attitudes and behavior on a myriad of contested issues: territory, including borders; refugees, including abandoned property; Jerusalem; and national security.

Israel–Syria

Attitudinal Prisms

Central to the Israel–Syria dyad in the Arab–Israel PC has been the *place of Syria in Israel's prism*. The preeminent element has been pervasive *hostility* by Israel's principal adversary, both in deeds and words, even before the formal onset of the Israel–Syria segment of the Arab–Israel PC—the proclamation of Israel's independence on 14–15 May 1948 and the immediate invasion of the new state by five Arab states, including Syria. Then, and in the decades that followed, until the onset of Syria's ongoing civil war in 2011, the near-universal *perception* by Israel's leaders, attentive public, and mass public was that Syria posed the *gravest threat to Israel's security* and was the *most relentless* among the Arab states in its hostility to the idea and the reality of a Jewish state in the Middle East. Territorial threats and existence threats were closely linked in Israel's psychological environment.

In *Syria's attitudinal prism*, Israel occupied the position of prime enemy for most of their PC—though there were glimpses of a possible breakthrough to peace as early as 1949, illuminated by one of Israel's leading scholars on modern Syria, Itamar Rabinovich, in a poignantly titled book, *The Road Not Taken* (1991) and, more promising, in extended negotiations in the 1990s aimed at a peace agreement (Rabinovich, *The Brink of Peace: The Israeli-Syrian Negotiations*, 1998). The importance of Israel's enemy role for Syria was acknowledged by former Syrian President al-Quwwatli: "the existence of Israel [has] been necessary for the Arabs for more than one reason: it has roused up their patriotic feelings and has stimulated their nationalism even outside the frame of their animosity to Israel. Their united hatred and action against Israel has brought about a fusion of their divergences" (Ma'oz, *Syria and Israel: From War to Peace-making* [New York: Oxford University Press, 1995, 35]).

Another crucial component of Syria's attitudinal prism was its longstanding self-proclaimed image as the "hotbed and the major center of the Arab nationalist movement" (Ma'oz, ibid., 12). An early Syrian president, Shishakly, reportedly acknowledged this role, with pride, in 1952: "it has become the duty of Syria, always the leader of the Arab people, [to] impose her will and recover her rights by force [in Palestine]." This comment also sheds light on another important element in Syria's prism—a long-held view that Palestine was part of southern Syria—and that several other neighbors, including Lebanon and Jordan, also belonged to "Greater Syria." Toward Israel, Syria's enmity was a product of national and religious differences, as well as its perception of insatiable Israeli aggrandizement, reinforced by the IDF capture of the Golan Heights during the June 1967 War, its extension of Israel law and administration throughout this territory in 1981, and its continuing occupation of the Golan, long an integral part of Syria's territory.

ARAB–ISRAEL PERCEPTIONS OF THE BALANCE OF MILITARY CAPABILITY

Throughout the *Israel–Palestine* segment of the *Arab–Israel* PC, the balance of military capability favored Israel. While Israel's military strength during most of the first war (1948–49) was inferior to the combined Arab military power, the Palestinian component of the Arab coalition was virtually nonexistent. There has never been an autonomous Palestinian army, though police-type security forces were formally sanctioned by several Israel–PLO agreements, especially since the Oslo Accord of 1993 and follow-up agreements until 1999, and again by informal agreements between Israel and the Palestine. Again, political after the passing of PLO leader, Yasser Arafat, in 2004. At no point did the Palestine military capability approach the level of the IDF, though PLO forces surprised superior-equipped IDF forces at the Battle of Karameh in 1968. Moreover, during both Palestinian uprisings (*Intifada*), late 1987–93 and from late 2000, after the collapse of the second Camp David peace process, to 2005, Palestinians were able to launch unconventional, guerilla-type violent acts. Only the *Hamas* regime in Gaza, except for *Hezbollah* in South Lebanon, succeeded in accumulating a substantial armory of short and middle distance rockets (since 2006) and causing Israeli casualties and material damage in Negev towns and settlements, in 2008–09, 2012, and 2014.

The two principal adversaries in the *Israel–Syria* segment of the Arab–Israel PC combined attitudes of *fear* of, and *respect* for, "the other's" *military capability*. This was already evident in their earliest military confrontation after their first war (1948)—over their Demilitarized Zone in the Huleh Valley (12 February–15 May 1951). Although Israel triumphed over Syria in three major wars that followed—June 1967, October 1973–May 1974, and June–August 1982 (the first Lebanon War), Syria was perceived by Israel to be its principal Arab military foe. The (failed) attempts by Syria in the 1970s, 1980s, and 1990s to achieve military parity with Israel sustained the latter's long-standing perception of a potential military threat from Syria. Moreover, the 2007 incident, in which Israeli planes destroyed what Israel suspected was an embryonic, Syrian nucleur facility, reinforced Israel's concern about Syria's military capability. A counterpart respect for, and fear of, Israel's military power by Syria was evident during most of the period of Hafiz al-Assad's domination of Syria (1970–2000) and was an important stimulus to Assad Sr.'s lengthy informal alignment with the USSR, the main supplier of Syria's armed forces since 1955. Only when he realized that military parity with Israel was unattainable and that he could not regain control of the Golan Heights by military pressure did Assad Sr. concentrate on the diplomatic track, including his (failed) attempt in 2000 to secure President Clinton's support for this Syrian goal.

CHAPTER 5

Israeli Leaders' Perceptions of the Arabs, the Arab–Israel Conflict, and Peace: Formative Generation, 1948–77

BEN-GURION AND SHARETT: TWO COMPETING PERCEPTIONS

The rationale of Ben-Gurion's view of the Arabs, the Arab–Israel conflict, and peace was conveyed orally, thus: "We Jews have been persecuted for two thousand years. At last, we have recovered this notch of territory in our historic homeland. The Arabs should have received us warmly as cousins; instead they are trying to create another ghetto by blockade, boycott, etc. Thus Israel must show its fist and display it often" (author's interview with Ben-Gurion, 1966). The policy consequence of this perception was that Arab–Israel reconciliation required Israel's possession and use of superior military power against its Arab enemies. The result was frequent Israeli resort to force, which was given its classic expression in the *policy of retaliation* under Ben-Gurion and Moshe Dayan, Chief of Staff of the IDF during 1955–56, during the 1956 Suez War, and Minister of Defense at the time of the June-Six-Day War in 1967 and the October-Yom-Kippur War in 1973.

The rationale of Sharett's very different perception was that the Arab–Israel confrontation is *not* an abnormal international conflict; rather, it is an acute and prolonged dispute but within the realm of the normal and should be treated as such. Further, the conflict cannot be resolved by a dramatic single act but only by a series of seemingly inconspicuous measures over time. Israel, initially the "David" in the region, became the "Goliath" by the end of the 1950s, and Israel should have taken the initiative for peace. In policy terms, the key is a lowering of the general level of tension by constructive acts, including attempts to create, however intermittent and indirect, Israeli contact with Arab leaders so that the transmission of ideas, proposals, and postures could be accomplished by mutually trusted third parties. *In sum*, Arab–Israel reconciliation could be best achieved through a rational search for moderate solutions (author's interview, July 1960).

Ben-Gurion was a hard-line "Ben-Gurionist" during most of his tenure in office (1948–53, 1955–63). Sharett adhered throughout to moderation and negotiation (1948–56). Yet Ben-Gurion did not always perceive the Arabs in suspicious, hard-line terms. From his reading of the Nasser-led revolution in Egypt (1952) and the failure of various *sub-rosa* efforts at negotiation—see below—he became committed to a Realist view. Its essence is that Israel lives in an inherently hostile Arab world, that the best one can work for is acceptance of Israel, and that the only way to achieve this is to hammer away at the Arab states whenever possible—a policy of strength—for this is all the Arabs respect. A soft-line, its argument proceeded, would weaken Israeli security by giving hope to those Arab groups who look for signs of Israel's weakness and an opportunity to destroy Israel. In short, one cannot buy security with concessions. Thus, Israel must persist with a strong line until the Arabs become reconciled to its existence.

The long-term goal, as with the Sharettist approach, was positive coexistence after 20 years or more of hostile acquiescence. Ben-Gurion asserted, however, that no alternative to a hard-line then existed, for the Arabs did not have a compelling motive for peace. The absence of an incentive for a settlement was attributed by him to three factors: *self-delusion*—the Arabs were victims of their own propaganda about Israel's survival potential; *idealism*—the Arabs genuinely felt the obliteration of the Palestine Arab community and the alienness of Israel, which they would like to eliminate; and *self-interest* in the perpetuation of the conflict—Israel provided an excellent focus for Arab unity. Nasser could always have negotiated with Israel—why now, the question was posed before the 1967 war. If Israel were to offer to repatriate 100,000 Arab refugees, why should Nasser accept this as sufficient for peace? He could take this as a starting point and wait for more; so too with territorial adjustments. Moreover, he could hope that Soviet arms and a shift in American strategic policy would enable him to destroy Israel. If not, he could always meet the Israelis at a later date. In short, as long as there was no Arab *need* for peace, there would be no peace. This Ben-Gurionist image and its policy consequence—firmness as the key to Israel's acceptance—commanded widespread support in Israel.

The critical question is whether this view was valid after the 1967 war. Most Israelis appeared to think so. Ben-Gurion himself did not, after that war. Only after the June-Six-Day War in 1967 did he perceive a compelling Arab need for peace—and the logical derivative—an Israeli policy of concessions. "We should evacuate all territories conquered in June 1967 except Jerusalem and the Golan Heights for a genuine peace," he declared often, including during my second interview with him, in May 1971. "There is enough room in Israel, as it was before the June-Six-Day War, to receive all future Jewish immigrants, and that is all that matters."

Notwithstanding his conviction, before the outcome of the June-Six-Day War, that the Arabs did not have a "compelling need for peace," Ben-Gurion revealed in June 1965, after he left office, "I personally was involved in four attempts at mediation with Nasser." One was by an emissary of President Eisenhower, Robert Anderson, a former US Secretary of Defense (the Anderson Mission of 1956). Another was "a very high State Department official." The third was via an English journalist who had interviewed Nasser. And the fourth, related to me in detail by Ben-Gurion during our July 1966 interview, was via an Israeli friend of Tito who had tried to establish contact with Nasser when he was in Yugoslavia in July 1956. According to Ben-Gurion, there were also two later abortive Nasser expressions of interest in meeting him, in 1963 and in 1970, eight days before Nasser's death (*Ha'aretz*, Tel Aviv, 12 October 1970). Nothing came of any of these initiatives.

My summary of Ben-Gurion's well-known Realist, hard-line image of Arab hostility to Israel before the 1967 war was presented to Sharett in July 1960. His response was revealing: "The summary is correct and the line is correct. However, this is not all. To demonstrate firmness and strength, yes. But one must also understand that the Arabs are proud and sensitive. The Arabs are people, not just enemies." When pressed to elaborate, he remarked that his difference with Ben-Gurion was one of "style not substance" and "tactics not strategy," a "mode of approach or language based on understanding of the Arabs' character." As an example, he referred to the expectation among Ben-Gurionists (but not by Ben-Gurion himself) that the Sinai Campaign (1956 Suez

War) would lead to peace. For Sharett, this was "an illusion, an absurdity, because the Arabs rally their people under pressure." (This view was borne out by the support of Egyptians for Nasser during his hour of greatest military defeat, in June 1967, and again in the winter–spring of 1969–70, during Israel's "deep-penetration raids" at the height of the War of Attrition.)

The most incisive comparison of the Ben-Gurion and Sharett images of the Arabs, the Arab–Israel conflict, and peace that I encountered in research on these two commanding figures in Israeli politics, during the first eight years of independence, was provided by Sharett himself in a brilliant lecture one year after the Suez War, in November 1957:

> Two approaches indeed exist.
>
> The *one approach* [advocated by Ben-Gurion until 1967] says that the only language the Arabs understand is force. The State of Israel is so tiny and so isolated ... that if it does not increase its actual strength by a very high coefficient of demonstrated action, it will run into trouble. From time to time, the State of Israel must give unmistakable proof of its strength, and show that it is able and ready to use force in a crushing and highly effective manner. If it does not give such proof, it will be engulfed and may even disappear from the face of the earth.
>
> As far as peace is concerned, says this school of thought, it is doubtful in any event; whatever happens, it is very remote. If peace comes, that will only be when the Arabs are convinced that this country cannot be brought to its knees .... The problem of peace, therefore, need not hamper our considerations when it comes to deciding on some large-scale show of strength to solve a problem of everyday security ....
>
> If we add to these arguments the natural human inclination to react; if we add the special sensitivity characteristic of the Jew that people may perhaps suspect him of weakness; if we add the proximity in time to the Golden Age of our triumph in war [in 1948 and 1956] ... we shall understand the factors behind the atmosphere fostering this approach, over and above the political and military considerations, which are very weighty in themselves.
>
> According to the *second school of thought* [Sharett's view], the question of peace must not be lost sight of for one single moment. This is not solely a political consideration; in the long view, it is decisive from a military point of view. Without diminishing the importance of considerations of day-to-day security, we must always bring the question of peace into our overall calculations. We have to curb our reactions. And the question always remains: has it really been proven that reprisals establish the security for which they were planned?

Those who support the first [Ben-Gurion] approach say that the development of events was inevitable. Arab hatred of Israel is an immutable element of the situation. The situation is grave; we do not claim that everything is fine as it is; but in our grim circumstances this approach has won us very considerable achievements.

"It is difficult, indeed, to query these achievements", Sharett continued. "Nonetheless it is possible to argue that if we had adopted a different approach, if we had sought to minimize incidents rather than play them up, if we had not taken the course of [retaliation raids] Qibya [December 1953], Gaza [February 1955] and so forth, then the political deployment of the other side would have assumed a different pattern. Nasser might perhaps not have been *forced* into the Czech [arms] deal [September 1955], and the Soviet Union might not have found such an easy opening for its penetration of the Middle East. We might have suffered a little more in the meantime, but our overall situation would have been less serious.

Who was right? It may be found that the two approaches should have been synthesized. It may be determined that such vacillation would have a harmful effect .... I cannot overlook the organic complexity of the problem. (An English translation of the bulk of the lecture appeared nine years later in the *Jerusalem Post*, 18 October 1966.)

LEVI ESHKOL: CHANGING VIEWS OF THE ARABS

Eshkol portrayed a calmer and more confident attitude to Israel's security problem, not the grim and ominous picture of the Middle East that was typical of the Ben-Gurion era. There was evident, too, more respect for the Arabs and their leaders, reflecting the Sharett (and Eban) perception of the Arabs—as a People, not merely an Enemy. Yet Eshkol remained a prisoner of his own life experience; that is, he perceived the Arabs through a Second *Aliya* (immigration) lens. Life in the Tsarist Pale, the area of the Russian empire in which Jews were allowed to live, had created a self-sufficient and internally tranquil Jewish existence, but it left the East European ghetto Jewish community isolated from the outer world. When he came to Palestine, Eshkol was preoccupied with the building of Zion. And he lacked knowledge about the Arabs as a people, culture, and society.

By the autumn of 1966 Eshkol's image of the Arabs had changed to the Ben-Gurion–type hard-line under the impact of the emergence of Arab guerrilla movements (*feda'iyun*, Arabic for "self-sacrificer for the cause," first organized by Egypt's army in 1955, later used for all Arab guerrillas) and mounting hostility from the Arab states. This is apparent in his address to the *Knesset*, Israel's parliament, on 17 October 1966 and even more so in his reply to the foreign policy debate a month later, just after Israel's retaliatory raid on the Jordanian village of El Samua: "We do not undervalue the friendship, goodwill and assistance of friendly nations .... But we must always remind ourselves that the safeguarding of our security, the defense of our survival, the building of our road to a safer future—all these things must be done first of all by ourselves." So it remained, his image of the need to "go it alone," until the grave political crisis culminating in the June-Six-Day War in 1967.

GOLDA MEIR: BEN-GURIONIST IMAGE OF THE ARABS

Like Ben-Gurion, but not Sharett, Meir's image of the Arabs derived principally from the Second *Aliya* prism and prolonged noncommunication with the other peoples of the region. In the ultimate shaping of Israel's destiny and the role of the superpowers, Meir was committed to Realism. External pressures, notably from the United States, might compel some adjustment in the application of this doctrine, but her predisposition was to view the Arabs through the Ben-Gurionist lens and to respond with *raison d'état*. Yet, among the four first-generation leaders of Israel, Meir held the most extreme view of the Palestinians: "there are no Palestinians," she declared often; "there are only Israeli Arabs." More than anything else Meir said or did as Foreign Minister (1956–66) and Prime Minister (1969–74), this denigration and denial of a Palestinian nation earned her irreversible enmity among the Palestinians and, more generally, the Arabs. It was the insulting counterpart of the Arab mantra, at least until the Egypt–Israel peace agreement of 1979: "there are no Israelis, only Jews who live among nations scattered throughout the world."

YIGAL ALLON AND MOSHE DAYAN: *SABRA* VIEWS OF THE ARABS AND ISRAEL'S STRATEGIC GOALS

There were two discernible tendencies in Allon's articulated image of the Arabs: the first displayed a conciliatory and cooperative approach; the second was much more hawkish in tone and substance. Arab enmity was perceived as a *constant* in his *Curtain of Sand* (1959), the result of diverse forces: xenophobia and religious fanaticism; the urge for revenge; inter-Arab competition for hegemony; domestic problems, requiring a diversionary external hate object; and Great Power rivalry for influence in the Middle East.

As with other components of his image of the Arabs, the similarity with Dayan's was striking. In Allon's view, prior to the 1967 transformation of the geostrategic balance of power between Israel and the Arab states, in favor of Israel, its strategic position was less than ideal. For one thing, Egypt had a natural base of attack in the Sinai Peninsula. Moreover, Jerusalem and most of central Israel were within artillery range from Jordan-controlled territory. And the Syrian army, encamped on the Golan Heights, threatened settlements in the Jordan Valley. Nor did Israel have any space for retreat. In addition, the danger of being severed at the waist was ever present. Finally, all of Israel was within a few minutes' bombing range of Arab airfields.

This perceived pervasive insecurity led Allon to advocate an "interceptive attack" as a necessary and legitimate form of defense. The essence of Allon's doctrine of interceptive war, perhaps the most innovative strategic concept developed and applied by Israel during the prolonged Arab–Israel conflict, was spelled out with utmost clarity in his *Curtain of Sand*, Chap. 11:

> As long as the Arab rulers refuse to make peace with Israel and continue to hope to overthrow her by economic blockade, or by direct military attack, the moral right and practical ability to carry out an interceptive counter-attack, whenever necessary, form the military guarantee for Israel's future existence .... Sometimes it must precede [Arab aggression] by months, sometimes weeks and sometimes even a few days .... When there is no choice ... by only a few hours, but precede it must.

Allon urged maximum caution before recourse to "active self-defense." He cited as *casus belli* a change in the *status quo* leading to the entry of non-Jordanian Arab troops into the West Bank, Syrian interference with Israeli development projects in the Huleh Valley, the effective creation of a Palestine army, and Egypt's closure of the Tiran Straits; in short, any substantive change in the existing Arab–Israel balance of power. As he remarked in 1960: "Nasser must know that, if he moves his troops through Sinai towards the Israel border, the Israel Army will intercept him. Israel will not act before the UAR (United Arab Republic—1958–61, the period of a merger of Egypt and Syria) or any Arab state begins to mobilize and concentrate on the border—but *it will intercept the Arabs before the attack begins.*" This indeed was the doctrine that guided the IDF's military action on 5 June 1967 after a growing

Egyptian military concentration in Sinai since mid-May and the closing of the Tiran Straits on 22–23 May set in motion what was perceived by Israel as a third Arab attempt to destroy it.

The main thrust of Allon's advocacy *vis-à-vis* the Arabs, from 1948 until his 1968 Allon Plan, which envisaged a two-state solution, was hawkish, like that of Dayan and Shimon Peres. This was most clearly evident in his consistent position on the core political–strategic issue of armistice or peace as the acceptable outcome of Israel's wars. Thus, in his recollections about the 1948–49 war of independence, he remarked: "we won the war but lost the peace." Moreover, during that war, he urged Ben-Gurion not to stop fighting until a peace treaty was assured and not to accept an armistice agreement. For this reason, too, he refused to serve on the Israel delegation to the Rhodes conference in 1949, designed to establish armistice agreements with Israel's neighbors. In 1956–57, too, he urged Ben-Gurion not to withdraw from Sinai and the Gaza Strip until further political goals were achieved (author's interview, August 1960). On these two occasions, Allon's advocacy was rejected. Only after Israel's greatest triumph in war, in 1967, did Israel's multiple administrations adopt a variation of Allon's advocacy, namely, no withdrawal until peace was achieved; this was implemented in the Egypt–Israel peace agreement of 1979, but only after a military impasse in the October-Yom-Kippur War of 1973. However, the exchange of territory for peace was abandoned in the negotiation of the Oslo Accord in 1993.

Dayan's conception of Israel's strategic goals in a period of limited war focused on explicitly limited goals: "Our strategy is to guard the Canal line and not to march on Cairo; to defend the Jordan river line, but not to conquer Amman; not to go to Damascus or Beirut, but to mount retaliatory raids – in depth, breadth, and locations that are unexpected; to retaliate, but to hit and return" (interview in *Ma'ariv*, Tel Aviv, 12 September 1969); it was a reaffirmation of the retaliation doctrine that Dayan had formulated in 1955, perhaps earlier.

Allon wrote a penetrating analysis of the Arab–Israel conflict and of many aspects of Israeli society, *Curtain of Sand* (1959) (in Hebrew), an account of the *Palmah* (in Hebrew), and two volumes on the evolution of Israel's armed forces since the early days of the Jewish Return to Zion. Dayan wrote at least three books, the widely known *Diary of the Sinai Campaign* (1966); *Story of My Life* (1976), an informative autobiography; and a revealing account of the peace process with

Egypt, *Breakthrough: A Personal Account of the Egypt–Israel Peace Negotiations* (1981).

ABBA EBAN: SHARETTIST VIEWS OF THE ARABS, THE MIDDLE EAST, AND PEACE

Eban, Israel's senior diplomat at the UN and the United States (1948–59 and 1950–59, respectively), and Foreign Minister from 1966 to 1974, stood apart from the two generals (Allon and Dayan) and the technocrat (Peres) on the optimal strategy and tactics for Israel during its first quarter-century of independence. The concept of a *pluralist, multinational,* and *multicultural Middle East* was to acquire the status of quasi-official Israeli doctrine. But no one gave it such plausible exposition as Eban, the supreme advocate, in a myriad of public speeches and publications.

On the critical question of *Israel's proper place in the Middle East*, Eban was conspicuously assertive. Like most Israeli leaders, he advocated a policy of cooperative coexistence in the form of a Mediterranean orientation. All this did not prevent Eban from recognizing Arab goals *vis-à-vis* Israel: to prevent its physical existence, to reduce its territory, to flood its territory with hostile refugees, to uproot Jerusalem, to thwart the development of its diplomatic relations, to bar it from international organizations, to hinder its trade; to prevent its immigration projects, to discredit Israel, and to undermine its relations with the new states of Africa and Asia. Yet, after almost two decades, he declared, the Arabs had suffered a "total strategic defeat": "not one of these aims has been attained; none of them is even remotely in sight."

Eban's persistent advocacy of keeping all options open to facilitate a negotiated compromise settlement, against the growing mood of "fortress Israel," most emphatically represented by Dayan and Peres (the latter, until his late years) indicated that Eban remained committed to a Sharettist moderate approach to the Arabs in the post-June-Six-Day-War phase of Israel's foreign policy.

SHIMON PERES: BEN-GURIONIST VIEWS OF THE ARABS AND THE MIDDLE EAST

While Eban may be described as a "cosmopolitan" in foreign policy outlook, and Dayan a "Middle Easterner," Peres was, in his earlier years, pre-eminently a "European" in his image. The task, he said, was to "de-Middle

Easternize" Israel and to place it in its proper European context! Israel, he added, had virtually no contact with Arabs and should ignore them, concentrating rather on internal development and security (author's interview, July 1960).

During the 1960s, Peres softened his rejection of Israel's Middle East environment. However, the Arabs remained for him merely *the enemy*; unlike Dayan and Allon, and especially, Sharett and Eban, he did not display empathy for the Arabs as a People until the 1980s; nor did he, like all three of his generational peers, seek insight into the Arab mind. Indeed, his image was permeated by Ben-Gurionist symbols only: Israel was in a permanent state of siege; Arab hostility was universal in time and space; the Arabs understand only force; concessions by Israel would be fraught with disaster, and so on. As in so many aspects of *perception* and *advocacy*, Peres was the most committed Ben-Gurionist.

In the ongoing Israeli debate over *borders*, the *occupied territories*, and *policy toward the Arabs in general, especially since the 1967 War*, Peres shared Dayan's advocacy in its entirety, that is, "strategic, secure borders," the "open bridges" policy, economic integration, and Jewish settlement in "the territories"—until the 1980s, when Peres began to see the merit of accommodation, compromise, and peaceful coexistence between Israel and Palestine. Since the early 1990s, he perceived the benefits of accommodation and compromise, and became a persistent advocate of peace with the Palestinians.

CHAPTER 6

Encounters with Arab Intellectuals and Officials: Views on Israel, Palestine, and Their Conflict (1975)

The encounters occurred in May–June 1975 during a visit to four Middle East states, Egypt, Israel, Jordan, and Syria, as a member of a group of 28 (mostly) academics, associated with American Professors for Peace in the Middle East (APPME). Notable among the 13 speakers who addressed the group in Cairo were: Ambassador Tahseen Basheer, then Press Counselor to President Anwar Sadat; Boutros Boutros-Ghali, then a professor of international law and political science at Cairo University and, later, Minister of State for Foreign Affairs, Egypt, and Secretary-General of the United Nations; Mahmoud Riad, then Secretary-General of the Arab League; Kamal Abu El Magd, Minister of Information; and three other academics—Yehia Eweiss and Ismail Ghanem (Ein Shams University), and Mahmoud Khairy Issa (Cairo University).

In Damascus, we were addressed by Abdul Ghani Rafei, Deputy Minister of Foreign Affairs; Abdullah El Khani, Minister of Tourism; and Abdul Mouhsen Abu Meizer, member of the Executive Committee and spokesperson for the Palestine Liberation Organization (PLO). In Amman, we received a stimulating overview of the state of the conflict from a talented US Foreign Service officer, then Ambassador Thomas Pickering, and standard fare for foreigners from two mid-level Jordanian officials.

In Israel, the speakers included: Shimon Peres, then Defense Minister; Teddy Kollek, a long-time and admired Mayor of Jerusalem; two knowledgeable academics—Yehoshafat Harkabi at the Hebrew University of Jerusalem, and Itamar Rabinovitch, a specialist on modern Middle East history and, later, president of Tel Aviv University, and chief Israel peace negotiator with senior Syria officials in the 1990s, along with several journalists.

Some of these talks were informative; most were set-piece presentations designed to generate sympathy and support for their inevitably biased interpretations of the causes of the Arab–Israel conflict and its persistence 27 years after its eruption in 1948. (At the time of writing, this conflict remains unresolved after 68 years, except for two formal peace agreements—Egypt–Israel in 1979 and Israel–Jordan in 1994, neither accompanied by any evidence of reconciliation between the adversaries.)

Among the many encounters, I conducted interviews with senior civil servants, politicians, military officers, journalists, and academics in Cairo. These provided insights into the attitudes of some talented Egyptian intellectuals and officials, who enhanced the value of these unrestricted exchanges by consenting to taped interviews. Given space limitations, four of these thought-provoking exchanges are presented below: they were designed to uncover *Egyptian attitudes* to, and *perceptions* of, the *basic causes* of the conflict—its *onset* and *persistence*, its *existing state* in 1975, and the *future prospects* for *termination*. One was with Mohammed Sayeed Ahmad, a Marxist intellectual–editorial contributor to *Al-Ahram*, Cairo's preeminent newspaper. Another was with Dr. Osama Al-Baz, then the National Security Advisor to President Sadat and, from 1981, for many years thereafter, to President Hosni Mubarak. A third was with Boutros Boutros-Ghali, then a professor of international law at Cairo University and, later, a Minister for Foreign Affairs during the Egypt–Israel negotiations that led to a peace agreement between Egypt and Israel in 1979. The fourth encounter was with a group of research scholars associated with the then premier Egyptian "think tank," the Al-Ahram Center for Political and Strategic Studies (1975).

MOHAMMED SAYEED AHMAD: COMMENTATOR, AL-AHRAM CENTER, CAIRO

Among the many persons encountered in Cairo in May–June 1975, one of the most insightful was a respected Marxist intellectual–commentator, Mohammed Sayeed Ahmad, author of an unconventional book by an Arab on the Arab–Israel conflict at the time, *When the Guns Fall Silent: Peace or Armageddon in the Middle East* (1976); most of the interview took the form of an exposition of its central ideas. An abridged version of the taped interview is presented here for the first time:

M.B.: In all candor, Mr. Ahmad, you were very highly recommended as someone I must talk to in Cairo.
We [a group of North American professors] have been here only a few days but I have talked with several other people and what I discern very clearly is what I would describe as a strong will among those I met for an accommodation with Israel or a settlement of this long-standing conflict between the Arab states and Israel. As a student of the region and of this problem for many years, I am puzzled by the very marked contrast between the written word in the Arab world from 1948 to 1973 on the issue of any kind of settlement, even to the extent that, in Arab newspapers, until about 1968, it was virtually impossible to mention the word "Israel," either without italics or the use of the term "so-called state."

M.S. Ahmad: Not after '67; for some years after '48, yes, the ambiguity was still there.

M.B.: This change seems marked, and I wonder whether you would share your analysis of the nature of the change and the reasons for this change.

M.S. Ahmad: I wrote an article last October [1974], to mark one year after the October War that I would recommend you to see in *Le Monde Diplomatique*. I think that, since the October War, there has been a turning point insofar as the Arabs have believed that they have acquired a certain common ability to deal with the opponent, an attitude that has removed many of the past inhibitions. There was no more the need for this discrepancy between strong [hostile] expression and weak ability. That's a very important change, I think, in the Arab world. This is the local [the Arab] component.

I mean the issue is much more complex than that. Another element, no less important, I think, is that, with international détente, the Middle East crisis had been one of the crisis situations in which the rules of Cold War and polarization had remained the longest. So, in a certain way, the October War has ushered the Middle East into the détente rules of the game.

I have a book just out on all this in Arabic. It's already made a bit of a noise in the Lebanese papers because I've been accused of recommending dealing with Israel. But the issue is much more complex than this.

One basic thesis in the book is what I call the rearrangement of contradictions: I say that détente is not a canceling of contradictions; it is a rearrangement of contradictions—a rearrangement made necessary by the fact that a certain set of contradictions has become more detrimental to all than beneficial to any, like, for example, nuclear warfare, like pollution, like spreading famines in the future. And this set of contradictions has to be frozen so that contradictions can express themselves otherwise. In fact, *when we say that in the Middle East today we are going towards a settlement, this settlement is a certain rearrangement of the contradictions in the Middle East.* One way of putting it, and that is what I put in the book, is a little bit a replacement of what I call vertical contradictions between the conflicting parts by what one could call horizontal contradictions within every previous part.

M.B.: Now, every previous part would include both the major parties to the conflict; that is to say, horizontal contradictions within Israeli society, and horizontal contradictions within the different components of Arab society.

M.S. Ahmad: Altogether.

M B.: Could you elaborate the nature and the substance of these horizontal contradictions that you discern?

M.S. Ahmad: The idea of horizontal contradictions could be first of all social contradictions. But in the case of Israel, it is not necessarily on a social level. I would put it more in terms, as least in the immediate future, of what I would call hawks and doves. In fact, hawks and doves are not necessarily altogether contradictory. They might be in a certain way complementary. What would be different is that the hawks would be those who emphasize the immediate interest ahead of the long-run interest, and that would be the policy of the state as having proved to be the most effective since the '67 War and in the complex of the pre-'73 situation.

Since the October War, the situation has been different, insofar as the doves have acquired a function more than being exclusively a décor. The doves' logic emphasizing the long-run interests was now taken sufficiently into consideration, not only short-run interests. But since the October War, the logic of the hawks has also changed. I mean the October War has been important enough to give to the doves a certain function but not important enough to cancel the logic of the hawks. I would say that both logics have validity now.

M.B.: And both perform a function within Israeli society?

M.S. Ahmad: And both perform a certain function within society. I mean what I would like to say is, what are the two logics? One is that what has occurred requires a complete reassessment of our policies so this is the last war of the century. That would be the dove logic. The hawk logic would be that certain links in the Israeli system of Defense had failed [in 1973], and because these things have failed, we must reinforce the system by replacing the failed things by stronger ones in the same logic—so both logics are there. And from this point of view, this is a horizontal contradiction in Israel which could go to the extent that, after the gods have failed, you see that the new leadership is more part of the mosaic than being above it. That could put us in front of the risk of a certain freezing of ability of taking the decisive decisions required. I mean Israel today might have a Heath, not a Churchill.

M.B: Everything you said suggests to me that, in your judgment, the October 1973 war was the inescapable catalytic agent to this kind of seismic change.

M.S. Ahmad: I wouldn't put it that way, but I put it that there was—I wouldn't say convergence—but a confluence of factors, forces at work which each had its own point of departure, but which at least blended together for this shock therapy.

The hawks in Israel are today less weighty than the other logic, the other logic being the idea of the possibility of a breakthrough towards a settlement. But I don't define a settlement as a canceling of the contradictions. I define it as a rearrangement of these contradictions; but this rearrangement does not exclude some forms of intercourse between all parts [of the Middle East], including Israel. I expect new forms of conflict in the region but not at all the classical ones, not the previous kinds. I see, at least at the moment, that the Middle East crisis might be losing its formal definition as being Arab–Israel and become an Arab conflict.

M.B.: All of these are in geographical–territorial terms. Could it be also in class–ideological terms?

M.S. Ahmad: No. I put it in territorial, geographical terms. I'll use another category, a crisis losing its geographical definition to acquire another more specific one. The Middle East Crisis is very much linked to the energy crisis and the monetary crisis and to raw materials vs. finished products. There is also the ideological element. I mean why were they attacking me on this book? Because I was saying in Arabic for the first time that there is a chance in the future of certain Arabs looking for complementarity with Israel. So this was very shocking.

I tried to make a prognosis on what would be the door in. I said the door in would probably be the idea of security because up till now security has been stated in terms of negative sanctions; but the next step in security is positive acceptance and that might be in the creation of economic linkages which would not be presented in terms of complementarity but in terms of security, and money might pour into the region for petrochemicals, for example, in this region: it is less costly than the arms race in the region. And then it might be contagious in a later stage.

Then I think that today the US might be interested in a settlement, in a breakthrough to something very important. I think that the Middle East is becoming more and more for the US a key issue for its superpower status the world over. The US is not really dependent on Arab oil, physically. But it is very dependent on Arab oil so far as it is very important for the US to keep its superpower status vis-à-vis Europe and Japan, who are much more dependent on Arab oil. And a certain decentralization of the industrial world is becoming also necessary. So this is also very important concerning a region where a raw material like oil is sold. So these are various regions where Israel might become a *buffer if it is to remain exclusively a state* [!] and might be much more useful as a *raison expertise* and as a sort of American control that this change in the Arab world does not go beyond the Western orbit.

M.B.: May I ask you in this context: what does this mean in terms of Soviet concerns—the Soviet penetration into the Middle East, the impact on détente, whether the Soviet Union itself is prepared to allow this natural process to fulfill itself?

M.S. Ahmad: Yes, that's very important. Let me say this. In a previous stage, one thing that was bewildering for the non-Communist world was the extent that the Soviet Union developed relations with a country like Egypt and under Nasser, though ideologically, it was obvious all through that there was no similarity between the two. There was a distinct difference in ideology. So how do you explain this dilemma? I would think that the basic idea during the polarized period for the Soviet Union was to circumscribe the polarized situation in Europe, let us say, amongst the developed capitalist countries and developed socialist countries by an opening into the Third World. At the time when the national liberation movement was going forward, where this issue was ambiguous insofar as it could be a reservoir for capitalism but also a potential possibility to go beyond into some socialist pattern, not necessarily Communist, but might. But there is another aim, too, which is to provoke peaceful coexistence, a key position here for various reasons. With the breakthrough of détente and Egypt's opening with the US, the 1973 détente was operational in the US. A breakthrough in the Middle East Crisis was not operational, and this was one reason why Sadat began getting very fidgety with his relations with the Soviet Union. He didn't feel that it was responding to what he wanted.

Now as to the future: The Nasserite pattern or similar patterns were islands in a wider Arab world. That was a first moment, islands of a progressive system within a conservative Arab world. For the problem of a Middle East settlement, there is another logic which is taking the fore. A dialogue with Americans has been the key.

M.B.: Let me move on from the Soviet role and strategy to one component of this which is almost universally ignored but which, in my judgment, is done so in great error, namely, the role of China in this. For a very long time, the Chinese presence in the Middle East has been marginal to nonexistent for all kinds of reasons which are internal to the Chinese set of priorities in terms of their national development and growth. Do you see in the period of a generation, a kind of penetration, intrigue, presence, whichever term one wishes to use, for the People's Republic of China in one or another segment of a divided community of Arab states which would have spillover effects both on the Arab–Israel conflict as it now exists and on the kinds of rearrangement of contradictions of which you spoke.

M.S. Ahmad: Yes, the logic of the Chinese is that this rearrangement of contradictions is just a sort of American–Soviet continuum: the realism in going upstairs and that, in fact, is an expression of chaos and not order. This has been basically the Mao Tse-tung logic.

M.B.: No one will be clear until the transition takes place in the succession to Mao and the new leadership.

M.S. Ahmad: This spectacular return of Deng is a little bewildering. I know that the Chinese have a certain logic in their behavior, with their alternating periods of ideology and technology. Their idea is that the only shortcut into development is to get movement by zigzags. This is Mao Tse-tung, you see—there are moments for cleaning house ideologically and moments for getting whatever you can get economically, even from the West, because with the Soviet Union, there is ambiguity that technology could eat ideology. Better to deal with clear-cut people, so Japan and the US are better.

M.B.: Where do you see, in the post-peace settlement period, assuming that this takes place, the role of Israel with a rather dynamic society, with a relatively high level of economic development, with the new horizontal contradictions replacing the vertical contradictions? What role does Israel play in this *new Middle East*?

M.S. Ahmad: Israel has played the role of economic model. In Africa, for example, for a long time, it has been able to project a certain ambiguity concerning itself: is it a part of the Developed World or is it a part of the Third World? And projecting itself as an outstanding experiment in the Third World, it could offer to Africa what the developed western countries couldn't sometimes offer directly. With more experience perhaps and more efficiency than Western countries concerning certain specific experiments in agriculture or others. Israel might strive towards playing the role of an economic model in the Arab world too, but there is one basic difference—basically land, territorial acquisition. Perhaps in the deep consciousness of Arabs, it is technological know-how and ability. But now, Arab wealth need not be easily absorbed by Israeli tech know-how.

M.B.: Which means competition and rivalry?

M.S. Ahmad: I mean a new sort of relationship. Can Israel afford becoming only an economic model in an Arab environment without losing its Zionist identity?

M.B.: What is your own judgment on this question?

M.S. Ahmad: My own judgment is that there is a serious danger that Israel could lose its identity for various reasons.

M.B.: When you say lose its identity, what precisely do you mean? What would happen?

M.S. Ahmad: I'll explain. Israel is constituted of very heterogeneous elements cemented together by the hostility of the environment. What will become of Israel if this hostility disappears? An important part of the Israel community is from the Arab world and might possibly return to the Arab world in this new situation. Israel is in a certain way strong to the extent that it appears weak

	and can get money from outside when it is threatened, but much less help if it is not threatened. All these are corrosive factors for its cohesion in the future. There might be a need for one or more other wars. Of course, wars have lost their character as that of eradicating one of the parts, but the wars still might remain a need for one part or another for the breakthrough towards peace.
M.B.:	Let me, on this point, ask a question about the Palestinians: what do you regard as the role of the Palestinians within the Arab world?
M.S. Ahmad:	There are enormous similarities between the Israeli experience and the Palestinian experience. The Palestinians are the most sophisticated Arabs with the highest per capita ratio of élites. The Palestinians are the only Arabs who have one foot in Israel and one foot out of Israel and would be the best of partners and the best of catalysts in a later stage. Probably, the Soviets and the Americans would pour in a fantastic amount of money into this Palestinian state the day it is considered practically relevant to bring it forward.
M.B.:	Do you mean a Palestinian state in the West Bank and Gaza?
M.S. Ahmad:	Yes, something of that sort. I don't know. Possibly the Palestinians will come up with '48, I mean '47 as the basis. I mean less than '67. They say it will be for more than '67 and everybody will get something, which will be some minor rectifications of '67. Put it this way: if there is a breakthrough towards peace and the recognition of a Palestinian entity, it will be a very potent catalyst. Until things settle down, we will have many stages in between but we will finish up with a settlement.
M.B.:	If we don't blow each other to bits!

M.S. Ahmad: If the Palestinians get nothing, there will be a blowing up.

M.B.: Are the Palestinians ready for a genuine settlement?

M.S. Ahmad: Yes, Yes.

M.B.: A settlement in which they abandon this notion of the ultimate transformation of Israel into an Arab state?

M.S. Ahmad: No, no. This will not happen this way. What will happen between Israelis and Palestinians will be similar to what is happening between the Soviet Union and the US. The Soviet Union has not given up Communism as its ultimate aim the world over. And the US is not giving up eradicating Communism the world over. Each side will have to give up requiring the ultimate goal of the other to be abandoned. You have to accept the ultimate goal. The question will be the modalities and leaving open for each side to prove by other means than those used until now, either that Israel is to remain Israel or becoming a democratic secular state. Each goes on fighting for its ultimate goal, but by other means than what was used up until now.

M.B.: What is the ultimate goal of the Palestinians?

M.S. Ahmad: The ultimate goal of the Palestinians is to replace or dismantle the Israeli state.

M.B.: What do the Palestinians perceive to be the ultimate Israeli goal which the Palestinians will not now require Israel to abandon?

M.S. Ahmad: Israel within some borders occupying a part of Palestine and not all. What borders exactly? That is to be decided upon. Let us say ultimately '67 or something around that.

M.B.:	But the Israelis, according to the Palestinians, have much larger ambitions.
M.S. Ahmad:	There is a certain ambiguity. When you have nothing, you assume the other wants everything.
	The Palestinians have a dilemma since the October War. Before the October War there were two logics which were just as valid theoretically in the Arab world. One was to a set of references going back to '67 and one was to make a set of references going back to '48. The Palestinians were going back to '48. After the October War, one logic has imposed itself upon the other logic, so the other has to accommodate. Now they are placed in a dilemma: either they say, "we go on with our '48 aim" and then we say—because we have to possess every bit of Palestinian land that can be liberated—we assert our right to this, every bit, and this implies implicitly a coexistence with Israel. They have chosen. They have chosen to take whatever bit they can get.
M.B.:	Have they chosen this in full recognition that, in reality, this means the acceptance and legitimacy of Israel combined with coexistence?
M.S. Ahmad:	For the moment, the difference between the Arab states and Israel is, Israel would like to be recognized by the Arab states but the Arab states won't recognize Israel. But the question of the Palestinians is more complex because neither Israelis recognize Palestinians nor do Palestinians recognize Israelis. So there is symmetry here, but this symmetry can be replaced by another symmetry.
M.B.:	Dual recognition?
M.S. Ahmad:	Yes, dual recognition.

M.B.: I have to go now but I want to thank you very much. It has been fascinating. I do hope your book is translated because I think the kind of analysis that you have given here is utterly unknown, not only in Egypt, but perhaps in many parts of the world outside of Egypt. I don't even know how well known it is in Egypt.

M.S. Ahmad: Not very well. I've been rewriting a lot of this, but not to this frankness. This is the first time I've been completely frank.

OSAMA AL-BAZ: NATIONAL SECURITY ADVISOR TO PRESIDENTS SADAT AND MUBARAK

On conflict, crisis, and war, Dr. Al-Baz was one of the most influential figures in Egypt's decision-making élite. An abridged version of the taped interview is presented here for the first time:

M.B.: I would like to begin, Dr. Al-Baz, by asking about the change that I and many others have discerned in the attitudes expressed to us during this visit, compared with a lengthy period dominated by the famous "Three No's of Khartoum" soon after the June-Six-Day War of 1967—the policy of *no negotiations with Israel, no peace with Israel, no recognition of Israel*, formally adopted by the Arab League at its Khartoum summit meeting. What do you think are the principal reasons for this rather dramatic change in policy?

Al-Baz: In my opinion, and I might be wrong, the Arabs feel stronger now and they are more secure. In the past, their attitude of total rejection [of Israel], no, no and negativism and so on was an expression of a complex on their part because they couldn't believe that the Israelis were able to establish their state in the midst of the Arabs by force. So, of course, it was fresh, the fact that Israel was established legitimately and was still a very living reality. Now the Arabs have more confidence in themselves, and the performance of both their leaders and their soldiers during the October War and after gave them the self-reassurance, self-confidence, and pride. No one is talking. Very few Arabs are talking of revenge now and of just rejecting, of negativism as a form of reacting. Now they think that they are masters of their own destiny and, like any other people, they can achieve, they can perform, they can fulfill. And there is no escapism anymore: they are not evading the issues and they are willing to face the future and to shoulder their responsibilities in this light. And they think they can deal with the Israelis. Everyone, this is an exaggeration, but most Arabs thought of Israel as a scheme, as a plot, a conspiracy that no one can control, and that if they come here, it is like an octopus, a cancerous mechanism that would swallow the rest of the Arab world. In other words, most Arabs thought that it is inconceivable for Israel to exist with the Arabs; but now this illusion has been smashed and the reality now is that Israel is a state like another state. It can be dealt with like any ordinary state, and in this respect, I think the defeat of the Israelis, at least in the first days, the early days of the October War, was in favor of Israel in the long run because it convinced the Arabs that the Israelis are just a normal, an ordinary state and the Israelis are just human beings like any others: they can be defeated, they could be dealt with as such. And this is important because it drove home to the Arabs the fact that they are not an octopus.

M.B.: One more point on this. I'm shocked by the fact that you've made no reference to the great economic problems of Egypt, and I wonder whether the domestic economic pressures and needs act as a kind of catalyst which project in this direction.

Al-Baz: No, no. I don't think so, because if the Egyptians were desperate, they couldn't care less because the economic problem does not appear today. In fact, most of our economic problems of today are remnants of the past, because in real terms, our economic situation now is much better than before. However, the fact is that when you are desperate, you have nothing to lose. Say damn it, I have nothing to lose. I can do anything. But now that the Arabs, let me confine myself to speaking about Egypt, the Egyptians have felt after the October War that they are secure enough and they can face any challenge easily and this is a bonus—not to talk about the economic factor. It was not in my opinion a main pressure for the Arabs to accept the proposition that they could live in peace with the Israelis.

M.B.: Most Egyptian officials that we have spoken to have talked in terms of a Palestinian state consisting of Gaza and the West Bank. Yet the few Palestinians we've talked to claim that their minimal position is 1947. What do you think is the Palestinian position?

Al-Baz: In my opinion, there are two Palestines in their minds, in the mind of every Palestinian, more or less. The realistic Palestine one would expect to see in our lifetime is the Gaza Strip and the West Bank. There is also an illusionary and imaginary Palestine, legally speaking, not de facto, but de jure in terms of a legal concept which consists of the 1947 part of Palestine that was allocated to the Arabs [in the UN General Assembly Partition Resolution].

M.B.: Then there is of course a third Palestine, all of the territory of the British Mandate, from the Jordan River to the Mediterranean.

Al-Baz: The third one is no longer Palestine. These are the only two Palestines that are considered by Palestinians. One of them is a reality and I think that it is feasible and that it should be implemented. It should be born. The second one is used only as a legal and juristic concept, so it is not really an expression on the part of the Palestinians that they should do that, but it is an expression of protest by the Palestinians of the fact that their rights were reserved and abused, and theoretically speaking, the most they could swallow is Israel within the 1947 borders. But this is theoretical only. Practically speaking, they know that the only Palestine which is viable and visible now is the Gaza Strip and the West Bank. The third one is not Palestine but it is an idea, probably an ideal—not one they would fight for but they would keep on advocating it, which is the secular, democratic state, a bi-national state consisting of both Arabs and Israelis. But everyone knows that this is a very remote proposition unless a strong movement in Egypt appears to advocate it. It cannot be achieved because no Arab is willing to advocate achieving that by force and most Arabs are not in favor of achieving the second Palestine by force. What remains as viable, as feasible, is the first Palestine.

M.B.: Is the Egyptian government making any efforts to try to persuade the Palestinians that this is the best that they can hope for and that they ought to take it?

Al-Baz: We are actually doing that. However, this is not of much help because they listen to Egypt, they listen to Algeria, they listen to some reasonable elements within the Palestinian movement. But then the acts and the behavior of the Israelis are not much help because it is very much the Israelis who are now behaving like the Arabs in the past. "No, No, No," the Israelis say; "the Palestinians are a bunch of terrorists. We are not willing to talk with them." Nothing. They are only willing to talk to King Hussein. The Palestinians now have their own representatives. Why not talk to them? "No, they are terrorists, say the Israelis, all terrorists." You know each other's language.

M.B.: Egypt is the premier Arab state in many respects. It has an opportunity—and some would say even an obligation—to try to get the PLO's responsible leadership at the top to understand that it is in their interests in terms of their three Palestines to make it clear in some way—whichever way seems appropriate to their need—that what they are talking about in reality is the only feasible Palestine: the one that involves the West Bank and Gaza. Now you may say, but, of course, the Israelis have to do the same thing.

However, I am asking you as a responsible Egyptian official, whether it is not possible for Egypt, as the leading Arab state, both in the confrontation with Israel and within the Arab world, to play a major role in this respect and to make the PLO understand that they are not functioning in a vacuum, but in a highly volatile situation in which their words, given their deeds, carry a great deal of weight.

We haven't heard any responsible Palestinian say that what they are prepared to accept is the West Bank and Gaza, but we have heard repeatedly a refusal to recognize the legitimacy of Israel. We heard it yesterday afternoon in front of 21 North American professors. This is why we raised the point. We put the question very seriously. We said: "even if you continue with your dream ...." The speaker seemed to be very moderate, but when we probed this .... We also had the Editor of *Al-Ahram*, who covers the PLO.

Al-Baz: Salbeck. He's a nice guy.

M.B.: Yes, but the same position was taken by him. In other words, the minimal position was '47. Now you know very well that to say to the Israelis the position is '47 is to close the door forever. If you suggest that to him, as we did, he looks at you and says, "how can we possibly expect anything else [than '47] or accept anything else." Doesn't Egypt have a potential role here? I know Egypt is busy with many things, but this happens to be one of the most complex, most difficult, most emotion-laden segments of the conflict. This is why I bring it to your attention.

Al-Baz: Sure. We do that within the following constraints. You realize that, in the final analysis, it is the Palestinians who must make a judgment as to what they should do and what they shouldn't do.

M.B.: I am not suggesting that you dictate, because I know you can't dictate.

Al-Baz: We don't even want to dictate, even if we can. I think we could dictate, but we don't want to dictate. We are advising the Palestinians. We are saying, "look, for you to reach your goal you have to be reasonable. We know that your goals are limited so don't make it sound like your goals are unlimited and they are endless, that if you have your way you are going to go all the way from Egypt to the Golan Heights. That's not the line to push."

M.B.: But is Egypt in fact acting in this direction?

Al-Baz: Egypt was. I'll tell you one of the leverages we used with the Palestinians. We worked very hard in the past 18 months to get them international recognition because we thought that international recognition will not only be a boost to their cause but it will also be a force towards moderation, and I think it moderated them tremendously, in my opinion. I know their views from the past and I know their views now.

M.B.: Many people thought that Arafat's speech at the United Nations was a historic missed opportunity to signal Israel in a way that was fundamentally different from what he did signal. Would you be inclined to agree with this?

Al-Baz: No, because given the fact that it was the first public statement of its kind given by a Palestinian leader, I think, he gave the message that they are willing to live in peace with the Israelis. When he spoke about the olive branch, he was sending that message. For the first, for a starter, I think it was not bad.

M.B.: How long is the gap in time between the starter and what is still yet to come, a long time?

Al-Baz: No, I think he has to follow it up. He has to follow it up, but they [the Israelis] have to reciprocate.

M.B.: One last point, in the form of a question. As you know, our group [North American academics] is going through several countries. We came directly to Egypt and have had the pleasure of a very fruitful stay. We go from here to Syria and then to Jordan, and then finally to Israel. Now I know very well that you have all kinds of ways of communicating your ideas to people on the other side; but is there anything that you feel we can do when we talk, as we will, to people on the Israeli side at the highest levels as we have here, in an attempt to bridge this gap, to contribute in some way to what I would call the lessening of this very thick wall of mistrust that still exists on both sides?

Al-Baz: If you just tell them what I've said—that there is a genuine mood towards peace in Egypt and in the other places you are going to visit, in case you find this to be true; and that the more the Israelis hold out in terms of getting into terms with the Egyptian leadership and so on, the more people will be disillusioned [with the present situation] and will start to question the wisdom and the validity of the claim that the Arabs could not live and coexist with the Israelis. And by this way, they are defeating their own cause, I think, by being intransigent because here really there is no limit. People are genuinely and honestly accepting the proposition that they could live with an Israel which is not expansionist and which is not an arsenal of arms and so on and which is not acting on behalf of a foreign power. If it is acting as a Middle East power, as a power like the rest in the area, that if it is not acting on the assumption that they are superior to us because definitely and, believe me, personally, I think that most Israelis think that they are superior to Arabs. They are not superior in terms of education. They are not superior in terms of technology, in terms of upbringing, in terms of heritage. Most of the ones who believe in that crap, they are Europeans because definitely, sometimes, someone coming from Poland or from Italy, Europeans, are known to be prejudiced against others: colored, Africans, Asians, the yellow race, non-Christians. For them to go to Palestine and to meet some Bedouins, some camel drivers with the kinds of images they had of the Arabs, it is very hard for them to conceive, to think of the Arabs in terms of equal people, and this is very wrong. There is no limit. If they are genuinely interested in peace, it is not only in our interests economically, but it is in our interests in every sense, culturally and otherwise. We have no hang-ups whatsoever, and our readiness to go toward peace is absolute and total.

M.B.: I would like to make one brief comment since I've travelled previously to Israel. There is no question that many are arrogant, but I think that you ought to be really disabused of the notion that it is against Arabs. It's against any non-Israelis.

Al-Baz: This is bad. Because we are non-Israeli.

M.B.: It's bad. But what I'm saying is that it's not a function of discrimination against Arabs. It's a function of a kind of sentinel mentality which they feel has forced them to be utterly self-reliant, tough, because they have lived in a period of collective horror.

Al-Baz: It is a backlash to the Nazis. The Nazis treated them as such. We're good and we're even as good as the Nazis.

I'm not trying to be malicious, but they [Israelis] behaved in many ways like the Nazis, thinking that sheer power per se could solve matters and that you can force your opponent by pushing them against the wall and you have to industrialize, you have to build a strong arsenal, you have to have this, you have to have that—this is a Nazi concept. And they were doing it. The symbol in Israel was not someone who is a philosopher. For years it was Dayan, until 1967—because he is a victor. When the Arabs talk about the Israelis as Nazis, they are not kidding. More Egyptians picture Dayan, although personally I know that Dayan is, relatively speaking, a moderate, but he is pictured in the eyes of most Egyptians and Arabs as another Hitler. Why? Because he symbolizes sheer force. Even the Israeli leaders who are, relatively speaking, knowledgeable of the Arabs, who know their culture, like Abba Eban—they are outnumbered, and even they are not really moderates in the universal sense of the word—they are moderates, relatively speaking, only because they are not as extremist as the rest of them. And this is a serious point.

M.B.: For many Israelis, if you've been at war for 27 years, it is hard to be in a position to cultivate trust.

Al-Baz: That's why we are saying that it takes some time. It has to develop gradually. It cannot be done quickly. And they [Israelis] say, "why should we take this chance?" Everyone is taking a chance. We are taking a chance in the presence of certain guarantees that would make it unlikely for war to break out again. It is not 100 percent. No one can get this. I think we are taking a big chance.

M.B.: What is that chance? If you regain your territories of '67, what are you risking?

Al-Baz: If I regain my land?

M.B.: You can close the canal again. You can close the Straits again.

Al-Baz: Why should I do that? Just for spite? There is always an assumption of rationality. Unless the Israelis are thinking that I am an irrational thing. There is an assumption of rationality if I get back my land, if I undertake a major reconstruction effort, why should I go fight Israel?

M.B.: Let me project another scenario, a reason that you and other Egyptian officials, I think, provided in the period between 1968 and 1971 in what was widely described in this country and in the press and in periodicals as the Two-Stage Plan. "We proceed in Stage One to regain through diplomatic and political means all of the territory lost in the 1967 war. And we give the necessary guarantees of course in order to achieve this, but we then create a situation in which Israel is then truly vulnerable—a Palestinian state in the West Bank and Gaza; Egypt in control once more of the Canal, of the Straits, not very far from the heartland of Tel Aviv and the surrounding populated areas; Syria, on the Golan Heights; Jordan back in the Old City, or Palestine back in the Old City of Jerusalem". Then, given the modern weaponry that is now available through the billions of petro dollars that are available to the Arab world, the second stage, rooted in what you and other Egyptian officials described as this profound conviction of the injustice created in 1947 [the Arab refugee problem]

	then becomes feasible. That scenario is not really as fantastic as it appears.
Al-Baz:	So for that reason we are more than willing to introduce any measures or arrangements or guarantees to make it clear that in case that happens, Egypt will not be able to do that. Limit the level of armament. Have all the big powers sign it. Have the Security Council support it. Have international supervision, provided it is both ways.
M.B.:	Is it correct, do you think, that it is much riskier for the Arabs than for the Israelis; but that the risks the Arabs are taking for peace is much less than maintaining the status quo?
Al-Baz:	If you look at the argument this way, that means they are preparing between two risks, and either way, they are losing, which is not necessarily true, because had Israel been courageous enough, they would have said the following after 1967: "we will give you back all your land provided you accept an unlimited peace with us."
M.B.:	Was that possible after "Khartoum" 1967 [the three No's]?
Al-Baz:	After Khartoum?
M.B.:	All this which was just two months after the '67 war? No recognition, no negotiations, no peace.
Al-Baz:	Sure.
M.B.:	Would you expect, within two months of the '67 war, any Israeli leader [except Ben-Gurion, who was no longer in power] to get up and say the war is over, now we return all the territory?
Al-Baz:	They would say the following: "Our objective was such and such, not to defeat the Arabs, not to occupy land, nor to expand. Our objective was to tell the Arabs that they cannot interfere with our right to exist here and that we are here to

exist and to continue. So if you Arabs like to live with us in peace we are offering you this: an olive branch. We can live in peace if such conditions are met and we are willing to do such and such. Go to the Security Council, hold a conference and get the guarantees of the two superpowers, and we will give you back your land because we are not interested in territorial expansion." They didn't do that. They took the land. This increased the image of the conspiracy. Many Arabs think that the Israelis are planning to control the entire world.

M.B.: That would be quite a feat for three million people to control the world.

Al-Baz: This is a revival of the Protocols of the Elders of Zion, the misconceptions that were exported from Europe to every place on Earth. Things like conspiracy. This is a great conspiracy—an invisible government in France. Most Arabs believe that Watergate was a Jewish conspiracy.

M.B.: The Final Settlement, Dr. Al-Baz: you said that you are prepared to consider all kinds of demilitarized arrangements. You recognized that, in a sense, the risks can legitimately appear to the Israelis as you have: to be rather larger than what they are to the Egyptians. Until we get to the peace settlement, could it not be perceived that the concessions, in order to convince the Israelis that they are not taking major risks, ought to be not necessarily evenly balanced?

Al-Baz: I agree with you. For that reason, we are willing to undertake not to resort to violence or to the use of force even though two-thirds of our territory was taken by force. This is a greater risk to accept the nonuse of force while two-thirds of Sinai is still occupied.

M.B.: Dr. Al-Baz, if I may be blunt: the kinds of concessions by Egypt which talk about eliminating the Arab boycott on five companies that trade with Israel as a gesture is a stingy gesture. What I mean to say: if I were an Israeli and you said to me "we'll reduce the boycott by a third and then we'll go on to something more meaningful," that would be a substantial concession.

Al-Baz: Let me put it this way. In terms of boycott, it will have to take place within an overall settlement. This is for the Arab countries in general, and Egypt cannot, in all honesty, break the boycott like that because it is an undertaking and we will do it together with the rest of the Arab countries. We cannot violate it just like that. The Arab countries chose the boycott as part of the confrontation with Israel. This confrontation is still continuing. It would be very immoral for Egypt to forsake the Palestinians. It is our duty to fight for the rights of the Palestinians because we feel that they have a sense of community with us, some kind of strong tie with us and we cannot let them down. So we cannot now lift the boycott. For the boycott to be lifted, it will have to be done, but why rush it. If you are genuine, I think the Geneva Conference could reach an overall settlement in two years and I'm not being unrealistic.

M.B.: All I can say is, I don't think you are right.

Al-Baz: Let us keep our fingers crossed.

M.B.: You've been most generous. Thank you very much.

Al-Baz: Thank you. I've enjoyed it.

BOUTROS BOUTROS-GHALI: PROFESSOR OF INTERNATIONAL LAW, CAIRO UNIVERSITY; LATER, MINISTER OF STATE FOR FOREIGN AFFAIRS, EGYPT, AND UN SECRETARY-GENERAL (1992–1996)

Dr. Boutros-Ghali was an influential academic in the field of international law and, later, as Egypt's Minister of State for Foreign Affairs. An abridged version of the taped interview is presented here for the first time:

M.B.: For those who favor a resolution of the Arab–Israel conflict, what kind of institutional setting would you advocate as conducive to achievement of that goal?

Boutros-Ghali: I was looking at Western Europe, hoping that Egypt's cabinet would accept the idea of a common market. I would say a common market is essential; without the common market, there would be no future for Europe. But then we are just talking about the same thing in this part of the world. However, the common market is only the first step. You know that, unless this common market will be transformed to a United States of Europe in the next 25 years, every scholar knows that there would be no future for the common market. The same applies to this region too.

M.B.: I don't think anyone in Israel would question the desirability of establishing a Middle East economic community comparable to that of Western Europe. Some would regard it as the first stage on the road to your idyllic federation. Some would regard it in more pragmatic terms as bringing benefits to the entire region. So I don't think this is the obstacle.

Boutros-Ghali: Would they accept the supranational body?

M.B.: Is there a supranational body in Europe?

Boutros-Ghali: Yes. Yes.

M.B.: But the European Economic Community (EEC) nonetheless does not detract from the fundamental sovereignty of all of its member states at this stage in the confederation. Let us remember also that, in Europe, nobody has asked Frenchmen to abandon French as their primary language, though they may learn German and English, and so do the Germans and the British. The fact of the matter is that, though federation and federalism are talked about as ideals by many people and have been for generations, the experiments that have taken place thus far, even within the Arab world, have demonstrated the extraordinary difficulties in reaching that stage. Should we not set our sights at least in the next generation at a lower level of integration which would bring economic benefits to the parties concerned through something like a Middle East economic community? I know on the Israeli side there is much discussion of this. There was an attempt, for example, when the negotiations took place for the European Economic Community to do so on what they called the three railroad lines of Lebanon, Jordan, and Israel. Now it wasn't possible then because the state of war was very intense. But is it not possible to contemplate that as one of the major transitional steps to be taken after the signing of a peace treaty.

Boutros-Ghali: No. For me, as long as the current establishment exists in Israel, forget about Jews. Who are the establishment in Israel today? German, Russian, and Polish. So this is a basic difficulty. You cannot have integration with a group of Poles and Germans. If the establishment had been Arab Jews, more often Algerian, then they would belong to the same family. It is exactly like you are talking about Quebec rather than 6 or 8 million French Canadians, you will have 6 or 8 million Indians.

M.B.: It seems to me you are making demands that are so excessive that they will be perceived by the Israelis, given the context of 27 years of warfare [since 1948] and a period even before that of hostility, as tantamount to requesting them to abandon the very essence, *the raison d'être*, of their state. Once you do that, you bring to the surface once again all the concerns, the fears, the insecurities that have plagued this conflict from the very beginning.

Boutros-Ghali: I completely agree. I never underestimated the difficulty, but you asked me: the first question was "How do you see to improve peace in this region?"

M.B.: But given the difficulty, can we not talk in terms of reaching something less which would terminate the state of belligerency and war, and begin the process of accommodation that might someday lead to your ideal form of federalism?

Boutros-Ghali: You see, this is the basic problem I tried to show you. I don't know how to express myself. As long as the establishment in Israel has the mentality of white settlers, it will be very difficult to obtain any real peace.

M.B.: No, I think that is not the correct designation of the Israeli mentality. I think we may be perfectly candid. We are trying, after all, as intellectuals to deal with this problem. What bothers you, it seems to me, and I don't deny you the right of being bothered by it, but what bothers you is that Israeli Jews don't think like Muslim and Christian Arabs. Now the truth is that they do not and will not, precisely because they are a different people who claim the same right of self-determination as a people within a territorial entity. When you use the word "Arabization," this is perceived as a demand for extinction of Israelis' unique identity. I would suggest that one must seek other ways of coming to a point of *rapprochement* which does not request of one party the total abandonment of that which permitted them, indeed induced them, to give expression, in territorial terms, to that wish for national self-determination. Your insistence on Arabization would seem to them, and I'm certain it does seem to them, as an insistence that they abandon not this white mentality but Jewish–Israeli mentality, which may have many components, including many of the Jews from Arab lands who have come to Israel and who do begin to exert more and more influence at different levels of the society. But to ask of them that they become simply another Egypt, another Lebanon, or another Syria is to ask of them to disappear. Not in physical terms but in their own unique cultural/linguistic/religious and related ways.

Boutros-Ghali: No, I'm not saying they will disappear. No, their culture will coexist. The Armenians in Lebanon have their own school, have their own church, have their own personality and still they are Lebanese.
What I'm saying about the Armenians in Lebanon, I'm suggesting for Israel in the whole Arab world. I'm just making a transposition. Just take the group inside the country. They have their own language, they have their own church, they have their own university, and they have their own school, which has the Armenian language and the Armenian Christian religion.

M.B.: But they don't have a political entity which expresses their wish to determine their own lives to the extent that any state determines its destiny.

Boutros-Ghali: That may develop. I may be thinking about a political entity at the level of Quebec and you are thinking of a political entity at the level of Canada. For me the solution is Quebec. For you the solution is Canada. My point of view is that you can afford to have Canada with I don't know how many kilometers—a huge country, but you cannot afford to have small states which represent half of Cairo. What I'm saying about Israel, I will say it about Lebanon, I will say it about Jordan; I will say it about the mini new state of Palestine. This is exactly the same. You cannot have any possibility of normal development with the existence of eight or ten mini-states, in which all of them claim complete sovereignty. Any students of International Relations and students of federalism will agree about this. We must agree that if you want to move to have developments that will be essential to obtaining implementation of real peace in this region—as you said, you can sign a lot of papers which mean nothing—you must move exactly the same way as happened in Western Europe and Central America, you move to a limitation of the sovereignty of the small states existing in this region. A limitation in favor of supranational system, a supranational organization which will build on a regional basis a federation.

I have no objection to begin with functional cooperation, but what must be clear from the beginning is that the ultimate goal will be a supranational system, not necessarily with all Arab countries. It can just be a group with, say, Syria, Jordan, Israel, Palestine, etc. But without this minimum of political association, in my point of view, we will never obtain any peace.

M.B.: Dr. Ghali, let me ask you in that connection. Do you think that at the present stage, given the character of the élite groups in Lebanon, Jordan, and the PLO or the future Palestinian leadership, do you think it is possible to conceive as a first stage towards functional integration within the period of the next decade that countries like Lebanon, Jordan, a Palestine located in the West Bank and Gaza, and Israel could enter into the equivalent of a European Economic Community in order to bring to all of these smaller states the mutual benefits that would accrue from enlarging the market in which all of them could participate and pool their resources. Is that politically feasible, let alone desirable from your point of view? Or is the background of hostility based upon a prolonged protracted conflict such that one cannot even think in terms of the feasibility of economic cooperation at the lowest level of functional integration?

Boutros-Ghali: Here again I repeat myself. If you have a change in the mentality in the Arab world and in Israel, I believe this is possible.

M.B.: But I'm asking you whether you think the change will take place on both sides early enough to permit this within the next decade?

Boutros-Ghali: This depends on the different establishments. If you have an establishment in Country A which has decided to push this kind of change.

M.B.: But as a specialist on this part of the world, we are asking for your expert evaluation of the probability that there would exist within these Arab states (Lebanon, Syria, Jordan, and Palestine) the kinds of establishments that would look favorably and indeed work towards the creation of such an economic community with Israel in the interests of all parties concerned or is that itself a kind of intellectual conceptualization that we cannot contemplate in practical terms in the near future?

Boutros-Ghali: No. I believe that this could be done. I believe that this could be done.

M.B.: What in your judgment are the kinds of things that would contribute to the creation of the conditions for this beyond the signing of a peace treaty, because obviously without a peace treaty, one cannot go anywhere?

Boutros-Ghali: And the peace treaty means nothing as such.

M.B.: Assuming that we begin from the point at which there is the formal end of a state of war, what would you ask those four states to do in order to achieve minimal economic cooperation?

Boutros-Ghali: Maybe I'm subjective belonging to the Arab side. I would ask more from the Israeli than from the other.

M.B.: What would you ask of Israel?

Boutros-Ghali: I'm repeating again. A transformation of the system, of the way of thinking.

M.B.: Can that be done in a decade even if they were prepared to do it, which I'm sure they are not? But even if assuming for argument's sake that they were prepared to do so, surely the process of cultural transformation is not something that takes place in a decade or even in a generation?

Boutros-Ghali: I will tell you why this could be done now because 'til now, you have in Israel around 50–60 percent of the population that talk Arabic and are of Arabic origin. So this is a chance, a unique chance for Israel to, if they want to do it, they can do it. After 10–15 years, this will already be too late and you will have a great majority of sabra, and for them, it will be more difficult to be readapted to let us say—using the word "Arabic language," as you know quite well it is not the Arabic language as such, but the whole mentality. So today they can still do it, I believe. I don't know if they will do it.

M.B.: What would you ask of the Arab parties to such an association, an economic community? What do they have to do? You've indicated what you think Israel should do in order to make this possible. Are there not things that would be required of Lebanon, Jordan, Palestine, and Syria?

Boutros-Ghali: Yes. I will say, just to open the door to accept the return of Iraqi Jews, Egyptian Jews to help the coexistence.

M.B.: But supposing they don't wish to leave Israel to return?

Boutros-Ghali: They are not only in Israel. They are in different other countries. Suppose that they don't want to return. This would be a new obstacle to the problem of integration.

M.B.: Are you suggesting then that all of the 600,000–700,000 Jews that came to Israel from Arab lands must return as a condition?

Boutros-Ghali:	I would not say must. But certain of them will return.
M.B.:	Perhaps a few would wish to, but I would assume that the overwhelming majority are now integrated into the society of Israel and are unlikely to wish to return.
Boutros-Ghali:	I am not so sure of this. You have been in Israel. I've never been in Israel. I'm not so sure. Certainly, you have the potentiality existing now in Israel to obtain this kind of transformation. In the next ten years, this potentiality will not exist.
M.B.:	Dr. Ghali, let me ask you another question which is not directly related to this but we have heard a great deal in Cairo and, of course, during our discussions and meetings elsewhere about the Arab will for peace, particularly in the last eight months through the words and some of the speeches of President Sadat. I have rarely heard the word "legitimacy" being used, that is to say, the acceptance of the legitimacy of Israel as a permanent, justifiable, acceptable, part of the Middle East as a sovereign state. Now is that an accidental omission or does it represent something deeper, namely, the psychological unwillingness on the part of Arab states, Arab peoples, and Arab intellectuals to accept, not in terms of a piece of paper, but to accept psychologically, the permanence of this reality as something which has a right to exist per se?
Boutros-Ghali:	I can't answer your question. To accept this reality, you must have contacts, and the day you have contacts, you will see whether you accept this reality or not.
M.B.:	Is it your judgment that, with contacts, acceptance will begin to take place or a greater rejection will take place?
Boutros-Ghali:	You may have a greater rejection. I don't know. But this is why I cannot answer your question. You see, as

long as you are accepting on a very symbolic way, you say, "yes, I'm accepting the existence of the state of Israel." So what?

M.B.: That's why I've asked the question.

Boutros-Ghali: Yes. I cannot answer your question.

M.B.: What would your expectation be? Does contact lead, you think, to friendlier relations or more hostile relations?

Boutros-Ghali: I don't know. I have no precedent. On a purely scientific weight, it is very difficult. The only comparison I have in mind is the relation between North and South Korea or the relations between East Germany and West Germany. I was just there 4–5 weeks ago in Berlin, and in spite of the different agreements that have been concluded, there is no contact, and this is contact between two groups in the same nation and the same language, so it is very difficult to answer your question.

M.B.: You have said it on a couple of occasions and I've heard it stated by others that, even if a peace treaty with Israel is signed, it is just a piece of paper; it doesn't mean anything. Why do you feel that way? Traditionally, peace treaties have been treated as though they represented a willingness or unwillingness but an agreement to abide by at the minimum, a state of nonbelligerency. Why then is there a tendency to dismiss making peace?

Boutros-Ghali: This is a very legal approach to a problem that must not be treated in a legal way. The treaty of peace as we discuss it—what will be after the treaty of peace? This is the basic element. I mean just look at the precedents in the history of the last 50 years. So this is why I return back to my first idea. As long as there is not a will coming from the different parts of the dispute to obtain a kind of association and to accept the limitation of their own sovereignty for the creation of a supranational system, you will never be sure to have any kind of peace. Just look at Western Europe during the last 50 years. And this was proved.

M.B.: But federal systems are not a guarantee of peace. After all, we look at the multitude of civil wars which have taken place in federal societies.

Boutros-Ghali: Yes, certainly I agree. Everything is relative, I agree. You see, again I will take a very important element; the region is so small, this is why you cannot have those mini-states. You must already think to the second stage and you must link the first stage with the second stage. Otherwise, the first stage means nothing. You cannot have city-states today in 1975.

M.B.: You have a great many of them in the world, as you know.

Boutros-Ghali: Singapore, Hong Kong, the Seychelles, Mauritius, and the Caribbean states.

I'm struck by the fact that, in Cairo, and I've met people and I've talked to people, the extent to which education, sophistication, economic desires for improvement, and standards of living seem to be common to a great many people, so why is there this assumption that there is somehow such a different mentality existing in Israel and Arab states, one that is unacceptable.

M.B.: Yes, but Dr. Ghali, with all due respect, I think what has to be accepted by Arab intellectuals, just as one has to demand of Israeli intellectuals to accept certain things about Arab aspirations and expectations, is that Israelis or the Jews who came from Europe to Israel never perceived themselves, do not perceive themselves in any sense as colonials as you define them. Yes, they

	live there and perceive themselves as an integral part of the area.
Boutros-Ghali:	Well, unfortunately, this is not the fact.
M.B.:	Well, I would put it differently. Unfortunately, it is not the perception held by Arab intellectuals. Perhaps the problem is a gap in those two perceptions, rather than a gap in the facts. What is a fact in this sense? These people have now lived—I'm not talking of those who lived through the centuries, I'm talking of those who have come in the last 90 years. They have lived there three or four generations of people.
Boutros-Ghali:	No. No. I'm sorry, you know the figures as well as I know.
M.B.:	Yes, I know the figure. They began to come in 1882. The great bulk of them came from 1914 onwards and, more particularly, 1933 onward. So we have a minimum of one-and-a-half generations.
Boutros-Ghali:	OK. You have four, five generations in Algeria from 1815 to 1960.
M.B.:	Yes, but the Frenchmen who settled in Algeria never thought of themselves as anything but an extension of metropolitan France. The Jews who came to Israel never thought of themselves as Europeans.
Boutros-Ghali:	As an extension of the international Jewish diaspora …
M.B.:	They thought of themselves as part of a nation called Jewry, which, for historic reasons which we need not enter here, for nineteen hundred years was dispersed, but they thought of themselves, you may regard indirectly, but what is important is that they identified themselves with this piece of territory as their homeland.

Boutros-Ghali: Exactly, the people of South Africa have the same feeling. And the French Algerian was looking when I was discussing Algerian French that had exactly the same feeling. The real problem of the French in Algeria was that they don't belong to the metropole and they were completely cut from the metropole. They had never been to the metropole.

M.B.: But they regarded themselves as part of the metropole.

Boutros-Ghali: No. No.

M.B.: Mentally, emotionally, they never thought of themselves as Algerians, did they?

Boutros-Ghali: No, they meant themselves as Algeri Frances.

M.B.: But the land of Algeria was never conceived by them as their historic homeland.

Boutros-Ghali: Yes. They claimed Algeria. Algeria was nothing. Exactly the same with the British in Rhodesia. They believe that the South African has created this land. In fact, they have created something in Israel from nothing, so they believe that this is their land. The same thing exists with the French.

M.B.: Are you suggesting that the Jewish–Israeli identification with this land, based on historic, traditional, emotional, cultural associations that run through the very heart of Jewry for a period of more than 2000 years, is simply a fiction? You cannot draw these comparisons.

Boutros-Ghali: I don't want to enter this long discussion.

M.B.: No, I don't want to go into a long discussion.

Boutros-Ghali: This is of no relation to the infrastructure of the problem. I'm not talking as a Marxist now. But the hard fact is there. The white settlers coming from Western Europe, from Europe, more sophisticated, more intelligent, with money. They pushed; they picked the land and created a state.

M.B.: You have just said that more than 50 percent, in fact, the figure is 65 percent, of the population is not white European.

Boutros-Ghali: Yes, this is a problem.

M.B.: Well, it cannot be both.

Boutros-Ghali: No. No. But the establishment. This is what I want to say when I speak again of the colonization of the mentality. The establishment is like this.

M.B.: But it is not colonial because they don't think of themselves as a colony of anybody but themselves.

Boutros-Ghali: They are acting as colonial.

M.B.: That's a matter of judgment, surely. They may regard you as acting as a permanent aggressor against them. You may regard them as permanent aggressors, but that will get us nowhere in the sense that if we begin with the premise that there is a reality in this part of the world and has been a reality for a period of 27 years or 50 years, surely one must move somewhere between the idyllic as you describe it, the present situation, which is clearly not to the advantage of anybody, and there must be paths which are pragmatic in the sense that they are acceptable to the parties to move in the desirable direction. I don't see what purpose is served by making a demand that you surely must know no Israeli society can possibly accept your concept of Arabization. To do so is to commit cultural, let alone political, suicide.

Boutros-Ghali: I completely agree with you.

M.B.: I'm speaking to you now if I may, in trying to communicate to you what I understand about the Israeli mentality since I am familiar with it to some extent.

Boutros-Ghali: And I'm trying to transmit to you as a scholar spending 25 years on this subject, how I see this in the next 25 years.

M.B.: Yes, which I welcome. I genuinely welcome your sharing your views.

Boutros-Ghali: I don't think you will have, in the next 25 years, around 70–80 million Egyptians, which will present the kind of demographic explosion which will be something essential for this region. Not only for Libya and Sudan, but for Israel too. You have to take into consideration this mass and you have to cope with this reality and the issues, and you have to be assimilated in this. You cannot create a kind of island. This is what I mean.

M.B.: All I'm trying to do here in this dialogue is suggest that words like "assimilation" and "Arabization" are perceived by Israelis and not only by the establishment but even by your Jews from Arab lands as extinction.

Boutros-Ghali: OK.

M.B.: Not physical extinction but cultural extinction.

Boutros-Ghali: Then what we must do is how to help them to know that Arabization must not mean this.

M.B.: But can you expect them to perceive it any other way in the context of this protracted conflict which is still not even at the first stage of a peace agreement? Surely, there is a correlation between the timespan of protracted conflict and the timespan at which enough trust enters so that the beginnings, not of assimilation in your sense, but the beginnings of convergence, I would use the term "convergences" rather than "assimilation" between the cultures of Israel, on the one hand, and her Arab neighbors, begin to take place. I think you expect of other people the kind of cultural transformation that has never been witnessed in history except by coercion, and I know that you are not talking about doing it by coercion. You are expecting it in the voluntaristic sense.

Boutros-Ghali: Certainly. If 60 or 70 percent of the Israelis were of Arab origin and were talking Arabic, the whole system would be rotten. To impose on them another language, Hebrew, would make difficult their integration into this region and its community.

M.B.: But are you then saying that the retention of Hebrew as the pervasive language of the territorial state called Israel is an impediment to integration?

Boutros-Ghali: No. I will say that you have to have Arabic near Hebrew. This has not been done.

M.B.: The fact that it has not been done is another casualty of the conflict [Boutros-Ghali says he agrees], and it will be done during that period when the conflict begins to take the form of peaceful coexistence and cooperation. But it must come from within. You know, with all due respect, Dr. Ghali, the suggestion that you make, and I know you don't make it in that sense, but the suggestion that you make as perceived by an Israeli, mainly assimilation, integration, Arabization, could easily, and I'm sure you must appreciate this, could easily be transposed in their lexicon to imperialism, colonialism, imposition. The words are different, but the impact of Arabization as you define it is the imposition from surrounding cultures, peoples, and states of their will through their culture by demanding the elimination of an autonomous culture, religious system.

Boutros-Ghali: No, we are not demanding elimination at all. We are speaking of a coexistence, and I was giving you a different case: your own country Canada, where you can have the coexistence of French and English, and of the two respective cultures. I never say that assimilation means you have to kill your own culture. You can have the coexistence.

M.B.: Yes, but in order to do that the French have had to assert themselves and have done so in the past 15 years. Indeed, they have had to perpetuate by conscious emphasis their culture and their distinctiveness. And it must be remembered that, in the Canadian federation, which is much more of a confederation than a federation, the distribution of powers is such that, on many vital issues such as education, the powers lie with the provinces, and not with the central government, so that you have a very loose confederation even in Canada.

Boutros-Ghali: In my Arab confederation, you will have a very loose confederation.

M.B.: Would such a confederation, in your judgment, be capable of allowing the continued existence of a state which, in many of the fundamental spheres that are required for the retention of the distinctive civilization, culture, and language and religion, that would permit a state of Israel within such a confederation to continue to exist in the form in which it exists today, though it might divest itself of some of its sovereign powers for the greater good of the confederation along those functional lines?

I think the notion of the Law of Return, which is absolutely one of the holy of holies in terms of the State of

	Israel—the right of every Jew should he so desire to emigrate and settle in Israel—would this still be a part of your list?
Boutros-Ghali:	This, certainly, is a very important thing. You say it yourself. This Law of Return must be changed, must have certain limitation to it. Otherwise you cannot have peace in this region. Suppose that you suddenly have three million Jews coming back to Israel in the next year. Do you believe that Israel could contain them, three million Jews? What is my main problem? It is that I will try in the next 20 years to create a kind of assimilation, to create a kind of contact with the Jews existing in Israel. But if after 20 years you bring me half a million Jews from Russia again, this complicates the problem of assimilation, of integration. You have to recognize this: in the case of my 40 million Arabs coming to Egypt, they belong to the region. They already speak the language of the region. They are already integrated in the region.
M.B.:	It seems to me, Dr. Ghali, that you are propounding here a kind of natural law doctrine which declares that the Middle East is a region in which the Arabs by virtue of their existence in the region for a specified period of time have a kind of inherent natural right to be in the region, and that anybody else who lives in the region has an obligation to justify his existence by becoming Arabized. That is the essence of the doctrine that I think underlies the conception that you are stating.
Boutros-Ghali:	No. If you just take the United States, any new immigrant coming to the US, if you want to be accepted in the US, has to adapt.
M.B.:	The US is one state.
Boutros-Ghali:	Exactly, one state. For me, this region would become one association, and if you just want to be admitted—

	an Algerian going to Paris or to France or working in the common market, if he wants after one generation to be admitted into the common market, he will have to accept the concepts.
M.B.:	But he may retain one of the seven languages.
Boutros-Ghali:	He may retain the language but he must be integrated in the common market.
M.B.:	Does it require cultural assimilation?
Boutros-Ghali:	No, it doesn't require cultural assimilation, but still it requires a minimum of assimilation with the majority. You are discussing how to obtain the integration of Israel in this part of the world.
M.B.:	No, I think that is what you're discussing. I am discussing rather how one proceeds to move from formal peace to a bona fide, a genuine relationship between Israel, as she exists today, and its Arab neighbors.
Boutros-Ghali:	In other words, you want to have your islands in the middle.
M.B.:	I don't regard it as an island. I regard it as a legitimate state in the same way that I regard Jordan as a legitimate state or Syria. Now it seems that you are regarding Israel as less than legitimate.
Boutros-Ghali:	I don't regard Syria as a legitimate state. You see my point of view.
M.B.:	The Syrians would not be very happy.
Boutros-Ghali:	I agree, but I'm telling you, if you ask my point of view, I don't consider Lebanon as a legitimate state; I don't consider Jordan as a legitimate state.

M.B.: But since the rest of the world does. Is Egypt a legitimate state?

Boutros-Ghali: No. As long as they have not moved to a second stage, which is a stage of very important association, so my point of view is not applying only for Israel. It applies to Jordan, Syria, Lebanon, to Egypt, to this entire group.

M.B.: In that long transition period?

Boutros-Ghali: It is not such a long transition period. If this does not happen in the next 10–20 years, then you will have no stability in this region. But you will have underdevelopment, maybe internal war.

M.B.: Internal war within the Arab world?

Boutros-Ghali: Within the Arab world, but believe me, if you are in the middle of the Arab community, you will be involved. It will be impossible to live as an island.

M.B.: Well, I can only conclude from this discussion so far that the picture you portray is one of unmitigated pessimism and I'll tell you why.

Boutros-Ghali: Yes. Yes. We agree.

M.B.: The reason why I say this is that, whether or not one agrees with your idea of a federation—which I happen not to agree with, but that's irrelevant—it seems to me inescapably true, on the basis of the historical record elsewhere, that the probability of achieving such a federation even within the community of Arab states, let alone Israel, is so low in the coming generation that, for all practical purposes of planning and serious intellectualization about what is likely to take place, we can eliminate it. If that is so, one must therefore infer the probability, as you set it out, of intra-Arab internal war spilling over between the Arab states or some of them and Israel. It means that you are portraying a future in which we move from protracted conflict with occasional wars to protracted conflict with near-permanent war. That's a very pessimistic picture.

Boutros-Ghali: Yes, I agree. I agree.

M.B.: Would you agree that my estimate of the probability of your pessimistic picture is accurate?

Boutros-Ghali: I disagree with you.

M.B.: Well, could you then perhaps provide some ray of light, of optimism, as to the reasons why you seem to be convinced that one can make this great leap forward from individual sovereign states to a federation of some kind.

Boutros-Ghali: 1. The demographic explosion of Egypt. You have to find a place for those 80 million Egyptians.
2. Money, which is a very important element.
3. And this is very important—a change of the foreign policy of the major countries, which during the last 25 years was against any kind of association in this part of the world.

M.B.: And now it is in favor?

Boutros-Ghali: Now they begin. The first step. The fact that the Arab League was not recognized by anybody. I remember the period when it took 5–6 years of negotiation to obtain the possibility of opening an office of the Arab League. It was considered like a kind of I don't know, this is not an organization. It is a kind of Mafia. So since then, that changed. Now they are asking for a kind of dialogue between Western Europe and the Arab world. So at least during the next 25 years, because Western Europe will need the oil and the US will need the oil of the Arabs, they will have a more positive attitude toward the problem of Arab integration.

M.B.: Are there other factors or forces at work within the Arab world, within the social structure and the new élites, the technocratic élites of the Arab world which, in your judgment, would also lead towards integration?

Boutros-Ghali: What you have now in the Arab world is an élite of technocrats who believe very deeply, like I believe, in the necessity of this kind of common market or this kind of association.

M.B.: Are these technocratic élites at a stage where they begin significantly to influence the shaping of political decisions?

Boutros-Ghali: Yes, just what happened during the last three years in this part of the world. Would you have believed this kind of oil which has been used? Could you have believed this kind of solidarity where millions of pounds have been given? They have not been given in the Western way in which you are accustomed to see it, but there is today Arab integration. There is integration at least of the brains. There are around 1 million intellectuals from between Syria, Egypt, Lebanon, which are distributed in all the other Arab countries, from the Gulf.

M.B.: Sounds like neocolonialism.

Boutros-Ghali: They call it neocolonialism. As long as they belong to the same community, this is not neocolonialism. They are intermarried. You cannot say he is a Syrian, he is a Lebanese, like he is from New Jersey or he is from California. Or he is an Italian or he is a Frenchman. Certainly, in Italy, they are speaking about French neocolonialism or the Italians speak of the country that you have Zurich speaking about the colonialism of Geneva, but I believe deeply that, in the next

10-15 years, you have a trend—transnational communications—you have the possibility of constructing infrastructure which will have this transnational counter and you will have the kind of very important association of the different elements belonging to this region.

M.B.: Dr. Ghali, let me ask you another question, if I may, in a quite different vein. It is felt by many people that, at the subconscious level, among many Arab intellectuals, there is a kind of concern, fear perhaps is too strong a word—a kind of concern that should formal peace be reached with Israel, the technological know-how of the Israelis, developed over the past 25 years, could represent a serious rivalry, a competition which people in the Arab world would regard as a dangerous intrusion. Let me spell out more specifically what I mean. It's been said by many that Lebanon generally fears peace because of the competition of the city and port of Haifa and Beirut.

Boutros-Ghali: I know. I don't believe it. I don't believe at all that there is any possibility of competition.

M.B.: Let me put it in more positive terms. Could you envisage in the transition period, following the piece of paper, a peace agreement, the use of Israeli economic skills and talents and resources in the way in which this was used, to some extent, in African countries during a period when the African states literally begged the Israelis to send very small groups of people to assist in their agriculture, in reclaiming zones, the whole range of economic problems?

Boutros-Ghali: I agree, but this is again, I'm sorry to tell you, to speak so frankly: this is a kind of Israeli propaganda. You can have the experts from the entire world, why do you want to bring the Israelis?

M.B.: Because we are talking about the conflict and you are talking about assimilation. I'm asking, would you object, for example, to Israeli technicians, who happen to be experts in a particular field of agriculture, to working somewhere in the Nile Valley or somewhere in the Euphrates Valley, to contribute their skills, and to have Egyptians going to Israel or Iraqis or Syrians with their special skills to assist, shall we say, in the schools to teach Arabic? In other words, I'm asking you whether you see this kind of assimilation at the functional/technical level as desirable, feasible?

Boutros-Ghali: Yes, it is desirable, and feasible. Yes, I answer yes to your two questions.

M.B.: I meant rather the use of skills of both parties to assist other parties in whatever special area they happen to be knowledgeable.

Boutros-Ghali: Since two years, the basic elements have changed very rapidly. The money in this part of the world, I agree with you, maybe this money will only be there for the next 23 years, but the amount of money is so big. It has changed completely the map for the possibility of cooperation.

AL-AHRAM CENTER FOR POLITICAL AND STRATEGIC STUDIES

The most insightful *group* encounter of the 1975 Middle East research visit was an intense exchange of ideas on the Arab–Israel conflict with five members of the premier "think tank" in the Arab world, the Al-Ahram Center for Political and Strategic Studies (ACPSS); *Al-Ahram*, as noted, has long been the most influential and semi-official daily newspaper in Cairo. Regrettably, but an indicator of the then existing nonrelations between Egypt and Israel—it was before Sadat's dramatic visit to Jerusalem in 1977 and the Egypt–Israel Peace Agreement in 1979—my interlocutors requested that their identities not be revealed: I recall that two of the participants were the Center's then Director, Al-Sayed Yassin and Abdel Moneim Said Aly, the later Director.

The dialogue began with an opening statement by the guest of the Center:

M.B.: I have been impressed during the few days that we [members of the American Professors for Peace in the Middle East (APPME)] have been in Egypt by what seems to be a fundamental change in the attitudes of some Egyptian intellectuals and governmental officials towards the conflict with Israel. The term that comes to mind is "articulated moderation," an expression of interest in an accommodation which is more than signing a scrap of paper.

I sense now, as I did on the Israeli side last year, that since the October 1973 War, there has been a basic change in attitudes to the conflict at various levels. I am impressed with change here and change there. I sense the change here, but I am not certain if this is correct; and, if so, why the changes have taken place; whether the 1973 War was indeed the great catalyst to change within Egypt, within the leadership of the Palestine Liberation Organization (PLO), and within other Arab confrontation states. On the Israel side, let me say this: If you wish to use the dove-hawk spectrum, one thing is perfectly clear—the gap has narrowed profoundly: the hawks are more dovish, the doves are more hawkish.

I do not have the feeling that this is fully realized here. There is a widespread realization in Israel that a solution which provides it with total security, which by definition means some insecurity for the other side, is impossible; that the bargaining process must take the form and character, and contain the components, of mutual concessions that characterize other international conflicts; that we are dealing with a situation in flux, in which the psychological dimension remains a great barrier. Yet the psychological change in the aftermath of the 1973 War is also a breakthrough. It is a turning point because of an emerging sense of exhaustion and of futility about the resort to war, a changing perception by some Arab states and leaders. There is (understandably) skepticism, but a skepticism which has begun to erode and give way to a willingness to take calculated risks.

It is important for you to understand the changing mood, the new polarization of forces in Israel, the new importance attained by those groups which are prepared to embark upon not just a dialogue, but a genuine negotiation process leading to a mutually accepted solution. But have no illusions: on the other side, they will not move towards a final, formal settlement without acquiring what they regard as indispensable, minimal conditions for Israel's security—as they, not you or the superpowers, define the *sine qua non* for Israel's security.

ARAB A: If I venture to answer the question you pose as to the reason for change in Egyptian attitudes, I can suggest one or two major reasons. One is: I think there has been an emerging recognition that there is no military solution to this problem. I hope that this conviction also exists on the Israeli side. I think Israel will never win a war of such magnitude as it did in 1967. The 1967 Israeli victory did not solve the problem.

I think it is very vivid in the verbal declarations of President Sadat, namely, we have to understand that there is no military solution to this conflict. It is a conflict that involves several variables—psychological, economic, political, and military. The military, therefore, should be looked at as merely one variable of the conflict. One should not exclude the possibility of a fifth war; but a fifth war could happen within the framework of a tendency towards a settlement.

The psychological impact of the (1973) October War, both on the Israelis and on the Arabs, has been much greater than its military impact. To put it differently, I would say that you have a sense of restoration of pride or recognition of the ability of Arab forces—Arab forces can stand up, fight, and score a victory, limited as it may be. And if it is limited this time, it could be more next time. Psychologically speaking, the effect was a greater Arab sense of equality, a greater sense of psychological reassurance on the part of the Egyptian leaders. They are moving now more from a position of confidence, from a feeling of trust in their own abilities; to put it differently, it was more difficult for Egypt, when it was defeated, to make an accommodation. It is easier when it is victorious.

This policy of accommodation, or whatever you want to call it, is part of a general reorientation now occurring in Egypt. Internally, we do not talk so much about social revolution; but we are talking more of social peace, of maintaining the status quo. *Vis-à-vis* the world, we are taking a more or less pro-Western attitude. And *vis-à-vis* the Arab–Israel conflict, we are taking a more or less accommodating stand. I am saying that the three go hand in hand.

What I am saying is the following: if the Arabs were ready to recognize—whether they like it or not—the existence of Israel, I would assume that some reciprocity would take place. It should take place.

The second question concerns the occupied territories. Again, I have not seen a declaration on the part of the Israelis saying, "we are ready, in some hypothetical situation, to go back to our territories before 4 June."

The third question is—what kind of Israel is going to remain in the area? If Israel is to be accommodated in the area, will it be 'the outpost of the white man?' I am looking at it from a cultural point of view.

ARAB B: There is one thing that comes as a result of 1973 and that is that it was not (and it is fully realized here) a total victory. It was a great success perhaps, compared with previous encounters with Israel, but it did not give the sense of complete fulfillment of objectives.

ARAB C: The spirit of moderation which exists in Egypt these days dates back before that. I would say that two months after the Khartoum Conference [in August 1967, which proclaimed the "three No's"—no recognition of Israel, no negotiations, no peace], Egypt accepted Security Council Resolution 242, which is the turning point in her attitude to Israel. Egypt's attitude to the existence of the State of Israel had undergone its most profound change when President Nasser accepted the 242 Resolution.

M.B.: All day yesterday I heard the question—why does Israel not define her borders? The obverse of this is—why does the Arab leadership never define "the legitimate rights of the Palestinians?" The PLO has defined them in the Palestine National Covenant, which was reaffirmed as late as 1974. If you take it literally, then I think you will have to agree that Israel's leaders would have to do the same—not to proceed to any substantive concessions until the Palestinians state unequivocally, "we now repudiate our goal of dismantling the State of Israel." As you know very well, no state voluntarily commits suicide; people do, but states do not.

ARAB D: I want to go back to your previous statement. You said that you have come to the conclusion that, both in Egypt and in Israel, there is a realization that the conflict cannot be solved by war. This is true. But if we are talking about military action with the object of starting a political process, perhaps, or jockeying for a better position, then I do not think that that option of limited military action has been discarded, either on the Egyptian or on the Israeli side. On the Egyptian side, the October War was a successful attempt to unfreeze a political block, and this would be resorted to again—this is my conviction—should the deadlock become more pronounced.

On the Israeli side, the October War strengthened the hands of those who said that Israel should have preempted. There seems to be a consensus in Israel, and even in world public opinion, that the minute Syria says, "I am not renewing the UN mandate," Israel will preempt. I would like to know your assessment—whether the resort to war for some kind of preemption, some kind of hypothetical threat, has been abandoned by Israel.

ARAB E: I am not worried about Professor Brecher's query concerning "what kind of legitimate rights." We don't have to define them. They are going to be defined. It is only seven years since we recognized a reality called the "Palestinian Question."

M.B.: There is going to be a correlation between an embryonic recognition of Israel by the Palestinian National Movement through PLO declarations [as occurred more than a decade later, in the PLO's Algiers Declaration of 1988 and in the 1993 Oslo Accord] and an increasing recognition in public by Israel—declarations of the legitimacy of the Palestinian National Movement [this too occurred in the 1993 exchange of letters between PLO President Yasser Arafat and Israel's Prime Minister Yitzhak Rabin].
In concrete terms, you move to dual recognition by statements and indicators from both sides of a willingness to accept, to begin with, the reality of the other party existing in a relationship which is not characterized by immutable total conflict. Our task is both to recognize it and to propel it forward. But our task operates at both ends of the spectrum. Those who talk constantly with PLO representatives must make them aware of the impact of their declarations and statements on Israelis. When Yasser Arafat spoke at the United Nations, he missed a historic opportunity to signal to the Israelis that the Palestinians are coming of age by saying something like this: "we recognize that there is another entity in that particular part of the Middle East called Israel, whose legitimacy may not be greater than ours, but it is not less."

ARAB A: Until 1948 this problem had the name, the "Palestinian Question." We never used the term "Arab–Israel conflict" prior to 1948. We have to understand that the Palestinian Question will always be the crux of the conflict.
What I am saying is that the main reason for Egyptian–Israeli hostility is the "Palestinian Question." If we accept that, then there would have been no "Arab–Israel conflict" if there had been no Palestinian problem. The Arab–Israel conflict is a byproduct of a more fundamental issue, which is the Palestinian problem. In the '50s and the early '60s, Palestine was a romantic call, which everyone would

repeat, without articulating clearly what they meant by that. Without the Palestinian problem, it would be difficult for me to conceive a major issue between Egypt and Israel.

M.B.: I disagree. I think that the rejection of the November 1947 UN Partition Resolution by the Arab states indicates that there was something much deeper than the Palestine problem, namely, the inability of Arab society to accept as a permanent reality and legitimacy a state which was not Arab in what was regarded as the heartland of the Arab world. There seems to have been a very deep-rooted psychological mechanism, if you wish, a rejection mechanism, which for a very long time could not cope with this notion. So the conflict goes far beyond Palestine.

ARAB C: I think what you said does carry an element of truth—the question of Arab culture not liking to see a non-Arab state. Sadat said, two or three times, that he conceives a Palestinian state in the West Bank and Gaza. So what I am saying is that he is setting the stage, the psychological environment of the Arabs, toward this kind of possibility.

M.B.: If one wants to take a pure position on the concept, "Arab territory"—the phrase, "total withdrawal from occupied Arab territory"—in the Palestinian view, Arab territory extends to the (Mediterranean) sea. One of the tragedies of the conflict is that there is ambiguity on both sides; both parties feel a sense of hurt that the other party will not place its demands on the table. The truth is that, in all conflict situations of this type, precise formulations are placed on the table not prior to the beginning of negotiation but in the course of negotiations.

Now I turn to the four questions posed to me at the outset. The first concerns *Israel's nonrecognition of the Palestinian reality*. If I had my materials with me, I could quote many statements by Eban and Allon and others about the reality of the Palestinians. *I am firmly convinced that, just as the process towards war gathers momentum and leads to war, the ongoing process towards accommodation has its own self-per-*

petuating mechanism with qualitative shifts in the direction of peace.

The *second* question was about *the territories*. There are, I think, three crucial problems in the issue of territories. One is *Jerusalem*. Another is *the ridge of the Golan Heights*. The third is *Sharm-el-Sheikh*. The question of Sharm-el-Sheikh is not a question of sovereignty. If I may put it in the terms of international law, the genuine right of innocent passage must be honored by Egypt. And that applies not only to Sharm-el-Sheikh; it also applies to Bab-el-Mandeb. Similarly, I would say about the Golan Heights that the issue is not whether the Syrians should get this territory back or that Israel should keep it; rather, it is that the Syrians must not be permitted to control a piece of land which has, in the past, wreaked havoc on a densely populated area, and which will not be allowed to happen in the future.

I have my own proposal for this: the disposition of the Golan Heights requires that the Syrians should not be confronted with Israel troops on the Heights acting as a direct threat on the plain leading to Damascus. And Israelis in the valley below should not be threatened by Syrian troops on the Heights. A possible solution is to establish a buffer Druze state. It is an area where no Syrian or Israeli troops would be allowed to enter.

Now to the *West Bank*. Here too, however, the concern is with security. The concern is simply that, if the West Bank becomes an independent Palestinian State, without any reservations whatsoever, then missiles could be set, placed, and aimed at targets—and could destroy in a moment the heartland of Israel.

Now, let's look at *Jerusalem*. I think there will have to be a complex formula which will retain Jerusalem's status as Israel's capital, along with the attainment of what seems to be a fundamental goal for the Arabs, and perhaps for all Muslims, that is, an Arab territorial presence in the Old City of Jerusalem. I do not know whether it has to be the Muslim Quarter or x part of the Old City: I am not engaged in the bargaining process.

Now I come to your "painful" question—*what kind of Israel?* I think it is morally wrong; I think it is a path of dead end, of total unproductivity, for anyone outside the State of Israel to attempt to intervene in its fashioning of legislation or social and ethnic composition within the recognized boundaries that will emerge from a peace settlement. In other words, to put it bluntly: have no illusions—the Law of Return is of the essence and the heart of Israel. That does not mean—here you make another major mistake—that the 16 million Jews in the world are going to come to Israel. They won't; they have not; and they are not doing so. But the Law of Return is the symbol of something which lies at the root of the restoration of the state. To rob it of that is to rob it of the dignity, the self-respect, the essence of that state.

Let me remind you: more than 65 percent of the present [1975] Jewish population of the State of Israel either migrated from, or are the children of people who come from, the North African rim and the Arab lands of the confrontation states, all the way to Iraq. You are making the further mistake of assuming that Israel does not change. All societies change. Israel has changed. I would venture to predict that the percentage I quoted will increase. But that is a natural process which will affect the culture and all its superstructural institutions.

The last question concerns the *internal politics of Israel* and her capacity to make "great" decisions. I agree with you about Ben-Gurion. I think he was a towering figure, not only in Israel terms, but also in a larger world context. He had the vision to create the state at the time that he did, and the vision—he displayed it also in the post-1967 period. I remember vividly interviewing him in 1971. He said, "For peace, genuine peace, not the paper agreement, but the reality of peace, return everything but the Golan Heights [security] and Jerusalem." Yet I think you make a fundamental error if you assume that human history is filled every 25 or 100 years with Ben-Gurion, or others whom you wish to include in the pantheon of great men of the contemporary era. This is not a stage in the conflict when a great man can make historic decisions and a lesser man cannot. It may be the reverse. It may just be that the lesser men who now lead both states are capable of making that jump, precisely because they are more closely attuned to the attitudes of their mass public. Ben-Gurion was ahead of his time. He was so far ahead that he would have had to drag his people into change. Rabin and Peres are much more in touch with the reality of their nation's mood. The error you commit is in trying to suggest that one must await another Ben-Gurion.

Let me put it in your terms. Nasser was in power for 18 years. He probably had much more unqualified power than any other Arab leader in modern times. Yet he could not make the great leap. Sadat, in a short period of time, with greater constraints, and without the charisma of leadership which Nasser had, could and is doing so.

I detect in Egypt the feeling that Israel's political system is too unstable now to make the necessary moves forward. I think that is totally wrong. The Israeli political system has an appearance of instability but it is among the most stable of multiparty systems. There are parameters which clearly define the points beyond which the frictions between parties, and between factions within parties, cannot go. In a participatory democracy in the true sense, one should not confuse the role of charismatic leadership with a mere ability to make decisions.

ARAB D: I think that there have been many signals coming from the Palestinians as well. You talk about Arafat's speech and missed opportunity. I agree with the missed opportunity but not so much from Arafat's as from the Israelis' point of view. Arafat speaks about the popular, secular democratic state as a dream. Now can we not envisage some kind of cohabitation of the dream with political reality? Take the situation of the division of Germany. You have in the West German constitution a notion of the unified German nation, which implies, of course, the disappearance of the name of the Democratic German Republic. Nevertheless, the situation exists.

ARAB C: If you compare the two sides during the last three years or, let us say, since 1973, there is a shortage of Israeli signals compared to the Arab side.

M.B.: I am not insisting that the Palestinians alone issue signals. It is a kind of locked-in situation in which the Israelis need evidence of recognition but the Palestinians may not be able to provide it. Similarly, the Palestinians need signals and the Israelis, because of their own constraints, may not be able yet to give them.

ARAB D: With one difference—who should make the signal first?

M.B.: Simultaneously.

ARAB D: The Palestinians do not have any ground to stand on besides their frustration, whereas the Israelis have their state. The Palestinians do not have their state. This is the point.

ARAB A: I would—with whatever sincerity I can—appeal to you not to publish this *idea of a Druze state*. And let me explain to you why: in the history of civilization, that has been the colonialist, imperialist proposal—to establish states for minorities. In Lebanon, France wanted to do something to establish a state for the Maronites, which did happen in the mid-nineteenth century. Your proposal will be perceived as a colonial model. So I think it can do more harm than good. I think we can think of other solutions for Golan—a buffer zone, UN troops, etc.
You made a very good point that there is *no necessary link between the withdrawal of Israeli forces from Sinai and the restoration of an Egyptian military presence*. And that idea does exist in Sadat's mind. He once said, "it is possible that at a future point of time, Sharm-el-Sheikh will be run by a civilian Egyptian administration and some sort of armistice committee or UN troops." So I think he toys with it. I think a similar arrangement could be thought of for the Golan ridge: either by a UN administration or Syrian civil-

ian administration, with UN troops—and not to be withdrawn except by order of the Security Council.
Let me tell you how classic Arab logic will go on the *Law of Return*. We have 18 or 16 million Jews in the world. At any moment of time, these could migrate—the theoretical possibility does exist. The piece of land which Israel is occupying now will not be sufficient. Then Israel will have an inherent imperative for expansion. What I am saying is that, if the arguments you have made (about not all Jews migrating to Israel) are clearly articulated by the Israeli leadership, that could alleviate the fears here. Israel should clarify some of what I would say are the very peculiar aspects of the kind of arrangements they have; one of them is the Law of Return.

M.B.: I understand the point you are making. I understand the kind of scenario that some Arab intellectuals could develop from this; but I am profoundly convinced that it is, like so many scenarios, nothing more than that. It seems to me that in this prolonged and, I fear, agonizing reconciliation that will take place, there is—to use the term that I heard in Luxor over and over again—more than one "holy of holies." Every temple, secular, religious, pagan, or other, has a "holy of holies." You must understand that one "holy of holies" for Israel as a state and society, and the conception of Judaism and Jewry that is associated with them, because of the particular historic experience of that people, is that Israel as the only Jewish state must provide the theoretical opportunity for any Jew who, for whatever reason, feels the need or the desire to migrate to Israel. I recognize the theoretical implication that you pointed out—but the probability that it would occur is virtually nil.

ARAB B: Perhaps what holds the same significance for the Arabs is the *territorial* question. It is not so much a question of rectification of borders—because Arab statesmen have expressed a willingness to make certain minor rectifications. Nor is it a question of certain arrangements for certain territories, such as demilitarized zones, a UN presence, a Great Power presence, and everything. Egypt and other confrontation countries have put forward so many proposals. But the crucial point is the question of sovereignty. And this is as holy to the Arabs as, perhaps, the Law of Return [is to the Israelis]. A territorial exchange cannot be included in a settlement, or else you will have a kind of settlement such as the Versailles Treaty, which will sow the seeds of a future war.

M.B.: The negotiators must find solutions that reconcile the need for Egyptian or Palestinian sovereignty with the need for Israeli security.

ARAB C: The French and German experience is interesting in this regard, because it seems to me that, if you look at the period from 1945 on, the reconciliation through the European Economic Community and related agencies—in the period of the Treaty of Rome [1957] onward—has been very rapid.

ARAB B: The minute nonbelligerency is declared, Israel has the right to pass through the Suez Canal. What does passing through the Canal mean? It means an Israeli ship, raising an Israeli flag, will pass through Egyptian territory. It means an Egyptian pilot will go on this ship. It means they will have to pay tolls through banks—a lot of relationships. They will need berthing rights. They will need services, and everything.

M.B.: Let us distinguish here between what I would call the peripheral trivia of shopping in the bazaars of Cairo and the real substance of relationships beyond signing a piece of paper. The notion of substantive relations to take place soon after a peace agreement is a fundamental indicator of the degree to which that piece of paper is meaningful. When the Israelis talk about normal relations soon after a peace agreement—after all they have normal relations with one hundred countries—what they are saying is that there is a correlation between the amount of time it takes to establish some semblance of normal Arab–Israel relations and the intensity of those normal relations, on the one hand, and the meaningfulness of the Arab commitment to a piece of paper, on the other. Now, you may say the Arabs cannot accept this. You may be right. But you must accept that the longer it takes, the more skeptical the Israelis will be about the meaningfulness of the Arab commitment in the light of the past 27 years. It works both ways.

ARAB B: I shall end the discussion here and give myself the last word. You said *territory* is not important to Israel, but only security. Well, as far as we are concerned, that is just fine. And I can promise you that, as far as Egypt is concerned, if we can find some solution for Sharm-el-Sheikh and, after that, for Sinai, that will give back sovereignty to Egypt, even though Egypt would be deprived of any possibility of using that stretch for military purposes, whatsoever the form—Americans, Russians, the UN, and the whole world—then I think that would be acceptable. I am positive about the Syrian ridge too, that they would accept such a settlement. About the *recognition of Israel*: when you get a statement from someone like King Khaled—he said that he agrees to it—that is a step that perhaps is not properly understood, because Khaled is Khaled and is not Arafat. My point is: you used the phrase "holy of holies," and I am afraid that a lot of "holy of holies" have been created recently, and especially since 1967. You began by asking us whether 1973 was a turning point in the change of attitudes in the Middle East. I want to ask you a question that can clarify lots of things for us. Do you think that the 1967 War was a turning point in a lot of Israeli attitudes? It is true that we talked of the Al-Aqsa Mosque a lot more after 1967 than before. But it is also true that, on the Israeli side, we have many, many things that have been transformed into "holy of holies"—the Wall and the Mosque of Abraham, for example. And "holy of holies" can be developed all the time. And in the West Bank ....

M.B.: The only "holy of holies" that I referred to explicitly by name was the Law of Return.

ARAB B: This is accepted.

There is misconception, distrust—and that is natural and human. I would understand that the Israeli side does not put on the table before negotiations even their willingness, at one point, to withdraw from all territories conquered in 1967. But what I do not understand is their going much further and saying, even before the negotiations, that "no, this is nonnegotiable—that there will be no return." I mean they should leave the thing to negotiations. I would accept that as a normal thing. What adds to the distrust is that they take the opposite stand and say "this is out" from the beginning.

M.B.: Let me say merely that I really and firmly believe that, at the negotiating stage, everything in dispute that has arisen following the 1967 War is, in the Israeli view, open to negotiation. I think what you have to do is to take the cumulative body of Israeli statements: and there I think the thrust is clear. The thrust is that territory is by no means the central issue. Territory was and is for the Israelis a bargaining device to attain the goal of security. I cannot overemphasize to you here, as I have tried to emphasize elsewhere in Cairo, that the issue of security is central, pivotal, and dominant. It is so overwhelming that, for Israel, it is the point of departure for discussions about an Arab–Israel settlement.

Rereading this dialogue 41 years later, I realized that it has, potentially, both archaeological and autobiographical interest. The Egyptian participants, it seemed to me then and later, articulated views that reflected Egyptian élite images at that time, clearly indicating a willingness to make peace with Israel. And my remarks during that intense exchange of views conveyed my considered thoughts on the conflict in *1975*, most of which, parenthetically, *remain my views in 2016*, with one important exception: *my studies of conflict resolution and crisis management since 1975* have generated a profound conviction that, *in a long-term conflict between adversaries with a large gap in military power, such as that between Israel and the Palestinians, the militarily stronger adversary must take greater risks and initiatives on the path to peace*. Regrettably, Israel has not accepted this view during the entire period since the Oslo Accords were signed in 1993.

In light of this gratifying discussion with Al-Ahram Center intellectuals—and similar exchanges with many Egyptian officials, other intellectuals, and journalists in 1975—I left Egypt with a much more optimistic view of the prospect for a breakthrough in the long-frozen path to peace with Egypt, the first, crucial accommodation between Israel and its Arab neighbors.

The most vivid image acquired in Cairo was that, after almost 30 years and five wars, the Egyptian élite was no longer prepared to carry the burden of the Palestinian struggle for statehood. It was now ready for peace with Israel, provided that the lost territory—the Sinai Desert, occupied by Israel during the 1967 War—was restored to Egypt. For this, Egypt was prepared to accord Israel full peace and normal relations: "land for peace," it was evident, was an acceptable formula for an end to the protracted conflict with Israel.

DISQUIETING REACTION IN ISRAEL

The views I encountered in Egypt were made known by me in an article in the weekly magazine of *Ha'aretz*, Israel's counterpart of the *New York Times*, on 14 November 1975. Earlier that summer, I was invited to give a lecture to the senior members of Israel's Foreign Office. They listened politely, but it was clear that I was addressing a closed-mind audience. I did *not* suggest that the same change was true of Syria; the difference in attitude encountered in Cairo and Damascus was glaring, and this contrast was conveyed.

The reaction was summed up by several questioners: "What a pity, Michael; you have been brainwashed; you simply don't understand the Middle East!" *Two years later, my discovery and assessment of a fundamental change in mood among Egyptian intellectuals and officials in 1975 was vindicated: President Sadat went to Jerusalem, addressed the* Knesset, *and the Egypt–Israel peace process was launched.* Not for the first time, the closed mind of Foreign Office experts—and many Israeli politicians, journalists, novelists, and academics—was incapable of assessing correctly the impact of the October-Yom-Kippur War. It was a very disquieting example of the inability to accept an adversary's readiness to end its conflict with a long-time enemy, and the pervasiveness of a *closed mind operating in a protracted conflict*. The Sadat visit to Jerusalem two years later was an historic and dramatic event. To the astonishment of many Israeli political leaders, intelligence agencies, academic experts, and others, Sadat took the initiative and went to Jerusalem in November 1977, and met with Prime Minister Begin and many Israeli officials.

Two years later, Egypt and Israel signed a peace agreement. While the Arab–Israel conflict persists 38 years after that agreement, especially *vis-à-vis* Israel and the Palestinians, Israel–Syria, and Israel–Lebanon, and while the Middle East remains a very rough, unstable neighborhood, the Egypt–Israel breakthrough, which had clearly been implied and advocated by so many Egyptians in 1975, became a reality.

CHAPTER 7

Conflict-Sustaining Acts in the Arab–Israel Protracted Conflict

As in almost all modern *interstate* protracted conflicts (PCs), the Arab–Israel PC, now approaching its seventh decade (1948–2016), with deep historical roots, has been sustained by four types of hostile acts between/among principal adversaries: *violence, political hostility, economic discrimination*, and *verbal hostility/propaganda*.

VIOLENCE

Viewed in terms of all the actively engaged *state* adversaries in this PC (Egypt, Jordan, Lebanon, Syria [the "frontline" Arab states], Iraq, and Israel), and three Arab *nonstate actors*, the Palestine Liberation Organization (PLO), *Hezbollah*, and the Islamic Resistance Movement (*Hamas*)—there have been nine large-scale Arab–Israel wars:

1. *First Arab–Israel War*: Arab designation, *al-Naqba*, The Catastrophe; Israel designation, *War of Independence*; 1948–49
2. *Suez War or Sinai Campaign*: Arab designation, *Tripartite Aggression* or *Second Arab–Israel War*; Israel designation, "Operation Kadesh," 1956
3. *June-Six-Day War*: Arab designation, *War of 1967* or *The Setback*; Israel designation, *Six-Day War*
4. *War of Attrition*; 1969–70.

© The Author(s) 2017
M. Brecher, *Dynamics of the Arab–Israel Conflict*,
DOI 10.1007/978-3-319-47575-2_7

5. *October-Yom-Kippur War*: Arab designation, *October War* or *Ramadan War*; Israel designation, *Yom Kippur War*; 1973–74
6. *Lebanon War I*: Arab designation, *The Invasion*; Israel designation, "Operation Peace for Galilee"; 1982
7. *Lebanon War II*: Arab designation, *July War*; Israel designation, *Second Lebanon War*; 2006
8. *Gaza War I*: Arab designation, *Gaza Massacre*; Israel designation, "Operation Cast Lead"; 2008–09
9. *Gaza War II*; Israel designation, "Operation Protective Edge"; 2014

Egypt was fully engaged in Wars 1–5, all before the Egypt–Israel peace agreement in 1979;
Jordan was an active adversary in Wars 1 and 3;
Lebanon was directly involved in Wars 1, 6, and 7;
Syria was an active participant in Wars 1, 3, 5, and 6;
Iraq was active in War 1 (and Gulf War I);
The *PLO* was active in War 6, *Hezbollah* in War 7, and *Hamas* in Wars 8 and 9;
Israel was an active adversary in all nine wars.

There were three *lengthy* wars: (1) *First Arab–Israel War*, 15 May 1948–7 January 1949; (4) *War of Attrition*, 8 March 1969–7 August 1970; and (5) *October-Yom-Kippur War*, 5 October 1973–31 May 1974.

There were two *short* wars: (2) *Suez War*, 29 October–6 November 1956; and (3) *June-Six-Day War*, 5–11 June 1967.

The other four wars were of *medium* duration: (6) *Lebanon War I*, 5 June–1 September 1982; (7) *Lebanon War II*, 6 July–23 August 2006; (8) *Gaza War I*, 27 December 2008–18 January 2009; and (9) *Gaza War II*, 8 July–26 August 2014.

Arab–Israel wars did more than any other type of hostile acts to sustain the Arab–Israel PC.

One or more wars occurred in each of the first six decades of this unresolved PC, some with far-reaching and enduring territorial consequences, notably (1) *First Arab–Israel War* (1948–49), (3) *June-Six-Day War* (1967), and (6) *Lebanon War I* (1982).

Israel triumphed in Wars 1, 2, 3, 6, and 8: there was no clear victor in Wars 4, 5, 7, and 9.

In addition to conventional *interstate* wars (1–5) and combined *interstate–nonstate actor* wars (6–9), noted above, there were two unconventional violent conflicts that occupied an important role in sustaining the Arab–Israel PC—the two Palestinian *Intifadas* (Uprisings) against Israel's prolonged occupation of the West Bank and East Jerusalem since 1967, and of Gaza from 1967 to 2005.

The First *Intifada*, also known as "the war of stones," because the mostly young participating Palestinians then lacked modern weapons, broke out in Gaza in December 1987. Triggered by a traffic accident between an Israeli truck and a Palestinian car, in which several Palestinians were killed, it began as a spontaneous expression of animosity toward Israeli rule and, for the most part, took the form of civil disobedience—demonstrations, strikes, boycotts of Israeli goods, withholding of taxes, with a prominent role played by young Palestinians throwing stones at Israeli security forces. Later, politicians from several Palestinian political organizations, the mainstream PLO, headed by Yasser Arafat until his death in 2004; *Hamas* (the Islamic Resistance Movement); and Islamic Jihad, "joined the bandwagon," but they never controlled the largely unorganized passive resistance activities of the First *Intifada*. It spread quickly through the Gaza Strip and the West Bank, and lasted until the Israel–PLO Camp David Accords were signed in September 1993, though it waned in 1991 at the time of the first Gulf War.

Its tangible accomplishments were few, if any; but intangibly, the First *Intifada* was the first manifestation of political action by Palestinians that cut across age, political organization, and ideological differences to create an emotional consciousness, especially among the youth, focusing on the challenge of attaining national goals, first and foremost, independence. Although hard evidence is lacking, it may well emerge in future research that the First *Intifada* contributed to the political process that culminated in the September 1993 Oslo Accords, in moderating the attitudes both of Palestinian political leaders and organizations and, possibly, of Israeli political leaders and organizations toward the idea of cooperation with "the enemy," at least to the idea of looking favorably on some kind of *modus vivendi* that could set in motion a meaningful peace process between the two core adversaries in this PC.

The Second *Intifada* lasted almost as long as the First (2000–05), with much greater violence and much larger casualties. The trigger is generally identified with the high-profile visit of Ariel Sharon, then a *Likud* Party candidate for the position of Israel's Prime Minister, to the Al-Aqsa Mosque in East Jerusalem, the third holiest shrine in Islam, on 28 September 2000. Israel's government sought—and received—permission from the mosque authorities for Sharon's visit, with assurances from Palestinian officials that no violence was expected as long as he did not enter the mosque, which he did not; but PLO leader, Arafat, and the Palestinian leader in Jerusalem, Faisal Husseini, called on Sharon to cancel his visit. Moreover, Sharon was still-remembered—and vilified—by the Palestinians as Israel's Minister of Defense during the 1982 invasion of Lebanon and as the person who was universally believed to have allowed the entry of Christian Lebanese Forces into Palestinian camps, where they committed the *Sabra* and *Shatila* Massacre of Palestinians. Even Israel's official commission of inquiry blamed Sharon for "indirect responsibility" for that traumatic event and recommended his dismissal from his post as Defense Minister, from which he later resigned. Moreover, the Sharon visit to the Temple Mount occurred barely two months after the collapse of another Camp David Summit (11–25 July 2000), this one initiated by US President Clinton, with Arafat and Israeli Prime Minister Barak failing once more to resolve the Israel–Palestinian conflict, amidst mutual recriminations for the cause of the failure. In these circumstances, violence ensuing from a highly publicized Sharon visit to the environs of a holy Muslim shrine in Jerusalem should have been assumed as highly likely to occur—it was not.

While there is no consensus about the exact date of the end of the Second *Intifada*, a plausible event was the declaration of a truce by PLO Chairman Abbas, the successor to Arafat, and Prime Minister Sharon, on 8 February 2005 at the Sharm el-Sheikh Summit, sealed by Sharon's commitment to release 900 Palestinians in Israeli prisons and to have the IDF withdraw from several West Bank towns. The casualties, on both sides in the Second *Intifada*, were very high—most sources agree that slightly more than 1000 Israelis and 4800 Palestinians were killed up to the end of April 2008, the latter figure including 575 Palestinians killed by Palestinians. In only two of the nine Arab–Israel wars were more Israelis killed than in the Second *Intifada*: the War of Independence (1948–49), 6373, of whom 4000 were soldiers, the rest, civilians; this was approximately 1 percent of the Jewish population of Israel in 1948, five times higher than the number of US combat deaths in World War II, as a proportion of population; and in the October-Yom-Kippur War (1973–74), 2520–2800 Israeli soldiers were killed in action, and 7250–8800 were wounded, along with 293 soldiers captured. In the June-Six-Day War (1967), 803 were killed, and 738 in the War of Attrition (1969–70).

The roughly comparable estimates of combined casualties of Arab participants in the 1948–49 *al-Naqba* war was 8000–15,000; separate figures for each Arab adversary are unavailable. For the 1973–74 October War, the lowest estimate of Arabs killed in action is 5000 for Egypt and 3000 for Syria, a total of 8000; the highest estimate is 15,000 for Egypt and 3500 for Syria, a total of 18,500 killed, with a combined estimate of 20,000 Arabs wounded. The Insight team of *The Sunday Times*, London, estimated 16,000 Arabs killed in action in the October War.

The formidable *conflict-sustaining role* of all the Arab–Israel wars and the two Palestinian *Intifadas* was enhanced by a large number of *violent crises*, all of lower intensity than the wars between Israel and one or more Arab "frontline" states and, in the Palestinian and two Lebanon wars, with a nonstate actor as the principal Arab adversary, the *PLO* and *Hezbollah*, respectively. (How the *violent crises* in this PC that *did not begin with, or escalate to, full-scale war*, as well as the *nonviolent Arab–Israel crises*, were *managed* is discussed in Chap. 8.)

Political Hostility

Like *violence*, the preeminent source of Arab–Israel conflict persistence, political hostility between the two claimants to the disputed territory between the Jordan River and the Mediterranean Sea, Israelis and Palestinians, was apparent from early in the twentieth century, escalating with increasing intensity during the 1930s, World War II, and the diplomatic struggle from 1945 to 1947. In the Israel–Palestinian domain, the territorial and identity core of this PC, the most visible expression of political hostility was *mutual denial*. As evident in the PLO's National Covenant, published in 1964 and revised in 1968, Jews were designated a *religious* community, not a nation, and therefore did not have a valid claim to a state. The PLO Covenant is replete with articles that emphasize this fundamental distinction between the two adversaries—Palestinians as a nation, with a natural right to statehood; Jews as a religious entity scattered among the nations, lacking a right to statehood. Even when PLO leader Arafat first acknowledged Israel's existence as a state, in a 1988 widely reported speech, he recognized the reality of a state, Israel, not a Jewish nation.

Israel's leaders reciprocated this hostile act of denial, though, for a long time, they did so by avoiding the topic, not by verbal denial of nationhood—until Golda Meir, Israel's Prime Minister (1969–74) declared, "there are no Palestinians": that is, no Palestinian nation; those residing in Israel are Israeli Arabs and, by inference, those residing in Jordan, Lebanon, and Syria are Jordanian, Lebanese, and Syrian Arabs. *In sum*, mutual denial between Israel and Palestine, specifically, the right of Jews and Palestinians to statehood, and the lengthy period of Arab states' denial of Israel's legitimacy as a state, reinforced the frequent resort to violence by the adversaries in sustaining, and often escalating, the Israel–Palestine PC. It was only in 1993, on the occasion of the inauguration of the Oslo Accord, that Arafat and Prime Minister Rabin, in an exchange of letters, acknowledged the legitimate existence of "the other," Israel and the Palestine Authority. Until then and, for political extremists among both adversaries, since 1993, mutual denial of a claim to nationality and statehood served as the ultimate rationale for mutual hostile political behavior toward the prime adversary.

Egypt and Jordan, too, engaged in denial of Israel's right to exist as an independent state during much of this PC—until their peace treaties with Israel in 1979 and 1994, respectively. Syria avoided the name "Israel" by referring to its prime enemy as the "Zionist entity" or "Zionist enemy," until Hafiz al-Assad, Syria's leader from 1970 until 2000, employed the name "Israel" in 1973; but Syria's officials and media continued to employ the pejorative terms of nonrecognition of Israel's legitimacy as a state. Political hostility was also conveyed—and sustained—by the absence of any formal relations between each of the "frontline" Arab states and Israel until their signed peace agreements with Israel—Egypt in 1979, Jordan in 1994, Lebanon's intention in its 1983 abortive peace treaty with Israel, and the Palestinians in the peace treaty expected to emerge from the 1993 Oslo Accord. There were, however, many informal relations between these primary adversaries-enemies, notably in the security and economic arenas after formal agreements had been signed and implemented.

Arab–Israel political hostility extended far beyond the essentially *passive* and *verbal mutual denial* of legitimacy by Israel and the PLO, and the longstanding denial of Israel's right to statehood by all the Arab states for lengthy periods of this PC. Notwithstanding attempts by Israel's first Prime Minister, Ben-Gurion, to initiate (indirect) talks with Egypt's leader, Nasser, in the mid-1950s, and other unpublicized initiatives, Egypt was unprepared for serious negotiations with Israel for almost three decades (1948–77), until President Sadat, politically strengthened by the outcome of the October-Yom-Kippur War (1973–74), set in motion the quiet diplomacy that led to the peace treaty with Israel in 1979. Serious negotiations between Israel and Syria did not occur until the early and mid-1990s. Talks between Israel and Lebanon in the early 1980s produced a draft peace treaty in 1983, but it did not come to fruition because of a decisive Syrian veto of Lebanon's ratification of that Israel–Lebanon agreement. The relationship between Israel and Jordan was the most accommodating—there were close to 30 secret meetings between King Hussein and Israeli senior ministers between 1968 and 1986, when the King and Israel's then Foreign Minister, Peres, produced a draft peace treaty. However, because of Jordan's weakness among the "frontline" Arab states, this agreement had to wait until 1994, long after the Egypt–Israel treaty had become a reality.

For Palestinians, virtually all Arabs, and many observers of the Arab–Israel PC, the most tangible expression of Israel's political hostility to its principal adversary was/is its policy and practice of building Jewish settlements in the disputed and (since the 1967 War) Israel-occupied, West Bank, East Jerusalem and, until 2005, Gaza. While it occurred earlier, occasionally—for example, during the *Hula* Drainage crisis between Israel and Syria in 1951, Israel dispossessed the Arab residents of the Demilitarized Zone (DMZ) and established paramilitary agricultural settlements—the Israel Settlement project, as a *state-directed and largely financed and supported national enterprise*, emerged from Israel's triumph in the 1967 War and its occupation of the entire West Bank, East Jerusalem, and the Gaza Strip. The first phase was launched and implemented by the Labor government from 1968 to 1977, mainly for stated strategic purposes. The second phase, implemented by *Likud*-led coalition governments from 1977 to 1992, was inspired by Revisionist Zionist ideology, in particular, the belief that the entire territory of the "Land of Israel" from the desert to the sea, including all of the West Bank ("Judea and Samaria"), belonged to Israel as a historic right, and was avidly supported by an ideologically driven, well-organized, and highly vocal Israeli settler movement. The second phase, since 1977, vastly expanded Israel's Jewish presence in the occupied territories.

The third, ongoing phase, since 1992, implemented by both Labor- and *Likud*-led coalition governments, continue to expand the Settlement project, despite strong criticism by many states, including Israel's most loyal patron, the United States, and unambiguous UN Security Council draft resolutions terming the settlements illegal. As of June 2010, there were 122 officially recognized West Bank Jewish Settlements beyond the pre-1967 War "Green Line," with an estimated Jewish population of 303,900, and a considerable number of "outposts" or aspiring illegal proto-settlements. There were also, in July 2009, an estimated 192,000

Israeli residents of disputed East Jerusalem, and approximately 20,000 in the Golan Heights: the Settlements comprised agricultural communities and frontier villages, urban suburbs and neighborhoods, with a total estimated settler population of 515,000. By 2016, that number had grown considerably during *Likud*-led coalition governments, under the leadership of Prime Minister Netanyahu. No other political act by Israel has aroused as much condemnation by Palestinian organizations and leaders, many Arab states, and states, organizations, and people beyond the Middle East, making the Settlement project, including its occupation of East Jerusalem and the Old City, Israel's most visible contribution to sustaining the Arab–Israel PC.

The Israel–Palestinian conflict over Israel's Settlements in the West Bank was long preceded by, and later reinforced, an intense Arab–Israel "political war" over a myriad of issues. These comprised: *violent crises* addressed by the UN Security Council, often generating calls for a cease-fire and/or condemnations, usually of Israel's behavior; *political crises*, in which threats of violence were conveyed by word or deed, but there was no violence; the unresolved *controversy over East Jerusalem*; *hostile political acts* by by one or more of the adversaries, other than Settlements; and competing claims that came before the Security Council and the General Assembly; and a veritable permanent Arab–Israel political war that accompanied this array of military confrontations, crises and, during the past near-half century, Israel's settlement activity.

Economic Discrimination

During the first three decades of the Arab–Israel PC (1948–79), there were no evident economic relations between the principal adversaries—because of a formal three-level Arab League boycott of Israel that was introduced in 1951, with the Boycott Office based in Damascus. The *primary* boycott, the only category widely enforced by Arab League members in the early years, applied to products and services that originate in Israel. The *secondary* boycott was intended to apply to firms or individuals from non-Arab states that do business with Israel. And the *tertiary* boycott referred to shipments by air or sea to Israel ports. The primary boycott, long enforced by Syria and Lebanon, became dormant after the 1973–74 War. The secondary and tertiary levels have never been enforced. And formal meetings of the Boycott Office have not been held since 1993 because of the lack of a quorum.

As for its goal—to wage economic warfare against Israel—the Arab League boycott has failed to impair, or slow the growth of, Israel's economy, which, since 2010, has been a member of the developed economies' club, the Organisation for Economic Co-operation and Development (OECD). Moreover, since Israel's peace treaties with Egypt and Jordan (1979 and 1994), economic relations between Israel and these Arab states, and others since then, have flourished. Nonetheless, the continued formal existence of the Arab boycott remained a high-profile symbolic act of economic discrimination, which helped to sustain the Arab–Israel PC.

There were several other high-profile *acts* of Arab states' *economic discrimination* against Israel, direct and indirect. One was Egypt's *denial of passage through the Suez Canal to Israeli shipping and ships of other states* seeking the right of passage to facilitate trade with Israel, until the 1979 Egypt–Israel peace agreement. Another was the *denial of passage through the Strait of Tiran to both Israeli shipping and the shipping of other states*. For Israel, this meant denial of access to the Red Sea and a direct route for Israel's shipping to and from states in East, South, and Southeast Asia, an increasingly lucrative export market for Israel's products, when many economies in these regions, notably Japan, South Korea, China, Taiwan, and, later, India and Indonesia, were undergoing rapid growth, leading to the prevention of an expansion of trade, both imports from and exports to Israel. Third, the Arab states' *use of their "oil weapon"* during the October-Yom-Kippur War, refusing to sell oil to oil-dependent states, notably in Europe, to bring about a more pro-Palestinian posture in their foreign policy behavior. A more effective Arab economic discriminatory act, though unorganized and fitful, was the economic boycotts by Palestinians in the West Bank and Gaza against the purchase of Israel products, and the nonpayment of taxes during the First and Second Intifadas, 1987–93 and 2000–05.

Israel, too, engaged in economic discrimination during this PC. Perhaps the most consequential specific conflict-sustaining economic act occurred during the First *Intifada*: 140,000 Palestinian workers in the agricultural, construction, and service sectors of Israel's economy were denied entry from Gaza and the West Bank into Israel on security grounds and, therefore, denied continued employment. Moreover, many of their replacements, workers imported from South and Southeast Asia, and Africa, remained in Israel after the *Intifada*, rendering the unemployment of Palestinians a long-term, for many a permanent, loss. More generally,

Israel's Settlement project led to an imposed large-scale transfer to Israeli settlers of agricultural land and resources from Palestinian residents in the West Bank since 1968, and in Gaza until Israel's unilateral withdrawal in 2005. The same transfer process occurred on the Golan Heights, where new Israeli settlements since 1968 reduced the land and resources available to Syrian residents for economic development. The cumulative result of these discriminatory economic acts by the Arab states and Palestinians and by Israel was to complement the conflict-sustaining effects of frequent resort to acts of violence and political hostility. In light of the combination of hostile acts by the principal adversaries, the persistence of this high-intensity PC is not, and should not, be surprising.

Verbal Hostility

All of the principal adversaries in this PC—Israel, the Palestinians (the PLO in the West Bank and *Hamas* in Gaza), and the "frontline" Arab states, Egypt, Jordan, Lebanon, and Syria—employed the full range of available media—print, radio, TV, Internet, sympathetic commentators—in a concerted effort to shape favorable external attitudes to their behavior in the conflict and unfavorable attitudes to that of their adversary[ies]; they used every forum that provided an opportunity to influence the world beyond the principal conflict adversaries. Each participant generated an array of official statements, speeches by political leaders, newspaper leaders-editorials, reporting of events, interpretations, and accusations relating to the steady flow of events that shaped the thinking and reaction of policy-makers and large sections of the publics in many states. The goal of this array of verbal expression was to influence the perceptions and actions of major global and regional powers, which were often capable of determining the outcome of a crisis; a response by the UN and/or regional organizations to claims made by one or more of the PC adversaries; and, in general, the response of the global and/or regional international system to the myriad of controversial issues brought to the attention of states and international organizations for debate and reaction, in the form of resolutions, condemnations, and actions of the adversaries. Most hostile verbal acts in the Arab–Israel PC were communicated within the framework of hostile political acts.

CHAPTER 8

Crises Within the Arab–Israel Protracted Conflict: 1948–2014

Among the 33 protracted *interstate* conflicts that have been active during the past near-century, the Arab–Israel conflict, in which one of the *principal adversaries* has been, and continues to be, a nonstate actor, the Palestine Liberation Organization (PLO), has generated 30 crises since its onset in 1948, the largest number of crises within any protracted conflict (PC): 15 were characterized by lesser degrees of violence, 9 were cases in which violence escalated to full-scale war, and 6 manifested perceptions of the likelihood of violence before the crisis ended, which did not occur.

EVIDENCE ON CRISIS TRIGGERS AND CRISIS MANAGEMENT

Violent Crises (Less than Full-Scale War) (15)

Sinai Incursion
(25 December 1948–10 January 1949, during the first [1948–49] Arab–Israel War): Israeli forces launched an attack, crossing into Egypt's Sinai Peninsula on 25 December 1948. Egypt called on the United Kingdom to press for a UN Security Council Resolution demanding withdrawal of the IDF. *Management* of this interstate intrawar crisis took two forms, *violence* and *diplomacy*: *Israel's shooting down of five UK planes over Israel's territory*, and the *IDF withdrawal from Sinai on 10 January*, in response to a UN Security Council Resolution strongly supported by the United States and the United Kingdom.

Hula Drainage

(12 February–15 May 1951): Israel's Palestine Land Development Co. (PLDC) began reclamation work on the Hula Drainage project in the 1949 Armistice Agreement Demilitarized Zone (DMZ) north of the Sea of Galilee (Kinneret, Lake Tiberias) on 12 February 1951, to drain the lake, reclaim 15,000 acres of land for agriculture, and use the water for irrigation purposes. Israel's controversial economic act in disputed territory triggered a crisis for Syria, which appealed to the UN Security Council to compel Israel to desist. Israel suspended work on the Hula project in March for a month. Seven Israeli policemen were killed by Syrian soldiers in early April. Israel retaliated with an air attack on a Syrian outpost and police station. There was further fighting in the first half of May, with many casualties on both sides. This crisis, too, was *managed* by a Security Council Resolution *calling for a cease-fire*, which Israel and Syria accepted, ending the three-month crisis on 15 May 1951.

Qibya

(14 October 1953–faded): IDF forces, responding to the killing of an Israeli woman and her two children by Jordanian infiltrators into Israel, attacked the Jordan village, Qibya, on 14 October, killing 69 civilians and destroying 45 houses. Jordan appealed to the UN Security Council and the Arab League, both of which *condemned Israel*, thereby *managing* informally a crisis that faded.

Gaza Raid/Czechoslovak Arms

(28 February 1955–23 June 1956): A series of guerrilla infiltrations from Egypt into Israel during the early 1950s led to five Israeli reprisals between 1950 and 1955, culminating in a large-scale Israel retaliation raid on 28 February 1955, killing 39 Egyptians and wounding 32. This "Gaza Raid" triggered a crisis for Egypt, which appealed to the UN Security Council and the Arab League in March and requested Soviet arms on 20 April, via China's Prime Minister Zhou en-Lai. A large-scale USSR-initiated arms agreement between Egypt and Czechoslovakia on 28 September 1955 ended Egypt's crisis—and triggered Israel's crisis. Israel responded by seeking and receiving French Mystère aircraft on 11 December 1955. Israel also launched another large-scale retaliatory raid into Gaza on 5 April 1956, causing 59 deaths and 93 wounded, and a week later, requested massive arms from France: these were provided on

23 June 1956, thereby providing temporary *management* of a long and complex Egypt–Israel crisis.

Qalqilya
(13 September–15 October 1956): Several infiltrations into Israel by Palestinian *feda'iyun* [guerrillas] from Jordan in July and August 1956, causing dozens of Israeli casualties, led to an IDF blowing-up of a police station in Jordan on 13 September, triggering a crisis for Jordan. After several other incidents from Jordan, including an ambush of an Israeli bus, there was another Israeli retaliatory raid—against Qalqilya on 10 October. An Iraq offer to send troops to Jordan escalated the crisis, and Israel threatened to retaliate. Crisis *management* was achieved on 15 October *by* a *Jordan declaration* that *Iraqi forces would not enter its territory.*

El Samu
(12–15 November 1966): The blowing-up of an Israeli army command car by infiltrators near Jordan's border on 12 November, with three soldiers killed and six wounded, triggered an Israeli raid on the village of Samu. Jordan mobilized its army, and heavy fighting followed. Israel withdrew hours later. The crisis was *managed* by *Jordan's termination of its army's state of alert* on 15 November.

Karameh
(18–22 March 1968): A violent crisis erupted on 18 March 1968 when an Israeli bus hit a mine near Jordan's border on 18 March, with 2 children killed and 28 wounded. Israel responded with a raid on the nearby village of Karameh, a Palestinian guerrilla base, on 21 March. Jordan sent troops to the site, where heavy fighting between IDF and PLO forces ensued, the first direct military confrontation between the IDF and forces of the PLO, with severe losses on both sides. The PLO base was destroyed, but the Palestinians stood their ground, emerging with a sense of military triumph against much-stronger Israeli forces. The crisis was *managed* the following day, when *Jordan reopened the Allenby Bridge connecting the West Bank and Jordan.*

Libyan Plane
(21 February 1973): IDF radar detected an unknown Boeing-727, with all shutters closed, on 21 February, heading in the direction of Israel's

nuclear center in the Negev town of Dimona. All attempts by Israeli fighter planes to secure identification failed. Israel's crisis was *managed* 30 minutes after its discovery, when the mystery plane, later discovered to be a Libyan civilian plane, with 113 passengers, was shot down at the order of the IDF Chief of Staff. There were no survivors. Israel was condemned by many states for "trigger-happy" *mismanagement*.

Litani Operation
(14 March–13 June 1978): The immediate background to the *Litani* crisis was an attack on 11 March 1978 by 11 Palestinians, who entered Israel by sea, on Israeli vehicles traversing the main Israel north–south highway north of Tel Aviv: 35 Israelis were killed and 70 wounded. Israel responded on 14 March, launching a major attack against PLO bases in southern Lebanon, triggering a crisis for Lebanon (as well as for the PLO). The Security Council, meeting at Lebanon's request, called for Israel's immediate withdrawal from Lebanon and dispatched a UN peacekeeping force (United Nations Interim Force in Lebanon [UNIFIL]) to the area occupied by Israel. The crisis was *managed* by *an IDF withdrawal*: hostilities ended by the end of March, but the crisis lasted until 13 June 1978, when the last stage of IDF withdrawal from Lebanon was completed.

Iraq Nuclear Reactor
(January–19 June 1981): This crisis was triggered by France's announcement in January 1981 that Iraq's *Osirak* nuclear reactor would be operational by 14 July. Israel's cabinet responded on 15 March by approving a preemptive strike as its *crisis management technique*: the *Israel Air Force destroyed Iraq's reactor* on 7 June. Initial world reaction was widespread condemnation of Israel's violent act, a public posture that changed in the West only in 1991 during the first Gulf crisis-war.

Al-Biqa Missiles I
(28 April–24 July 1981): The trigger to this Arab–Israel crisis, which overlapped with the dramatic *Iraq Nuclear Reactor* crisis (January–June 1981) was an air incident: on 28 April 1981, Israeli planes shot down two Syrian helicopters carrying supplies to Syrian soldiers on Mount Sannine overlooking the strategically located town of Zahle, then occupied by Lebanon's largest anti-Syria Christian militia, the Lebanese Forces. Syria responded by deploying SAM-3 ground-to-air missiles

in Lebanon just beyond the Lebanon–Syria border. Israeli planes destroyed these Syrian missile bases on 28 May, amidst accusations by Israel and Syria, alleging "the other's" violation of their 1976 Red Line Agreement, which specified the limits of Syria's military presence in southern Lebanon. Effective *management* of this crisis was complex. The *United States intervened* with a *mediation* mission and *a temporary freeze on its delivery of F-16 planes to Israel* because of its bombing raids against Syrian and PLO forces from 10 to 17 July. *Mediation* and *pressure*, by the *United States on Israel* and by *Saudi Arabia on Syria, led to a cease-fire*, as did *US mediation leading to a cease-fire between the PLO, formally Lebanon, and Israel*, on 24 July, ending this complex crisis for all the adversaries.

Al-Biqa Missiles II
(19 November 1985–15 January 1986): Two Syrian MIG aircraft were shot down on 19 November by two Israeli planes over Lebanon, triggering a crisis for Syria. It responded on 24 November by deploying SAM-6 missiles in the Biqa Valley and along the Beirut–Damascus road, but these were withdrawn, under US pressure. Then, on 15 December, Syria redeployed missiles close to the Lebanon border. On 27 December, Israel's Defense Minister threatened to respond "whatever the cost." This crisis was *managed* by *US mediation* and *concessions by the two adversaries*, including the decisive step—*Syria's withdrawal of its long-range missiles from Lebanon*, announced on 15 January 1986.

Operation Accountability
(10–31 July 1993): Several attacks by Lebanon's predominant Shiite militia, *Hezbollah*, in Israel's self-created "Security Zone" in southern Lebanon, on 10, 19, and 23 July, with considerable Israeli casualties, led to Israel's massive retaliation on the 25th, "Operation Accountability." This catalyzed a flight of half a million Lebanese refugees to the capital, Beirut, but Israel's basic goal, curbing *Hezbollah*'s attacks on the "Security Zone" via pressure on the Lebanon government to act against its most powerful political and military rival in Lebanon, was not achieved—*Hezbollah* had become a "state within a state" during Lebanon's civil war (1975–90). The UN Secretary-General condemned Israel for creating a massive refugee problem, and the Security Council called for Israel's withdrawal from all Lebanon territory (which occurred only seven years later). Effective *management* of this crisis was achieved

by *US mediation* on 31 July 1993, *in the form of a cease-fire between Israel and Hezbollah*, which lasted for almost three years.

Operation Grapes of Wrath/"April War"
(11–27 April 1996): The 1993 crisis, dominated by Israel's "Operation Accountability," was replicated almost three years later. The prelude to the 1996 crisis was spasmodic but frequent *Hezbollah* rocket attacks on towns and villages of northern Israel. Israel's massive response, the 16-day "Operation Grapes of Wrath," designed to end the shelling of northern Israel by *Hezbollah*, triggered another massive flow of Lebanese refugees from the South to the Beirut area. As in 1993, this crisis was *managed* by a *US-mediated cease-fire*, aimed at restoring the oft-violated Israel–*Hezbollah* "rules of the game": both adversaries again renounced military acts against civilians in the Israel–Lebanon border area.

Haifa Suicide Bombing
(4 October–2 December 2003): A crisis was triggered for Israel on the eve of *Yom Kippur*, 4 October 2003, by a suicide attack on a sea-side restaurant in Haifa, killing 21 persons: Islamic Jihad claimed responsibility. Israel responded on 5 October, with an air attack on a training camp near Damascus allegedly used by Islamic Jihad and *Hamas*, triggering a crisis for Syria, which claimed that the camp was a shelter for Palestinian refugees. Syria moved a resolution before an emergency meeting of the Security Council, accusing Israel of violating the UN Charter and international law. Many Council members—China, France, Germany, the United Kingdom—and the European Union (EU) condemned Israel's air strike, with Russia calling for an end to attacks against Israel, along with condemnation of Israel's air attack. The United States asserted Israel's right to defend itself against terrorist attacks and threatened to veto any resolution that did not condemn Palestinian terrorism. There was no vote on Syria's draft resolution and no further discussion by the UN. The crisis was *managed* after almost two months by Syrian officials' less hostile statements on Israel at the end of November, emphasizing the Arab–Israel peace process, culminating in a *conciliatory interview in the* New York Times *by Syria's President Bashar al-Assad* on 1 December, welcomed by newspaper editorials in both adversaries and by some Israeli officials the next day: these *verbal acts* ended the crisis.

Crises That Escalated to Full-Scale War (9)

Palestine Partition/Israel Independence
(29 November 1947–20 July 1949): There were six *crisis actors*—Egypt, Iraq, Israel, Jordan, Lebanon, and Syria—in this lengthy multistate crisis that escalated to full-scale war. The crisis was triggered *for the five Arab states* by an international *verbal-political act*, the adoption of the UN General Assembly's Resolution 181 on 29 November 1947, which called for *the creation of two states* in the territory that had been the British Mandate for Palestine since 1923, *one Arab, the other predominantly Jewish*. The initial response by the Arab states was intensified attacks on Jewish settlements in Palestine, until 14–15 May 1948. Three events led to escalation of the violence to war: the termination of the Mandate and the departure of the UK Mandatory power on 14 May 1948, the proclamation of the State of Israel on 14–15 May, and the invasion of Israel on the 15th, triggering a simultaneous *interstate crisis for Israel* and the *First Arab–Israel War*. The crisis-war was *managed* by UN-initiated and mediated *armistice agreements* with pairs of adversaries at different dates: Israel–Lebanon, 23 March 1949; Israel–Syria, 20 July 1949, though violence on those two fronts ended on 30 October 1948; Egypt–Israel, 24 February 1949, ratified by Israel on 10 March 1949, though fighting ended with Egypt's defeat in Sinai, in early January (see Sinai Incursion crisis, above); Israel–Jordan, 3 April 1949; and Israel–Syria, 20 July 1949; there was no formal agreement between Iraq and Israel, but fighting ceased on that front by 18 July 1948. Most of these agreements resulted from persistent and skillful mediation by UN Under-Secretary-General, Ralph Bunche.

Suez Nationalization Crisis-War
(26 July 1956–12 March 1957): This crisis, which later escalated to the *Suez War*, was triggered by another *verbal-political act*, the proclamation of the nationalization of the Suez Canal Company by Egypt's President Nasser on 26 July 1956, the fourth anniversary of the military regime's assumption of power in Egypt. Initially, this act triggered a crisis for France, the prime mover in the construction of the Canal, which opened in 1869, and the United Kingdom, which then exercised the role of protector in Egypt. Bilateral talks between the two Western powers and then three rounds of multilateral conferences in August and September failed to manage the crisis between France–United Kingdom

and Egypt. The deadlock led to a tripartite attack on Egypt by Israel on 29 October 1956 and by France–United Kingdom two days later. A threatening series of messages by the Soviet Union to France, Israel, and the United Kingdom triggered a serious crisis for all three states. France and the United Kingdom agreed to a cease-fire on 6 November—before their forces had achieved the goal of restoring international control of the Suez Canal; and Israel, notwithstanding the rapid advance of the IDF in Sinai, agreed to a cease-fire on 8 November and to the withdrawal of its forces once arrangements for an emergency international peacekeeping force had been concluded. The two humiliated Western powers evacuated their forces within days of the cease-fire. Israel's withdrawal, in stages, ended on 12 March 1957. As with the winding down of the 1948–49 Arab–Israel War, the crucial role in crisis management was played by the UN General Assembly, where the *cease-fire-withdrawal formula* for crisis management was conceived and implemented.

June-Six-Day War
(17 May–11 June 1967): A crisis for Israel was triggered by two high-profile, *nonviolent military acts* of Egypt on 17 May 1967: an overflight of Israel's nuclear center at Dimona, the "Holy of Holies" in Israel's military capability, and the dispatch of two additional Egyptian divisions into Sinai, reinforcing others dispatched there during the two preceding days. The perceived threat by Israel was increased on the 18th by UN Secretary-General U Thant's acquiescence in President Nasser's demand to withdraw the UN Emergency Force (UNEF), which had successfully prevented contact and conflict between Egypt and Israel for a decade, a legacy of successful UN management of the Suez crisis-war in 1956–57. This 18 May act led to mobilization of army reserves by both Israel and Egypt on 19 and 21 May. The decisive escalation to war occurred on the 23rd, when Egypt announced the closure of the Straits of Tiran, thereby blockading the port of Eilat, Israel's gateway to Africa and Asia. A defense pact between Egypt and Jordan on 30 May escalated the crisis further. So too did a failed effort by the United States and the United Kingdom to create a naval flotilla to restore unhindered access by Israel to the Afro-Asian world via the Strait. On 4 June, Israel decided to launch a pre-emptive strike, which was implemented the next day, the outbreak of the *June-Six-Day War*; the result was an overwhelming military triumph for Israel. The United States perceived a crisis on 6 June, as a result of a *threat of military intervention by the USSR*, which reached its peak in a "hotline"

telephone message from Soviet Premier Kosygin to President Johnson on 10 June, threatening the dispatch of mobilized Soviet airborne divisions to support Syria's defense of the Golan Heights, unless Israeli forces ceased their advance on the Heights, which had begun the preceding day. On the 10th, Israel and Syria accepted the Security Council Resolution calling for a Cease-Fire, which was initiated by both the United States and the USSR. In essence, successful *management* of the 1967 crisis-war was achieved by a (unenthusiastic) consensus among the United States, the USSR, Israel, and Syria that continuation of the war on the Golan Heights would threaten all of their interests. For the two principal adversaries, the cost could be very high: for Israel, the likelihood of direct military intervention by Soviet forces on the Golan Heights and war between Israel and the USSR; for Syria, the risk that, with US involvement, to counter Soviet military intervention, the entire Golan Heights and other parts of Syria would be lost to Israel; both found a cease-fire to be a more tolerable outcome, with fewer benefits for Israel and less severe costs for Syria. The UN role in crisis management was *pro forma*—to provide international legitimacy for crisis termination through a US–USSR-initiated Cease-Fire Resolution.

War of Attrition
(8 March 1969–7 August 1970): The trigger to both phases of this two-stage crisis-war between Egypt and Israel, with high involvement by both superpowers, was a *violent act*—Egypt launched the *War of Attrition* on 8 March, with intense artillery fire against Israel's "Bar-Lev Line" on the east side of the Suez Canal. Israel's response to limited, though increasing, losses was belated: only four months later, on 20 July, did Israel react with air raids, triggering a crisis for Egypt. However, these raids were suspended on 28 July, terminating the first phase of this crisis-war. It resumed in October, when Israeli air raids destroyed valuable USSR-supplied SAM batteries and antiaircraft systems in Egypt. However, the significant catalyst to crisis-war escalation for Egypt was Israel's *deep-penetration raids* in Egypt's heartland, which Nasser perceived as a serious threat to his regime. The USSR responded to his personal request for Soviet military advisers and advanced missile air defense systems. Their arrival in Egypt in mid-March 1970 triggered the second stage of Israel's crisis-war, to which it responded with sustained bombing of the antiaircraft weapons supplied by the Soviet Union to Egypt, beginning on 24 March and continuing until early August 1970. This crisis was *managed* by a *cease-fire*

agreement, attained by intense US pressure on the two adversaries and formalized in US Secretary of State William Rogers's Plan, designed to end the War of Attrition: the cease-fire was accepted by Egypt and Israel on 7 August, marking the end of the longest crisis-war, with the fewest casualties, among all the violent crises in the Arab–Israel PC.

October-Yom-Kippur War
(5 October 1973–31 May 1974): The *principal adversaries* in this crisis-war were Egypt, Israel, and Syria, with the United States and the USSR as highly engaged *crisis actors* from its onset. A *crisis* for *Israel*, the first state to experience higher-than-normal value threat, time pressure for response, and a higher-than-normal likelihood of war, in this very long, two-phase crisis-war in the Arab–Israel PC, was triggered by an observed movement of Egyptian forces toward the Suez Canal on 5 October, in a shift from a defensive to an offensive posture. The *October-Yom-Kippur War* began the next day, in a simultaneous attack on Israel, from Syria in the North and Egypt in the South. A few hours before the Egypt–Syria attack on the 6th, Israel decided against a preemptive air strike. However, the immediate and rapid advance of Arab armies on both fronts led Israel to a potentially grave decision on the 7th—in favor of the "Samson Option," the use of nuclear weapons if Egyptian–Syrian attacks penetrated deeply into Israel's coastal plain. This did not occur. By 10 October, the tide of battle in the North had changed, triggering an intrawar *crisis* for *Syria*, and Israel's nuclear weapons were returned to storage. On the 12th, Israel agreed to a cease-fire in place, but it was rejected by Egypt and Syria. The turning point in the South was a massive tank battle in Sinai on 14 October, reputedly the largest tank battle in history, in which Egypt suffered a major defeat. On the 16th, IDF forces crossed the Suez Canal, threatening to surround and destroy Egypt's Third Army. This triggered an *intrawar crisis for Egypt* on the 18th; Egypt responded by pressing the USSR to arrange a cease-fire. This cease-fire was accepted by Egypt, Israel, and Syria on 22 October—under pressure from both the United States and the USSR. A resumption of hostilities by Israel soon after triggered *a crisis for the Soviet Union*, which reportedly mobilized seven paratrooper divisions and threatened direct military intervention on the Sinai battlefield if Israel did not cease military operations in the South. This triggered a *crisis for the United States*, which responded by pressing Israel to accept a ceasefire and to allow food and other nonmilitary supplies to reach the beleaguered Egyptian Third Army. The Egypt–Israel

segment of this crisis-war was *managed* by a US–USSR-sponsored UN Security Council Cease-Fire Resolution, adopted on 26 October by Egypt and Israel, thereby ending military hostilities in the South. On 21 December, Israel agreed to withdraw its forces to 20 kilometers from the Canal, and the size of Egypt's and Israel's forces in Sinai was reduced. A Disengagement Agreement, on 18 January 1974, ended the Egypt–Israel phase of the October-Yom-Kippur crisis-war.

The process of terminating Israel–Syria hostilities was more complex and continued another four months. As with the de-escalation of the Egypt–Israel crisis-war, but even more significant in achieving termination, US Secretary of State Kissinger played the decisive role in *crisis management* and *war termination*, in a crucial mediating role, including a month of "shuttle diplomacy" between Damascus and Jerusalem in May 1974. The Disengagement Agreement between Israel and Syria, including the return to Syria of part of the largest town on the Golan Heights, Quneitra, and the creation of a UN buffer zone on the Golan Heights, and a US Memorandum of Understanding with Israel, as in the negotiations leading to the Egypt-Israel Agreement, was signed on 31 May 1974, ending the October-Yom-Kippur crisis-war in the *unresolved* Arab–Israel PC.

War in Lebanon
(5 June 1982–17 May 1983): This crisis-war between Israel and Lebanon, with Syria as the third crisis actor, was triggered by Israel: in response to a rare incident, not a full-scale *interstate* crisis, in the *Arab–Israel* PC, a Palestinian attack in London that gravely wounded Israel's ambassador to the United Kingdom, Israel invaded Lebanon on 5 June, along three fronts, triggering, simultaneously, a *crisis* for *Lebanon* and *Lebanon War I*. Although Syria was not directly involved in the bilateral crisis, the rapid IDF advance in the Biqa Valley of Lebanon, very close to Syria's border, on the 7th, triggered a *crisis* for *Syria*. That crisis escalated on 8–9 June as a result of an air battle, in which many Syrian planes were shot down. A US-initiated mediation led to a short-lived cease-fire on 11 June. However, the IDF success in cutting off the strategic Beirut–Damascus highway, linking the two capitals, by 24 June, created a threat to Syria's control over Lebanon, escalating the crisis. In July, Beirut was besieged by the IDF. Ultimately, this crisis-war was *managed* by successful US mediation, in which special envoy Philip Habib generated a viable, complex agreement between Israel, Syria, and, informally, the PLO in Lebanon on 1 September 1982. The agreement provided for the completion of: the

withdrawal of Syrian forces from Beirut by that date; the withdrawal of PLO forces from Lebanon and their dispersion to nine parts of the Arab world, and the evacuation of IDF forces from the outskirts of Beirut. However, a formal peace agreement, initialed by Israel and Lebanon on 17 May 1983, largely at the behest of the United States, was never ratified: its most controversial article, authorizing the creation of an Israeli "security zone" in southern Lebanon, to protect Israeli settlements in northern Israel against potential PLO or other attacks, was vigorously opposed by Syria, then and until the end of Lebanon's civil war (1975–90), the dominant power in all matters relating to Lebanon. Not deterred by the abortive agreement, Israel created a "security zone" in southern Lebanon unilaterally, which it retained until 2000, when the recently installed Labor Prime Minister unilaterally terminated an 18-year occupation that, by then, was perceived as an escalating image and financial burden for Israel.

Lebanon War II
(12 July–8 September 2006): The second full-scale crisis-war between Israel and Lebanon was triggered by Lebanon's most powerful militant group, *Hezbollah*, on 12 July 2006: guerrillas crossed the Israel border, attacked an IDF patrol near Shtula, killing three soldiers and taking two soldiers as hostages; they also launched rocket attacks on several villages and Israel arms posts. Israel responded the same day with a major assault on southern Lebanon ("Operation Just Deserts"), triggering a crisis for Lebanon. *Lebanon War II* escalated quickly—Israel air raids and sea blockades of Lebanon and *Hezbollah* rocket attacks on northern Israel, leading to a large-scale evacuation of Lebanese abroad and a large-scale departure of Israelis from the North to the Center and South of Israel. There were a substantial number of casualties, as always in the Arab–Israel conflict, many more Arabs than Israelis: more than 1125 Lebanese, mostly civilians, and 119 Israeli soldiers and 45 civilians.

Calls for a cease-fire—from the UN, US Secretary of State Condoleezza Rice, and from an *ad hoc* meeting in Rome on 26 July of officials from the EU, the UN, the United States, the World Bank, and several other states, which called for an additional UN force to support the existing UNIFIL, in an attempt to restore stability, were of no avail. In mid-August, the Security Council adopted Resolution 1701, calling for the end of all attacks and military operations, and for deployment of 15,000 Lebanese troops to support UNIFIL peacekeeping operations. The UN cease-fire was due to go into effect on 14 August, but *conflict management* was delayed for three weeks—until *Israel*, after intense negotiations with the UN, lifted its *air blockade on Lebanon on 7 September and the sea blockade on the 8th*, ending this crisis-war.

Gaza War I
(Israel designation, "Operation Cast Lead"; Palestinian designation, *Arab Massacre*) (27 December 2008–18 January 2009): A week after the end of a mutually agreed—and implemented—six-month *Hamas*–Israel cease-fire (19 June–19 December 2008), Israel triggered this crisis, which escalated instantly to *Gaza War I*, by launching a military campaign in Gaza on 27 December 2008, designed to terminate *Hamas* rocket attacks on southern Israel and arms smuggling via tunnels into Gaza. The crisis began with the resort to Israeli air power in the Gaza Strip and escalated on 3 January 2009 with a ground invasion. *Hamas* responded by escalating its rocket and mortar attacks on southern Israeli towns and villages, including cities not targeted before this resumption of substantial military hostilities, Beersheba and Ashdod. It was a relatively short campaign, though longer than the June-Six-Day War in 1967: the ground war ended after 15 days; the crisis and war were *managed* after 21 days of intense violence, by mutually agreed *Israel and* Hamas *unilateral cease-fires*, announced on 18 January 2009; and Israel completed its withdrawal from Gaza on 21 January. The casualties during Gaza War I, as always in the *Arab–Israel* PC, were strikingly uneven. Of an estimated 1166–1417 Palestinian casualties, the IDF reported 25% were civilians (B'Tselem, an Israeli human rights nongovernmental organization, placed this number at 25%, while the Palestinian Center for Human Rights placed it at 65%).

Gaza War II
(Israel designation, "Operation Protective Edge") (8 July–26 August 2014): Gaza War II was one of the most destructive full-scale wars in the *Arab–Israel* PC, in both human casualties and material damage: as usual, estimates vary, but there was a consensus that more than 2200 Gazans and 73 Israelis were killed, with thousands of Palestinians wounded or injured, and enormous physical destruction of public buildings and 130,000 homes in Gaza destroyed or damaged during the 50-day war. The catalyst was the kidnap and murder of three Israeli teenagers. The emotional impact on Israelis was profound and facilitated the immediate Israel military response, which concentrated on, and severely weakened, the

Hamas-supporting underground in the West Bank and quickly escalated the near-permanent level of violence between Israel and the *Hamas*-ruled regime in Gaza. Eventually, as in all Arab–Israel crises and wars, Gaza War II yielded to mediation and cease-fire, with Egypt serving as the only third party that both adversaries, Israel and *Hamas*, were prepared to accept as a reliable and effective mediator.

There have been other military incidents in the Israel–Palestine domain of the *Arab–Israel* PC between 2009 and the 2014 upheaval. Only two were larger than an incident but less severe than a full-scale war. One was *Gaza II*, the Gaza–Israel clashes, triggered by the IDF's "Operation Returning Echo" (9–14 March 2012), with 26 Palestinians killed and 74 injured; this crisis was *managed* by Egypt, in the form of a *cease-fire*. The other, *Gaza III*, triggered by Israel as "Operation Pillar of Defense" in late October 2012, was essentially a contest between Israel air strikes and Palestinian rockets, with various estimates of casualties: 5 Israelis and 158 Palestinians, according to a Palestinian source; 177 Palestinians, according to the IDF.

Management of *the Gaza War II* (2014) crisis-war was not simple, given the extreme hostility between the adversaries—and their mutual commitment to the destruction of "the other." There was a 72-hour pause and then an extension of the halt to hostilities for five more days, until 18 August, secured by Egypt's mediation and pressure. Both adversaries had clearly indicated goals and conditions. For the Gaza regime, these were an end to Israel's blockade of Gaza, an extension of its maritime and security boundaries, the building of a seaport, and the reopening of its sole airport. For Israel, the demands were an end to rocket firing from Gaza into Israel, demilitarization of Gaza, the shift of control over management of Gaza's border with Egypt from the *Hamas* regime to the Palestinian Authority under President Abbas in the West Bank, and the termination of *Hamas*'s smuggling of weapons, through tunnels it had successfully constructed. Two years after the final, enduring cease-fire on 26 August 2014, none of these goals, beyond the virtual cessation of military acts by both adversaries, a not-unimpressive achievement, has been achieved. There were accusations of war crimes committed by both Israel and *Hamas*, but these petered out; and the international community pledged large-scale financial support for rehabilitation of Gaza, though the pledges have not yet been fulfilled. The Israel blockade has been loosened, allowing the import of essential materials for Gaza's reconstruction. Overall, the Israel–*Hamas*

conflict has not been resolved, and is unlikely to end until the *Israel–Palestine* segment of the *Arab–Israel* PC is terminated.
(Other important dimensions of the nine Arab–Israel wars, notably their *duration, participants, casualties,* and *conflict-sustaining role* in the *Arab–Israel* PC were discussed in Chap. 7.)

Nonviolent Crises (6)

The *Arab–Israel* PC has also experienced nonviolent interstate crises, in which one or more of the principal adversaries perceived a higher-than-normal likelihood of violence before the crisis was resolved, but violence did not ensue. These nonviolent crises are discussed below, in chronological sequence.

Rottem

(15 February–8 March 1960): A message from the Soviet embassy in Cairo to President Nasser on 15 February, alleging that IDF forces were massing on the Syrian border, with the intention to launch an attack, triggered a crisis for Egypt. Nasser responded with army maneuvers in Sinai, in the direction of Egypt's border with Israel, which counter-responded by moving its forces southward, in the Negev. This crisis was *managed* by *conciliatory acts on the part of the two principal adversaries.* On 1 March, Egypt's forces in Sinai began to return to their bases. Israel reciprocated. And on 8 March, Israel's Prime Minister Ben-Gurion departed for an official visit to the United States. These accommodating acts terminated a crisis in which anticipated violence was avoided by both adversaries.

Jordan Waters

(11 December 1963–5 May 1964): A statement by Israel's Minister of Labor on 11 December, that Israel's National Water Carrier would be operated, despite pressure from Arab states, triggered a crisis for Egypt, Jordan, Lebanon, and Syria. President Nasser responded on the 23rd, calling for an Arab Heads of State meeting, with the goal of avoiding war with Israel, which had been proposed by Syria. At their summit meeting on 13–16 January, all thirteen Arab Heads of State voted not to go to war, which they perceived to be a likely threat, but to divert the three Jordan River tributaries and to create a joint military command for the

affected four Arab states. The summit announcement triggered a crisis for Israel, which perceived a serious threat to its water supplies. Israel reiterated its plan to utilize the waters of the Jordan River and announced the plan's starting date. The United States, the USSR, and the UN warned the adversaries against resort to force. The crisis ended on 5 May, when Israel announced completion of its project and that the project would begin to operate in the summer of 1964. The Arab states *managed* this nonviolent *interstate* crisis by *acquiescing in Israel's decision to activate its Jordan Waters project* on 5 May 1964.

Beirut Airport
(28 December 1968–January 1969): An attack on an Israeli civilian plane at Athens Airport by members of the Popular Front for the Liberation of Palestine (PFLP), on 26 December, led to an IDF retaliation raid on Beirut Airport on 28 December, destroying thirteen Middle East Airlines planes. This act triggered a foreign policy crisis for Lebanon, home of the PFLP. Lebanon complained to the Security Council and mobilized reserve forces. There was widespread criticism of Israel's raid by France, the United States, the USSR, and the UN. The only violence was the killing of a passenger on an Israeli plane in Athens.

Israel Mobilization
(10 April–late June 1973): An Israel military intelligence report reached the IDF Chief of Staff on 10 April 1973 that Egypt planned to attack on 15 May, with fighter plane support by Iraq and Libya. Although Israel's Intelligence expressed its conviction that Egypt would desist from the plan, General Elazar placed the IDF on alert on 13 April, canceled army leaves, and ordered reserve units into active service. Near the end of June, the Chief of Staff became convinced that Egypt would not initiate war, *managing* that military-security crisis without resort to violence, ironically, not without a serious consequence: the Chief of Staff was criticized by Israel's Finance Minister for "wasting funds," leading to his reluctance to order general mobilization on 6 October 1973, the first day of the *October-Yom-Kippur War*, amidst the correct report, but disbelieved by Israel's political decision-makers, that Egypt would attack Israel that day; as noted above, it did.

Entebbe Raid
(27 June–4 July 1976): An Air France plane en route from Tel Aviv to Paris on 27 June was hijacked by the PFLP during a stopover in Athens.

The plane was forced to fly to Libya and then to Entebbe, Uganda, where non-Jewish passengers were released, while Israelis and Jews were held captive. Israel, perceiving a grave humanitarian crisis, decided on a rescue mission, on 1 July. Commandos landed in Entebbe on 3 July; a one-hour battle with Ugandan soldiers at the airport led to the hostages' release and return to Israel the next day. This crisis was primarily an act of Palestinian *political* hostility: it qualified as a military-security crisis because Israel's decision-makers correctly perceived high threat to the Israeli passengers, acute time pressure, and violence as highly likely before Israel could effectively respond; in fact, minimal violence occurred. This crisis was *managed* by Israel's successful resort to an unorthodox technique of crisis management, *a surprise, minimally violent intervention by IDF forces* that prevented any casualties among the passengers.

Syria Mobilization
(21 November–13 December 1976): Syrian troops began to move from their base in Lebanon's Bekaa Valley toward southern Lebanon on 21 November. This act triggered an immediate Israeli perception of threat to the Israel–Syria tacit Red Line Agreement, which forbade Syrian troops access to Lebanon's territory south of the Litani River. Israel responded the next day by concentrating tanks and infantry along its border with Lebanon. Negotiations between Israel and the United States, at the level of Prime Minister Yitzhak Rabin and Henry Kissinger, and their ambassadors in Tel-Aviv and Washington, reaffirmed their alliance. *The tacit Red Line Agreement between Israel and Syria was restored* by 13 December, after the Syrian forces halted their march to the south of the Litani River, thereby *managing this Arab–Israel crisis* without violence.

CHAPTER 9

The Arab–Israel Military Balance: 1967 and 1973

MILITARY LINEUP IN 1967[1]

Arab Forces

On the eve of the June-Six-Day War in 1967, political fragmentation within the Arab world gave way to unity, the goal being to crush Israel. During the peak prewar *crisis period*, there were many pious declarations of military support for the frontline Arab states, Egypt, Syria, and Jordan. In fact, they received very little aid, partly because of the gap between stated and real intentions,[2] and partly because the war was over within six days.[3]

Land Forces
In early June 1967, Egypt's estimated regular armed forces were 180,000–200,000 men (not including the National Guard). Of these, about 30,000–35,000 were stationed in Sinai. An expeditionary force of approximately 30,000–40,000 was fighting in Yemen. Syria's armed forces comprised about 60,000–70,000 regulars and 40,000–45,000 reservists. Jordan's Arab Legion consisted of about 50,000–55,000 regulars, and its National Guard units consisted of 15,000–20,000 men (Table 9.1).

© The Author(s) 2017
M. Brecher, *Dynamics of the Arab–Israel Conflict*,
DOI 10.1007/978-3-319-47575-2_9

Table 9.1 Arab military forces, early June 1967

	Egypt	Jordan	Syria	Iraq	Total
Troops					
Infantry brigades	6	6	6	1	19
Mechanized brigades	8	1	2	1	12
Armored brigades	8	2	2	2	14
Special troop battalions	15		2	1	18
Armor					
Tanks and self-propelled guns	1380	200	500–550		2080–2130
Armored personnel carriers	1160	250	500	200	2110
Artillery	1200	200	1200		2600
SA-2 Batteries	18		10		28
Air Forces					
Fighters	400	22	100		522
Bombers	70		6		76
Helicopters	60	3	10		73
Transport	90	6	5		101
Trainers	120		20–30		140–150
Naval Forces					
Destroyers	8				8
Submarines	12				12
Motor torpedo boats	32		12		44
Missile boats	18		4		22

Israel Forces

Published estimates of Israel's armed forces in May 1967, including those in the London-based International Institute for Strategic Studies (IISS) Military Balance, erred on some important items. The data given in Table 9.2 are taken from Professor Nadav Safran's estimates (with some adjustments based on my judgment) from other sources mentioned above.

Forces Committed on 5 June 1967

In Israel's opening air strike, virtually its entire Air Force was committed to the destruction of the main protagonist, Egypt's Air Force; 12 planes were left to protect Israel's air space. After the destruction of the larger part of Egypt's Air Force and airports, all of Jordan's 22 Hawker Hunter fighters and half of Syria's Air Force were destroyed. The principal task of Israel's Air Force from the second day of the war was ground support.

Table 9.2 Israel armed forces, May 1967

Troops	
Infantry brigades[a]	23
Armored brigades[a]	8
Artillery brigades	12
Armor	
Tanks and self-propelled guns	1050
Armored personnel carriers	1000
Planes	
Fighter-bombers	200–230
Bombers	25
Trainers/ground attack planes	60
Transport	20
Helicopters	25
Naval Units	
Destroyers and frigates	4
Submarines	2
Motor torpedo boats	12

[a]Including mechanized units
The number of men in the IDF, on full mobilization, was estimated to be 270,000–300,000

During the first four days, Egypt, and then Jordan, joined the battle. Syria stayed out, her army contained by the reduced units of Israel's Northern Command, as well as by IDF air strikes.

Israel's land assault on the Sinai front on 5 June involved the larger part of its mechanized infantry and armored strength. Organized in three IDF Corps, the forces advanced along three axes in the northern part of Sinai. On its eastern border, as Jordan began an artillery bombardment all along the line and an infantry attack in Jerusalem, Israel committed five infantry and three armored brigades; of these, two infantry and one armored brigade were assigned to the battle for Jerusalem.

By 5 June, Egypt had concentrated close to 100,000 combatants in Sinai, including some who were hastily recalled from Yemen. Two reinforced divisions were placed in the northern approaches to Sinai, including the Gaza Strip. Two divisions controlled key positions in the second line and around the strategic crossroads of Bir Hama and Bir Hassna, while the Fourth Armored Division held the mountain passes leading to the Suez Canal. Forces of more than one division strength controlled a third line, further south. In addition, the so-called Shazli Task Force, composed of three brigades and 200 tanks, was poised opposite the southern Negev, with orders to cut off the southern part of Israel, including Eilat.

Jordan committed almost all of its armed forces in the developing battle. Two of the armored brigades, kept in the Jordan River valley until 5 June, were seriously weakened by IDF air strikes as they advanced. By the second day of fighting, King Hussein admitted that the war was lost and asked for a cease-fire.

Qualitative Balance

It is unreliable to compare military data on a one-to-one basis. First, there are significant differences between plane and plane, their concentration or dispersal, their tactical use, and so on. Secondly, leadership, training, technology, motivation, and organization cannot be quantified but are of crucial importance nonetheless.

In June 1967, Israel had two qualitative advantages over its adversaries: surprise and motivation. Its devastating air strike on the 5th caught Arab leaders totally by surprise and ensured Israel's aerial supremacy for the rest of the war. In fact, Israel's victory was certain within the first three hours. As to motivation, the concentrated outpouring of Arab hatred during the prewar crisis period had convinced Israelis, from members of the Cabinet to the man in the street—but not the IDF General Staff—that once again they were fighting for survival. The superior quality of IDF leadership and training, and the quick exploitation of the tactical advantages gained on the first day—air supremacy and the breakthrough of the Arab front line—led to disarray and retreat among the Arab land forces.

The armies of Egypt and Syria had been equipped with sophisticated Soviet weapons in the years prior to the 1967 War, including MiG-21 fighters, SA-2 missiles, and the latest models (T-54 and T-55) of Russian tanks, at the time. Israel's military experts admitted after the June-Six-Day War that Soviet armor was superior to Israel's. But these weapon systems were not yet fully integrated into the Arab armies and were used, if at all, less effectively in battle conditions. Moreover, in sharp contrast to 1973, the Egyptian army was badly led in 1967.

The combined Arab armed forces were superior to the IDF quantitatively and qualitatively. "Because of this, knowledgeable and qualified observers did not anticipate anything approaching the actual course of the war."[4] The combination of superior motivation, leadership, and training, and the tactical exploitation of surprise, speed, and air superiority more than made up for those Arab advantages.

THE ARAB–ISRAEL MILITARY BALANCE: 1967 AND 1973   149

MILITARY LINEUP IN 1973

Arab Forces

Two years after the *October-Yom-Kippur War*, Major-General Shlomo Gazit, the IDF's Director of Military Intelligence, provided the following figures for the Arab armed forces facing Israel in the 1973 War. The figures were "based on what we knew before the war, and especially on whatever we found out after the war when a lot of documents and thousands of prisoners fell into our hands."[5] Two Egyptian armies faced Israel across the Suez Canal: the Second Army in the north and the Third Army in the south. They included five infantry, three mechanized, and two armored divisions. In addition, several Arab states dispatched expeditionary forces to the Suez Canal front when war broke out; thus, the IDF had to fight a formidable adversary. Overall, according to Defense Minister Dayan, the "Arabs have, on both fronts, 820,000 soldiers"; while Prime Minister Meir's estimate was 800,000.[6]

Arab Air Forces (Table 9.3)

Table 9.3   Egypt, Syria, and Jordan air forces, early October 1973

	Egypt	Syria	Jordan	Total
Fighters	653	388	55	1096
Bombers	39			39
Helicopters	160	58	6	224
Transport	61	6	11	78
SAM batteries	146	34		180

Arab Naval Forces (Table 9.4)

Table 9.4   Egypt and Syria naval forces, early October 1973

	Egypt	Syria	Total
Destroyers	5		5
Frigates	3		3
Submarines	12		12
Missile boats	19	9	28
Torpedo boats	34	13	47
Mine sweepers	14	4	18

Arab Land Forces on the Egyptian Front (Table 9.5)

Table 9.5 Arab land forces on Egyptian front, early October 1973

Troops	Egyptian	Algerian	Kuwaiti	Libyan	Moroccan	Sudanese	Tunisian	Total
Infantry brigades	15	1			1	1		18
Mechanized brigades	15							15
Armored brigades	10	1		1				12
Additional infantry Battalions			1			1	1	3
Special troop battalions	24							24
S/S rocket brigades	2							2
Armor								
Tanks	2200	130		100	12	30		2472
Armored personnel carriers	2985	30				30		3045
Artillery (units)	2200	18		18		12–14		2248–50
S/S Scud Launchers	9							9
S/S Luna Launchers	12							12

Arab Land Forces on the Syrian Front (Table 9.6)

Table 9.6 Arab land forces on Syrian front, early October 1973

Troops	Syrian	Iraqi	Jordanian	Kuwaiti	Moroccan	Saudi Arabian	Total
Infantry brigades	9	2	6	1	1	2	21
Mechanized brigades	5	2	3				10
Armored brigades	10	4	6			1	21
Special troop battalions	7	2	3			1	13
Additional armored car battalions						1	1
S/S rocket brigades	1–2						1–2
Armor							
Tanks	1650	500	480	40	30	36	2736
Armored personnel carriers	1500	700	550				2750
Artillery (units)	1200	150	320			54	1724
S/S Luna Launchers	36						36
AML 90						40	40

IDF Chief of Staff Elazar stated that the ratio of the number of tanks was 2.5:1 in the enemy's favor; that of planes, 2:1.[7] This would imply about 2000 Israeli tanks and 650 Israeli aircraft of all types, numbers larger than those enumerated by the IISS Military Balance.

Arab Forces Committed on 6 October 1973
The Egyptian leadership decided during the planning stage "to strike the strongest possible blow [in the first assault] that we are capable of."[8]

The Egyptian High Command allotted to the first assault wave, on the northern (Second Army) sector, three infantry divisions and three additional tank brigades; to the southern (Third Army) sector, two infantry divisions, two additional tank brigades, and one mechanized brigade. One mechanized and one infantry brigade, supported by several commando battalions, were allotted the task of conquering the Ras-Sudar-A-Tur section of the Sinai coast (south of the Third Army's section); and one infantry brigade, supported by several commando battalions, was ordered to conquer, in an independent effort, a triangle in the northernmost section of the Suez Canal front.[9]

Along the Canal were arrayed almost the total artillery force of Egypt, 2000 units, which, at 14:00 on 6 October, opened a barrage along the entire front, firing 3000 tons of shells at a rate of 175 shells per second, for 53 minutes. The first assault was also supported by a wave of 240 Egyptian planes, sent to bomb airfields and missile sites. In sharp contrast to the Syrians (see below), the Egyptians committed mostly infantry forces in the first assault, and only a small part of their armor by night; about 100,000 Egyptian soldiers and 400 tanks (of a total of 2200) had crossed the Canal.

Syrian Front
On 6 October, Syria had concentrated along the front line of the Golan Heights three infantry divisions, which together included 540 tanks. The two supporting armored divisions had 460 tanks. All told, the Syrian Army on the Heights disposed of approximately 1500 tanks. In addition, they had moved 140 batteries of artillery to the front line.[10]

These five divisions were opposed on 6 October by two IDF armored brigades: the Barak Brigade in the southern part of the Golan Heights and the 7th Armored Brigade in the northern part, together with 177 tanks; there were also 11 batteries of artillery and 2 battalions of infantry.[11]

Israel Forces

There are no official figures on the overall strength of Israel's armed forces and their equipment—planes, tanks, guns, and missiles. Most of the educated guesses on Israel's military strength in October 1973 are based on the figures for July 1973, published by the IISS. They are quoted here from the Institute's annual survey, *The Military Balance 1973–74*. The Egyptian military intelligence assessment of Israel's armed strength, as of 1 September 1973, tended to be higher.

The IDF's defense, along the first line, comprised 436 soldiers in a series of fortifications, the Bar-Lev Line, "7-8 miles apart and three tanks actually on the water-front."[12] In the second line, there were 275 tanks, divided almost equally among three brigades. These tanks were not in position. Major-General Mendler, the Commanding Officer, had orders to move them into position, according to the guidelines of "Operation Dovecote," at 16:00 on the 6th, in order not to create unnecessary tension until the last moment before the attack, expected at 18:00. Israeli armor suffered heavy casualties while moving forward—from aerial bombardment as well as from Egyptian infantry units equipped with antitank missiles, by then in large numbers, on the east bank of the Canal. "On Sunday [7 October] at 5:00 in the morning, there were about 110 tanks and about 500-550 soldiers defending the state [Israel] on the southern front."[13]

QUALITATIVE BALANCE

In 1973, in contrast to 1967, the Arab armies were better trained and equipped, and they had higher motivation because they were fighting to regain occupied territories. Israel's army, because it was convinced it could not afford a single defeat, fought with the same commitment as in previous wars.

In the 1973 War, the Arab armies had the advantage of surprise, tactical as well as strategic. Egypt had meticulously planned the first assault across the Canal for four years—and carried it out well. But after 14 October, when the massive Egyptian armored attack in Sinai was stopped (250 tanks destroyed against marginal IDF losses of 5 tanks destroyed and 10 damaged), some of the organizational weaknesses of Egypt's army, and Israel's qualitative superiority, reasserted themselves. That prompted Bar-Lev to inform Meir: "Golda, it will be all right. We are back to being ourselves and they [the Egyptians] are back to being themselves."[14]

According to Egyptian sources, as well as military analysts, Egyptian field commanders reported to general headquarters (GHQ) accurately as long as the battle went reasonably well. But as of 14 October, old habits of misreporting resurfaced. Thus, the crossing of the Canal by Israeli forces was brought to the notice of Egypt's GHQ 16 hours after it actually took place, though frontline observations had been reported at least 6 hours earlier.[15]

There was a massive, concentrated use of antitank and antiaircraft missiles by the Egyptians: Sagger missiles by Egyptian infantry who had crossed the Canal, and the Strella and SAM 2, 3, 6, and 7 missiles fired by infantry or from static or mobile batteries. The latter provided an effective umbrella against the known superiority of the Israeli Air Force during the first week of the war.

For Israel, perhaps the greatest qualitative difference in the 1973 War was surprise: it took a week until the IDF recovered; much of the confusion and many of the losses of that week were attributed to this factor.[16] However, by quickly adapting tactics—for example, making the destruction of SAM missile batteries by infantry and armor the first priority after crossing the Canal—the superior technical proficiency of Israeli armor and air power was reasserted.[17]

NOTES

1. The data for the 1967 Crisis and War are based on the following sources: Eliyahu S. Levi, ed., *This Was Goliath: Facts and Figures on Arab Military Strength in the Six Day War* (Tel Aviv: IDF Information Office, October 1967); Nadav Safran, *From War to War: The Arab–Israel Confrontation, 1948–1967: A Study of the Conflict from the Perspective of Coercion in the Context of Inter-Arab and Big Power Relations* (New York: Pegasus, 1969), Chaps. 4, 5, and 7, and Appendices B and C; Daniel Dishon, ed., *Middle East Record: 1967* (Tel Aviv: Israel Universities Press, 1971), 205–207; International Institute for Strategic Studies, London, *The Military Balance, 1966–67* and *1967–68* (London: International Institute for Strategic Studies, 1966 and 1967); A. Legler and W Liebisch, "Militärische, Ereijuisse im Nahen Osten, June 1967, Eine Documentation," *Bibliothek fur Zeitgeschichte Jahres-Bibliographie* (Stuttgart: 1967), 321–395; Edgar O'Ballance, *The Third Arab–Israel War* (London: Faber and Faber, 1972); and Major Yonah, "The Background of the Six Day War in the Eyes of

the Arabs: Egypt and Her Entry Into the War," *Ma'arakhot* 191–192 (June 1968), 37–40, 73–103. For an analysis of the Military Balance, 1967–73, including the qualitative aspects, see Ahmed S. Khalidi, "The Military Balance 1967–73," in *Middle East Crucible: Studies on the Arab–Israel War of October 1973*, ed. Naseer H. Aruri (Wilmette, IL: Medina University Press International, 1975), 21–63.

2. The story of the Kuwaiti regiment, as told by Mohamed Heikal, a confidante of Nasser, was typical of this gap: "One of the strangest incidents of the day centered on a battalion of the Kuwaiti Regiment which had been sent to Egypt as a propaganda move to demonstrate Arab solidarity. It had been dispatched to El Arish on the understanding that it would not be involved in any trouble .... But the only welcome the Kuwaitis got at El Arish came from Israeli planes strafing the station. The moment they got out of the train they were ordered to make their way back to Suez" ("The 1967 Arab–Israel War," *Sunday Telegraph*, 28 October 1973).

   The data on Arab forces are limited to those of Egypt, Jordan, and Syria (Lebanon stayed out of the 1967 War), plus the Iraqi forces which had been dispatched to Jordan prior to the outbreak of hostilities.

3. Of the Arab countries without a direct border with Israel, small units from Iraq already in positions in Sinai took part in the fighting. Of the reinforcements under way from Algeria, Iraq, Sudan, Morocco, Tunisia, and Saudi Arabia, only two squadrons of Algerian MiGs reached the front. There were some air strikes by Iraqi planes from an Iraqi airfield. An Iraqi division, reinforced by a battalion of Palestinian troops, which had entered Jordan on 4 June reached the Jordan River on the day of the cease-fire with Jordan, having been slowed down and severely mauled on the way by Israeli air strikes.

4. Safran, *From War to War*, 319.

5. Shlomo Gazit, "Arab Forces Two Years after the Yom Kippur War," in *Military Aspects of the Israeli-Arab Conflict: Proceedings of the International Symposium Held in Jerusalem, 12–17 October, 1975* (Tel Aviv: University Publishing Projects, 1975), 188–195.

6. Respectively: Moshe Dayan, "Interview on Israeli Television, 14 October 1973," in special issue, *Ma'arakhot* (November 1973): 232–233; and Golda Meir, "Speech to the Knesset, 16 October

1973," *Divrei Haknesset* [*Parliamentary Proceedings*] 68, 4474, in *Israel's Foreign Relations: Selected Documents, 1947–1974,* ed. Meron Medzini (Jerusalem: Ministry of Foreign Affairs, 1976): 1044–1051.

7. David Elazar, "The Yom Kippur War: Military Lessons," in *Military Aspects of the Israeli-Arab Conflict: Proceedings of an International Symposium Held in Jerusalem, 12–17 October 1975* (Tel Aviv: University Publishing Projects, 1975), 245–250.
8. General Hafez Ismail, interview by Mohamed Heikal, *Al Anwar*, 18 November 1973; cited in Avi Shay, "Egypt before the Yom Kippur War: War Aims and Plan of Attack," *Ma'arakhot*, 250 (July 1976): 18.
9. Shay, "Egypt before the Yom Kippur War"; Chaim Herzog, *The War of Atonement, October 1973* (Jerusalem and Tel Aviv: Steimatsky's Agency, 1975), 150–151.
10. Herzog, *The War of Atonement*, 61, 63–64.
11. *Ma'arakhot*, special issue (September 1974).
12. Herzog, *The War of Atonement*, 151. Haim Bar-Lev mentioned 352 soldiers in 14 fortifications along the Canal, "and that included cooks, medics, radio-men, drivers and other service personnel," three tanks and five batteries of artillery, with several battalions of artillery in the second line ("We Knew Where the Egyptians Would Attack and How – But We Made a Mistake about the Timing," *Ma'ariv*, 1 August 1975).
13. Shmuel Gonen, "Interview with Major-General Gonen on the Fourth Anniversary of the Yom Kippur War (Hebrew Calendar)," *Yediot Aharonot* 21 September 1977.
14. Bar-Lev, interview, *Ma'ariv*, 21 September 1977.
15. See excerpts from the top-secret Third Army daily journal of messages, captured during the war and published in *Ma'ariv*, 14 September 1975.
16. Major-General Y. Tal, IDF Deputy Chief of Staff in 1973, interview, *Yediot Aharonot*, 21 September 1977.
17. For analyses of the military aspects of the 1973 War, see Herzog, *The War of Atonement*; Zeev Schiff, *October Earthquake, Yom Kippur 1973* (Tel Aviv: University Publishing Projects, 1974) and his articles on the battle of 8 October and on the encirclement of the Third Army, *Ha'aretz*, 25 and 30 September 1974 and 14 September 1975; Shay, "Egypt Before the Yom Kippur War";

Ma'arakhot 232 and 233 (November 1973) and 240, special issue on the first anniversary of the war (September 1974); Mohamed Heikal, *The Road to Ramadan* (London: Collins, 1975); the series of interviews with Sadat by Mousa Sabri, ed., *Akhbar el-Yom*, 1974, in *Ma'ariv*, 13 September 1974; the Insight team of *The Sunday Times*, *The Yom Kippur War* (London: Andre Deutsch, 1974); Elizabeth Monroe and Anthony Farrar-Hockley, *The Arab–Israel War, October 1973: Background and Events* (London: The International Institute for Strategic Studies, 1974), Adelphi Paper No. 111 (Winter 1974); and Martin van Creveld, *Military Lessons of the Yom Kippur War: Historical Perspectives*, The Center for Strategic and International Studies, Georgetown University, Washington, D.C., The Washington Papers, vol. 3 (London and Beverly Hills: SAGE, 1975).

CHAPTER 10

Israel's Behavior in the 1967 and 1973 Wars: Overall Findings

DECISIONS, DECISION-MAKERS, DECISION PROCESS: PREWAR CRISIS PERIOD (17 MAY–4 JUNE 1967)

Decisions

For Israel, the 1967 higher-than-normal stress crisis period began on 17 May and lasted until the Cabinet decision on 4 June to initiate a war. Following the three decisions of the precrisis period, there were 14 others during the next 19 days. These decisions can be divided into three phases (Table 10.1).

Decision-Makers

Almost all decisions in the prewar, high-stress crisis period were taken by the 18-member, 5-party coalition Cabinet and their advisers. The decisions on war were made by the National Unity Government, enlarged to 21 on 1 June with the addition of two ministers from *Gahal* and one from *Rafi*. The Cabinet met almost daily throughout the 1967 prewar crisis, sometimes around the clock, and was engaged in what one civil servant termed "an exercise in collective cable reading."[1] Its composition is given below (Table 10.2).

© The Author(s) 2017
M. Brecher, *Dynamics of the Arab–Israel Conflict*,
DOI 10.1007/978-3-319-47575-2_10

158 M. BRECHER

Table 10.1 Israel's decisions: May–June 1967 crisis-war

Decision number	Date	Content
Phase I: Apprehension and mobilization (17–22 May)		
4.	17 May	Prime Minister–Defense Minister Eshkol and IDF Chief of Staff Rabin decided on further mobilization.
5.	19 May	Eshkol and the IDF General Staff decided on large-scale mobilization.
6.	19 May	The General Staff decided to change the disposition of the IDF forces from a defensive posture to a buildup toward offensive capability.
7.	21 May	The Cabinet approved the large-scale mobilization decision of 19 May.
Phase II: Delay and diplomacy (23–28 May)		
8.	23 May	The Cabinet, acting as the Ministerial Committee on Defense, decided to postpone a decision on whether or not to go to war.
9.	23 May	The Cabinet, acting as the Ministerial Committee on Defense, approved Foreign Minister Eban's journey to Washington to explore US intentions.
10.	25 May	Eshkol approved a move to warn the US administration, through Eban, that there was a danger of an imminent Egyptian attack.
11.	26 May	The Cabinet, acting as the Ministerial Committee on Defense, decided to await Eban's return before taking a decision on the opening of the Straits.
12.	28 May	The Cabinet decided to opt for further waiting, to leave time for action by the maritime states.
13.	28 May	The Cabinet decided to keep the army on full alert.
Phase III: Preemption (29 May–4 June)		
14.	30 May	Eshkol, in consultation with other ministers and bureaucrats, decided to send Intelligence Head, Major-General Amit, to the United States to ascertain American intentions.
15.	1 June	Eshkol accepted the formation of a National Unity Government, with Dayan as Defense Minister.
16.	2 June	Dayan approved military plans to strike along three lines of advance into Sinai, instead of one.
17.	4 June	The Cabinet decided to go to war.

Table 10.2 Israel's decision-makers, 1967 crisis-war

Labor Alignment	Portfolio
Mapai	
L. Eshkol[a]	Prime Minister (and Defense Minister till 1 June)
Z. Aranne[a]	Education and Culture
A. Eban[a]	Foreign Affairs
H. Gvati	Agriculture
P. Sapir[a]	Finance
E. Sasson[a]	Police
Y.E. Shapiro[a]	Justice
Z. Sharef	Industry and Commerce
Y. Yeshayahu	Posts
Ahdut Ha'avoda	
Y. Allon[a]	Labor
M. Carmel	Transport
Y. Galili[a]	Without Portfolio (in charge of information)
Mapam	
Y. Barzilai[a]	Health
M. Bentov	Housing
Other parties	
National Religious Party	
Y. Burg H.	Welfare
H.M. Shapira[a]	Interior
Z. Warhaftig[a]	Religious Affairs
Independent Liberals	
M. Kol[a]	Tourism and Development
As of 1 June	
Gahal	
M. Begin[a]	Without Portfolio
Y. Saphir[a]	Without Portfolio
Rafi	
M. Dayan[a]	Defense

[a]Members of the Ministerial (Cabinet) Committee on Defense, as of 1 June 1967

Other party leaders and persons who participated in the deliberations of the prewar crisis period were:

S. Avigur	The "eminence grise" of Israel's military-security establishment
D. Ben-Gurion	"Father of the Nation" and Prime Minister–Defense Minister for most of the period, 1948–63
Z. Dinstein	Deputy Minister of Defense
G. Meir	Secretary-General of *Mapai* during the 1967 Crisis
S. Peres	Secretary-General of *Rafi* and a central figure in the 1967 domestic political crisis
Y. Yadin	Former Chief of Staff, archaeologist, and an Eshkol confidant

Civil servants and diplomats of consequence during the prewar crisis period, apart from Ya'acov Herzog, included: Aviad Yaffe, Eshkol's Head of Bureau; Harman and Evron, Ambassador and Minister at Israel's Washington Embassy, respectively, who helped to decipher the attitudes and policy of the US administration; Levavi, who, in Eban's absence, often represented the Foreign Ministry in Cabinet discussions; Rafael, who implemented Israel's policy at the UN; and Moshe Bitan, Assistant Director-General of the Foreign Ministry in charge of US affairs. From the IDF, Generals Rabin, Yariv, and Weizman continued to be actively involved in the consultation process. They were joined from 1 June by the newly appointed Deputy Chief of Staff, Major-General Haim Bar-Lev.

Decision Process

The 1967 prewar crisis period was triggered by three dramatic events on 16 and 17 May: first, Egypt's request to the UN to withdraw the UN Emergency Force (UNEF), and UN Secretary-General U Thant's immediate response, which conceded Cairo's right to unilateral termination of the UNEF presence on Egypt's territory; second, the crossing of two additional Egyptian divisions into Sinai; and third, the overflight of Israel's nuclear weapons center at Dimona for a minute.[2] The crisis period may be divided into three distinct phases, as follows: phase I: apprehension and mobilization, 17–22 May; phase II: delay and diplomacy, 23–28 May; and phase III: resolution, 29 May–4 June.

PHASE I: APPREHENSION AND MOBILIZATION (17–22 MAY)

The events preceding 17 May were links in a chain of controlled tension that was an integral part of a protracted conflict (PC). Even the movement of Egyptian troops into Sinai on 14 and 15 May—and their reinforcement on the 16th—belong to the qualitatively lower-stress precrisis period: they were perceived by Israeli decision-makers as a repetition of February 1960, a show of force within the inter-Arab domain and not a threat to Israel's security.

The events of 17–22 May surprised Israel's political and military élites, and induced precautionary acts that became part of the escalatory process of stimulus–response for both principal adversaries. And yet, until Nasser's *closure of the Straits* on 22–23 May, war was still not perceived as certain. That act was, for Israel, the watershed of the 1967 Crisis. In the words of Major-General Meir Amit: "The basic evaluation was correct: Egypt was not ready for a war; and Nasser did not want a war. Until 23 May, I thought that there is a possibility for maneuvers, that there is leeway for alternatives. But when Nasser closed the Straits, I said: 'This is it; there is no way to avoid war.'"[3]

Wednesday, 17 May

Egypt's demand for the withdrawal of the UNEF troops was broadcast by Radio Cairo at 06:00 hours, Israel time. By 11:00, the Ministerial Committee on Defense was in urgent session. The rest of the day was devoted to intense formal and informal consultations within the fairly large circle of participants in the deliberative processes of the 1967 Crisis: the Cabinet, either in full or its Defense Committee (comprising more than half its members); the *Knesset* Foreign Affairs and Security Committee, broadening the consultative circle to include the main Opposition parties; and the military and foreign affairs élites. After the meetings of the Cabinet Defense Committee and the *Knesset* Foreign Affairs and Security Committee, there were seven hours of small group consultations, involving Eshkol, Eban, and Galili of the Cabinet; Rabin, Weizman, and Yariv from the IDF General Staff; Herzog and Yaffe from the Prime Minister's Office; and Levavi, Bitan, Tekoah, and Lourie from the Foreign Office. The upshot of these consultations was several reactive decisions and moves in the military and diplomatic issue-areas. The Prime Minister and the Chief of Staff decided to call up further military reserves at a late evening meeting (Decision 4).[4] The Foreign Minister instructed Rafael, Israel's Representative to the UN, to bring to the attention of the UN Secretary-General the commitments given by his predecessor—Dag Hammarskjold—in February 1957, to prevent belligerency in the Straits of Tiran and to undertake consultations in the UN if the question of the removal of the UNEF was raised.[5]

Eban was told by Rabin that the IDF needed time to complete its defenses in the South. In fact, during the Cabinet session, Rabin even suggested that Israel initiate a meeting of the Security Council, to gain time. Eban, after consultation with members of Israel's UN delegation, who were against it, rejected the idea.[6] His reasons were the possibility of an adverse decision and an expected Soviet veto, which might have encouraged Nasser even further. And "I knew from long experience that it was easier to turn on the tap of United Nations debate than to turn it off."[7] Instead, he tried, through Rafael and leading members of the Security Council, to induce U Thant to visit Cairo and Jerusalem.[8]

Events were overtaking decisions. The process imposed massive pressures on Israel's decision-makers, as they were to do during the next 20 days, as well as sharply limited the practical possibility of keeping everybody concerned informed. By the time Rafael saw U Thant and Bunche the next day, the Egyptians had decided to demand total, immediate withdrawal of the UNEF.[9]

In other capitals, as in Jerusalem, the mood was still tranquil. In Washington, Eugene Rostow again advised Harman that Israel should not act. In Paris, Eytan was told by Herve Alphand, then Director-General of the Foreign Ministry, who had just returned from Cairo, that Nasser was still interested in the presence of the UNEF, as protection against Israel. In London, the general appreciation was that, though the situation was dangerous, it would not reach a critical stage. Yet, by the end of the day, the decisions regarding the UNEF were taken and the facts already established.

Thursday, 18 May

The day began—and ended—in Israel with security consultations between Eshkol and Rabin. They were joined in the morning by Eban, Amit, Yariv, and other IDF officers. The daily intelligence estimate was that war was a remote possibility. While in consultation, around 09:00 am, President Johnson's first communication of the 1967 Crisis to Eshkol arrived. It was, in effect, outdated by this time, for it dealt with the Syrian situation; Johnson also warned Israel against retaliatory action[10]:

> I want to emphasize strongly that you have to abstain from every step that would increase the tension and violence in the area. You will probably understand that the United States cannot accept any responsibility for situations that are liable to occur as a result of actions in which we were not consulted.[11]

This warning was to be repeated again and again in the following days. The other item of discussion was Egypt's request for the total withdrawal of the UNEF. This unexpected reaction of Nasser to U Thant's challenge turned apprehension into consternation. Eshkol and Rabin, later in the day, reportedly expressed their belief that there might be war.[12]

Eban called in the ambassadors of the United States, the United Kingdom, and France to express Israel's objections to the removal of the UNEF. He reminded them again of Western commitments made in 1957 and warned about the serious consequences of upsetting the *status quo*. In the afternoon he drafted a reply for Eshkol to Johnson's letter. The substance of the letter stated:

1. The serious crisis presently threatening the Middle East originated in the attitude of Syria.
2. Egypt has spread out over the Sinai Peninsula an offensive force of at least 500 tanks. It is advisable to insist that that country return its forces immediately to the other side of the Canal.
3. The UN Force should not abandon its positions. The Secretary-General of the United Nations ought to inform Egypt that only the General Assembly can order the evacuation of the UNEF.
4. The United States should publicly reaffirm the guarantees it has given Israel in the past, notably from Johnson to Eshkol in 1964.[13]

Eshkol approved the calling up of further reserves and the speeding up of deliveries of war material that might be necessary—a constant source of concern to Israel's decision-makers. Eshkol and Rabin were "especially alarmed" by the report that U Thant was about to order the UNEF's withdrawal, which raised the possibility of the closure of the Straits. Eshkol also held consultations on civil defense preparations, and he decided to acquire, at all costs, gas masks in sufficient quantities. (These were to be located and supplied at the height of the crisis, somewhat reluctantly, by the Federal Republic of Germany.)

The focus of the crisis on 18 May remained for the last time, until the outbreak of war, at UN headquarters. In the forenoon, Rafael called upon U Thant and Bunche to warn against the removal of the UNEF and the situation on the Israel–Syrian border. U Thant stated that he had seen no legal grounds for refusal (of Egypt's request) and countered with the suggestion that the UNEF be transferred onto the Israeli side of the border. Rafael refused on the spot.[14] The same suggestion was raised that day, and in the days to come, by the United States, the United Kingdom, and— very strongly—by Canada.[15]

Rafael was immediately followed by El-Kony, with Egypt's Foreign Minister Riad's note, calling for the termination of the UNEF presence.

U Thant, after some hasty consultations with leading members of the Security Council, called, for the first time, a meeting of the UN Advisory Committee on the UNEF at 17:00 New York time: he told them of his decision to evacuate the UNEF. Serious misgivings were expressed, particularly by the representative of Canada, but no one challenged his decision, a fact that U Thant and his defenders later recalled to justify his action.[16]

Within the Arab world, 18 May marked the beginning of intra-Arab coordination. Noteworthy was Syria's announcement that the mobilization of its reserves was now completed. And Egypt let it be known that its secret missile bases were in a state of alert. That day also marked the first significant break in the intense hostility between the "progressive" and "traditional" regimes in the Arab world, with Saudi Arabia's Crown Prince openly supporting Syria on grounds of "our religion, Arabism, and brotherly bonds."

Friday, 19 May

On Friday, 19 May, "alarm bells rang at one and the same time in several chancelleries of the world."[17] In Israel, the adjustment to the unexpected gravity of the situation was rapid, although it was decided to continue, officially, the evaluation of "demonstrative moves" and to belittle the danger. The closure of the Straits was now considered a distinct possibility.

At eight o'clock in the morning, President Shazar left for an official visit to Canada; it had been decided upon the night before as part of the drive to underline the "business-as-usual" atmosphere. By 09:30, Eshkol and Rabin had returned to the Ministry of Defense, first for a consultation with the Chief Scientist of the Army and then for a meeting with the General Staff, where the daily intelligence report was evaluated. Gone was the appreciation that Nasser would not be ready for war until 1970. Gone, too, was the view that he would not risk war while he was tied down in Yemen. Instead, the report contained the new realities: the presence of 70,000 Egyptian soldiers and 600 tanks in Sinai; an Egyptian infantry and two tank battalions recalled in secrecy from Yemen and sent straight into Sinai; Sharm-e-Sheikh occupied by Egyptian units; and the Gaza border manned by units of the Palestinian Liberation Army. The outcome of this meeting was the decision to order large-scale mobilization of reserves, effective immediately (Israel's Decision 5). Another decision was to replace the previous tactical plans for the buildup and disposition of Israeli troops along the border, with plans for a buildup to enable a preemptive strike into Sinai (Decision 6).[18]

The Foreign Minister decided on a last attempt to enlist Soviet support for a policy of restraint. He summoned Soviet Ambassador Chuvakhin and proposed "a reciprocal de-escalation of troops in the South." He asked "the Soviet Government to cooperate to this end," as well as in the prevention of sabotage from across the Syrian border, and he suggested international consultation on the consequences of the removal of the UNEF. He added that everything now depended upon Egypt: "There will be no war unless the Egyptians attack our territory or violate our rights of free navigation." Chuvakhin replied that the present situation was created by Israel's aggressive propaganda against Arab states, especially Syria, and its attacks on Syria. "History will pass judgment on Israel for having played with fire." He was not prepared to discuss troop concentrations and acts of sabotage because they were not within his competence. "As for UNEF, its presence on the territory of any state depended on the free consent of that state, which had full power to demand its removal." Eban came away from the meeting with the impression that "it was indecently clear that what the Soviet Union had in mind was not how to reduce tension, but how to bring it swiftly to the boil," and that Chuvakhin's demeanor "expressed an almost sadistic delight in Israel's predicament."[19]

Eban and Eshkol now proceeded, on a broad diplomatic front, to try to preserve Israel's freedom of navigation in the Straits. The Prime Minister wrote to de Gaulle: "Israel on her part will not initiate hostile acts but she is firmly resolved to defend her territory and her international rights. Our decision is that if Egypt will not attack us, we will not take action against Egyptian forces at Sharm-e-Sheikh—until or unless they close the Straits of Tiran to free navigation by Israel." This assurance was repeated the same day in a personal note by Eban to French Foreign Minister Couve de Murville. Eban reminded him that France had in the past confirmed, and identified herself with, former Foreign Minister Meir's statement of March 1957, in which Israel stated: "Interference with free passage will be regarded by Israel as an attack entitling it to exercise the inherent right of self-defense under Article 51 of the United Nations Charter."[20] Israel's policy, he added, remained unchanged. A similar message was sent to Britain's Foreign Secretary, George Brown.[21]

Eshkol and Eban also acted to restrain all official Israeli public pronouncements so as not to aggravate the pressures now piling up on Nasser. And with the exception of *Ha'aretz* ("Tension Grows in the South"), the Israeli press still expressed the relatively tranquil mood of the preceding days.

U Thant decided to fly to Cairo. In Washington, the administration was being urged to extend public support for the integrity and independence of Israel. Instead, President Johnson opted for "semi-quiet" diplomacy. George Brown announced the postponement of his visit to Moscow. And Moscow stated that it would not stand idly by if Israel attacked Syria.

Saturday, 20 May

During the day, Eshkol and Rabin toured the southern front. The previous day's mobilization order was to be completed by nightfall. In the evening, Dayan received Eshkol's permission to tour IDF forces in the Negev. The first answer to Eshkol and Eban's communications came from UK Prime Minister Wilson. Although sympathetic in tone, it foreshadowed the line to be taken in Washington and Paris as well: support for the freedom of navigation, but international action only through the United Nations and only if the Egyptians in fact imposed an embargo:

> I am on public record as saying that the Straits of Tiran constitute an international waterway which should remain open to the ships of all nations. If it appeared that any attempt to interfere with the passage of ships through the waterway was likely to be made, we should promote and support international action through the United Nations to secure free passage.[22]

Other communications from London stressed that Israel should not act prematurely.

In Paris, Israel's Ambassador suggested that de Gaulle add his prestige and influence to that of Johnson and put pressure on Kosygin to restrain the Egyptians. The French government was reminded of its repeated commitments (in 1950, 1957, 1960, and 1964) to Israel's security and to the free passage of Israeli shipping in the Straits.[23]

In Washington, Harman and Evron had another meeting with Eugene Rostow and continued to press for a public statement of American support. But the reaction was cautious and hesitant. Rostow raised the suggestion that the UNEF be placed on the Israeli side of the border; again the idea was rejected. All through the conversation, Rostow stressed that, at that stage, the crisis should be handled through the UN and that Israel should abstain from unilateral actions.

By the end of the day, the Israeli government was biding its time, still slightly hopeful about possible developments, in spite of the bad news beginning to arrive from Western capitals. Late in the evening, Eshkol was somewhat encouraged by the news of U Thant's forthcoming visit. Another encouraging sign was the passage of a cargo ship bound for Eilat through the Straits, unmolested.

Sunday, 21 May

Before the regular Sunday morning meeting of the Cabinet, Eshkol and Rabin met briefly to review the situation. The Cabinet session was, according to several accounts, acrimonious.[24] Much had happened since the last meeting of the Cabinet five days earlier, most of it unexpected, and all of it unpleasant.

The subjects discussed included the concentration of Egyptian troops on the southern border—reported by Rabin to be by this time up to 70,000 men; the state of inter-Arab coordination; diplomatic efforts made by Eshkol and Eban; intelligence evaluation of possible developments, including an Egyptian surprise attack; Soviet intentions; and U Thant's forthcoming visit to Cairo. The predominant mood was that of emerging anxiety, and several Cabinet ministers strongly demanded that everything be done to avoid war. In Rabin's opinion there was no need for further mobilization: the Egyptian buildup was still defensive. The Cabinet approved the large-scale mobilization of 19 May (Decision 7). The Cabinet also approved Eshkol's intention to make a statement on the situation at the opening session of the *Knesset* the next day, but anxiety was such that several ministers, particularly H.M. Shapira, asked to be shown the draft of the Prime Minister's speech.[25]

Incoming cables at the Foreign Office showed a similar pattern: the advice of the Western powers was to lay the burden on the UN, and official France was covered in "thunderous silence."[26] One of the most important inputs to Israel's decisions on the 21st was a letter of caution from the State Department:

> The United States' position is that the present grave problem should be handled, in a peaceful manner, preferably through the United Nations.[27]

In Washington, the answer to the first overtures of the United States to the Soviet Union arrived. Although recent developments were blamed on Israel for its aggressive intents, Washington did state that the Soviet Union was interested in the preservation of peace in the area. In Canada,

Prime Minister Pearson used the occasion of Shazar's visit to sound out the Israelis on ways to save the UNEF presence, either through transferring to the Israeli side or through a considerable increase of the United Nations Truce Supervision Organization (UNTSO). Again, though informally, the first suggestion was turned down. The second—to which Israel was not totally averse—was soon to be overtaken by events.

The Arab world on 21 May was mainly concerned with the question: will Nasser decide to close the Straits to Israeli ships? The Syrians and the Lebanese openly demanded it; so did the Jordanians and the Executive Committee of the Arab Socialist Union. The political consolidation of the Arab world continued; so did military preparations. Egypt now proclaimed total mobilization of reserves, and Nasser announced that he had accepted the President of Iraq's offer to send units of the Iraqi army, armor, and air force.

One other important event on the 21st, within Israel, was a meeting of *Rafi* leaders and sympathizers, convened by Shimon Peres. The meeting was attended by a galaxy of public figures, among them: Ben-Gurion and three former IDF Chiefs of Staff—Dori, Zur, and Dayan. There seems little doubt that the meeting was called to lay the groundwork for an attempt to topple Eshkol and reinstate Ben-Gurion as Prime Minister and Minister of Defense. In any case, it marked the beginning of an internal crisis, a crisis of confidence in Eshkol's government and leadership that culminated in the formation of a National Unity Government and Dayan's appointment as Minister of Defense ten days later. A meeting between Ben-Gurion and Rabin later in the evening did not dispel the former's doubts about Israel's military prospects: he accused the IDF Chief of Staff of escalating the crisis through wide-scale mobilization, at a time when the IDF was not adequately prepared and Israel was without an ally. In Israel and the United States, official optimism was still prevalent.

Monday, 22 May

On Monday, 22 May, Nasser decided to close the Straits. But during the day, until his decision became known, world attention was focused on Israel, specifically on Eshkol's anticipated statement. The major external input into his final draft was another Johnson letter, in answer to Eshkol's of 19 May, containing clarifications of the US position. The President wrote that the United States would support "suitable measures in and outside the United Nations."[28] He referred to his contacts with Soviet leaders:

The Soviet leaders have no illusions about the pledge of the United States to prevent, either through the United Nations, or independently of that international organization, all aggression in the Middle East. This policy has been defined and confirmed by four American presidents: Truman, Eisenhower, Kennedy and myself. It is also contained in the three-power agreement of 1950.[29]

Johnson also suggested that Israel work toward the renewal of the 1950 Tripartite Declaration, support for which was officially announced by the State Department.

After appearing before the *Knesset* Foreign Affairs and Security Committee at 15:00, Eshkol read his prepared statement before the *Knesset*. It was a very cautious, moderate reaction to a dangerous situation; the possibility of the closure of the Straits was not mentioned once. He called upon the powers "to exercise their full influence," in order to remove the danger of conflagration in the Middle East, laying "particular responsibility" on the Soviet Union. He demanded a return to the status quo on both sides of the border and called for a complete cessation of acts of sabotage.[30] During the subsequent debate, many parliamentarians called for stronger measures to counteract Egyptian moves—and for a clarification of the government's position that it was ready to go to war to defend Israel's rights.

In Washington, Harman warned Assistant Secretary of State Lucius D. Battle that if Nasser were for a single moment to believe that the US attitude were as indicated in the 21 May letter, he would regard this as an invitation to interfere with shipping in the Straits. In New York, Rafael handed U Thant an Eban letter which emphasized Israel's determination to defend freedom of navigation. He also asked the Secretary-General not to commit himself in matters which needed Israel's agreement.

During the day, there were other contacts between Evron and Harman, and Evron and the Rostows (senior officials in the Johnson administration). The Rostows reinforced the tenor of Johnson's letter, making a public announcement conditional upon U Thant's trip, as well as on a Security Council debate. Ways of defusing the crisis through some UN machinery were also discussed, with the Americans suggesting a revitalization of the Egypt–Israel Armistice Agreement and the Israelis giving an indication of a willingness to consider this.

Toward evening came news of further setbacks for Israel—the French and British statements disavowing the 1950 Tripartite Declaration. The

French position was that the guarantees were now outdated, while the British stated that they were only restating a policy announced by Prime Minister MacMillan in 1963 and reaffirmed by Prime Minister Wilson in 1965. Their timing indicated the reluctance of two of the signatory states to get involved in Israel's confrontation with the Arabs.[31]

In Sinai, at the Bir Gafgafa airbase, Nasser made his fateful announcement about the Tiran Straits:

> Under no circumstances can we permit the Israeli flag to pass through the Gulf of Aqaba. The Jews threaten war. We say they are welcome to war, we are ready for war, our armed forces, our people, all of us are ready for war, but under no circumstances shall we abandon any of our rights. These are our waters.[32]

Upon his return to Cairo, Egypt's President told the Soviet Ambassador that the Soviets were responsible for what had happened.[33]

The crucial role of the decision to close the Straits as a trigger mechanism for Israel's subsequent behavior in the 1967 Crisis was noted by President Johnson in his 19 June 1967 address: "If a single act of folly was more responsible for this explosion than any other, I think it was the arbitrary and dangerous announced decision that the Straits of Tiran would be closed."[34]

Phase II: Delay and Diplomacy (23–28 May)

The second phase of Israel's prewar crisis period began and ended with Cabinet decisions to opt for diplomatic rather than military means to resolve the 1967 Crisis. Nasser had challenged the basis of Israel's security policy, the concept of deterrence, that is, the capability of the IDF to prevent encroachments upon Israel's vital interests. The announcement of the decision to close the Straits was, for Israel, a major escalation; in fact, it was a point of no return on the path to war.

Tuesday, 23 May

The news reached IDF headquarters between 02:00 and 04:00. At 04:30, Rabin phoned Eshkol; Eban was informed by Army headquarters at 05:00. Eshkol's first reaction was: "This cannot continue. We shall have to call upon the whole people and the whole Opposition."[35] Consultations with Herzog and Yaffe began at 06:10. At 06:40, they left together for a meeting at IDF General Staff headquarters in Tel Aviv, which began at 08:30. En route, Herzog suggested that Opposition leaders be brought into the consultations, and Eshkol readily agreed.[36] Some military leaders were of the opinion that Israel's deterrent credibility was at stake. Others expressed concern over large-scale war and destruction, along with the view that war would be a matter of life and death for Israel. This discussion was followed by a meeting of the Ministerial Committee on Defense, at 09:30, attended also by Eban's advisers, with Rabin, Weizman, Yariv, and Meir. After the departure of three ministers, Aranne, Sapir, and Carmel, the meeting was enlarged to include Coalition and Opposition leaders, who had arrived in the interval: David Hacohen of the Labor Alignment, Chairman of the *Knesset* Foreign Affairs and Security Committee; Almogi, Peres, and Dayan from *Rafi*; and Begin, Ben-Eliezer, Landau, Rimalt, and Serlin from *Gahal*. The ministers who remained were Warhaftig and Galili. It was in this large forum that most of the alternatives open to Israel for action were considered. However, the basic decision to wait and opt for diplomacy, including the possibility of the Foreign Minister's journey to Washington, was taken at the Ministerial meeting at 09:30. The larger group was not informed of the decision authorizing a possible journey by Eban to the United States; and Eban's decision to see de Gaulle en route was arrived at by neither forum, but rather in the evening.

The Defense Committee meeting had begun with a review of the military situation by Rabin. The Egyptian buildup was not yet offensive, he observed; the pivotal Fourth Armored Division was still on the western side of the Canal, and nothing had yet moved on the Jordanian front. He did not make a proposal for immediate action but indicated that the sooner Israel acted the better. He also pointed out that if Israel were to take military action, it would not be feasible to strike at Sharm-e-Sheikh alone: "That would be to start the war at the worst and most difficult place."[37] The only viable alternative to an all-out assault would be to hit the Egyptian Air Force, then to occupy the Gaza Strip and hold. Although the IDF Command was certain of victory, "I cannot promise a walk-over," said Rabin. "This will not be similar to Sinai [1956]; it will not be easy. There will be sacrifices."[38] In reply to a question from Eban, whether anything would be lost by a few days' delay for intensive diplomatic activity, the military commanders present concurred that all nonmilitary possibilities should be exhausted first. They affirmed their agreement to a postponement of military action—for 48 hours—at the Ministerial Committee meeting and during the consultation with the larger group of the political élite.[39]

Eshkol expressed the view that Egypt's challenge could not remain unanswered. Already en route to Tel Aviv, he had remarked to Yaffe that "it seems there is no way out."[40] Eban dominated the rest of the substantive discussion, by virtue of his mastery of the details of the commitments (as he saw them) made by the Western powers and other maritime states to Israel in 1957. And his views and proposals carried the day.

"The question," Eban began, "is not whether we must resist, but whether we must resist alone or with the support and understanding of others." However, before Israel responded militarily, there were several powerful reasons for diplomatic activity: to explore Soviet intentions, to test the willingness of the Western powers to fulfill their 1957 commitments to break Israel's isolation, and to consult with friendly states, first and foremost with the United States, in order to assure their diplomatic support if victory were achieved on the battlefield. "Otherwise we may win a war and lose a victory."[41] And finally, diplomacy was designed to ensure US support, especially the delivery of arms, in case of war. Eban analyzed the reactions of the Western powers to recent diplomatic moves. Then he read out a cable from Evron, which contained a formal request by Under-Secretary of State Rostow, on President Johnson's behalf, that Israel take no decision for the next 48 hours and that it consult with the United States. Again the President warned that he would not take any responsibility for actions on which he was not consulted. Eban suggested that Israel agree to this: the time could be put to good use to test the 1957 commitments; and "if we didn't do it, they would say afterward that we missed an opportunity to solve our problem in cooperation with them."[42]

Eban's presentation contained elements that would satisfy everyone—the hawks and doves, even Ben-Gurion's followers. No one opposed the basic concept, though Dayan and Peres expressed their belief that nothing would come of diplomatic maneuvers. Dayan stated that only Israel would open the Straits—though he was willing to let others have the honor (he was to express himself in a similar vein at his 3 June press conference). What he emphasized was that, in diplomatic contacts, no official Israeli commitments should be given to the principle of prior consultations. Further, "at the end of forty-eight hours, we should launch military action against Egypt."[43] It was clear to many, as Eshkol, Sapir, and others observed during the discussion, that 48 hours would turn into 72 or more.

Eshkol summed up the debate in the Ministerial Defense Committee by stating that the closure of the Straits was a warlike act and that every hour that passed was fraught with danger. He proposed cautioning Washington that a longer period of waiting might turn into a victory for Nasser. Thus the crucial ministerial session of 23 May ended with Israel's leaders opting for diplomatic action.

The most acrimonious discussion—in the Ministerial Committee only—revolved around implementation. H.M. Shapira suggested that Eban get in touch with those states which had committed themselves to freedom of navigation and possibly even visit them. Aranne opposed this, declaring that it would invite pressures on Israel for concessions; while Carmel opposed the whole idea, for it might tie Israel's hands. Eban countered that pressures could be applied just as well through ambassadors and that it was important that Israel's position be explained at the highest level abroad, directly by a high-ranking member of the government. He emphasized that the most important place to visit was Washington, while Meir still believed that clarifications of de Gaulle's intentions had priority. A consensus was reached that US intentions ought to be clarified. Then the question of the emissary was raised. Again the mistrust of Eban surfaced. Eshkol proposed that Meir be sent, but Eban vigorously opposed this and other suggestions, including the dispatch of Amit. In the end, Eban's view triumphed. The Ministerial Committee finally took the following formal decisions:

1. The blockade is an act of aggression against Israel.
2. Any decision or action is postponed for forty-eight hours, during which time the Foreign Minister will explore the position of the United States [Decision 8].
3. The Prime Minister and Foreign Minister are empowered to decide, should they see fit, on a journey by the Foreign Minister to Washington to meet President Johnson [Decision 9].[44]

Most of the participants now left for Jerusalem. Eshkol proceeded to work on his reply to the *Knesset* debate over his statement of the previous day, but much had changed since then. His statement, delivered at eight o'clock in the evening, was short and restrained and was devoted exclusively to the announced closure of the Straits: "Any interference with the freedom of navigation in the Gulf and the Straits ... is an act of aggression against Israel." The upshot of the past few days' consultations with other states that supported the freedom of navigation was "that I can state that the international support for these rights is serious and widespread.... I call upon the powers once again to act without delay for the maintenance of the right of free passage to our southern-most port."[45]

Eshkol proposed that the debate be continued, in secret, in the *Knesset* Foreign Affairs and Security Committee. The vote expressed the growing national (as distinct from political) cohesion: all parties except the Communists voted in favor, 89 to 4. Even the minority resolutions submitted by the two Communist parties affirmed Israel's right to freedom of passage.[46] Nasser had succeeded in uniting Israeli society, an element that he always underestimated in his calculations.

Earlier, at 18:00, there was a second informal meeting of seven Cabinet members. Eban's proposed trip abroad was not discussed. Throughout the afternoon and evening, the Foreign Office tried to arrange a meeting between Eban and de Gaulle for the following day. The cable also notified Paris of Eban's arrival in the morning. When the Foreign Minister left Israel, however, he did not know whether or not he would be able to see the French President.

When the news of Eban's journey to Washington became known in the *Knesset*, there was great dissatisfaction in Opposition circles; they had not been told during the consultations in Tel Aviv.[47] It strengthened their resolve to take part in the decision-making process in a formal capacity only: if they were to become an integral part of the process and share responsibility for decisions, they would insist on proper authority.

At IDF headquarters there was another meeting in the afternoon presided over by Rabin. The Chief of Staff felt faint, was taken home, and was ordered complete rest for the next 30 hours. His place was taken temporarily by Weizman.[48] On the same day, too, almost unnoticed at the time, Nasser raised the stakes further: the first Egyptian statements were published denying Israel's right to a presence on the shores of the Gulf, that is, to Eilat.[49]

The procession of Arab leaders to Cairo reached a high point. By that time some members of the UN Security Council had lost their patience: Canada and Denmark insisted upon convening the Council, and it met the next day, 24 May. The US administration was galvanized into action on a broad diplomatic front by Nasser's announcement. Strong warnings were sent immediately to Syria and Egypt—through U Thant as well— that the US government supported Israel's right of navigation in the Gulf of Aqaba. The USSR was similarly informed. There were also immediate consultations with Britain.

The strongest pressure was put on Egypt. A message from Johnson to Nasser stressed in general terms the need to avoid fighting. He promised to send Vice President Hubert Humphrey for talks with Egyptian, other Arab, and Israeli leaders "if we come through these days without hostilities."[50]

The US government note was stronger and more explicit. It warned against "misadventure or a miscalculation. Those in power in the area are likely to misunderstand or misinterpret the intentions and actions of others." Then it emphasized three aspects of the situation that "cause us special concern: the continual terrorist acts carried out against Israel with Syria's agreement, some of which at least are carried out from Syrian territory"; the removal of the UNEF; and the mobilization of forces on both sides. It continued: "We take this opportunity to reaffirm our continuous commitment to the freedom of passage in the Gulf of Aqaba for all ships." The verbal message was blunt and menacing:

> The U.S.A. feels that: (1) the UNEF should remain in Gaza and Sharm-e-Sheikh until a decision is issued by the UN General Assembly. (2) No armed forces should proceed to Sharm-e-Sheikh until the UAR Government issues an official statement confirming the freedom of navigation in the Straits of Tiran, the entry to the Gulf of Aqaba, without any conditions. . . . (3) No Egyptian armed forces should enter the Gaza Strip. (4) The UN and its agencies should remain responsible for the administration of the Gaza Strip until the issue is settled. (5) The Egyptian military concentration which is now taking place in Sinai is a serious matter. The Egyptian forces in Sinai and the Israeli forces massed opposite them in the Negev should return to their previous positions.[51]

In Washington, Johnson decided to publish a statement—after the release of the expected Soviet announcement. An early draft was read over the phone to Evron by Roche. It was a noncommittal text, mainly calling on both sides to abstain from aggravating the issue. Evron "lost his temper" and told his White House contact that if that is the best the President could do, he better not make any statements at all. Johnson was angry at first but later decided to make the statement stronger. The main part of the President's statement read:

> The purported closing of the Gulf of Aqaba to Israeli shipping has brought a new and grave dimension to the crisis. The United States considers the Gulf an international waterway and feels that a blockade of Israeli shipping is illegal and potentially disastrous to the cause of peace.[52]

Moreover, units of the Sixth Fleet were ordered toward the Eastern Mediterranean.

Evron cabled home that the United States had decided to approach the Security Council because it was essential to use the UN platform before a unilateral position was adopted. He added the reassurances of a senior American official that "we could rely on the President," and that the senior official confirmed that the President has told USSR Premier Alexei Kosygin of US commitments.[53]

In Moscow, after a meeting of the Soviet government, the TASS News Agency released its Statement on the Situation in the Near East. It stressed Israel's aggressive intentions toward Syria and praised the action of Arab states and the UAR "honoring its allied commitments for joint defense with Syria." The closure of the Straits was not even mentioned. The final passage stated:

> But let no one have any doubt about the fact that should anyone try to unleash aggression in the Near East he would be met not only with the united strength of Arab countries, but also with strong opposition from the Soviet Union and all peace-loving states.[54]

In London, the British government went into special, urgent session, under the impression that "at any moment it seemed that war might break out, with either side seeking to gain the advantage to be derived from a preemptive strike."[55] The British Cabinet decided to work, with other maritime nations, toward the assertions that the Gulf of Aqaba and the Straits were international waterways.

There was no official reaction from the French government. As the tense day came to an end, world attention began to focus on Eban's forthcoming visit to Western capitals.

Wednesday, 24 May

On this day, discussions were held at the highest level in several capitals: their purpose was to try to gain time, for different reasons. U Thant finally met Nasser and continued his meetings with Egyptian Foreign Minister Riad. George Brown met with Kosygin and Gromyko in Moscow. British Minister of State Thomson began his talks with the US administration in Washington. At the center of attention were Eban's meetings with de Gaulle and Wilson, in Paris and London. In New York, the Security Council met for the first time to deal with the crisis.

Eshkol spent the morning dealing with matters affecting the crisis tangentially—finance and internal security. He had lunch with Weizman, *de facto* IDF Chief of Staff during Rabin's illness, and he met with the General Staff for three hours in the afternoon. Mobilization of reserves was about to be completed; and Weizman used this opportunity to discuss military plans with the Prime Minister–Defense Minister. Three alternative possibilities were reportedly discussed: occupation of the entire Sinai Peninsula, part of Sinai, up to El Arish, or only the Gaza Strip. Bar-Lev, present at the meeting, claimed that the first alternative emerged as the dominant view; but his version was contradicted by two authoritative sources. Weizman stated at the end of the meeting: "Mr. Minister of Defense, *Tzahal* (the IDF) is prepared and ready for war, as of tomorrow, that is, as of May 25."[56]

That afternoon, Allon returned from the first special visit by an Israeli Cabinet minister to the Soviet Union.[57] He immediately held a two-hour conference with Galili and, at IDF General Staff headquarters, with Bar-Lev. Eban left Israel at 03:30 in an empty El Al plane, flying to France to load military equipment. During the forenoon, Israel's ambassador to France, Eytan, succeeded in arranging the meeting with de Gaulle. Eban knew that during the past few days the French had raised the question in official talks whether the economic value of trade through Eilat was sufficient to justify war. The time had come to put these doubts to test.

Eban's meeting with the French President began at noon, with Foreign Minister Couve de Murville also present.[58] De Gaulle asked him to present his case but first stated the basic French position:

> Israel must not make war unless she is attacked by others. It would be catastrophic if Israel were to shoot first. The Four Powers must be left to resolve the dispute. France will influence the Soviet Union toward an attitude favorable to peace.[59]

Eban then spoke for 12 minutes. He had come to consult with Israel's great friend. "Israel was faced with Syrian terrorism, Egyptian troop concentrations and the blockade of the Straits; the last was an act which must be rescinded." He reminded de Gaulle of the strong French declarations of 1957 in favor of Israel's rights in the Straits. In reply to de Gaulle's interposed question, "What are you going to do?" he stated: "Si la choix se pose entre l'abandon et la resistance, Israel va résister. La décision est prise [If the choice lies between surrender and resistance, Israel will resist.

Our decision has been taken]." But Israel would not act immediately. She wished to explore the attitude of the powers to their previous commitments. "If there is concerted international action ... Nasser will yield."

De Gaulle emphasized again that Israel should not declare war—at least, it should not fire the first shot. He did not accept Eban's interposed remark that Nasser's acts had already opened hostilities: opening hostilities meant firing the first shot. He disengaged France from her 1957 position: 1967 was not 1957. He emphasized the importance of the role of the Soviet Union: "In our days there are no more Western solutions, and therefore coordination between the four powers has to be achieved, the Straits opened, and war is to be avoided." Specifically, he was skeptical about any Western naval action. The Soviet Union had to be part of any peaceful solution, to be achieved by a concerted action of the Big Four. "The more Israel looks to the West, the less will be the readiness of the Soviet Union to cooperate." He greatly minimized the closure of the Straits, placing it at the level of another "incident" in a long series of incidents since 1957. He upheld the freedom of the seas and suggested that an agreement could be sought "as in the Dardanelles."

Finally, Eban—in an obvious reference to arms supplies—thanked France for her "reinforcement of Israel's strength and spirit." De Gaulle's reply contained the first hint of the reversal of France's position in this matter as well: "Israel was not sufficiently established to solve all her problems herself."[60] He concluded by once again repeating his warning: Israel should not open hostilities; it should leave time for international consultation.

As he later recalled, Eban's immediate summary of the meeting was that "I had been an eye-witness to the death of solemn commitments." Expressions of support were vague, advice to abstain from "resistance" direct and specific. De Gaulle's solution was a four-power consensus with all that it entailed.

Eban then proceeded to London for an exchange of views with the British Prime Minister. Wilson was skeptical about four-power consultations, but, he added, he had declared the British government's willingness to put the idea to test. Eban stated that "Israel would not live without access to Eilat or under the threat of Egyptian encirclement. Israel's choice was either to fight alone or to join with others in an international effort to force Nasser's withdrawal." He had come to test the purpose of the maritime powers.

Wilson told him that the Cabinet's decision was that the blockade ought not to succeed. "Britain would join with others in an effort to open the Straits." He handed Eban a copy of a speech he had made that morning, at Margate, which included the following passage:

> It is the view of Her Majesty's Government in the United Kingdom that the Straits of Tiran must be regarded as an international waterway through which the vessels of all nations have a right of passage. Her Majesty's Government will assert this right on behalf of all British shipping and is prepared to join with others to secure general recognition of this right.[61]

Wilson had already sent Thomson to Washington to discuss plans for common action—"nuts and bolts" talks. In reply to Eban's question, he stated that Britain would act within the UN, if possible, but could "take measures of her own outside the UN," if necessary.[62] When the talk ended, Eban noticed that Wilson had confined himself to an analysis of Britain's position: "He had not given me any counsel on the advisability or timing of Israel's resistance."

In Washington, the White House and the State Department kept officially silent. But unofficially a mood of caution and reserve was communicated. Publicly, members of the House of Representatives signed a statement calling on the President to do everything possible to defend Israel. On the other hand, the powerful Senate leaders, Mansfield and Dirksen, added their weight against any unilateral US action outside the UN. Ambassador Harman flew to Gettysburg to clarify with Eisenhower the commitments given by him in 1957 and to urge him to support Johnson. Eisenhower declared that, if he were asked by journalists, he would state that the Straits were an international waterway, as he and Dulles stated in 1957, and that the denial of rights of free passage would be illegal.[63]

In New York, the Security Council convened at the request of Denmark and Canada. Two meetings were held during the day, but there was no vote taken, nor was a date fixed for the next meeting. In Moscow, George Brown met with Gromyko and Kosygin. It soon became clear that, while the Soviets were not interested in an outbreak of war, they were in no mood to cooperate with the Western powers in restraining Nasser, either within the UN or through four-power consultation, or through pressure upon the Arab states.

Thursday, 25 May

From this day onward there was increasing pressure on Prime Minister Eshkol by Israel's military leaders—with the exception of Bar-Lev—to go to war; the time limit given to the political decision-makers on the 23rd, 48 hours, was running out. The trigger seems to have been the news that the Egyptian Fourth Armored Division had crossed into Sinai that morning. The first manifestation of IDF pressure occurred in a meeting at the armored division headquarters of Major-General Tal, at 11:15. The assembled officers presented to Eshkol the war plans of the Southern Command, which had been told that D-Day had been set for the morning of the 25th and then postponed by 24 hours.[64] Then General Ariel Sharon expressed his dissatisfaction with the hesitations of the government in the face of the increasing strengthening of the Arab forces. War could not be avoided any more, he declared; and the earlier the power of the Egyptian Army was broken, the more easily Israel's goals concerning the Straits would be achieved.[65] There was no doubt that Sharon was expressing the views of the field commanders.

During that morning's consultations, Yariv presented the daily intelligence appreciation, which showed the building up of a serious Arab military threat. As a result, Eshkol approved the sending of a cable to Eban informing him of the sudden Arab escalation and asking him to explain to President Johnson that the danger no longer lay simply in the closing of the Straits but also in the concentration of troops in Sinai and in the prospect of an Arab attack on Israel.

In the evening, Eshkol approved a rather controversial and uncharacteristic venture in Machiavellian statesmanship, about which Dayan expressed disquiet (Decision 10).[66] The process was best described by Rabin:

> After the closing of the Straits, in order to test where Israel stood and to what extent she was not to depend completely on herself, the Director-General of the Prime Minister's Office, the late Ya'acov Herzog, in a conversation with me, suggested that we send a telegram to the Foreign Minister, Abba Eban, who was then in Washington, and in it we would say that according to the information in our hands, there may occur the development of an Egyptian offensive initiated against Israel as the events evolve. And Mr. Herzog further suggested to me that we ask Mr. Eban to clarify to what extent the United States is prepared to make good on obligations, given in the past to Israeli leaders, for real help in such an event.[67]

It was typical of the hectic pace of consultations by that time that Eshkol accepted the idea and approved the second telegram to Eban as well, without thinking too much about its consequences. While the first telegram was merely informative, the second warned about an immediate attack. It stated:

> As a result of events during the last twenty-four hours, be advised that we expect *a surprise attack from the Egyptians and the Syrians at any moment.* The United States Government should declare at once that any attack on Israel would be regarded as an attack on the United States. It should also issue instructions in that spirit to its forces in the area. It is recommended that you show this cable to the highest officials, the President himself or the Secretary of State.[68]

Immediately upon his arrival in Washington, Eban received the second telegram, signed by Eshkol: he was asked to convey the Israeli evaluations to the American leadership "in the most drastic and urgent terms." While deliberating whether to ask for further details, the first telegram was delivered to him, seemingly underscoring the contents of the one previously received. In spite of his misgivings, as Eban later noted, he decided that he could not hesitate any longer and asked for his scheduled meeting with Dean Rusk to be advanced from 18:00 to 17:00.

The meeting, also attended by Eugene Rostow and Lucius Battle, was brief. Eban read the telegram to the Americans. Rusk, surprised, asked for an immediate adjournment in order to enable him to inform the President and the Secretary of Defense of this development. He remarked that there was support for Israel's cause but only if the United States did not have to act unilaterally; Israel's demand raised constitutional problems.[69]

Eban returned to the State Department for a working dinner, accompanied by Harman and Evron. The discussion was devoted almost exclusively to ways of opening the Straits. The Americans were rather optimistic about the planned maritime action. It provided for: (a) a declaration by maritime powers on the right of free passage, open to adherence by all, including Israel; (b) the enforcement of this declaration through a naval patrol by a group of maritime states; and (c) the two steps to be connected by recourse to the Security Council. Eban was alarmed by an undertone of some possible limitations on Israel's rights in the Straits. At midnight, he sent Harman back to the State Department to make it clear, through E. Rostow, that the Israeli government expected "absolute precision about where you stand in the matter." He was told: "On the determination of the United States to ensure that the Straits would be open Eban would have to hear from the President himself."[70]

After the dinner, Eban and Harman had a second meeting with Rusk. By that time the Secretary of State had seen the President, who had just returned from Canada, and had consulted General Earl Wheeler, Chairman of the Joint Chiefs of Staff. He told Eban that "the United States did not share the appraisal that any Arab state was planning an immediate attack on Israel."[71] The President had also told him that he did not have the authority to act without full coordination with Congress. What Israel was requesting ("any attack on Israel would be regarded as an attack on the United States.") had been stated only in the NATO (North Atlantic Treaty Organization) treaty, and even there only after a long and heated debate. Then he gave the President's views on the crisis—views that were to be repeated, sometimes in identical terms, twice the next day, in Johnson's conversations with Evron and Eban. The President would act to live up to American commitments, and he was taking a strong political and diplomatic stand in Cairo, as well as in other capitals. But it was absolutely essential for him to act with the approval of Congress and public opinion, and in the meantime, Israel should not take preemptive action. Thus, the Israeli government was aware of the broad outlines of the American position the next morning, Friday, 26 May.

Harman cabled to Jerusalem the results of the discussions during the working dinner, while Eban sent Eshkol a short cable, on Friday at 01:30, New York time, summarizing the results of the three meetings. The latter cable emphasized the seemingly positive aspects of the talks:

> It appears that the President is likely to discuss a program for opening the Straits by the maritime powers, led by the United States, Britain and perhaps others.... The second stage ... would be the dispatch of a naval task force which will appear in the Straits. Some officials here predict that the President will make a pledge that the Straits will be opened, even if there is resistance.[72]

The growing clamor in Egypt and the Arab world to "wipe Israel off the face of the earth" became an important input into the Israeli decision process. It could no longer be ignored or discounted. The air was full of martial songs, bloodcurdling threats, cries of exultation, and calls for total extermination of the Jews. Two illustrations will suffice. Radio Cairo announced: "The Arab nation is determined to wipe Israel off the face of the earth and restore to Falastin the Arab honor." Ahmad Shukeiry's answer to an interviewer's question as to what would happen to Israelis born in Israel: "Those who survive will remain in Palestine. I estimate that none of them will survive."[73]

Another significant event on the 25th was the announcement by US Sixth Fleet headquarters in Naples that six US ships, with 2000 Marines on board, had sailed toward the eastern Mediterranean: the movements of the Sixth Fleet were carefully watched by Nasser and the Soviets as tangible evidence of American intentions.

Friday, 26 May

Eshkol presided over a six-hour meeting of the Ministerial Committee on Defense, in which the Director of Military Intelligence, Yariv, gave the latest intelligence report, and Rabin evaluated the developments of the past ten days. The atmosphere was tense. The "doves," headed by Warhaftig, expressed doubts and fears about the feasibility of armed resistance. Further, it was necessary that all sectors of the nation be represented in the government: even to decide to postpone action required courage and daring—and the sanction of a National Unity Government. Ben-Gurion's views—partly included in Warhaftig's remarks—were discussed at length, sowing further doubt. The "hawk" view was expressed by the *Ahdut Ha'avoda* ministers. To Allon, one of its leaders, a delay in decision could be disastrous, while Carmel and Galili, the other ministers from that Left-Nationalist party, suggested that the Prime Minister be empowered to take appropriate action in case of necessity. Eshkol, in his summary of this security debate, stressed the change of Israel's primary focus from the Straits to the concentration of Egyptian forces along the Israel border. If it were only the problem of the Straits, Israel could be satisfied with promised American assistance, he said; but there was now a greater danger.

On Sharef's suggestion, the Committee decided to wait for Eban's return from Washington with clarifications and to postpone discussions until then (Decision 11). Sapir then laid before the Committee plans for mobilizing resources—inside and outside Israel—to enable Israel to hold out, even during a prolonged siege. After the session of the Ministerial Defense Committee, Allon met with Eshkol to persuade him of the necessity of an early Israeli military initiative. He reportedly told him: "This is one of the great issues in Jewish history. I believe you can go down in Jewish history as another King David—if you decide to act now." He persuaded Eshkol to cable Eban instructions to emphasize, in his meeting with the US President, not the closure of the Straits and its possible reopening, but the threat posed by the Egyptian army massed on Israel's border. According to Allon, this meeting was decisive in making up Eshkol's mind to go to war.[74]

At 16:00, the *Knesset* Committee on Foreign Affairs and Security convened to discuss the security situation. Again, Eshkol emphasized the change of focus from the Straits to the Sinai troop concentrations. Israel was still determined to exhaust all diplomatic possibilities, even though the results of Eban's contacts were not satisfactory. The prevalent atmosphere of hesitancy and doubt penetrated the *Knesset* Committee as well. At 19:00, *Mapam* Left Socialist leaders, Ya'ari and Hazan, met with Eshkol: the discussion centered on the warnings about the IDF's preparedness, which they had heard about from *Rafi* leader Shimon Peres the previous day and from Ben-Gurion that day. Eshkol finally retired after a meeting with Dayan, further consultations with leaders of world Jewry, and an evaluation of the military situation by Allon, Rabin, and others.

Friday, 26 May, was no less hectic and tense in Washington. Secretary of State Rusk phoned Ambassador Harman, in an attempt to gain some time, and asked whether Eban would be staying until Saturday, for by that time the results of U Thant's visit to Cairo would be known. Eban phoned back immediately and told Rusk that he had to be back in Israel the next day. A Cabinet meeting was planned for Sunday, possibly the most crucial in the history of the state, and the Cabinet's decision would be heavily influenced by what President Johnson told him. The results of U Thant's mission were not decisive for Israel: Israel, in Eban's view, might have to face hostilities the next week. There was an act of blockade which had to be resisted.

Then, as planned, Eban went to the Defense Department for a meeting with McNamara, General Wheeler, and other Pentagon officials. While this meeting was in session, the cable containing Allon's suggestions arrived; Eban now emphasized the concentration of Egyptian armed forces in Sinai. But Wheeler again stated that Israel would succeed, whoever took the initiative. To him the idea that Israel might have to act in desperation, in a mood of "now or never," was inconceivable, in view of the facts of the situation, especially Israel's air superiority. McNamara bluntly opposed the idea of a naval task force. For Israel, this was not a tactical question of using foreign ships to ply the Straits, but a *casus belli*; and the problem was first of all an Israeli one. General Wheeler expressed himself in similar terms: the breaking of the blockade by an international flotilla would not solve the problem. Because of fear of the charge of collusion, the Israelis were never told they should go to war; but neither did the Pentagon representatives say they should not.

Eban was informed of a further delay in the meeting with Johnson by W. Rostow. In the meantime, Eshkol cabled that he must return the following night: there were growing demands for a decision from political as well as military circles. Rostow called the President and informed him that Evron had given assurances that there would be no publicity given to his conversation with Eban. Johnson instructed him to fix the meeting for 19:00 and asked him to send Evron to see him. Late in the evening, Evron cabled the following report about his conversation with the President:

> When I entered his room, the President told me that he fully understood the gravity of Israel's position. His reaction to the Foreign Minister would be in accordance with what Mr. Eban had heard from Rusk and others that morning, namely, that any American involvement would require Congressional support of the intentions and decisions of the President. The first step would have to be the laying of a Congressional basis for any support of Israel's position. The President emphasized that he was working energetically in that direction. The United States had pledged itself to preserve freedom of passage in the Straits of Tiran: and the United States would carry out that obligation. But anything involving even a possibility of force would be impractical and would boomerang unless the proper Congressional basis was laid in advance. The President agreed that the United Nations in its present composition would not be able to do anything; no result would come from its discussions. Yet those discussions were vital in order to give proper support to the President, in the Congress and the public, as well as in the international domain. The President spoke without confidence about the result of the Secretary-General's mission to Cairo, but said that it would be foolish to ignore the effect of his report. Any action by any member-state before the report was published would be received badly in many places. The President spoke optimistically about the possibility of setting up a structure with the active support of Britain and other maritime powers after the conclusion of a quick debate at the United Nations. Here he mentioned several countries that might be willing to cooperate. He had taken counsel with some of his leading advisers. All of them could be described as friends of Israel. They had expressed their support in the following formulation:

The objective is to open the Straits for navigation by all states including Israel and this objective shall be carried out. Mr. Johnson made it clear that the appraisal in Jerusalem about an imminent Egyptian surprise attack was not shared by the United States. Israel was a sovereign Government, and if it decided to act alone, it could of course do so; but in that case everything that happened before and afterwards would be upon its responsibility and the United States would have no obligation for any consequences that might ensue. He refused to believe that Israel would carry out unilateral action which was bound to bring her great damage. But, he added, this was Israel's affair. As President of the United States he must carry out American commitments to Israel in a way which seemed to him best, within the framework of American interests. He emphasized several times, that Israel could depend on him. He said that he was not a coward and did not renege on his promises, but he was not prepared to act in a manner which seemed to him to endanger the security of the United States, or to bring about the intervention of the Soviet Union, in the event, simply because Israel has decided that Sunday is an ultimate date.[75]

The formal meeting with Eban started a little late, around 19:15. Eban began by giving the President the essence of information which had reached him the previous day about the possibility of an Egyptian attack and a summary of Israel's concern. Johnson reiterated that he had said publicly an illegal action had occurred and that the Gulf was an international waterway. The question was when and how to act. Only if the Congress and the American people felt that Israel had justice on her side could he respond firmly. Moreover, the UN channel must first be exhausted. He needed a very short time and British help to develop an effective solution. He suggested that "it would not be wise at this stage to call Nasser's hand. If your Cabinet decides to do anything immediately and to do it on their own, that is for them. We are not going to do any retreating. We are not back-tracking. I am not forgetting anything I have ever said." But there were constitutional constraints, and a statement to the effect that an attack on Israel is an attack on the United States was beyond his prerogatives. "What you can tell your Cabinet is that the President, the Congress and the country will support a plan to use any or all measures to open the Straits. But we have to go through the Secretary-General and the Security Council and build up support among the nations.... Israel will not be alone unless it decided to go alone.... If you want our help in whatever ensues, it is absolutely necessary for Israel not to make itself responsible for the institution of hostilities."[76]

At the end of the meeting, the President handed Eban the following aide-memoire:

> The United States has its own constitutional processes, which are basic to its actions on matters involving war and peace. The Secretary-General has not yet reported to the Security Council and the Council has not yet demonstrated what it may or may not be able or willing to do, although the United States will press for prompt action in the United Nations. I have already publicly stated this week our view on the safety of navigation and on the Straits of Tiran. Regarding the Straits we plan to pursue vigorously the measures which can be taken by maritime nations to assure that the Straits and the Gulf remain open to free and innocent passage of all nations. I must emphasize the necessity for Israel not to make itself responsible for the initiation of hostilities. Israel will not be alone unless it decides to do it alone. We cannot imagine that Israel will make this decision.[77]

Harman notified the Israeli government:

> The Foreign Minister left without being able to report on his talk with the President. Brings with him full protocol.[78]

En route, Eban went to see Arthur Goldberg in New York. UN Security Council proceedings were coming to naught, he was told. And U Thant had been totally unsuccessful in Cairo, except for Nasser's promise not to start an armed assault. Goldberg stressed that Eban should pay particular attention to what the President himself had said: the alternatives open to America were now so fateful that the President's own words were decisive. At midnight, Eban began his journey back to Israel.

The 26th marked another escalation of the crisis by Egypt. Heikal, who was close to Nasser, wrote in his weekly column that morning that war was inevitable because Israel had no choice but to go to war, and hostilities could break out any moment. A more important input to Israel's decision process was Nasser's speech to a delegation of the Damascus-based Arab Workers Conference, which had come to Cairo to inform him of the Conference's resolution. The three significant elements of the speech were: his declaration that the closure of the Straits meant total war with Israel, his emphasis on the readiness of Egyptian and other Arab armed forces to win such a war, and his statement that the aim of the war would be the destruction of Israel—as compared with the aims of restoring the pre-1956 situation and supporting the rights of the Palestinians, stated in his Bir Gafgafa speech four days earlier.

At UN headquarters, U Thant submitted a report to the Security Council on the results of his mission to Cairo; his main recommendation was to gain time, a "breathing spell," in order "to allow the Council to deal with the underlying causes of the present crisis and to seek solutions."[79] In spite of the urgency, the Security Council was not convened until 29 May, three days later.

Another noteworthy event on the 26th was an announcement by Cairo Radio, quoting London sources, that a British ship arrived at Jordan's port of Aqaba without having been stopped and searched. Cairo Radio announced a compromise explanation (clearly in line with U Thant's suggestion to Nasser): ships which pass through the Suez Canal would be allowed to pass through the Straits without inspection.[80]

Saturday, 27 May

This day's events began with a concerted, deliberately dramatic move by the Soviet Union in both Israel and Egypt to prevent the outbreak of war. In Israel, the government sat until after four o'clock the next morning (the 28th) to try to decide whether or not to go to war.

At 02:00 on 27 May, Bykov, First Secretary of the Soviet Embassy, phoned Yaffe at the Dan Hotel in Tel Aviv and insisted upon an immediate meeting between Eshkol and Ambassador Chuvakhin. The meeting began at 02:35 and lasted until about four o'clock in the morning. Levavi, Yaffe, and Bykov were also present.[81] The Ambassador gave Eshkol a note from Prime Minister Kosygin, whose main passages were:

> According to the latest information reaching the Government of the USSR, the tension on the borders of Israel, the UAR and Syria is mounting more and more.... It would be a tremendous error if circles eager for battle, unrestrained by serious political thought, gained the upper hand in such a situation, and arms were to begin to talk. We would like to appeal to you to resort to all measures to prevent a military conflict.... We are convinced that, however complicated the situation in the area of the borders of Israel, Syria and the UAR may be, it is necessary to find means to resolve the conflicts by non-military means, as it is easy to ignite a fire but putting out its flames may not be nearly as simple as those pushing Israel to the brink of war imagine.[82]

It was the most restrained Soviet official communiqué of the 1967 prewar crisis until that date: it did not even mention the standard Soviet accusation that Israel was to blame for the tense situation.[83]

Eshkol replied that Israel had mobilized only in direct response to Egyptian and Syrian threats, and therefore the Soviet government should direct its pressure toward these governments. But Chuvakhin was rudely insistent: his concern was Israel, and he demanded, four times, to know whether Israel would undertake not to fire the first shot. Eshkol would not commit himself. Finally, Israel's Prime Minister totally lost his temper and answered: Egypt had blocked the Straits, and her planes had penetrated over Israel—weren't these "first shots"? If Israel shot down such a plane, would that be the "first shot"? In great anger he told Chuvakhin:

> The function of an Ambassador ... was to promote friendly relations to the best of his ability, with the country to which he was accredited. It did not seem to him that Chuvakhin had cared or tried to do this. Since this was the case, he would be pleased to welcome a Soviet Ambassador who held this conception of his role.[84]

He questioned, sarcastically, the Soviet motives in their support for Syria: "Who are we to be compared with Syria, with its six million socialists?" He offered to travel to Russia, any time, to speak with Soviet leaders, in order to promote Soviet-Israeli friendship.[85]

At 09:30, Eshkol met a group of his colleagues, including Meir, Galili, Allon, Sasson, Rabin, Yariv, Herzog, and Levavi, to tell them about the "pajama conference."[86] Some interpreted Kosygin's message as an attempt to gain time while closely coordinating Soviet actions with the Egyptians, as proved by Egyptian War Minister Badran's visit to Moscow. Most thought Israel had no choice but to act. Rabin came away from the morning consultations convinced that Eshkol had made up his mind to go to war, and he hinted at this when he returned to IDF headquarters.[87] At a meeting of the *Knesset* Foreign Affairs and Security Committee, called for 11:45, Eshkol reported on his early morning conference with the Soviet Ambassador, thereby informing the Opposition as well.

The Cabinet session of 27 May, in which Israel's decision-makers came close to deciding to go to war, began late in the evening, around 22:30, and lasted for more than six hours. It was attended as well by Dinstein, Rabin, Weizman, Yariv, and Bar-Lev. The very fact of the Cabinet meeting was secret at the time. Parallel to it and in close vicinity, a session of the *Knesset* Foreign Affairs and Security Committee took place. It lasted until 3:30 the next morning. Eban, who went straight to the Cabinet session on arrival from abroad, around 22:00, attended both meetings and reported to both of them.

The Cabinet first heard reports by Yariv on the military situation and Levavi on international contacts. Eshkol reported on his talk with Chuvakhin. When Eban arrived, he gave a brief review of his talks in Paris and London and a long survey of his discussions in Washington. However, the accumulated information was unable to produce a consensus: the Cabinet divided evenly, 9–9, between those who advocated going to war immediately and those who opted for a further waiting period.

In order to reconstruct the essence—and the atmosphere—of the deliberative process on 27 May, it is well to note the reported views of the principal participants and groups at that meeting.[88] I begin with Eban, whose report focused and shaped the discussion.

Eban acknowledged his failure to convince de Gaulle of Israel's view of the situation. The United States perceived its interest as vital that Egypt should not achieve a diplomatic victory. At the same time, there were some suspicions that Israel was trying to involve the United States in a military confrontation it did not want. American leaders did not promise anything concrete, but they were acting on the matter of the Straits. Wilson would cooperate, outside the UN as well, but only in concert with the United States. Eban suggested that the Cabinet decide to wait another 48 hours. A further round of consultations with the United States was necessary because of steps undertaken by the United States in the wake of Israel's warning about an impending Egyptian attack. If Israel wanted to preempt on the 28th, said Eban, it should not have asked the Americans on the 25th to restrain Egypt.[89]

Eshkol stated that he was against the intervention of a third party; he did not see what another 48 hours would give Israel; the powers would continue to advise Israel to wait. Israel's deterrent power was being undermined; if it did not act, it would be considered a sign of weakness. But, as usual, he was willing to listen to what his colleagues had to say. After the war, he declared:

> I know that if I would have pressed them I would have received the support of the majority.... Had I banged the table and insisted, no one would have resigned from the Government. I did not do that.... I do not regret it.[90]

Allon believed that Eban's journey was a mistake; its outcome had limited Israel's freedom of action. Time was working against Israel, and waiting for the international flotilla would lessen considerably Israel's chances for a preemptive strike, and he expressed his certainty that Israel could win, even if it had to fight on three fronts, which he saw as a distinct possibility.[91]

Carmel agreed that a decision not to act would have very dangerous connotations. He felt that there was no prospect whatsoever that the Straits would be reopened. And even if, by some miracle, they were, that would not solve the main problem—the threat of the massed Egyptian troops poised along Israel's southern border. "I feared their military initiative.... There was the overall military-political view of the necessity for us to take our fate in our own hands and to smash the aggressive Egyptian build-up."[92]

The Allon–Carmel (*Ahdut Ha'avoda*, Left-Nationalist) views were opposed by the Mafdal (National Religious Party, NRP) and Mapam (Left Socialist) ministers. The former termed the Eban report encouraging, and in any case, it would never be too late to fight. The latter agreed that Egypt, not the Straits, was the central problem but argued that Nasser would not attack; there was still time to exhaust diplomatic opportunities.[93]

For immediate action were: Eshkol, Allon, Carmel, Galili, Gvati, Sasson, Y.S. Shapira, Sharef, and Yeshayahu.

For a period of further waiting: Aranne, Barzilai, Bentov, Burg, Eban, Kol, Sapir, H.M. Shapira, and Warhaftig.

Eshkol suggested to his colleagues that they adjorn the deliberations ("sleep it over"), that Israel could not go to war on a split vote (9-9) and that they would reconvene the next afternoon. This was accepted; though some, along with other political leaders and advisers, continued the discussion with Eshkol for another hour. Several of his colleagues later stated that Eshkol's 27 May behavior—not to press for a decision by a tired group of men—was typical of his essential humanity. His method, what some have termed "open deliberation," was to achieve a broad consensus, particularly on momentous decisions.

The meeting of the *Knesset* Foreign Affairs and Security Committee was no less tense. There, too, opinions were sharply divided. Some members from *Mapai*, the largest party in the governing Coalition, *Mafdal*, the National Religious Party, and *Mapam*, the Zionist-Left Socialist party, supported Eban's suggestion for a further period of waiting. Others did not, arguing that the United States would not be able to assure free navigation permanently and that time was running out; the latter also rejected the American view that the Egyptian buildup was defensive. Deliberations ended as inconclusively as in the Cabinet.

Israel's frontiers were now "coming alive." An IDF border patrol vehicle hit a mine near the Gaza border and seven soldiers were wounded. From that day on, there were to be almost daily incidents, increasingly violent, in which shots were fired and people were wounded or died.

In Washington, there was relative calm after the previous day's feverish activities. Reports which reached Israel that day regarding the maritime action to reopen the Straits were still optimistic: E. Rostow told Harman that Britain and Holland had joined, and that Canada had promised a ship for the naval patrol; further, that the United States would act alone, if necessary. Reports from other capitals showed that Belgium and Norway, too, would sign the statement.

In London, the press was informed that the Cabinet had decided "to go to the UN," without any real hope that anything would come from that step. The British government was still willing to act outside the UN, together with the United States, but the latter was not prepared to do so. In Moscow, Kosygin met Badran, the Egyptian War Minister, for the second time. The world was tensely awaiting news from Israel.

Sunday, 28 May

The Israeli Cabinet reconvened at three o'clock in the afternoon of the 28th. In the interim, a spate of notes and other inputs to Israel's decision process arrived from abroad: all influenced Eshkol and, later, the Cabinet to opt for a further waiting period of two or three weeks (Decision 12). Of these, the most important were from the United States: a note from Johnson, a dispatch from Secretary of State Rusk about Eban's discussions with Johnson and his advisers, and an addendum to this dispatch, which was probably the most decisive in influencing Israel's leadership to leave more time for international action in the Straits to materialize. Additional information was contained in cables from Harman on his meeting with E. Rostow and other contacts. Other inputs were a message from Prime Minister Wilson and reports from Israeli Ambassadors Eytan in Paris and Remez in London on their contacts and discussions there.[94]

President Johnson's note was received at 11:00 am, Israeli time. He wrote that Moscow claimed to have information about Israel's preparations for military action, to provoke a conflict. "The Soviets state that if Israel starts military action, the Soviet Union will extend help to the attacked states." The President repeated his concern about the safety and vital interests of Israel and continued: "As your friend, I repeat even more strongly what I said yesterday to Mr. Eban: Israel just must not take preemptive military action and thereby make itself responsible for the initiation of hostilities."[95] The British Prime Minister was more sympathetic. He said, *inter alia*: "We understand that you have reached the moment of decision. We urgently request you to maintain your attitude of restraint, as long as efforts are being made to solve the problem through diplomatic channels."[96]

The US Secretary of State first dispatched to US Ambassador Barbour a resumé of Eban's talks in Washington, officially confirming their substance from an American source. Secretary Rusk's report to Ambassador Barbour ended: "During the course of the conversation Eban said: 'Can I take it that I can convey to my Prime Minister that you have decided to make every possible effort to assure that the Straits and the Gulf would be open to free and innocent passage?' The President responded 'yes.'" Only the words *every possible effort* might be construed as differing from Eban's report to the Cabinet: they were less firm than *decided to assure that the Straits would be open....* To Johnson's letter, Rusk instructed Barbour to add the following explanation for Eshkol and Eban:

> The British and we are proceeding urgently to prepare the military aspects of the international naval escort plan and other nations are responding vigorously to the idea. The Dutch and Canadians have already joined even before a text was presented to them. With the assurance of international determination to make every effort to keep the Straits open to the flags of all nations, unilateral action on the part of Israel would be irresponsible and catastrophic.[97]

The Israeli Cabinet session on 28 May was relatively short: it began at 15:00 and lasted for two to three hours. Eban reviewed the diplomatic contacts of the preceding hours and stated that Johnson was willing to reopen the Straits, even to do it alone. Several states—the United Kingdom, Canada, and Holland—had already agreed to cooperate. It would take about two to three weeks. Eshkol was not as sanguine, but he agreed that Johnson's message had to be taken into consideration—and that a further waiting period of two to three weeks ought to be accepted in principle, though the IDF would remain mobilized.[98] And there would be a continuous follow-up of Nasser's moves. Should the situation worsen, the Cabinet would be called into session immediately. That suggestion was supported by the

Mafdal (Religious Zionists) and Mapam (Left Scocialists) ministers, while Allon and Carmel expressed doubts about the advantages of further waiting. They were also concerned about the military situation two to three weeks later. In this they were supported by Rabin.[99]

The Cabinet decided to delay military action, taking note of the promise of the President of the United States to undertake efforts to assure freedom of navigation in the Straits. At the same time, it decided to leave in force the mobilization of the reserves and the state of alert in the IDF (Decision 13). Although not formally inscribed as such in the Cabinet's final decision, the decision was to wait at least another two weeks. This is evident from Eshkol's cable to Johnson of 30 May: "The international naval escort should move through the Straits within a week or two." It is also apparent from remarks to E. Rostow and Rusk by Israeli diplomats a few days later.[100]

The decisive role of US pressure in that decision was confirmed by the Prime Minister some months after the June-Six-Day War:

> Had we not received Johnson's letter and Rusk's message, I would have urged the Government to make the decision to fight; but their communications pointed out not only that unilateral Israel action would be catastrophic but also that the United States was continuing with its preparations for multilateral action to open the Gulf to shipping of all nations. I could not forget that the latter was signed by the President who had once promised me face-to-face: 'We will carry out whatever I ever promise you.' I did not want him to come afterwards and say, 'I warned you in advance and now you cannot make any claims whatever on the United States and its allies.'[101]

The Cabinet also decided to reject the several suggestions voiced by Western states regarding the reactivation of UN machinery, and it empowered the Foreign Minister to attend the meetings of the Security Council, if he deemed it necessary. It also approved Sapir's journey abroad to organize an emergency financial appeal among world Jewry, to be directed personally by him.[102] The Opposition was informed of the Cabinet's decisions by Eshkol and Eban at a meeting of the *Knesset* Foreign Affairs and Security Committee which began at 17:30. Begin went on record that the Opposition was not informed in advance and that the decision to delay was that of the government alone.[103]

De Gaulle's answer to Eshkol's letter of 19 May was also delivered on the 28th, but its contents became known after the Cabinet session and thus cannot be considered an input into the Israel Cabinet's decisions of 28 May. President de Gaulle wrote:

> For you the matter at issue is the threat which weighs upon your frontiers and the freedom of navigation in the Gulf of Aqaba. Indeed, it is legitimate to fear that the situation, suddenly tense and disturbing, in the region of which Israel is the geographical center, may deteriorate into an armed conflict. However, there is nothing to indicate that either of the parties at issue has any interest in such a development. It is not necessary for me to say that this is the case with Israel. Your message testifies to this fact in the most authorized fashion. It seems to me that this is also true for Syria and for Egypt. That is why it is essential in present circumstances that no party should give a pretext for dangerous reactions.... As for the question of free navigation in the Gulf of Aqaba, I know the importance which this has for Israel. In this connection, you know how deeply France is attached to the maintenance of the status quo which ultimately seems to us to be essential in the Middle East both for Israel and for the other states in the region.
>
> My Government has moreover proposed that the four Great Powers which are members of the Security Council, should coordinate their action on the situation in the Middle East. The need is above all to insure that these Powers abstain from intervening in order to impose their own solutions; and that none of them undertakes any action or gesture which could be interpreted as taking sides. We hope that this initiative will first of all support a reduction of tension. Thereafter cooperation between these four states should take place for the establishment of peace and the settlement of the more burning questions which arise in the Middle East.[104]

This letter finally convinced Israel's decision-makers in the pre-June-Six-Day War Crisis that France was advising Israel to acquiesce in Nasser's *fait accompli*. Indeed, the last sentence implied even further pressure, for, according to the Arabs, the "most burning question" in the Middle East was the very existence of the State of Israel, termed by Nasser a 19-year-old aggression.

The Cabinet also decided to inform the nation and the world of its delay decision and entrusted Eshkol, Eban, and Galili to draft the announcement. Eshkol broadcast the announcement live over *Kol Yisrael* at 20:30. The substantive contents were almost forgotten in Israel's history. What remained etched in everyone's memory was its mode of delivery and the disastrous effect it had on the nation's morale. The worst incident of the delivery was described thus:

'Furthermore,' continued Eshkol, 'lines of action were decided for the removal....' Eshkol suddenly stops. His breathing can be heard, picked up well by the sensitive mike, as well as his whisper: 'What's this?' The word—removal—does not please him. And thus he includes in his deliberations his listeners who are in a state of high tension. He changes the word to 'movement' (of military concentrations on the southern border of Israel).[105]

Eshkol's trials were not yet over. The Prime Minister knew that since the morning of 27 May, the IDF General Staff had been expecting the decision to go to war: in contacts during the last two days, they had been led to understand that such a decision was imminent. Eshkol now had to tell them that the Cabinet had opted for further delay. Rabin told him that, as Defense Minister, it was his duty to inform them of the government's decision. Eshkol proceeded to General Staff headquarters, where most of Israel's military leaders were assembled, waiting for him. He was, as yet, completely unaware of the effect of his radio broadcast. He explained the reasons for the Cabinet decision; again he emphasized the importance of not isolating Israel, of securing the cooperation of the Western powers. He also told them of his confrontation with the Soviet Ambassador. Then he asked for their opinions freely: "You can and should say anything you like to me. Talk as if you were out of uniform."[106]

Despite the previous indicators of dissatisfaction with the government's hesitation, particularly among field commanders—the 25 May confrontation and Rabin's obvious reluctance to inform his colleagues—Eshkol was totally unprepared for the storm that broke. He was told by Sharon, M. Peled, and Avraham Yaffe—with Allon, Rabin, and Bar-Lev standing aside silently—that there was no way to avoid war anymore and that every day that passed might increase the losses. The generals expressed their concern with the effect of further waiting on the IDF's and the public's morale, and the possible effect on the enemy; and Yariv particularly stressed the dangers of a first Egyptian strike. Eshkol, clearly shaken, tried to reassure the generals. According to Bar-Lev, he answered substantially thus: "We have to have patience. I am sorry that you feel the way you do. It is necessary to continue negotiations, in order to exhaust all other possibilities, before going to war. This was also necessary in order to avoid a repetition of the post-Suez [1956] Crisis, when Israel was forced to withdraw."[107] After he left, he held another meeting with his Labor Alignment colleagues (at 22:30), where again the Cabinet's decision was discussed.

In Egypt, the central event of 28 May was Nasser's press conference, broadcast live over Cairo Radio. It was one of his most brilliant performances. Incisive, biting and sarcastic, moving at times, baring his teeth at the Western powers, particularly the United States, he projected total confidence in the will and capacity of Egypt and the Arab world, and in the righteousness of their cause. While restating, in substance, the extreme Egyptian position—the threat to the very existence of Israel—he managed to avoid giving it an extreme formulation and even succeeded in putting the onus for a probable outbreak of war on Israel, leaving some doors open for possible *ad hoc* accommodation.[108]

Washington, on the surface, was relatively quiet on Sunday, 28 May. The Israeli Embassy was swamped with queries: "When will you react?" NATO headquarters in Paris and Brussels were put on a state of alert.

PHASE III: PREEMPTION (29 MAY–4 JUNE)

The deliberations in Israel during the week before the outbreak of war were dominated by Israel's domestic political crisis: this left very little time and energy for the critical foreign policy issues. The rest of the world seemed ready to accept the altered balance of power in the Middle East, with jubilation in one camp, resignation in the other. The momentum for action by the maritime states clearly had petered out by the end of that week, and all alternatives involved some compromise solution at the expense of Israel's vital interests in the Gulf of Aqaba. This final phase of the prewar crisis was divided in two: 29 May–1 June, characterized by growing pressure to form a National Unity Government, with General Moshe Dayan as Minister of Defense; and 2–4 June, during which the decision process leading to war was crystallized.

Monday, 29 May

The Israeli press reported Eshkol's stuttering radio broadcast, emphasizing its negative effect on morale. Even the pro-government daily *Davar* carried calls for a widening of the government and for the co-option of Ben-Gurion or Dayan into the government. In the late afternoon, Eshkol informed the *Knesset* that Israel had opted for a further waiting period and was continuing its diplomatic efforts. After describing the events of the previous week, he stated:

The Government of Israel has repeatedly stated its determination to exercise its freedom of passage in the Straits of Tiran and the Gulf of Aqaba, and to defend it in case of need. This is a supreme national interest on which no concession is possible and no compromise is admissible.[109]

In Cairo, Nasser reaffirmed his ultimate aims in his last major policy statement before the June-Six-Day War: "Just as we have been able to restore the pre-1956 situation, we shall certainly, with God's help, be able to restore the pre-1948 situation.... We want the full and undiminished rights of the people of Palestine."[110] In Syria, President Attasi, accompanied by Foreign Minister Makhus and Information Minister Muhammad Zubi, left for what even Radio Damascus termed a "hasty" visit to Moscow.

Conflicting signals reached Israel from the United States on the 29th. Rusk was continuing his efforts to mobilize wide support for the maritime declaration. Walt Rostow assured Harman that the maritime action plan was serious and that it would be transmitted the same day for President Johnson's approval, after which it would take 10–14 days to finalize detailed plans. On the other hand, Eugene Rostow, in his contacts with Harman and Evron, kept on emphasizing the Straits issue, thus minimizing what Israel now perceived to be its dominant problem—a direct military threat.

In New York, the UN Security Council convened for another inconclusive meeting. Elsewhere, West Germany finally informed Israel that the gas masks it sought would be delivered. And the French notified Israel that the USSR had turned down the four-power consultation formula because of disinterest on the part of the Arabs and US involvement in Vietnam. The same day, too, a Liberian tanker under an American captain tried to force the blockade. He disregarded Egyptian warnings and changed course only after an Egyptian torpedo boat fired a warning shot.

Tuesday, 30 May

The major event on the 30th was King Hussein's dramatic journey to Cairo and the signing of the UAR–Jordan Defense Agreement. In Israel, the internal crisis was reaching its climax; by then, it dominated Eshkol's activities.[111]

Early in the morning, Eshkol asked Eban to hold a press conference in order to clarify Israel's determination not to wait too long for US and/ or Western action in reopening the Straits. He also entrusted Eban with drafting a reply to President Johnson's letter of 28 May. There were by now clear signs that US "action," in the sense of the use of force, was becoming more and more illusory. Moreover, Harman cabled that contacts with several other maritime states—Canada, Denmark, and Norway—had shown that support for the use of force had quickly evaporated—and that Israel would be offered economic aid to compensate for the strain of mobilization and waiting.

Uncertainty about US intentions led Eshkol to decide to send Meir Amit, the head of Israel's Intelligence Service, to Washington (Decision 14). As Amit later recalled:

> The American intentions were not clear; better stated, there was not sufficient light. I believed that I could fathom their real intentions, and I succeeded in this. A second aim of my mission was to make the Americans realize, in direct contact, the seriousness of the situation, to make them see that Israel had been forced into a situation where there was no way out, and hear their reactions. Both aims were fully achieved: it became clear that here, in Israel, there existed certain misperceptions. It became totally clear that they [the U.S.] were not planning to do a thing.[112]

Eban's press conference was held around noon. He emphasized the problems of the Straits and the "build-up of Egyptian troops on the Israel frontier" and, repeatedly, the importance for Israel that "these changes be rescinded ... within the shortest possible time." If international action would not materialize, Israel reserved for herself the right of self-defense: "Normal rationality suggests a policy: alone if we must, with others if we can." The press conference was also an occasion for an unparalleled attack by Eban on the UN, and specifically on U Thant's decisions.[113]

In the afternoon, Eban formulated Eshkol's reply to Johnson, which was sent the same day. The Prime Minister stated:

> A point is being approached at which counsels to Israel will lack any moral or logical basis. I feel that I must make it clear in all candor that the continuation of this position for any considerable time is out of the question.... It is crucial that the international naval escort should move through the Straits within a week or two.

Eshkol reminded the President of commitments made a few days earlier and in 1957. He also stressed that history showed the futility of trying to appease an "aggressive dictator."[114]

The signing of the UAR–Jordan Defense Agreement—which placed Jordan's armed forces under Egyptian command—came as another surprise and shock to Israel's decision-makers. It caused a flurry of military consultations in the afternoon and gave added urgency to Amit's mission. Five years after the 1967 War Rabin stated that "in my opinion Israel should have fought on the 30th of May."[115] And Eban recalled: "By his journey to Cairo on May 30 Hussein had made it certain that war would break out."[116] The Opposition was informed, as usual, at a meeting of the *Knesset* Foreign Affairs and Security Committee.

By the night of the 30th, Coalition and Opposition parties had practically united on the need for a National Unity Government. Only Eshkol himself and *Mapam* still held out. Nerves were strained to the breaking point. The following incident was symbolic of the atmosphere existing at the time: Michael Hazani, Member of the *Knesset* (MK) for the *Mafdal* (and later, Minister for Social Welfare), returned to the *Knesset* from a day-long tour of southern border settlements and started shouting in the corridors: "This cannot go on any longer.... The army is breaking up.... What are you doing? ... Take a decision, and quickly." And Carmel told a group of Alignment Ministers and MKs standing in the corridors: "Everything is on fire. What are you discussing? What is it you are holding on to? There is no solution without the enlargement of the Government!"[117]

Messages of congratulation poured into Egypt from Arab governments, with the notable exceptions of Syria and Saudi Arabia. King Hussein publicly invited Iraqi troops into Jordan, and President Aref agreed. Morocco promised to send troops. Rashid Karame, the Premier of Lebanon, came out with a strong statement of support. In Washington, the Israeli Embassy was informed by the State Department that preparations for the formation of a multinational naval force, as well as the declaration in support of free passage, were in an advanced state. Letters had been sent to 25 states, and the administration was now awaiting their reactions. The significance of the sharp drop from the US plan to approach 90 states on 26 May could not have been lost. In New York, the UN Security Council continued its futile debate. In Paris, official circles remained silent. In London, the British Cabinet, at its weekly meeting, decided to soften its determined stand on action to open the Straits, in the face of American hesitancy. Another significant development was the growing, shadowy confrontation between the naval forces of the two superpowers in the eastern Mediterranean. Publicity was given to the fact that the main force of the US Sixth Fleet was concentrated in the Sea of Crete. The Fleet was now within easy striking distance of the center of the conflict: 370 miles from Egypt, much less from Syria—one day's steaming distance for warships, 20 minutes' flight time for many of the planes on board the carriers. The Turkish authorities announced that, in the first week of June, ten Soviet warships would pass through the Dardanelles, on their way to the Mediterranean.

Wednesday, 31 May

This was a day of quiet, intense diplomacy in the capitals of the world. In Israel, the domestic political crisis dominated. The main inputs into its foreign policy process were the news, evaluations, and after-effects of the Egypt–Jordan Defense Pact, and the weakening of the Western powers' resolve on the reopening of the Straits. Israeli press editorials that day and the next all dealt with the Pact, underlining its serious implications.[118]

At 11:00, there began a long session of the Labor Alignment's Political Committee, which included members of the Cabinet and other party leaders. By now, it was clear to all but Eshkol himself that a new Minister of Defense had to be appointed. Eshkol met Dayan at 16:30 and offered to appoint him as Deputy Prime Minister, but Dayan refused: he was not interested in an advisory position; if he could not be responsible for defense matters, he preferred to serve in the IDF, for example, as Commander of the Southern Front. Eshkol accepted the suggestion, and by evening he received Rabin's reluctant agreement to replace Gavish with Dayan. For a few hours, Eshkol believed that his troubles were over.[119]

In Washington, disagreement was evident when W. Rostow called Evron to the White House to discuss a passage in Eshkol's letter of the previous day: it referred to "the assurances that the United States would take any and all measures to open the Straits of Tiran to international shipping." The President was disturbed by this formulation, which did not reflect accurately what he had said to Eban, since such a commitment went beyond presidential prerogative. Evron asserted that the statement was based upon a verbatim report of the Johnson–Eban conversation prepared by Harman immediately after the meeting on 26 May. He added that these statements, reinforced by the letter from Rusk, particularly his addendum to the President's letter, which all reflected the same policy, had been decisive in Israel opting for a further waiting period on 28 May. The matter was not pursued any further, but the nature of the query itself, and its source, again cast doubts on the strength of the US commitment.[120]

There were other disquieting indicators of the US position. Rusk reportedly told the House of Representatives Foreign Affairs Committee that Washington was not planning any unilateral move, but only within the framework of the UN. And Goldberg stated in the Security Council that the purpose of a fresh US resolution was "to insure a cooling-off period ... without prejudice to the ultimate rights or claims of any party."[121] In London, Wilson and Brown made extensive statements in the House of Commons on the crisis, revealing a cautious retreat from the Prime Minister's Margate speech on 24 May. The Soviets continued to give all-out public verbal support to the Arab cause. However, in private contacts with Israeli and American diplomats, they stressed their desire for a diplomatic solution of the crisis.

Thursday, 1 June

This was the day when Israel's internal agony ended: everybody—including Eshkol—gave a sigh of relief and settled down to deal with a threat that most decision-makers and the public perceived as an issue of Israel's survival. It was well characterized thus:

> Thursday, 1 June 1967, will be recorded as the longest day of Israel's first twenty years of existence. Every second was like 24 hours. The citizens of Israel wherever they were—the citizens of the home front, the regular and reserve soldiers on the front—are like a spring coiled to its utmost point of resistance. Nasser continues in his mad rush toward the borders of Israel and the news arriving from Washington underlines the weakening of hopes for the creation of an international naval force, supposed to break through the Straits.[122]

It was also the day that Eban withdrew his opposition to military action. There were several reasons. First, since 28 May, there had been no US pressure on Israel to wait for any length of time. Second, there was the Egypt–Jordan agreement and the encirclement of Israel, which "had shortened all previous ideas of the time available for an impending storm." Third, the days of waiting had achieved their desired results—military action now by Israel would be greeted with relief, not condemnation, in most Western capitals. And finally, Amit's first report arrived on 1 June, stating: "From hints and scattered facts that I have heard, I get the impression that the maritime force project is running into heavier water every hour."[123]

By the time the *Mapai* Secretariat convened, at 10:00 on 1 June, several of its members had been informed by Peres that Dayan would accept the Ministry of Defense. Finally, in the afternoon, after further meetings with Coalition colleagues and Opposition leaders, and continuous reports about the debate in the Secretariat—all indicating the wish for the appointment of Dayan—Eshkol yielded. In a meeting at 16:15 hours, he offered the Defense Ministry to Dayan, either as a representative of *Rafi* or in his personal capacity, and Dayan accepted—on both counts. At 17:15, at a meeting of the Labor Alignment ministers, Allon announced that, for the sake of national unity, he withdrew his candidacy for the Defense portfolio. Then Eshkol announced his decision to transfer it to Dayan. The decision was submitted to, and approved by, the *Mapai* Secretariat, which reassembled at 20:00 hours to hear Eshkol's further report. It was also approved in the *Rafi* caucus, which met about the same time in Ben-Gurion's home.[124]

The Cabinet met at 21:30 to formally approve the creation of the National Unity Government (Decision 15). And at 22:00, Dayan and Begin, the latter as Minister-designate Without Portfolio, joined the meeting. (The second representative of *Gahal*, Y. Saphir of the Liberal faction, joined the Cabinet deliberations the next day.) Eshkol and Eban reviewed the political situation, and Rabin gave a military account. After a brief exchange of views, the Cabinet decided to postpone the discussion of military matters to a meeting of the Ministerial Defense Committee, set for the morning of 2 June. Dayan, however, stated that if it would be decided not to attack, then 50 percent of the reserves ought to be released and the rest should dig in. This would also mean acceptance of the fact of the closure of the Straits.

In Cairo, Nasser met with Robert Anderson, President Johnson's personal emissary. Anderson left the same day for Lisbon and reported from there to Johnson that there was little chance to persuade Nasser to accept any compromise on the Straits. The concrete outcome of the meeting was that the United States and the UAR agreed to an exchange of vice-presidential visits, suggested by Johnson in his letter to Nasser of 22 May: Zahariyah Muhi-a-Din of Egypt would visit Washington on 7 June, with Humphrey's return visit thereafter to follow soon. Although the meeting was arranged secretly, it soon leaked to the press and became known to the Israeli Embassy in Washington the same day.

It was becoming clearer that the maritime force was breaking up before it ever assembled. Wilson arrived in Ottawa to try to persuade Canada to join the international maritime force with two destroyers. Pearson, under the pressure of sharp Egyptian protests, had by now retreated from his previous position of strong support for the freedom of navigation. In Washington, Rusk, leaving a meeting of the Senate Foreign Relations Committee, stated that the United States had no immediate plans to test the blockade or to act unilaterally. Both Rusk and Humphrey emphasized on that occasion the importance of action through the UN. E. Rostow again anxiously asked Harman about any Israeli intentions to send a ship through the Straits, stressing once more that the President had not yet decided what to do next. He also reemphasized that it was a vital US interest not only to prevent an Arab–Israel war but also to prevent a diplomatic victory for Nasser, for that would endanger all the pro-Western Arab regimes, particularly Saudi Arabia.

At UN headquarters, there was intensive activity behind the scenes. Israel's Representative, Rafael, met with Hans Tabor, President of the Security Council, and tried to persuade him to terminate the debate the next day; but Denmark's representative stated that it could not do so without a resolution, and there was no hope of arriving at one so soon. Rafael also tried (unsuccessfully) to persuade UK Representative Lord Caradon not to submit a draft resolution which would touch upon the basic problems of the Arab–Israel dispute. It was stopped only on Wilson's direct orders, after an Israeli intervention in London.

Friday, 2 June

Israel's Ministerial Committee on Defense met from 09:15 until noon, with Eshkol, Allon, Dayan, Eban, Rabin, and their advisers continuing discussions for another hour. Present, too, were most of the IDF commanders. Yariv began with a report on the military situation. Then Rabin gave an overall view of Israel's military plans; the emphasis was on a decisive blow to the Egyptian army, with Sharm-e-Sheikh incidental to the strategic plan. Jordan's entry into a war was also considered a possibility. But in all these presentations, the focus was not on what the military aims were, but on how to achieve them. The implications of the plans were a deep thrust into Sinai and then action according to developments, but no one spoke of how far the IDF should advance or where it should stop. Begin described the atmosphere at the meeting thus:

The commanders ... revealed their basic concern that every additional day without a decision would increase our losses when the hour of implementation arrived. They had no doubts of victory. They expressed their belief not only in the strength of the army but also in its ability to rout the enemy.[125]

Again there was no decision. Begin asserted later that, after leaving the meeting, he and Dayan agreed they would leave the Cabinet if a decision were not taken.

Dayan devoted the rest of 2 June to briefings at Army headquarters. There is a broad consensus that his appointment gave a tremendous boost to the country's morale, including the High Command and the army: it was interpreted as a sign of Israel's determination to resist encroachment upon its vital interests. What is also certain is that the decision to break the Egyptian army with an all-out attack and then to occupy Sharm-e-Sheikh was finalized on the 2nd and subsequent days.[126]

The military plans of Israel and the changes effected during the crisis were summarized by the IDF historian as follows:

> Two plans for counter-attacks were prepared in the period between the evacuation of UNEF and the closure of the Straits: a limited and a broad one. The starting point of both was the destruction of the Egyptian air force by surprise, and the difference lay in the deployment of ground forces. The broad plan envisaged the occupation of the forward area of Sinai, while avoiding a frontal attack on the Um Katef-Abu Ageila strongholds; while the limited plan was directed toward the occupation of the Gaza Strip alone. After the blockade of the Straits by Abd el-Nasser, Prime Minister and Minister of Defense Levi Eshkol was presented with a plan to advance along the Northern axis, until the Suez Canal.... With this, the limited plan was put aside.... The final plan, which was approved by Defense Minister Moshe Dayan on June 2, 1967, stipulated—because of calculations connected with the "political clock" ticking away—a minimal span of time between the air force's first strike and the first breach of the ground forces in the Egyptian arena. The phase after the first breach was not planned in detail. In a plan of operations, prepared by Yitzhak Hofi, the Chief of the Operations Department, all that was stated was that in the breaching phase, the forces are to establish a line—*not east* of the line of El Arish-G'ebel Livni, i.e., short of the Canal and to be in a stage of preparedness for moving toward the Suez Canal and Sharm-e-Sheikh.[127]

To this should be added that, according to Ezer Weizman, Chief of Operations, the broad plan was presented to Eshkol, there was a consensus, but nothing was formally decided. Further, Gavish, OC Southern

Command, stated that the limited plan was actually put aside on 2 June, under the impact of Dayan's appointment. And Sharon, OC of one of the three corps on the southern front, stated that Dayan also decided, on assuming office, to order a simultaneous advance by all three corps, along three axes, instead of the existing plan of advancing along the northern axis (Decision 16).[128] Dayan was to write later about his dissatisfaction with existing IDF plans as early as 23 May, especially the concentration on capturing the Gaza Strip, which 'was not an outright military target' and would not attain the key goal—the destruction of much of Egyptian military strength. He repeated these objections to Major-General Amit, Head of *Ha-Mossad*, on the evening of the 26th. And on 2 June, at a meeting of the inner circle— Eshkol, Eban, Allon, and Rabin—he urged a full-scale attack on the 5th, 'to destroy the Egyptian forces concentrated in central Sinai. We should have no geographical aim whatsoever and we should not include the Gaza Strip in our fighting plans. . .' Just before that, he told the General Staff that he envisaged a two-stage campaign—'first, capture of northern Sinai; second, capture of the Straits and Sharm-e-Sheikh.'[129]

Another element of the public argument about Dayan's role revolved around the decision to go to war, with Dayan and Begin and, more vociferously, their supporters claiming that the Cabinet's hesitancy came to an end with their entry.[130] Dayan's appointment made such a decision inevitable and possibly accelerated the decision process.

On the evening of 2 June, members of the government fanned out all over the country to inform and calm the public: the people needed reassurances, and the proven valor of Dayan satisfied this yearning. Reports from all parts of the world served to reinforce the belief that the time for diplomatic efforts was over.

A note from the Soviet government was more menacing than Kosygin's letter of 26 May. Although repeating Kosygin's statement that "the Soviet Government desires once again to state that it will do everything possible to prevent an armed clash," it continued with a threat: "but if the Government of Israel should decide to take upon itself the responsibility for the outbreak of war, it will have to pay the price in full."[131]

No less worrying was an official statement issued at noon in Paris, after a meeting of the French Cabinet. Bearing the unmistakable imprint of de Gaulle, it read:

La France n'est engagé à aucun titre ni sur aucun suject avec aucun des États en cause. De son propre chef, elle considère que chacun de ces états a la droit de vivre. Mais, elle estime que le pire serait l'ouverture des hostilités. En conséquence l'État qui le premier et oïl que ce soit, emploierait les armes n'aurait ni son approbation ni, a plus forte raison, son appui.

[France is not involved in any form or in any way with any of the States concerned. On her part, she considers that each of these States has a right to live. But, in her opinion the touchstone will be the opening of hostilities. As a result, the state which will be the first to open hostilities will have neither her approval nor her acclaim.][132]

The French Cabinet also decided to declare an embargo on arms deliveries to the Middle East, officially effective as of 5 June, but in fact, in some cases of equipment, effective immediately. The delivery of planes to Israel was stopped; that of spare parts and other vital equipment would now depend on the individual goodwill of French officials and the interests of the French High Command. It was yet another event that limited the perceived time available for action by Israel and thus achieved exactly the opposite effect of what de Gaulle intended.

In Washington, the major event of that day was Prime Minister Wilson's talk with Johnson, with no joint communiqué being issued. It was decided to bring Ambassador Harman back to Israel the same day to report the results of his discussions with US officials. Harman asked that any decision be held up until his arrival, although he already hinted guardedly that his report would not include new, positive developments. At the Israeli Embassy in Washington, Harman, Amit, and Evron had a final consultation about the Harman–Amit report to the Cabinet. All three agreed that their advice had to be that there was no alternative to war.[133] Just before he left for Israel, Harman had a final meeting with Rusk and E. Rostow. Although the Americans continued to assure him that the maritime plan was going well, that within seven to nine days plans would be completed, and that the Australians had promised ships for the naval patrol, there were also disquieting equivocations in their views on Soviet intentions and the probable US response, and the interpretation of the 1957 American "commitments," regarding the Straits.

In Moscow, Gromyko again warned Israel, through Ambassador Katz, not to start a war and that Israel was endangering her future with her aggressive policy. In Paris, the French continued to insist that Nasser would not escalate further, that a compromise on the Straits could be achieved, and that the Soviet Union would have to play a decisive role in negotiations and ought to be persuaded to work together with the United States toward a reduction in tension.

Saturday, 3 June

Several crucial inputs—from the Near East core, the United States, and France—crystallized the resolve taken at an *ad hoc* meeting of Israel's political and bureaucratic élites to propose military action at the Cabinet meeting, scheduled for the next day. At the same time, Dayan and his associates made an effort to create the impression that Israel would wait a little longer, a week or two, in order to regain the basis for tactical surprise. These efforts succeeded brilliantly.

Of all the rumors, statements, and declarations emanating from Arab sources about the flow of reinforcements to the fronts, one solid fact emerged that day: an Iraqi armored division had entered Jordan on its way to the Israeli border. This was perceived as a clear and present danger.

Another letter arrived on the 3rd from Johnson, in answer to Eshkol's letter of 30 May. The President again emphasized as "vital national interests of the United States" the right of free and innocent passage through international waterways, of which the Gulf of Aqaba was one, and the territorial integrity and political independence of all countries in the Middle East. But there was no specific commitment for immediate US action. On the contrary, Johnson repeated his warning: "I must emphasize the necessity for Israel not to make itself responsible for the initiation of hostilities; Israel will not be alone, unless it decides to go alone."[134] On the possibility of naval action, the President was vague.

Harman and Amit arrived from Washington in the afternoon. Harman's full report about his contacts with the US administration again showed that measures to be taken by the maritime powers were still under consideration but that nothing had been firmly decided. The evening meeting was held at Eshkol's Jerusalem home, beginning at 23:00. Present were: Allon, Dayan, Eban, Dinstein, Rabin, Yadin, Amit, Yariv, Herzog, Levavi, and Harman. The central issue was whether or not the United States and the Soviet Union would be aligned on the same side, against Israel, if hostilities began. Although Harman expressed the view that Israel ought to wait another week, because of the US belief that they had been given that much time to complete their plans, there was a broad consensus that nothing further could be gained from additional waiting. Amit concurred and the day's events tended to support this assessment. Further, Amit's judgment was that if Israel decided to act alone, the United States would not resist. Those present agreed with Eshkol's and Eban's view that the United States would extend diplomatic support in the aftermath. There was also agreement that the Soviet Union would not intervene militarily.[135]

Military plans, too, were discussed at the meeting, especially those approved the previous day by Dayan. "It was decided to stage for the time being a holding operation against the Syrians in the North, and not to attack Jordan unless Jordan attacked first.... The main blow was to be directed against the Egyptians."[136] The meeting ended with unanimous agreement to recommend to the Cabinet the next day the decision to go to war.

During the same day, thousands of soldiers, released for the weekend, joined the crowds at the beaches, thus becoming a visible sign of relaxation of tension. Dayan, in personal meetings with correspondents, as well as in his two press conferences—one public, at 16:00, immediately followed by one for military correspondents—succeeded in convincing a hardened audience that war was not imminent; many of them so reported and left Israel the next day. Dayan's press conference was attended by hundreds of reporters and was immediately broadcast all over the world. Two of his statements made a particular impact on his audience. Asked about the loss of time because of the "long drawn out diplomatic action," he answered:

> I accept the situation as it is. I know it is always easy to say last week we were in a better position. This is not the point. The point, I should think just now, is that it is more or less a situation of being too late or too early—too late to react regarding our chances in the military field—on the blockading of the Straits of Tiran—and too early to draw conclusions as to the diplomatic way of handling the matter.

On promises given by other governments, he stated:

> I do not know whether we got such promises or not, but let me say that I, personally, do not expect and do not want anyone else to fight for us. Whatever can be done in the diplomatic way I would welcome and encourage, but if somehow it comes to real fighting I would not like American or British boys to get killed here, and I do not think we need them.[137]

At his meeting with military correspondents, he again emphasized the element of further waiting: "The Government of Israel had decided upon diplomatic steps and you have to give this a chance. Until when? Until the Government decides."[138]

In Washington, General Wheeler, Chairman of the Joint Chiefs of Staff, had told the President the previous day that war was now inevitable and that Israel would be victorious within two weeks, but the toll of destruction might be quite heavy. In New York, Prime Minister Wilson met with U Thant for two hours. Again, during a press conference, his statements were noncommittal. The problem was that of averting disaster; the matter was urgent, but he had no timetable for the issuing of the maritime declaration. In Paris, Israel Ambassador Eytan had a meeting with de Gaulle, who tried to frighten Israel into following France's advice ("A war would be disastrous for Israel even if she won. There would be enormous losses"). But by this time it had no effect on Israel's decision-makers.

Sunday, 4 June

On Sunday, 4 June, Iraq acceded to the defense pacts. An Iraqi division was advancing into Jordan, and two battalions of Egyptian commandos were flown there—clear indications to Israel's military leadership of an intent to attack at an opportune moment. By that time, however, no further stimuli were necessary to strengthen Israel's resolve. At a seven-hour meeting, broken up from time to time for group consultations, the Cabinet reviewed the situation once more and then decided to go to war.[139]

There were, in fact, three meetings, each flowing into the other. It all started at 8:30 as a meeting of the Ministerial Committee on Defense. This continued, at 11:00, as a full Cabinet meeting. And this then went on once more, after a pause, as a meeting of the Ministerial Committee on Defense. The deliberations were opened by Dayan, who reviewed the strength of the Arab armies confronting Israel. There were 100,000 Egyptian troops in Sinai, 60,000 in reserve; 1000 tanks, mainly of the Soviet T-54 and T-55 types; and 400 interceptors and fighter-bombers. The Syrians had 50,000 men lined up on the border, 200 tanks, and 100 aircraft, 32 of which were MiG-21s. Jordan had 50,000–60,000 men, 250 Patton and Centurion tanks, and 24 British Hawker Hunter fighters. They were reinforced by the Iraqi division, moving to take up positions on the Israeli border.[140]

The Cabinet then heard Eban's final evaluation of the international situation, including Johnson's message. The Foreign Minister emphasized that he believed the Americans were now committed, at least to the extent that the 1956 situation would not be repeated: Israel would not be isolated after an armed clash. As for the Soviet Union, Israel could expect her to remain hostile politically, but there was no indication of armed intervention. Eban also told the Cabinet about de Gaulle's warning to Eytan the previous day, at which Israel had been notified of the arms embargo. He concluded by advocating military action, for Egypt had started the war by all known rules of international law.

Eshkol stated that Israel had to act soon and at her own initiative. He believed that Johnson had softened his stand and would give Israel political support. De Gaulle's actions worried and puzzled him. There was a movement toward a search for compromise, at Israel's expense. Interior Minister Shapira declared that he felt it necessary to recapitulate the views of Israel's elder statesman, Ben-Gurion, whom he had seen on Friday. Ben-Gurion said that it was very dangerous to initiate a war where Israel would have to fight alone, and mobilization had been a grievous mistake. Israel should hold out, even for several months, until it could find an ally who would stand by her side and enable her to take up arms against the enemy, as in the Sinai Campaign. Dayan rejected the implications of Shapira's statement—and Ben-Gurion's advice—by replying that, until somebody found Israel an ally, it was doubtful whether the country would still exist. He also rejected the idea of a test ship, for the same reason as that given by Rabin—it would be a clear signal to Nasser that Israel was about to attack. The time to act was now. There was increased danger on the Jordanian border, coupled with the possibility of a preemptive attack by Nasser, which could cause serious damage to Israel's hinterland. "Put bluntly, I [Dayan] said, our best chance of victory was to strike the first blow. The course of the campaign would then follow our dictates.... Considering the situation in which we found ourselves ... it would be fatal for us to allow them to launch their attack."[141]

The *Mapam* ministers, Barzilai and Bentov, were taken aback by the change in attitude of colleagues who, until then, had advocated further diplomatic efforts (Eban and Shapira, among others). Yet they did not dissociate themselves from the general trend—after their proposed resolution for further delay and diplomacy received only two votes. Rather, they reserved the right to consult senior party colleagues, notably Ya'ari and Hazan. Begin supported the Prime Minister's proposal and suggested sending emissaries abroad, particularly to the United States, to explain the real situation as presented to the Cabinet that day.

Eshkol called for a formal vote at the end of the meeting. Eighteen members of the Cabinet voted for the Dayan-initiated resolution. (Finance Minister Sapir was abroad.) The two *Mapam* ministers added their assent after consultation, thus making it unanimous. The resolution, the text of which was published five years later, stated:

> After hearing a report on the military and political situation from the Prime Minister, the Foreign Minister, the Defense Minister, the Chief of Staff and the head of Military Intelligence, the Government ascertained that the armies of Egypt, Syria and Jordan are deployed for immediate multi-front aggression, threatening the very existence of the State.
> The Government resolves to take military action in order to liberate Israel from the stranglehold of aggression which is progressively being tightened around Israel.
> The Government authorizes the Prime Minister and the Defense Minister to confirm to the General Staff of the IDF the time of action.
> Members of the Cabinet will receive as soon as possible the information concerning the military operation to be carried out.
> The Government charges the Foreign Minister with the task of exhausting all possibilities of political action in order to explain Israel's stand to obtain the support of the powers.[142]

The Cabinet session ended at 15:00. The official communiqué was as innocuous as it could be under the circumstances: "The Cabinet at its weekly session ... heard reports on the security situation by the Prime Minister and the Defense Minister-designate, and a survey of political developments by the Foreign Minister." The rest dealt with routine matters—approval of draft laws and ratification of treaties.

Dayan returned immediately to IDF headquarters to supervise the final preparations. The forces on the borders of Syria and Jordan received strict instructions to stay in defensive position and to advance to limited strategic strongholds inside the enemy territory only if attacked. After a tour of the Northern Command, during which he told its commander, David Elazar, that, because the campaign against Egypt would be difficult, he would have to do with the forces he had. Dayan returned to Army headquarters and informed Ben-Gurion late at night of the Cabinet's decision. Ben-Gurion gave him his blessings.

Eshkol returned to his home and had a final consultation with Allon, Eban, Galili, and advisers. At 20:00 in Tel Aviv, he received the report of the Navy Commander about the first action of the War, the dispatch of frogmen to the port of Alexandria, making 4 June the chronological first day of the 1967 War.

The pace of diplomacy was slowing down: Israeli diplomats and their counterparts abroad—Evron with W. Rostow in Washington, Rafael with Goldberg in New York—went over familiar ground.[143] A meeting between Tekoah and Chuvakhin can be characterized as one between two deaf men.

In the Arab states, as in the rest of the world and—seemingly—in Israel, it was a day of relative relaxation. The streets of Cairo filled again, diplomats and soldiers took off for a day of long-delayed relaxation, and journalists were leaving the scene in droves. In a speech at the ceremony of Iraq's accession to the Joint Defense Pact, Nasser declared that Egypt would regard a maritime declaration as an act of aggression and a prelude to hostilities. In an interview with Anthony Nutting, published in the *Sunday Times*, he declared that he planned no further escalation. King Hussein held a press conference to explain his decision to sign the Joint Defense Pact. In Baghdad, President Aref opened a conference of the "Arab Oil Producing States." He threatened the oil companies that their property would be "seized, placed under tutelage, liquidated," if they supplied oil to Israel.

In Washington, Senator Mansfield released a report on the Senate Foreign Relations Committee's discussions with Humphrey, Rusk, and McNamara. There was a sharp distinction between the passage of American ships and the passage of Israeli ships through the Tiran Straits, in terms of a declaration and the use of force.[144] Italian and Japanese officials announced that their states would not sign the declaration for the time being. A French government spokesman once more made it clear that France would not sign.

British newspapers speculated that, after Wilson's return from the United States, the British Cabinet would change its policy, since Wilson had not found energetic support for his initiative in Washington. Intermittent firing broke out in Jerusalem early in the afternoon, in the vicinity of the Mandelbaum Gate. An additional Soviet destroyer passed through the Dardanelles, on its way to the Mediterranean. By now, a sizeable British force had assembled off Aden: the aircraft carrier Hermes, four frigates, four minesweepers, and three other vessels. The bulk of the US Sixth Fleet was still stationed off Crete. Full-scale war was hours away.

Decisions, Decision-Makers, Decision Process: Before and During October Yom Kippur Crisis-War (5–26 October 1973)

The brief prewar international crisis of 1973 was dominated by the 1973 October War, designated by Israel and the world media as the Yom Kippur War, and termed by one incisive commentator the "October Earthquake."[145] Signals of its impending outbreak escalated on the morning of 5 October and culminated in information which reached IDF Intelligence at 03:40 on the 6th. This triggered all three necessary conditions of a grave foreign policy crisis, notably a perception on the 6th, of the near-certainty of war, by the senior decision-makers of one of the principal adversaries, Israel. War broke out at 14:00 that day. The war, between Egypt and Israel, continued until 26 October, when the second UN-sponsored cease-fire between these adversaries took effect. The state of war between Israel and Syria continued until a cease-fire on 31 May 1974. [Because of space constraints the analysis of Israel's behavior in the 1973 October War will focus exclusively on the Egypt–Israel segment of that war.]

Decisions and Decision-Makers

The 1973 high-stress crisis period escalated to full-scale war within a day, from 5 October until the full-scale coordinated attack on Israel by Egypt and Syria on the 6th. There were 18 discernible Israeli decisions during that crisis-war: six taken by the Cabinet, seven by the Prime Minister in consultation with other ministers or the IDF Chief of Staff, three by the Prime Minister's "Kitchen Cabinet," and two by the IDF General Staff with the Defense Minister. [The first two decisions preceded the high-stress crisis period.] Not all of these decisions were important. Some were of a formal, authorization nature. The consultative process varied, as did the size of the decisional unit (Table 10.3).

Decision Process

Phase I: 5–6 October

Three events triggered the 1973 high-stress crisis period: the hasty evacuation of Soviet dependents from Egypt and Syria, the findings of a crucial Israeli air reconnaissance mission over Egyptian lines, and an intelligence

Table 10.3 Israel's decisions and decision-makers, 1973 crisis-war

Decision number	Date	Content
3.	5 October 1973, 09:00–10:00	The IDF Chief of Staff and the Defense Minister, with members of the General Staff present, decided to place regular IDF forces on (the highest) alert "C" and the Air Force on full alert.
4.	5 October, noon	An extraordinary Cabinet meeting, with seven ministers present, approved all IDF measures taken thus far and empowered the Prime Minister and Defense Minister to mobilize all reserves, if necessary.
5.	6 October, 08:00–09:45	At a meeting of the "Kitchen Cabinet," the Prime Minister decided against a preemptive airstrike.
6.	6 October, 08:00–09:45	The Prime Minister, with the "Kitchen Cabinet," decided in favor of large-scale mobilization.
7.	7 October, 17:00–18:00	The "Kitchen Cabinet" empowered the IDF Chief of Staff to decide about a counterattack after he studied the situation on the southern front.
8.	8 October	The Defense Minister, in consultation with the IDF Chief of Staff and the General Staff, decided to concentrate IDF action on the northern front, including the bombing of military targets deep inside Syria (Damascus, Homs, and Latakia). This was subsequently approved by the Cabinet.
9.	9 October, morning	The Prime Minister, after consulting Dayan, Allon, and Elazar, decided to place Bar-Lev in charge of the Southern Command; that is, he was made *de facto* Officer Commanding.
10.	9 October	The Prime Minister, after consulting Dayan, decided to fly to Washington on a secret mission (abortive decision).
11.	10 October, evening	The "Kitchen Cabinet," in consultation with the IDF General Staff, approved a plan to launch a general attack on Syria, in the direction of Damascus, but not to attempt to occupy Syria's capital.
12.	12 October, morning	The "Kitchen Cabinet," in consultation with the IDF Chief of Staff and several other generals, decided to postpone a decision on an attempted crossing of the Canal until Egyptian armor on the east bank had been defeated in battle.
13.	12 October, afternoon	The Prime Minister decided to accept a US suggestion for a cease-fire in place.
14.	14 October, evening	The Cabinet approved a proposal to cross the Canal.
15.	19 October, morning	The Prime Minister approved Dayan's suggestion to press forward on the west bank of the Canal but not to advance on Cairo.

(*continued*)

Table 10.3 (continued)

Decision number	Date	Content
16.	21/22 October, midnight	The Cabinet decided to accept the US–Soviet call for a cease-fire.
17.	22 October, evening	The Cabinet decided to continue IDF operations if Egypt did not obey the cease-fire.
18.	23 October, dawn	The Prime Minister approved continued IDF advances on the west bank of the Canal because of continuing Egyptian attacks.
19.	26 October, 04:00	The Cabinet, after a six-hour debate, decided to accept a second and third call for a cease-fire.
20.	26 October, evening	The Cabinet yielded to US pressure on the issue of providing supplies to Egypt's encircled Third Army.

report from the IDF Southern Command. As noted, information on the Soviet airlift of advisory personnel from Egypt and Syria, which reached AMAN (IDF Intelligence) during the night of 4–5 October, did not fit the existing Israeli evaluation of Arab intent. Preliminary analysis suggested three interpretations: (1) that the Russians were aware of an Arab plan to attack Israel and were attempting, openly and drastically, to prevent it; (2) that Egypt and Syria had requested the Soviet Union to withdraw all its advisers because of a deterioration in their relations; and (3) that Moscow was dissatisfied with its clients' behavior and had decided to act. The last two interpretations were unconvincing to the IDF Director of Military Intelligence, General Zeira, who conveyed his disquiet to the IDF Chief of Staff.[146] The results of the aerial reconnaissance mission along the Canal reached IDF general headquarters (GHQ) at the same time and "attested to the reinforcement of the Egyptian deployment in a threatening and warning manner."[147] This was further supported, at dawn on 5 October, by an intelligence report from the South showing that "the Egyptian army along the Suez Canal had reached a degree of emergency deployment and dispositions such as had never been observed previously by the IDF."[148] These included the strengthening of frontline forces along the Canal with dozens of artillery units, hundreds of tanks, and advanced preparations for a crossing.[149]

The direct result of these inputs was evident at the IDF General Staff's weekly meeting on Friday morning, 5 October. In Dayan's presence,

ISRAEL'S BEHAVIOR IN THE 1967 AND 1973 WARS: OVERALL FINDINGS 217

the Staff "again decided to order 'C' Alert, the highest alert, for the army and a full alert for the Air Force" (Decision 3).[150] The "C" alert, declared at the beginning of the week, had been relaxed for some units on the previous day, 4 October.[151] At 09:45 on 5 October, Dayan, Elazar, and Zeira met with Prime Minister Meir to inform her of developments and IDF actions. At both meetings, the estimates of the probability of war were revised slightly upward, but it was still considered "low."[152] The outcome was a decision to convene a Cabinet meeting with those ministers present in Tel Aviv—it was the day before Yom Kippur—and to inform the United States of the situation, along with a request that the US attempt to restrain Egypt through the Soviet Union. Although the warnings were transmitted, they did not achieve any effect, because of the prevailing Central Intelligence Agency (CIA) estimate of war as "unlikely" and because of communication failures between Washington and New York.

The Cabinet meeting on 5 October was attended by the Prime Minister, the Defense Minister, and five other ministers—Bar-Lev, Galili, Hazani, Hillel, and Peres—and by Elazar, Zeira, and Gazit. The Director of Military Intelligence reportedly declared that an attack was not likely, that "it was most improbable that the Egyptians would cross the Canal in large forces, though they might open fire and attempt raids."[153] Elazar supported the AMAN estimate but added that there was no evidence that the enemy was not going to attack. Again he noted that he had ordered the highest alert in the regular forces, including the cancellation of all leaves on both fronts and in the Air Force, and had alerted the mobilization centers, "but the mobilization of reserves and other measures were delayed until [the receipt of] further indicators."[154] Meir recalled about that meeting: "Not one minister ... said a word about the need for total mobilization. [The experts] ... said on Wednesday and on Thursday, even on that last Friday before the war, that war is unlikely."[155]

To be on the safe side, after Galili had raised the question, the Cabinet decided to empower the Prime Minister and Defense Minister to call up all the reserves, if necessary (Decision 4).[156] It also approved the dispatch of a message to Kissinger, via Israel's Embassy in Washington, requesting him to inform Egypt, Syria, and the Soviet Union that Israel had no aggressive intentions but to indicate that, if attacked, it would respond forcefully. The message also contained the prevailing Israeli Intelligence evaluation: that Syria was reacting to a perceived possible Israeli move against it, and that Egypt was engaged in maneuvers, which were expected to end on Sunday, 7 October. Inexplicably, the message was not sent until the evening. Brigadier-General Scowcroft, the Deputy Director of the National Security Council, received it at 17:30, that is, 23:30 Israel time. The message reached Kissinger at 20:00 New York time.[157]

This delay in informing Washington underlines the fact that, until the end of 5 October, time salience for Israel's decision-makers did not extend to hours and minutes. Nevertheless, the pace of consultation and action quickened. The IDF's Northern Command decided to prepare for a limited Syrian assault. The Southern Command undertook some preparations called for by Alert "C," but it denied requests made by the OC Armored Corps, South, General Avraham (Albert) Mendler, for additional forces. More serious, Mendler was unable to undertake some of the redeployment called for by "Operation Dovecote." Even as late as the morning of the 6th, he received instructions from the OC Southern Command not to undertake any movements (i.e., of tanks) to forward positions in Sinai that could arouse Egyptian suspicions of a planned Israeli attack.[158]

Between 03:30 and 04:00 on 6 October, the Director of Military Intelligence was notified by an Israeli spy in Egypt that Egypt and Syria would attack Israel before sundown; the Director immediately informed the Defense Minister and the Prime Minister's military Aide-de-camp.[159] The timetable of events from the receipt of this message until the outbreak of war at 14:00 is as follows (Table 10.4).

The consultative process during these fateful hours revealed the effect of intense time pressure. A realization that war had become a near-certainty[160] led to a purely internal Israeli decision process without external, primarily US, pressure—unlike 1967.[161] The two major decisions—to order large-scale mobilization and not to preempt—were taken at the same meeting by the Prime Minister, almost intuitively, though she was formally empowered to do so during the previous day's Cabinet session.

Elazar opened the meeting, which began at 08:00 on 6 October, advocating the mobilization of several army divisions and of the entire Air Force.[162] To the Prime Minister, he said, pointedly: "I want you to know that our air force can be ready to strike at noon, but you must give me the green light now."[163]

Dayan recalled the deliberations thus:

> We were faced with four principal issues: mobilization of reserves and reinforcement of the fronts; a possible pre-emptive strike by our Air Force; evac-

Table 10.4 Israel's decisions, decision-makers, and decision process, 6 October 1973

03:30–04:00	The message was received by the Director of Military Intelligence, Zeira, who informed Meir, Dayan, and Elazar, the Prime Minister, Defense Minister, and IDF Chief of Staff.
04:00	Meir instructed ADC Lior to ask Dayan, Allon, Galili, and Elazar to be in her Tel Aviv office before 07:00.
04:05	Meir phoned Dayan, who informed her that he would meet with the IDF Chief of Staff to assess the situation; the meeting at the Prime Minister's office was postponed to 08:00.
04:40	The IDF Chief of Staff phoned Air Force Commander Peled and asked him to specify the earliest feasible time for a preemptive aerial strike against Syria. Peled indicated between 12:00 and 13:00. Elazar issued an order to prepare for such a strike.[a]
05:15	An IDF General Staff meeting was held with Elazar, Zeira, Peled, Tal, and other ranking officers, but without the regional commanders. Zeira still estimated the probability of an attack to be "low," but this was rejected by Elazar and others. The Chief of Staff informed the meeting that he intended to propose full mobilization of the reserves and had given the necessary preparatory orders, including the mobilization of Civil Defense.
05:45	Dayan met General Shlomo Gazit, in charge of the Administered Territories (West Bank), and they decided on an increased alert in his Command.
05:50	Dayan held a meeting with Elazar, Tal, Zeira, and others from the IDF General Staff, as well as Lior. Elazar advocated almost total mobilization—"about 200,000 men"—and a preemptive strike by the Air Force either against Egypt and Syria or against Syria alone. Dayan rejected both ideas and was willing to agree only to mobilization of forces needed for defense.[b]
07:15	The IDF Chief of Staff met with the OCs of Northern and Southern Commands, Generals Hofi and Gonen, and other members of the General Staff. He issued "general instructions" for war, emphasizing that the first phase would be a holding operation and that all forces must be ready to move over to a counterattack as early as possible.[c]
08:00	The (enlarged) "Kitchen Cabinet" met at the Prime Minister's office in Tel Aviv. Present were Dayan, Galili, Allon (who arrived late), Bar-Lev, Elazar, Zeira, M. Gazit, and Zvi Zur, Assistant to the Defense Minister. The Prime Minister decided in favor of large-scale mobilization of reserves, but against a preemptive airstrike (Decisions 5 and 6).
10:00	Meir met US Ambassador Keating and his Counselor, Veliotis. Also present were Allon, Zeira, Aharon Kidron, Director-General of the Foreign Ministry, and Simha Dinitz, Israel's Ambassador to the United States. The Prime Minister informed Keating that Israel had reliable evidence that the "attacks would start late in the afternoon and that we would not strike first."[d]

(continued)

Table 10.4 (continued)

11:00	Dayan joined the "Kedem" Operational Consultative Group chaired by Elazar to discuss preparations to stop the Egypt–Syria assault.
12:00	The Cabinet convened in Tel Aviv, with all members present except two *Mafdal* (National Religious Party) ministers, Burg and Warhaftig, who were in Jerusalem; Eban, who was in New York; and Sharef and Gvati. War broke out at 14:00 while the Cabinet was still in session.

[a]Bar-Tov, *Dado*, vol. 2, 9–10; Nakdimon, "New Revelations"
[b]Nakdimon, "New Revelations"; Dayan, *Story of My Life*, 376; Bar-Tov, *Dado*, vol. 2, 12–13
[c]Herzog, *The War of Atonement*, 53; Bar-Tov, *Dado*, vol. 2, 15–16
[d]Meir, *My Life*, 359; Michael Brecher, interviews with Kenneth Keating and US Embassy officials, 30 July 1974

uation of children and women from our frontier settlements in the Golan Heights; and delivery of a warning to Egypt and Syria.

In our preliminary consultation [at a meeting], I told the chief of staff that I agreed to his request for the immediate mobilization of the reserves required for the defense of the two fronts on as full a scale as he found necessary. But I decided to bring before the prime minister the questions of a pre-emptive strike and the immediate mobilization of all the reserves needed under the contingency plan to go over to counter-attack.

The pre-emptive strike which the chief of staff recommended, after consultation with the Air Force, was to be directed against Syria alone ... only against air bases deep inside Syria – and even that not before twelve noon.

I rejected the idea of a pre-emptive strike by the Air Force as well as the mobilization of more reserves than were required for immediate defense.

These points were thoroughly reviewed at our meeting with the prime minister and it was finally resolved, at her decision, to order the mobilization of ... 100,000 to 120,000 men, in addition to the regular army; not to carry out a pre-emptive air strike; to evacuate children and women from the Golan settlements; and to send a warning to Egypt and Syria through the United States.[164]

Elazar's account of what took place in the discussion with Dayan before the eight o'clock "Kitchen Cabinet" was diametrically opposed to the latter's memoir:

> During my meeting with the Minister of Defense on the morning of Yom Kippur, I demanded again and again a full mobilization of reserves, but the Minister of Defense argued that a small deployment of two divisions

would be sufficient. During the investigation, I was asked by the [Agranat] Committee if there was an agreement between the Minister and me to mobilize two divisions. My repeated answers were that during the meeting on the morning of Yom Kippur, it was not agreed to mobilize two divisions. I testified that at a certain point during this discussion, the Minister ordered his Military Secretary to ask the Prime Minister for approval by telephone to mobilize two divisions. I clarified that that would not be enough. The Minister cancelled his order to his Secretary and agreed that both proposals would be brought to the Prime Minister for her decision.... As a result of the disagreement between the Minister of Defense and me, the Minister decided to bring both proposals to the Prime Minister, and until her decision was made, he did not give his approval to any mobilization.... It should be noted that a request to the Prime Minister for the mobilization of reserves is the privilege of the Minister of Defense only.[165]

The essential difference between the two advocacies was cogently summarized as follows:

Elazar deduced his policy recommendations from the assumption of the worst case—the Arab intent to attack—and the subsequent necessity to increase Israel's defensive capability. Dayan deduced his proposals for partial mobilization and no pre-emption from a lower estimate of the probability of attack, reinforced by assumptions of miscalculation and escalation.[166]

Both men insisted upon clearly defined, explicit terms in the decision, and when they could not agree, Dayan passed the burden—for a crucial military decision—on to the Prime Minister. The Prime Minister recalled her consternation: "My God, I have to decide which of them is right?"[167]

The Prime Minister's decision in favor of Elazar's suggestion for large-scale mobilization was due to a single calculus, as noted earlier: "If there really was a war, then we had to be in the very best position possible." Similarly, as noted, she decided against a preemptive strike because "there is always the possibility that we will need help, and if we strike first, we will get nothing from anyone."[168] That decision, she later revealed, was made almost instantly: she made her calculation by drawing upon Israel's experience in the 1967 crisis period, before the June-Six-Day War, when, even with Nasser's provocative acts, "we witnessed the 'great support' given to us by the whole world."[169] Elazar replied that it was, of course, reckless not to preempt but that it would not make things too difficult for Israel.[170]

The acrimonious debate between Dayan and Elazar was thus resolved and the orders given to mobilize. The Agranat Commission blamed Elazar for the delay, and it was the main reason for his resignation after the Commission's first interim report was published on 3 April 1974.[171]

At the 10:00 meeting with Keating, the Prime Minister informed the US Ambassador that, "according to our intelligence, the attacks would start late in the afternoon and that we would not strike first.... We would not make a preemptive strike."[172] Keating recalled the incident vividly. He had received a phone call at 08:30 from the Prime Minister, asking for a meeting at 10:00:

> The Prime Minister said to me that she had unqualified and undeniable evidence that the Arabs intended to strike massively against Israel by sunset of that day. The Prime Minister urged me to communicate this information to the Secretary of State and, through him, to contact Soviet officials and those of Egypt and of Syria and to tell them that Israel knew of their plans, was ready, but did not want war. I asked the Prime Minister: 'In the light of the information is it Israel's intent, and has Israel made a decision, not to pre-empt?' And the answer was firm and clear: 'Mr. Ambassador, we have decided not to pre-empt.' Thereafter, Keating left to communicate this significant information to Washington.[173]

At the same time, US Embassy personnel informed Washington that they expected to be notified by the Israeli government within a few hours that there were too many risks involved and that it had decided to preempt massively. Thus, for several hours after the outbreak of war, the United States was not certain who attacked whom.[174]

The noon Cabinet meeting, in Meir's terse summary, "heard a full description of the situation, including the decision to mobilize the reserves and also my decision regarding a pre-emptive strike. Nobody raised any objections whatsoever."[175] One of the reasons for unanimity, and a key to Israeli decision-making throughout the 1973 prewar crisis period, was noted by a participant: "The issue was discussed at the noon Cabinet meeting, but you must remember that Golda had great authority. Once she decided and gave her reasons, the others would accept her decision."[176]

Dayan confirmed the essence of the meeting more precisely:

> The government approved what had been decided upon at my earlier meeting with the prime minister, including partial mobilization—of 120,000 reservists. There was a brief discussion of how we might act if Egypt alone

opened hostilities, namely, whether to wait until Syria joined in or to make an advanced strike on Syria. The Cabinet was also informed that the United States had been in touch with Egypt, directly, and with Syria, through the Soviet Union, telling them of Israel's report that they intended to attack and asking for clarification. The Egyptians had not yet replied, but America warned us not to take any provocative action, adding that news had reached them that we were proposing to attack within six hours. Nor had the United States received any response from the Russians.[177]

Bar-Lev challenged the assumption that the Egyptian-Syrian attack would begin at 18:00, on the grounds that it did not make military sense, and he wondered whether the intelligence information might be incorrect. The same objection was raised by Allon. But Elazar was categorical about the timing.[178] While the Cabinet was still in session, at 14:00, news arrived that war had broken out.[179] During the next few hours, there were intense consultations centering around Meir in the Prime Minister's office and Dayan at IDF GHQ. In the evening, there was a second Cabinet meeting, and from then on until the end of the 1973 crisis period, as in 1967, there was a continuous round of Cabinet meetings, averaging two per day, at the Prime Minister's Tel Aviv office.[180] There were also many informal consultations at political and bureaucratic levels, and daily meetings of the *Knesset* Foreign Affairs and Security Committee, the first at 14:00 on 6 October, at which time Opposition Leader Begin proposed a political truce until the end of the war. The Prime Minister readily agreed.[181]

The second Cabinet meeting that day started at 22:00 and lasted until midnight, with the first three-quarters of an hour devoted to a report on the military situation by the IDF Chief of Staff and the Defense Minister. Elazar did not conceal the heavy losses sustained during the first hours of the fighting, but "despite this, [he] was relatively optimistic.... Israeli army reserves would reach both fronts within 24 to 48 hours. Their arrival would tilt back the balance of forces and enable us to retrieve the initiative."[182] Dayan's own evaluation was much less sanguine:

> I felt heavy of heart, and I did not share the optimism of the Chief of Staff and GOC Southern Command. The Egyptians had already achieved powerful gains, and we had suffered a heavy blow. They had crossed the Canal, established bridges, and moved armor, infantry, and anti-tank weapons across them. Not only had we failed to prevent this, but we had caused the Egyptians relatively little damage.

The critical battlefield was the Canal Zone.... We would need a good deal of luck to end the next day's battles in our favor. After that, on the third and fourth days of the war, Monday and Tuesday (October 8 and 9) we should have all the planned armored force in the south, and we would be able to carry out tank warfare. It would not be simple, but the prospects for success were good.

It seemed to me, therefore, that in the south we should retire to a second line, fight the Egyptians within a belt of twelve miles from the Canal, and build up our strength. In the north, I expected that we would succeed in stopping the Syrians at the frontier.[183]

The Cabinet was also informed of steps taken to keep Jordan out of the war; as in 1967, a warning was sent together with assurances that Israel would not start a third front.[184]

The issue of a cease-fire arose at the outset of the war. As Gazit remarked: "We were in favor of a cease-fire right from the beginning. But the decision ... was not made on the first day. Even later, the request to the U.S. to arrange a cease-fire was not to arrange it on the ground but rather to restore the status-quo-ante."[185] Eban concurred—and shed more light on this controversial matter:

On the first day of the war there was some discussion of a cease-fire, in a talk I had with Kissinger about its timing. Kissinger said, 'We are working toward a cease-fire, the sooner the better.' In that sense there was talk about it. But the Arabs were taking their time; they wanted a demonstration [of support] in the General Assembly, on Monday. I think it became clear on Monday how serious the situation was. Then a cable arrived from Mrs. Meir stating that we should wait for a cease-fire until Wednesday [the 10th], because by that time the situation should have turned to our advantage.[186]

This accords with the mood of optimism about the outcome that prevailed among Israel's decision-makers on the evening of the 6th. Moreover, at the UN, Israel, like the Arab states, did not request an urgent meeting of the Security Council: it merely conveyed to the Council's President and the Secretary-General a charge of Egyptian and Syrian aggression. The first meeting of the Council did not take place until Monday, 8 October, in the evening. On that same date, there was also an inconclusive debate in the General Assembly at the initiative of the Arab states.[187]

Phase II: 7–14 October
Sunday, 7 October, was a day of desperate fighting on both fronts to stop the advance of Syrian and Egyptian armor and infantry. IDF reserve units were thrown into battle as they arrived, and losses in manpower and equipment were mounting sharply. By the end of the day, the Syrian advance had been temporarily contained. On the southern front, the Egyptians were still advancing methodically, the Second Army in the northern sector of the Suez Canal and the Third Army in the southern section.

Early in the morning, Elazar reported to the Cabinet the estimates of front commanders that the advances of the Arab armies had been contained. He also reaffirmed his evaluation that the Egyptians could be thrown back to the other side of the Canal within a short time. Dayan was absent, having left for a tour of the fronts. After the Cabinet meeting, Elazar left for a similar tour.

At 16:00 and 17:00, respectively, when Dayan and Elazar returned, they met with Meir, Allon, and Galili There was a sharp divergence in their assessment of the situation. The Defense Minister advocated a substantial retreat—evacuation of the Canal strongholds and the establishment of a new line "some distance from the Canal," to be held at all costs. The Chief of Staff, on the other hand, suggested a counterattack to begin the next morning. The meetings ended with a decision to empower the Chief of Staff to fly south, study the situation, and "decide about a counterattack" (Decision 7). But Dayan's evaluation was so shocking to the Prime Minister that she called a Cabinet meeting at 20:00; it approved the decision taken. The Prime Minister also decided to relieve former IDF Chief of Staff Bar-Lev from his duties as Minister of Industry and Commerce, and to send him to the northern front to assess the situation.[188]

The heavy IDF losses in equipment—40 planes downed by missiles during the first 24 hours and 200 tanks—led to urgent requests for planes and tanks from the United States. However, only on Tuesday, 9 October, did these needs seemingly become so imperative that Israel put immense pressure on US leadership, through several channels, for an immediate airlift of vital supplies. In reality, except for 155 mm artillery shells, Israel's pre-6 October resources were adequate for the conduct of the 1973 War.[189] Nevertheless, to continue the war with rapidly dwindling stockpiles would have placed an intolerable strain on the IDF and its leaders. Moreover, and no less important, the fact of the US airlift, in the face of an all-out resupply of Arab armies by the Soviet Union, was instrumental in restoring the diplomatic balance and laid the groundwork for an end to the war. At the same time, the negotiation process exposed Israel's dependence upon US support in a PC.

On the morning of 8 October, the southern part of Israel's Golan Heights Front Golan Heights front collapsed and there was a danger that Syrian armor would reach Israeli Jordan Valley settlements. Furthermore, in the early afternoon, Syrian armored units suddenly appeared next to a military camp in the center of the Golan Heights (Nafekh); again there was grave danger that these units might reach Israeli Huleh Valley settlements by crossing over the B'not Ya'akov bridge, only six miles away. These advances were contained (a) by intensified IDF air attacks on Syrian armor; and (b) by using newly arrived reserve units in desperate blocking operations. By the evening, Syrian attacks were checked and the danger of a breakthrough was averted, with heavy fighting still continuing.

IDF operations on the Egyptian front that day were a dismal failure. The counterattack ordered by Elazar on the morning of the 8th did not achieve its aim—namely, to throw the Egyptians back across the Canal, and Israel again suffered heavy losses. The Agranat Commission issued a harsh verdict on the battle of 8 October:

> Although in the *execution* of the operations of that day some of the effects of the initial surprise are still discernible, the IDF were by then in a position to determine the timing and plan of attack.... What caused—*inter alia*—the offensive to go wrong was an erosive deviation from the objective of the battle, as defined by the Chief of Staff, as well as a lack of control on the part of the Command, and its inability to read correctly the course of the battle.[190]

An early result was the Prime Minister's decision the following day to replace Gonen as OC Southern Command by Bar-Lev, as the Chief of Staff's Personal Representative (Decision 9).

The UN Security Council met for the first time during the 1973 crisis-war on the evening of 8 October (New York time). Although the US initiative was based upon an agreement reached in an exchange of messages between Nixon and Brezhnev the previous day, it soon became apparent that the cease-fire proposed by Ambassador Scali would not be accepted. Eban's very short speech was noncommittal, its main purpose being to reserve Israel's right of further communication. The Council adjourned without deciding anything, even the time for its next meeting, after less than two hours of discussion.[191]

The 9th of October became a turning point in US and Soviet attitudes to the 1973 War: "From the perspective of Washington," wrote William B. Quandt, "the war entered a new and acute phase on October 9." Until then, the CIA evaluation was that Israel would be victorious within a week—Kissinger had called the Arab attack military madness. At that day's two meetings of the US National Security Council's Action Group, Kissinger reported Israel's urgent needs for military equipment, received through Dinitz that morning. The Israeli Ambassador had also reported the heavy IDF losses, especially of planes on the Syrian front. Quandt continues: "The two recommendations that emerged from these sessions were presented to Nixon by Kissinger at noon. First, some arms must begin to reach Israel quickly, without violating the principle of maintaining a low American profile in the conflict. Second, a new formula for a cease-fire should be explored."[192]

The Soviet attitude toward the 1973 War had been relatively reserved thus far. While providing political support to the Arab cause publicly and in the UN, the style was restrained and mild.[193] Moscow revealed a readiness to cooperate in a political solution, stressing, as Brezhnev did on 8 October, "guaranteed security for all countries and peoples of the area." But after the early successes of the Arab armies, the Soviets decided to take a more active role. On 9 October, they began a massive supply of military aid by air and sea to Egypt and Syria, designed, as Galia Golan put it, "to supply the wherewithal for a total Arab victory now that the Arabs had proved their worth in battle."[194]

Dayan returned from the South with Elazar in the early morning of the 9th. His gloomy assessment of the situation on that front—overly pessimistic as events would show—received full expression in an off-the-record briefing for Israeli editors that evening.[195] Stating over and over again that Israel did not have the strength to push the Egyptians back across the Canal, he strongly urged that the IDF establish new defense lines near the Canal, dig in, and conserve its forces. The worst was over on the northern front, he argued, but the war in Sinai could be a drawn-out affair: "I don't think that the affair will be over in ten days," for the Egyptians "have unlimited equipment..., it's fantastic, it is terrible to fight against such a thing." Although unlikely, he did not rule out Egyptian gains in southern Sinai, at the Abu Rodeis oilfields, or even the occupation of Sharm-e-Sheikh.

Dayan had presented this morbid evaluation at the morning Cabinet meeting. The Cabinet approved a decision, taken by the Defense Minister the day before, to concentrate IDF efforts on defeating the Syrians while containing Egyptian advances in the South. It also approved the bombing of military targets in Damascus and elsewhere well inside Syria, partly in retaliation for the use of ground-to-ground intermediate-range Frog-type missiles against targets inside Israel, and partly to ease the pressure on the IDF front line (Decision 8).[196] The Cabinet also approved a request for large-scale military supplies from the United States. The only good news of the day was that Jordan and Lebanon had not—as yet—entered the War. Dayan believed that, if Syria could be beaten quickly, they would not do so.[197]

The initial US response to Israel's early requests for arms during the October-Yom-Kippur War was discouraging. The United States agreed to supply only two Phantom planes and electronic equipment—no tanks, artillery, or other weapons. On the 9th, Meir asked Allon to meet the US Ambassador to clarify Israel's position and needs. At the meeting with Keating and Veliotis, Allon indicated that Israel had succeeded in stopping the Syrians in the North and was about to turn her attention to the Egyptians. However, in order to be able to do this, Israel required very substantial, indeed massive, US military support. The word "airlift" was not mentioned, but it was clear from the context that military support of that magnitude would have to be transported in American planes.[198] As noted, the same request was submitted, through Dinitz, to Kissinger, and had reached the Secretary of State by 08:00 (New York time).

The Prime Minister, in consultation with the Defense Minister, decided on an even more drastic step—to fly to the United States for a secret meeting with President Nixon, in order to explain, face to face, Israel's needs in view of the strength of the Arab forces (Decision 10). She was dissuaded only when the President sent her a message of assurance on his decision to resupply Israel. Meir's immense relief is evident in her letter to Nixon on 10 October: "Early this morning I was told of the decision you made to assure us of the immediate flow of U.S. material.... I knew that in this hour of dire need by Israel, I could turn to you and count on your deep sympathy and understanding."[199]

The structure and style of Israel's decision-making unit during the early days of the 1973 early war period was accurately portrayed by Schiff:

Grandma Will Decide
    Golda Meir almost unwillingly becomes the generalissimo. It is strange to see a warrior of seven campaigns and brilliant past-Chief of Staff of

the IDF [Dayan] bringing clearly operational subjects to a Jewish grandmother for decision. Golda doesn't shirk responsibility. Of itself, neither appointed nor elected, a "War Cabinet" arises alongside Golda; but not her famous "Kitchen," which disbanded at the outbreak of war. Abba Eban is in the United States. Finance Minister Pinchas Sapir is also abroad to collect money. Agriculture Minister Haim Gvati is ill, while Justice Minister Shapiro—Golda's friend and veteran adviser—is not at home in war consultations. Yigal Allon and Yisrael Galili remain by her side and, with Golda, form the regular War Cabinet. Moshe Dayan oscillates between the Supreme Command, the war fronts, and the Cabinet Room. He reports to meetings where vital points are resolved but doesn't spend much time with the decision-makers. Dayan noticeably prefers battlefield tours to conference rooms and command bunkers.[200]

Moreover, Bar-Lev was acting as Commander in Chief on the southern front. In short, Cabinet sessions were, in most cases, attended by ten ministers: Meir, Allon, Galili, Hillel, Ya'acobi, and Zadok from the Labor Party, and Burg, Hazani, and Warhaftig from the NRP, with Dayan attending occasionally. Among them was an inner circle of four—Meir, Dayan, Allon, and Galili—who took decisions between Cabinet sessions.

On Wednesday, 10 October, the mood in Israel's decision-making group improved somewhat. Not only were there US assurances about the resupply of military equipment, but also the Syrians had been pushed back beyond the 5 October cease-fire lines, with most of the armored equipment of their assault divisions destroyed or damaged. There was also more confidence about the southern front, for an Egyptian brigade probing in the direction of Abu Rodeis had been decimated. As Herzog noted, after 9 October, "the Egyptians did not advance one yard during the remainder of the war."[201]

It was time to determine the next moves—to stop in place, continue the advance on the northern front in the direction of Damascus, or regroup and make a renewed effort in the South to push the Egyptians back. These options were considered at a series of meetings, beginning on the afternoon of 10 October and lasting for six hours: two at IDF GHQ, the first attended by Dayan, and a third, extending beyond midnight at the Prime Minister's Tel Aviv office, with Dayan, Allon, Galili, Elazar, Tal, Zeira, and Peled present. The last of these discussions was recalled by Dayan as follows:

> On the southern front, the Egyptians had captured a strip along the east bank of the Canal, and if we could not drive them out at once, we should

try to seize part of their territory west of the Canal. We would then have something with which to bargain, or at least even up the score. Bar-Lev of Southern Command said he agreed with the political considerations which called for the conquest of territory west of the waterline, but at the moment Southern Command was unable to do this. I replied that I thought it would be possible to transfer units from Northern to Southern Command, and Bar-Lev agreed that we should plan an action which would give us a hold west of the 1967 lines.

Various places were mentioned.... At all events, the guideline of our next step was clear to me. Either in the Golan Heights or in Sinai we had to go over to the attack. And indeed, after midnight, at a meeting with the Prime Minister, it was resolved that our forces would attack on the Syrian front with the objective of advancing as far as possible in the direction of Damascus. There was no intention of capturing Damascus or even of bombing it.[202]

The upshot of the discussions was a decision to press the advance on the northern front (to begin at 11:00, the next day, 11 October), in order to put Damascus within IDF artillery range, though not to occupy it, and thus exert powerful pressure for a cease-fire with Syria (Decision 11). As for the southern front, it was decided to prepare forces for an attack across the Canal, to occupy territory, and thus balance Egyptian gains on the Sinai side of the Canal.

Israel's decision-makers were now beginning to be aware again—as they were in the 1967 War—of the ticking of the political clock. Dayan recalled: "There was now 'powerful pressure,' according to our representative in Washington, for an unconditional cease-fire. The Soviet Union had approached President Nixon with this suggestion, and the United States, in its anxiety to avoid deterioration in its relations with Russia, was likely to respond positively. This would mean victory for the Arabs.... I felt we should do whatever we could to prevent an immediate cease-fire decision."[203]

The attack on the northern front began, as planned, at 11:00 on 11 October, but it proved to be heavy going. The Syrian defenses were not broken. In fact, their forces in the prewar defense perimeter around Damascus, which had not participated in the initial attack on 6 October, were now strengthened by the remnant of their assault troops, together with a brigade of tanks from Jordan, an Iraqi division, and troops from other Arab states.[204] During the next three days, the IDF advanced ten kilometers beyond the line of 5 October, putting its long-range artillery within range (25 miles) of the outskirts of Damascus. From 13 until 22 October, the day Syria accepted a cease-fire, heavy fighting continued, but the Syrian front line held. The IDF improved its position mainly on the southern part of the Golan Heights.[205] A stronghold on Mount Hermon was recaptured by Israeli forces during the last day of the War.

Israel's actions in the North were calculated mostly in terms of Soviet behavior. On 9 October, Moscow began a massive resupply of the Arab armies, first and foremost that of Syria. This was accompanied by increasingly threatening verbiage as Israeli troops advanced into Syria.[206] In the South, fighting continued, with limited Egyptian attacks repulsed by Israeli forces, causing heavy losses in men and equipment to the Egyptians.

The idea of an IDF counterattack across the Canal had been discussed, heatedly, from the beginning of the 1973 War. With the enemy contained, the commanders on the southern front, headed by Bar-Lev, considered the various alternatives on the evening of the 11th. Bar-Lev decided in favor of a crossing between the territories held by the Second and Third Egyptian Armies, at Deservoir—but only after Egypt had transferred a major part of its forces still on the west side, committed them to battle, and saw them defeated.

These recommendations were put the next day before the GHQ, with Dayan, Elazar, and Bar-Lev present. Because of Dayan's indecision, the issue was brought before the "Kitchen Cabinet." Present were Meir, Dayan, Allon, Galili, Elazar, Bar-Lev, and several other generals. While the discussion was going on, news arrived that Egyptian armored forces on the west bank had begun to cross the Canal. On Bar-Lev's suggestion, the Israeli decision on the IDF crossing was postponed until after the breaking of the expected Egyptian attack (Decision 12). The high level of stress among the decision-makers is evident in the accounts of these events.[207]

On the Prime Minister's instructions, Eban met with Kissinger in Washington on the evening of Friday, 12 October; also present were Dinitz and Shalev. Eban again demanded the speeding up of US arms deliveries, with Kissinger replying that everything was being done to get the airlift into motion. When Eban's report of his meeting reached Meir, indicating further delay, she dispatched a personal note to President Nixon, asking for the immediate, direct delivery of military supplies. Nixon summoned the National Security Council on the 13th and, after discussion, ordered the use of American military cargo planes immediately. The former President recalled the incident, so crucial for Israel, as follows:

> The way that we worked was that he [Kissinger] would come in with options; and the option that he presented was that the Defense Department thought we should send three of these big cargo planes; and then, of course, he gave his own opinions as to their reasons and reasons which he thought I ought to have before me; that politically it would be perhaps dangerous for us to send a greater number and that it would destroy the chances for negotiation in the future if our profile was too high.... And I said: "Look, Henry, we're going to get just as much blame for sending three if we send thirty, or a hundred, or whatever we've got, so send everything that flies. The main thing is – make it work."[208]

It was the cumulative stress from two sources—delay of the US airlift, while the Arab armies were being lavishly resupplied, and continued fighting on both fronts, with reinforcements pouring in from Saudi Arabia, Iraq, and Jordan that led Meir to agree on 12 October to a renewed Soviet proposal for a cease-fire in place (Decision 13).[209] The cable was transmitted by Eban and Dinitz directly in Washington that day. Eban recalled the episode:

> I went to Washington on the 12th to try to get a cease-fire in place, immediately. Things were not going too well. We had had some successes in the North, but in an exhausting way. In the South we were in the mountains.... Then Kissinger worked out a scenario with the Soviets, but they wanted an Israeli retreat to June 1967. The British were involved. But by October 14, and according to my instructions, I refused it—to Kissinger's surprise.[210]

Quandt's account of this Israeli decision, as viewed from Washington, is revealing:

> Prime Minister Meir, under pressure from the United States to accept a cease-fire in place, apparently appalled by the mounting casualties, and realizing that American arms might not be readily forthcoming if she refused, finally agreed to accept a cease-fire in place. Her acceptance was accompanied by an urgent personal appeal to President Nixon to order an immediate resupply of arms to Israel. She went so far as to raise the specter of an Israeli military defeat. On October 12, late in the evening, Ambassador Dinitz met with Kissinger at the White House. He conveyed Israel's acceptance of the principle of a cease-fire-in-place and Golda Meir's urgent request for arms.[211]

According to I. Disentshik of *Ma'ariv*, the request for a cease-fire, to be submitted by the British, came from Meir but on condition that the British were not told the source of the request.[212]

Kissinger tried to arrange a cease-fire through the British UN Delegation, but he could not get the necessary agreement. His scenario called for a British proposal without prior consultation with Sadat. But the British did consult with Sadat. Egypt's President told the British Ambassador at a dawn meeting on the 13th that a cease-fire was unacceptable.[213] The issue never came before Israel's Cabinet or even the "Kitchen Cabinet." "In fact," noted Matti Golan, "till this very day her [Meir's] desperate telegram has not been entered into the official records of the government."[214]

Superpower involvement had become more pronounced. And with the primary Arab states' military danger contained, it played an increasing role in Israel's decision-making process. On the one hand, Israel was finally notified on Saturday, 13 October, that the United States would deliver military supplies, even refueling fighter planes—Phantoms and Skyhawks—in the air. The first huge transport planes, Galaxy C5s and C141s, landed at Lod the next day.[215] On the other hand, Soviet pressure became more intense. Israel's government was notified that Ambassador Dobrynin had informed Kissinger of the alert of two Soviet airborne divisions—and of Kissinger's reply that the United States would not want the Soviet Union to do anything irresponsible.[216]

There were other noteworthy military movements. On the previous day, during an Israeli naval attack on the Syrian port of Latakia, a Russian freighter, the Ilya Michnikov, had been sunk. In its wake, the Soviet navy had concentrated missile boats to protect the port, and units of the US Sixth Fleet were ordered close to Israel's coastline.[217] As in 1967, movements of the Sixth Fleet were used to signal US political decisions. And as in 1970, Israel shied away from giving the Soviets grounds for direct intervention; the IDF ceased the attacks on Latakia.

Another recurrent legacy of the past became a focus of decision. Allon had, for years, been advocating that Israel encourage the creation of an independent Druze state in the southern region of Syria, including parts of the Golan Heights. After the June-Six-Day War, he had stated publicly that Israel had erred in not reaching Mount Druze, the center of the Syrian Druze minority. At a Cabinet meeting of 13 October, he urged a push toward Mount Druze, but the idea was dropped because of Dayan's sharp opposition.[218]

The expected Egyptian attack on the east bank of the Canal began at 06:00 on 14 October and lasted until 15:00, with close to 1000 tanks, hundreds of artillery pieces, and scores of planes taking part. It was a major IDF victory, with 260 Egyptian tanks destroyed or damaged, against the loss of only a few Israeli tanks. Bar-Lev phoned the news to Meir in the evening and strongly urged her to approve the crossing of the Canal, planned for the next day. The Prime Minister brought it before the Cabinet, then in session. Elazar explained the proposal, and it was passed unanimously (Decision 14).[219]

Phase III: 15–23 October
The IDF crossing of the Canal was to begin at 19:00 on the 15th. In fact, the first IDF units crossed by rubber boats and floats at 01:30 on the 16th, and it took another day-and-a-half of heavy fighting to enlarge the beachhead and complete a pontoon bridge. At one stage, when the fighting around the bridgehead became very heavy, Dayan suggested withdrawal; but he accepted Bar-Lev's decision to continue as planned, subject to a bridge being completed quickly.[220]

Meir had called a Cabinet meeting for 19:00 on the 15th. Because of the delays in IDF crossing of the Canal, ministers stayed all night, awaiting information from the front. News of the Canal crossing was announced by the Prime Minister during the first *Knesset* session since the outbreak of the October-Yom-Kippur War, on the afternoon of 16 October. The main thrust of her speech was the justification of Israel's policy since 1967, the "evil role" of the Soviet Union, and Israel's war aims. On the subject of feelers for a cease-fire, she stated, disingenuously: "Until now there has not been offered to the Government of Israel any suggestion from any source for a cease-fire. This being the case, we do not have to discuss the subject."[221] By contrast, Sadat publicly stated for the first time on the 16th that Egypt would agree to a cease-fire—if Israel would return to the 4 June 1967 borders. He also disclosed, ominously, that Egypt possessed surface-to-surface missiles "aimed at Israel's largest cities."

Premier Kosygin's unexpected and unannounced arrival in Cairo the same day heralded a sharp escalation in superpower involvement in the war. While both superpowers, the United States and the USSR, mainly with the help of monitoring devices and satellites, were generally well-informed of what took place on the Arab–Israel battlefield, there was no photographic coverage of battlefield events available on the 16th. Such photos reached Kosygin on the 18th, and he immediately showed them to Sadat. Egypt's President did not mention the IDF crossing to the Soviet Premier on the 16th, though he was aware of it; and on the 17th they did not meet.[222] Yet Kosygin's efforts to persuade Sadat to accept a cease-fire failed.

The Israeli Defense Minister remained in the South to observe IDF advance and blocking actions, while the Chief of Staff shuttled back and forth between the fronts, GHQ, and Cabinet meetings in Tel Aviv. Dayan phoned the Prime Minister every evening to report on the progress. On the evening of 17 October, after another day of heavy fighting, Israel's armored brigades crossed to the west side of the Canal on a pontoon bridge.

This change in the balance of military power was immediately reflected in diplomatic activity. Kosygin, using the photographic evidence of the seriousness of Israel's penetration, persuaded Sadat on the 18th to accept a cease-fire.[223] The same day, after a delegation of Arab Foreign Ministers from nonbelligerent states had met with Nixon and Kissinger to explore the US position on a cease-fire, the Organization of Arab Petroleum Exporting Countries (OAPEC) declared an oil embargo.

Use of the oil weapon had no effect on the outcome of the war; this was decided on the battlefield and in Washington and Moscow. The main effect of the oil embargo was a sharp increase in the price of oil, causing economic hardship all over the world. However, the panic caused in Europe and Japan contributed substantively to the growing pressure on Israel after the 1973 War, causing its isolation in many diplomatic forums, including the UN.

Parallel to Kosygin's role in Cairo on the 18th, USSR Ambassador Dobrynin called upon Kissinger and demanded a cease-fire, linked to a gradual Israeli withdrawal from all occupied territories. Kissinger accepted the call for a cease-fire but not withdrawal.[224] These proposals were communicated by General Scowcroft to Israel Ambassador Dinitz, who immediately informed Meir in Tel Aviv and Eban in New York. Eban cabled Meir that Israel ought to accept the call for a cease-fire in principle, even a reference to Resolution 242, on condition of an exchange of prisoners. In any case, she should suggest to Kissinger that Israel needed to gain time to complete its military activities. Eban repeated these suggestions to Kissinger in a telephone conversation two hours prior to his (Eban's) departure for Israel on the 18th. He was not informed of Kissinger's intended trip to Moscow.[225]

These inputs reached Israel on the morning of 19 October. Dayan stated that Ambassador Dinitz "informed us of feverish negotiations between the Americans and the Russians to sponsor an agreed cease-fire resolution by the Security Council, and it was clear that only a few days remained before the end of the war."[226] This was reinforced later in the day by a message from Nixon to Meir, explaining that a cease-fire also served US interests. He reminded her that the United States had supplied Israel's needs in aircraft and other vital equipment and would continue to do so; moreover, he was submitting to Congress a request for 2.2 billion dollars for emergency defense assistance to Israel.[227]

At a meeting between the Prime Minister and the Defense Minister, it was decided to press forward on the west bank of the Canal but not to press too far inland toward Cairo (Decision 15). On the northern front, an all-out effort would be made to recapture former IDF positions on Mount Hermon before a cease-fire came into effect.

The dramatic events of 19 October, involving the two superpowers, had no immediate effect on Israel's decision-makers; they were not aware of them. Summarized briefly, the "hotline" between Moscow and Washington was activated that morning. Brezhnev notified Nixon that the Soviet government was about to take a decision from which there would be no retreat, and he urged that Kissinger come to Moscow immediately. The President agreed, perhaps in part because, by that time, the Americans knew of a considerable Soviet military buildup, including the introduction into Egypt of MiG-25 squadrons flown by Soviet pilots.[228]

Bernard and Marvin Kalb noted that, prior to his departure to Moscow, Kissinger

> talked at length with Dinitz about a cease-fire scenario. In rough terms, Kissinger knew what the Russians were proposing, and what the Egyptians were willing to accept, however reluctantly: a cease-fire-in-place, linked to an Israeli withdrawal to the 1967 line. The Israeli Ambassador rejected this proposal as unrealistic. He recommended instead a cease-fire linked to direct negotiations between the two sides that could lead to withdrawal and peace. Kissinger set his sights on achieving a solution that accented direct negotiations. If Brezhnev really needed American cooperation to rescue his Arab clients and to preserve detente and its dividends, then the Russians might be made to pay a high price.[229]

Dinitz informed Jerusalem of his talk with Kissinger, adding that the Secretary of State intended to provide sufficient time for Israel to complete her military victory.[230]

Kissinger arrived in Moscow on the evening of 20 October. The next day an agreement was hammered out, according to which US and USSR representatives would submit a draft resolution to the UN Security Council calling for an immediate cease-fire in site, linked to Resolution 242. Most of the day's negotiations were taken up by the Soviet insistence on linking the cease-fire to a call for total Israeli withdrawal to the 4 June 1967 borders. However, because of the rapidly worsening plight of the Arab armies, the Russians suddenly dropped that demand and accepted Kissinger's proposals. The basic framework of a peace conference under joint superpower auspices was also agreed upon. And the Soviet Union promised to undertake efforts to expedite an exchange of prisoners of war.[231] As a result, the UN Security Council passed Resolution 338 on 22 October 1973:

The Security Council

1. Calls upon all parties to the present fighting to cease all firing and terminate all military activity immediately, no later than 12 hours after the moment of the adoption of this decision, in the positions they now occupy;
2. Calls upon the parties concerned to start immediately after the cease-fire the implementation of Security Council Resolution 242 (1967) in all of its parts;
3. Decides that, immediately and concurrently with the cease-fire, negotiations start between the parties concerned under appropriate auspices aimed at establishing a just and durable peace in the Middle East.

Israel was kept informed, from time to time, of the progress of the Moscow talks on the 20th; but then, because of a "technical hitch" in transferring news from Moscow, it received no further reports.[232] By that time, it had become sufficiently clear to the Israeli government that they had only a day or two until a cease-fire agreement was imposed; Southern Command was so informed by Elazar.[233] Finally, Israel was notified of the US–Soviet agreement on a cease-fire when General Haig, Kissinger's deputy, called on Dinitz on the 21st and presented him with the text. It was not open to argument. Dinitz immediately cabled it to Tel Aviv, as well as phoning the Prime Minister to convey its content. The news reached Israel around 17:00.

Upon receipt of the messages, Meir called a Cabinet meeting, which began at 22:00. While the Cabinet was still in session, at 01:00 on 22 October, a message arrived from Nixon, in which he urged the Israeli government to accept the text of the cease-fire agreement to be submitted the next day. The Cabinet decided unanimously to accept the cease-fire (Decision 16).[234] The next day, Meir described the reasons for its acceptance, in a speech to the *Knesset*:

> In connection to paragraph 2 of the proposed decision [the reference in Resolution 338 to Resolution 242], the Government instructed its Representative at the UN to include in his speech in the Security Council, a passage to clarify that our agreement to this paragraph is given subject to its meaning as specified by Israel when it decided, in August 1970, to respond to the U. S. initiative for a cease-fire. Israel's agreement to a cease-fire with Egypt is subject to Egypt's agreement and not subject to Syria's agreement to a cease-fire with her, and vice versa. We saw fit to respond to the U. S. initiative and that of U.S. President Nixon, because:
>
> a. Israel, by her very nature, does not want war
> b. The proposal for a cease-fire has come when our situation on both fronts is firm; when our achievements are of great value and justify an agreement to a cease-fire, despite the enemy's achievement on the east bank of the Canal.
> c. We responded to the U.S. call and that of its President in appreciation and esteem of the positive policy of the U.S. in the Middle East at this time.[235]

Meir notified the US government of Israel's acceptance at 03:00 on 22 October and then informed the *Knesset* Foreign Affairs and Security Committee of the Cabinet's decision, in terms of a *fait accompli*.

At Israel's request, Kissinger paused in Tel Aviv, en route from Moscow to Washington, to clarify the agreement reached with the Soviet Union; Kosygin flew to Cairo for the same purpose. During his four-hour visit on 22 October, Kissinger met first with Meir alone and then with Meir, Eban, Dayan, Allon, and Galili and reported on his Moscow talks. Dayan's memoir version is as follows:

> As to a cease-fire agreement, we made the categorical demand that there be an exchange of prisoners. We considered this a prime condition: 'No prisoner exchange, no cease-fire.' Kissinger was unwilling to agree to such an extreme formula. He promised to act and to ask the Russians to help. He cited promises which he had received from Moscow but he avoided giving us an iron-clad undertaking that there would be a prisoner exchange. His reassurances were bound by such expressions as 'We'll work for it.' 'We'll try.' 'We'll make a supreme effort.' As for getting exit permits for the Jews of Syria, he was even less forthcoming

The impression created was that we were treading a tightrope which soared above a canyon of monstrous danger but which stretched toward a gleam of light in the distance. We would reach that light only if we learned to tread along the thin cord with wisdom.

Furthermore, the United States supported the cease-fire because a continuation of the war would lead to the radicalization of the Arab world, to the fall of moderate governments, and their replacement by extremist regimes.[236]

The results of the discussion with Kissinger were brought before a Cabinet meeting that evening. The Cabinet decided that "if the Egyptians failed to live up to the cease-fire, the Israel Defense Forces will 'repel the enemy at the gate'" (Decision 17).

Israel announced at 18:05 her acceptance of a cease-fire which was to go into effect on 22 October at 18:52. Radio Cairo had announced Egypt's acceptance at 14:30 the same day. Syria announced at 06:15 on 23 October her acceptance in principle and on condition that Israel withdraw to her pre-4 June 1967 borders.

Fighting continued on the Sinai front, however, with conflicting views on responsibility. IDF forces in the rear of the Third Army received orders and ceased fire at 19:00, while those on the outskirts of Ismailia continued for another four hours in order to extricate their dead and wounded. But when the Egyptians continued to send commando and infantry teams during the night to destroy Israeli tank concentrations, in order to open an escape route for the Third Army, fighting was resumed at dawn with the Prime Minister's approval (Decision 18). There are strong indications that Israel's military leaders were hoping for such an eventuality in order to complete the encirclement of the Third Army.[237] This was attained by midnight of 23 October. And the IDF gained control of part of the town of Suez, as well as the port of Adabiyah, thus sealing the Third Army off from all supplies.

Phase IV: 23–26 October
Israel came under mounting US pressure to stop the fighting, including a phone call from Kissinger to Meir on the evening of the 23rd; the Secretary of State emphasized his commitment toward the Soviet Union on a cease-fire.[238] At UN headquarters, the Security Council passed another cease-fire resolution (339) on 23 October, this time calling for the immediate dispatch of UN observers to supervise it:

The Security Council,
Referring to its Resolution 338 (1973) of 22 October 1973,

1. Confirms its decision of an immediate cessation of all kinds of firing and of all military action, and urges that the forces of two sides be returned to the positions they occupied at the moment the cease-fire became effective;
2. Requests the Secretary General to take measures for immediate dispatch of United Nations observers to supervise the observance of the cease-fire between the forces of Israel and the Arab Republic of Egypt, using for this purpose the personnel of the United Nations now in the Middle East and first of all the personnel now in Cairo.[239]

Sadat, fearing that IDF advances since the first cease-fire call would erase all his gains in the field, now called upon the Soviet and US leaders to send troops to ensure the cease-fire.[240] His letter to Nixon reached Washington at 15:00, 24 October (21:00 Israel time). Six hours later, a letter reached the President from Brezhnev; it warned that if Israel would not observe the cease-fire and the United States refused to cooperate in enforcing it, "we should be faced with the necessity urgently to consider the question of taking appropriate steps unilaterally. Israel cannot be allowed to get away with the violations."[241]

Nixon recalled this grave incident as follows:

> The [Brezhnev] note had an ominous sound to it because he, in effect, said that the United States and the Soviet Union should move in as the Egyptians had requested. He knew we had rejected that and he said '... if you cannot restrain the Israelis ....' It's my recollection he said: 'It will be necessary for us to move unilaterally ... into the situation.' Now that to me was a code word. For the Soviet Union to move any kind of forces into the Mid-East would, first, tip the balance so that Israel would have been down the tube. But even more important, it would have established the precedent where the Soviets had a presence in the Mid-East.... And so it ran the risk of a great power confrontation.... I just said, in my reply: we would not agree to go in. Second, we would be glad, of course, to participate in a UN group with a number of advisers. And third, we took a very dim view—I used stronger words than that—a very dim view of any unilateral action on their part of moving in.[242]

The United States also signaled Moscow by placing most of its armed forces on "Defensive Condition 3," including the Strategic Air Command with its nuclear capability. This became known almost immediately. And CIA reports reached Washington that, in the early hours of 25 October, a Soviet ship suspected of carrying one or several nuclear warheads had docked in Alexandria.[243]

By the afternoon of the 25th the crisis of superpower confrontation began to abate when it became known that the USSR had accepted the American formula (at 15:00) for the setting up of a UNEF "composed of personnel drawn from state members of the United Nations except permanent members of the Security Council."[244]

Parallel to these UN efforts, US pressure was put on Israel to accept the second cease-fire call, without the surrender of Egypt's Third Army and, in fact, with a flow of supplies to the beleaguered force. In Israel, Keating and Veliotis went to see Meir and Allon to communicate the urgency of the situation. In Washington, Kissinger kept in constant touch with Dinitz and, by phone, with the Israeli Foreign and Defense Ministers. There was even, reportedly, a phone conversation between Nixon and Meir.[245] The Americans argued that it was in the highest US and Israeli interests to accept the cease-fire. There were too many unknown factors: Soviet intervention, the effect on détente, and future peace talks. In terms of the future, it would be better to keep the Third Army alive. There was no talk of stopping the airlift.

The Israel decision process leading to its Decisions 19 and 20 was recalled by Dayan as follows:

> We were first told by the Americans that they had information that we were attacking the Third Army. This, they said, was a breach of the cease-fire agreement, and we had apparently failed to understand the grave steps the United States was likely to take against us. Half an hour later, following a strong denial from Jerusalem, our Washington embassy received a correction: The Americans had discovered in the meantime that indeed it was not we but the Egyptians who were continuing hostilities! However, they added, this information was not 'relevant.' The crux of the problem was the situation itself—the isolation of the Third Army, with all the complications that arose therefrom. The Americans could not allow this Egyptian army to be destroyed, or left hungry, or weakened by thirst, or taken prisoner. If the Third Army could not receive supplies in any other way, the Soviet Union would send them, and such a move, they said, would be tantamount to Soviet military intervention. It would be a blow to American prestige. No matter how, the Third Army had to be saved from its plight.... Finally, the Americans presented their demand more or less in the form of an ultima-

tum. It had crystallized into the requirement that we grant a one-time permit allowing an Egyptian supply convoy of non-military equipment, food, and water to pass through our lines to the Third Army. If we did not agree to this proposal, we would find ourselves in a crisis situation with the United States. Israel gave approval for one hundred supply trucks to be sent from Cairo.[246]

At the Cabinet meeting, which began late at night on 25 October and lasted until 04:00 on the 26th, Meir, as noted, gave US pressure as the reason for Israel's acceptance of the cease-fire call. Eban's recollection of the deliberations and the reasons for acceptance was as follows:

> Yes, consideration was given to the possibility that American supplies would be stopped, though this was not said in the [Nixon] letter. It was a matter of casualties if the war goes on, the Soviet threat, and a break with the U.S. The continuation of good relations with the U.S. was more important than a greater military victory. If we had two or three more weeks ... but these were just not available. If it would have been a matter of two or three days, Nixon might have gone along with it, because he wanted an American success vs. a Soviet one.
>
> The threat of Soviet intervention was real and visible. This time, unlike in 1967, there was a concentration of troops, and they were now operating in UN interests, come as it were, to carry out the world's will—there has to be an end to the war. The feeling was that there could very well be a Soviet military intervention in the Middle East, unless the U.S. put up a very strong show. All that night [the 25th] we sat up, until 04:00 o'clock, while the Security Council was waiting. In the Cabinet there was a consensus that the Soviets might intervene unless the Cabinet responded, it was that persuasive. There was physical evidence of Soviet strength.
>
> The Cabinet meeting of the 25th lasted until 04:00 in the morning. The entire meeting was devoted to the question, do we accept the second cease-fire or do we not? The decision was unanimous. The decisive factor was the Soviet threat, and the preparedness of the U.S. for a confrontation. This was different from 1956 and 1967 because the evidence was there. The Soviets then solved it by retiring from the idea of Soviet intervention and accepting this rather innocuous form [Resolution 340].[247]

The October-Yom-Kippur War ended on 26 October. For Egypt, it was a prestige victory, along with a little-noted military defeat. As against the two Egyptian footholds on the eastern side of the Canal, Israel held a substantial enclave on the western side; and on the northern, Syria, front, the IDF had not only expelled all enemy soldiers from positions gained during the first days of surprise, but also advanced to within artillery range of Syria's capital.

The cost to both sides, for a short war, was high. In absolute terms, the Arab armies suffered more casualties than Israel (table 10.5).[248] Material losses were made up so quickly by the superpowers that, within several weeks, Israel and Syria were better equipped than before the war. But in relative terms, Israel's losses in manpower, dead and wounded, were a heavy blow to a small nation. The 1973 War followed the pattern of its predecessors. Israel's war aims were victory on the battlefield, destroying as much as possible of her opponents' military capability. The Arab war aims were victory if possible, but, if not, to use the fighting as an extension of diplomacy to break a political stalemate.

As long as the Arab side had the upper hand, there was no pressure from the international system, specifically from the superpowers. But the moment Israel began to triumph on the battlefield, there was intense pressure from the superpowers, directly and through the UN, for a cease-fire, coupled with demands for Israel's retreat to prewar positions. The Soviet Union used military threats to achieve its aims; the United States used pressure.

Table 10.5 Estimated Arab military losses

	Egypt	*Syria*
Planes		
Fighters	222	117
Bombers	1	0
Helicopters	42	13
Tanks	1000	1113[a]
Armored personnel carriers	450	400
Artillery units	300	250
SAM Batteries	44	3
Missile boats	6	3
Torpedo boats	4	1

[a]Includes Iraqi, Saudi Arabian, and Jordanian equipment

See S. Gazit, "Arab Forces Two Years after the Yom Kippur War," 189–195. Figures for Israel are not known precisely. Chief of Staff David Elazar has stated that the ratio of losses in tanks was 4:1 in Israel's favor; that of aircraft, 5:1 (Elazar, "The Yom Kippur War: Military Lessons," 245–250). This would mean approximately the loss of over 500 tanks and about 80 planes. Other sources put the number of Israeli aircraft lost at between 94 and 112; see Avnery, *Red Sky*, 259–270

There were two differences in the military domain between the June-Six-Day War and the October-Yom-Kippur War: (a) because the latter lasted three weeks instead of six days, both sides had to be resupplied by their superpower patron during the war; and (b) the Soviet military threat was much more credible in the October-Yom-Kippur War because of the buildup of an impressive Soviet military presence at or near the scene of fighting: a vast armada in the Mediterranean, including landing craft with tanks and troops; squadrons of MiG 25s in Egypt, as well as brigades armed with ground-to-ground missiles; alerted airborne divisions near airfields around the Mediterranean; and—possibly—nuclear warheads for missiles in Alexandria. As in the 1967 War, so in the 1973 War, the military moves of both superpowers were carefully calculated to signal political aims and interests to the other side. And in both cases, at the height of the war, there was a direct confrontation between them, including, in 1973, the resort to a nuclear alert.

NOTES

1. Michael Brecher, interview with Ya'acov Herzog, 10 August 1968.
2. The first two of these events occurred on the 16th, but they were unknown to Israel's decision-makers until the morning of the 17th. The significance of the second and third events was affirmed by General Yariv in a conversation with Brecher on 27 July 1977. Thus the beginning of the 1967 prewar crisis period is designated as 17 May.
3. Meir Amit, interview by Benjamin Geist, 13 July 1973.
4. Levi Eshkol, Appointments Book (AB) as Prime Minister for 14 May to 10 June 1967; Michael Bar-Zohar, *Embassies in Crisis: Diplomats and Demagogues Behind the Six Day War* (Englewood Cliffs, NJ: Prentice-Hall, 1970), 39.
5. U Thant noted in his 26 June 1967 report that Hammarskjold took the following position, in reply to a question on 26 February 1957 on the withdrawal of the Force: "An indicated procedure would be for the Secretary-General to inform the Advisory Committee on the UNEF, which would determine whether the matter should be brought to the attention of the Assembly" (Theodore Draper, *Israel and World Politics: Roots of the Third Arab–Israel War* [New York: Viking Press, 1968], 190). The

Israeli Cabinet was also informed of a relevant passage in Hammarskjold's 5 August 1957 private memorandum: "Egypt would declare to the United Nations that it would exert all its sovereign rights with regard to the troops on the basis of a good faith interpretation of the tasks of the Force. The United Nations should make a reciprocal commitment to maintain the Force as long as the task was not completed. If such a dual statement was introduced in an agreement between the parties, it would be obvious that the procedure in case of a request from Egypt for the withdrawal of UNEF would be as follows: The matter would at once be brought before the General Assembly. If the General Assembly found that the task was completed, everything would be all right. If they found that the task was not completed and Egypt, all the same, maintained its stand and enforced the withdrawal, Egypt would break the agreement with the United Nations" (Rosalyn Higgins, *United Nations Peacekeeping, 1946–1967: Documents and Commentary*, vol. 1, *The Middle East* [London: Oxford University Press, 1969], 363–366).
6. Foreign Ministry sources.
7. Abba Eban, *An Autobiography* (Jerusalem and Tel Aviv: Steimatsky's Agency, 1977), 324; also cited in Robert St. John, *Eban* (Garden City, NY: Doubleday, 1972), 413.
8. US Ambassador Goldberg suggested it to U Thant the next day. The forthcoming visit—to Cairo only—was announced on Saturday 20 May.
9. In a message in U Thant's report on the withdrawal of the UNEF, 26 June 1967 (*UN Monthly Chronicle* 4, no.7 [July 1967]: 140), addressed to the UN Secretary-General, the Foreign Minister of Egypt stated: "The Government of the United Arab Republic has the honor to inform Your Excellency that it has decided to terminate the presence of the United Nations Emergency Force from the territory of the United Arab Republic and Gaza Strip. Therefore I request that the necessary steps be taken for the withdrawal of the Force as soon as possible." Gideon Rafael's description of this meeting throws considerable light on Bunche's and U Thant's perceptions, on which they had based their fateful decision the day before. As he recalled in an interview in *Yediot Aharonot* (4 June 1971): "I asked Ralph Bunche, what happened to the deceased Hammarskjold's commitment of 1957 that no

change will be made in the deployment of UNEF without a previous agreement of the General Assembly. Bunche answered that the Secretary-General had recently received an explanation from his legal adviser that the presence of UNEF is dependent only on the agreement of the host government. Bunche did not share our evaluations. He explained that through this announcement U Thant intends to bare the fact that Nasser's message is a bluff. He is convinced that faced with the situation that would be created by the departure of the Force Nasser will reconsider and back down." For another version, see Ralph Bunche, Letter to the Editor, *New York Times*, June 11, 1967.
10. Lyndon B. Johnson, *The Vantage Point: Perspectives of the Presidency, 1963–1969* (New York: Holt, Rinehart and Winston, 1971), 290.
11. Moshe A. Gilboa, *Shesh Shanin, Shisha Yamim* [*Six Years, Six Days: Origins and History of the Six Day War*] (Tel Aviv: Am Oved, 1969), 115.
12. Bar-Zohar, *Embassies in Crisis*, 46.
13. Ibid., 44–45; Gilboa, *Six Years, Six Days*, 145 (in part).
14. Rafael, interview, *Yediot Aharonot*, 4 June 1971; Gideon Rafael, "May 1967—A Personal Report," *Ma'ariv*, 18 and 21 April 1972; and Charles W. Yost, "The Arab–Israel War: How It Began," *Foreign Affairs*, 46, no. 2 (January 1968): 313.
15. "The first time I heard about the demand for the withdrawal of UNEF," recalled Israel's Ambassador to Canada during the 1967 Crisis, "was when Paul Martin [Canada's External Affairs Minister] called me and told me that the Force was in danger, that its withdrawal would mean war, and that events are developing so fast that if something is to be done, it has to be done within hours. 'I propose, therefore,' said Martin, 'that you accept UNEF on your side of the border, as we originally proposed. I know that Israel is against it, and all the reasons for it, but this is no time for diplomatic niceties. You can call it a temporary step, or anything you wish, but the main thing is to save the Force.' I cabled this home and asked for instructions; I never received any" (Gershon Avner, interview by Benjamin Geist, 25 February 1973).
16. Canada's position was clearly stated in Parliament that day and a few days later: "It is now the prerogative of the UN rather than of the UAR Government to determine when the UN Force has

completed its task of restoring peace and when it should be withdrawn" (Canada, Parliament, House of Commons, *Debates*, 27th Parliament, 2nd session, vol. 1, 8 May–5 June 1967, 342, 416).
17. Michael Bar-Zohar, *The Longest Month* (Tel Aviv: Levin-Epstein, 1968), 59.
18. Eshkol's AB; Levi Eshkol, "Eshkol's Broadcast to the Nation, 28 May 1967," television broadcast, BBC, 30 May 1967; Israel Foreign Ministry sources; Draper, *Israel and World Politics*, 75; Bar-Zohar, *Embassies in Crisis*, 47. The transfer of Egyptian troops from Yemen to Sinai was, for Israel's decision-makers, a very significant indicator of Nasser's intentions: one of the pillars of the forecast that Nasser would not be ready to wage war against Israel for years to come was that a large part of his army—60,000 to 70,000 troops—was bogged down in Yemen. But there is some doubt whether, in this field of military intelligence, Israel's leaders had wholly accurate information. Nasser stated, in an interview in *Newsweek*, 10 February 1969: "In fact, three of our best divisions were in Yemen at the time, and had we been preparing for an attack, it would have been logical to bring them home first." Mohamed Heikal, in part of a series on the June-Six-Day War, published in *Ma'ariv*, 9 November 1973, stated that sizable units, with armor, were returned from Yemen only toward the end of the crisis period, and it seems to be the correct version. In *The Third Arab–Israel War*, O'Ballance wrote that "on June 4 two infantry brigades and some logistic units, and about 10,000 soldiers, were in transit back to Egypt" (96).
19. Israel Foreign Ministry sources. Also discussed in Eban, *An Autobiography*, 325.
20. Eban, *An Autobiography*, 327; Israel, Ministry of Foreign Affairs, Cables and Communications, Jerusalem, 1967.
21. The vigorous language of these Eban communiqués explains the virtual panic caused in Washington, London, Paris, and other capitals on 23 May by Nasser's announcement of the closure of the Straits. The Western powers expected Israel to go to war within hours. When it did not, and Eban's trip was announced, these powers could only conclude that Israel was hesitant; her credibility suffered as a consequence.
22. Eban, *An Autobiography*, 327.

23. 1950: Tripartite Declaration; 1957: declarations in March at the UN; 1960: at de Gaulle's meeting with Ben-Gurion, where he stated that "if Israel is threatened, we shall not let you be destroyed." In 1964, de Gaulle repeated the same assurances to Eshkol, during the latter's visit to Paris.
24. The following reconstruction is based upon: Israel Foreign Ministry sources; Shlomo Nakdimon, *Likrat Sha'at Haefes* [*Toward the Zero Hour: The Drama that Preceded the Six Day War*] (Tel Aviv: Ramdor, 1968), 28; Zeev Schiff, "The Three Weeks that Preceded the War," *Ha'aretz*, 4 October 1967; and Gilboa, *Six Years, Six Days*, 124.
25. Winston Burdett noted in *Encounter with the Middle East: An Intimate Report of What Lies Behind the Arab–Israel Conflict* (London: Andre Deutsch, 1970), 237, that Herzog was instrumental in drafting a mild speech, so "that nothing should be said that might be seen as inflaming Nasser, lest in the future the world hold Israel responsible for overacting."
26. Abba Eban, interview, *Ma'ariv*, 2 June 1972; and St. John, *Eban*, 413–415.
27. St. John, *Eban*, 414.
28. Eban interpreted Johnson's phrase as a retreat from previous statements: in 1963, President Kennedy's declaration spoke of "adopting other courses of action of our own," while Johnson wrote of supporting measures, presumably initiated by someone else. Eban elaborates on this in his *An Autobiography*, 329. Harman's further clarification had elicited the response that the United States preferred to await the result of U Thant's visit to Cairo, before putting any pressure on Egypt.
29. Bar-Zohar, *Embassies in Crisis*, 68; and Israel Foreign Ministry sources.
30. Israel, Knesset, *Divrei Haknesset*, 49 (1968), 2225–2227; and Draper, *Israel and World Politics*, 248–254.
31. *New York Times*, *Davar*, and *Jerusalem Post*, 23–24 May 1967. It was also reported over Radio Cairo on May 22. The Tripartite Declaration had been dead ever since the Sinai Campaign; its resurrection at this stage was a US idea.
32. Fuad A. Jabber, ed., *International Documents on Palestine 1967* (Beirut: The Institute for Palestine Studies, 1970), 538.

33. Mohamed Heikal, "The 1967 Arab–Israel War," *Sunday Telegraph*, 21 October 1973, translated in *Ma'ariv*, 9 November 1973, purports to give a verbatim report of the discussion between Nasser and Soviet Ambassador Pozhidaev. Nasser is supposed to have said: "I want you to understand that you are the reason for everything that has happened today—the closure of the Straits—you are the reason. The confirmation by Moscow of the movements of the Israeli Army was the deciding factor that set everything into motion. When you told us that there are 11 Israeli regiments ready to attack Syria and occupy Syrian territory, we decided that matters cannot be left to fate. But now I realize that the Israeli concentrations in the North are thinned out and they are moving toward us. We have become the front."
34. *New York Times*, 20 June 1967.
35. Reported to Benjamin Geist in confidential interviews, 1973.
36. Michael Brecher, interview with Ya'acov Herzog, 10 August 1968; and Menachem Begin, eulogy for Ya'acov Herzog, March 1972. See also Burdett, *Encounter with the Middle East*; *Middle East Report* 196; and Nakdimon, *Toward the Zero Hour*, 43–46. The following reconstruction of the 23 May decision process is based upon: Israel Foreign Ministry sources; Eshkol's AB; Eban, *An Autobiography*, 332–338; Abba Eban, "Revelations from the Waiting Period," *Ma'ariv*, 6 May 1973; Menachem Begin, "A Chapter from a Book to Be Written," *Ma'ariv*, 18 June and 2 July 1971; Joseph Serlin, interviews, *Yediot Aharonot*, 26 May and 5 June 1972; Aviad Yaffe, "The War of Twenty-Seven Days," *Nitzoz*, September 1967; St. John, *Eban*, 417–420; Moshe Gilboa, "The Crisis that Reached the Top," *OT*, 31 May 1973; Nakdimon, *Toward the Zero Hour*, 43–60; and Schiff, "The Three Weeks that Preceded the War."
37. See Eban, "Revelations from the Waiting Period"; Nakdimon, *Toward the Zero Hour*, 48. Although Yitzhak Rabin later stated in an interview in *Ma'ariv*, 4 October 1967, and in "Six Days and Five More Years," *Ma'ariv* 2 June 1972, that he perceived the closure of the Straits as a declaration of war, participants and observers at the 23 May 1967 meeting have stated that he did not propose war at that or at a later stage. There was no pressure on the 23rd May meeting from the military for "immediate action," as claimed by Walter Z. Laqueur, *The Road to War 1967: The*

Origins of the Arab–Israel Conflict (London: Weidenfeld and Nicolson, 1968), 124; Draper, *Israel and World Politics*, 88; Nakdimon, *Toward the Zero Hour*, 49; Gilboa, *Six Years, Six Days*, 127; and David Kimche and Dan Bawly, *The Sandstorm; The Arab–Israel War of June 1967: Prelude and Aftermath* (London: Secker & Warburg, 1968), 138–139. All noted that the military leaders agreed to further waiting, to explore political opportunities, as well as to give the IDF a little more time for preparations. Major-General Ezer Weizman (interview by Dov Goldstein, *Ma'ariv*, 5 June 1973) confirmed this as well, as did Moshe Bitan (interview by Michael Brecher, 8 August 1968).

38. St. John, *Eban*, 418, and Eban, "Revelations from the Waiting Period."
39. It was, according to the very reliable Nakdimon (*Toward the Zero Hour*, 51), the main factor which persuaded *Rafi* and *Gahal* leaders to acquiesce in the government's proposal of 23 May to opt for diplomatic action. See also Weizman, interview by Dov Goldstein, 5 June 1973.
40. Schiff, "The Three Weeks that Preceded the War."
41. Eban, *An Autobiography*, 334. Not all have cast the "waiting period" in such a positive light. Teddy Kollek, a long-serving, popular Mayor of Jerusalem, in his memoirs a decade after the events, poured scorn on Eban's interpretation: "It seemed to us that Eshkol's hesitation about attacking derived from weakness, not wisdom. Later, his supporters gave statesmanlike reasons for the endless delay.... .Much of this was nonsense (even after the American or British ships would have gone through, the Straits could have been closed again). It was good for some favorable editorials in newspapers and a few kind words on American television, yet it made no more difference in the United Nations than if we had attacked on May 15.... The fact that all turned out well was his [Eshkol's and, by clear implication, Eban's] good fortune and a result of Moshe Dayan's leadership and the army's state of preparedness" (Teddy Kollek, *For Jerusalem* [Jerusalem and Tel Aviv: Steimatzky's Agency, 1978], 190).
42. Eban, *An Autobiography*, 335. For further details on Eban's views, see Eban, interview, *Ma'ariv*, 2 June 1972. In a 22 July 1968 interview with Brecher, the then Foreign Minister stated that there was unanimity in the Cabinet on 23 May that war lay

ahead, but nobody advocated going to war immediately. This is confirmed by other sources, including expressed opinions of those present at these meetings.
43. Moshe Dayan, *Story of My Life* (Jerusalem and Tel Aviv: Steimatzky's Agency, 1976), 254.
44. Eban, "Revelations from the Waiting Period." The English translation is quoted from his *An Autobiography*, 337; it also appears in St. John, *Eban*, 420. St. John points out, correctly, that Eban's journey was authorized (by delegation) by the Cabinet. What he fails to note is that: (a) the decision was taken at the fairly brief Ministerial Committee meeting, and that during the wider consultation forums with party leaders this was not mentioned; and (b) the Ministerial Committee did not authorize his meetings with de Gaulle and Wilson. Menachem Begin, interview, *Yediot Aharonot*, 2 June 1967, and Moshe Carmel, interview, *Jerusalem Post*, 2 June 1972, carefully point out these distinctions.
45. Henry M. Christman, ed., *The State Papers of Levi Eshkol* (New York: Funk & Wagnalls, 1969), 89–94.
46. Moshe Sneh, the leader of *Maki*, the Israel Communist Party, explained after the war in an interview in *Yediot Aharonot*, 16 June 1967: "On one side we saw a pan-Arabic front, almost total, whose aim was to destroy Israel; on the other, we saw a lone Israel, fighting for its very survival. There couldn't be and there weren't any differences of opinion among us as to the fact that the Israel Communist Party would join the ranks with the whole nation in this campaign of resistance."
47. There was dissatisfaction among Coalition partners as well; see Carmel, interview, 2 June 1972. The most extreme criticism of Eban's meeting with de Gaulle came from Ben-Gurion, who later termed the mission "a silly mistake" and claimed that "it could be that this meeting caused substantially, maybe even decisively, de Gaulle's change of relationship and the imposition of the embargo" (interview, *Ma'ariv*, 13 November 1970). Just as Ben-Gurion earlier accused Eshkol of being the cause of the deterioration of relations between France and Israel (see Gilboa, "The Crisis that Reached the Top"), so too, later, he blamed the Israeli side—Eban—for the failure. That he was wrong is perhaps best shown by de Gaulle's views, expressed in remarks to Wilson in Paris soon after the June-Six-Day War—on 19 June 1967.

48. On the occasion of Rabin becoming a candidate for the Premiership, reports about a document were published in *Ha'aretz* and *Ma'ariv* on 22 April, and in the *Jerusalem Post* on 23 April 1974. The document, an *aide-mémoire* prepared by Weizman on 6 November 1967, stated, according to *Ha'aretz*, that "from the beginning Mr. Weizman felt that the COS's steadfastness is crumbling. Rabin got in touch with Weizman at 8 in the morning [on the 23rd] and asked him to come to his home immediately.... When he arrived ... the COS told him in a weak voice: 'I have involved the nation in the biggest and most difficult war because of mistakes I have made.' He asked whether Weizman was willing to take over the job, but Weizman refused and encouraged him.... [A]n army doctor told him that the COS suffers from acute anxiety. It was decided to inform the Prime Minister and to let it be known that Rabin was suffering from nicotine poisoning."
49. Radio Cairo, 11:30 GMT, 23 May 1967.
50. Johnson, *The Vantage Point*, 291.
51. BBC, 26 June 1967.
52. Michael Brecher, interview with Ephraim Evron, 3 March 1972; *New York Times*, 24 May 1967.
53. Israel, Ministry of Foreign Affairs, Cables and Communications; Levi Eshkol, interview by the editors, *Ma'ariv*, 4 October 1967.
54. *New York Times*, 24 May 1967.
55. Harold Wilson, *The Labour Government 1965–1970: A Personal Record* (London: Weidenfeld and Nicolson, 1971), 395.
56. See *Encyclopedia Hebraica* 23, cols. 725–726, s.v. "The Six Day War"; and Weizman, interview by Dov Goldstein, 5 June 1973.
57. In an interview on 26 July 1968, Yigal Allon told Brecher his reasons for not returning from the Soviet Union earlier: (1) In the USSR, it was very difficult to make correct judgments on what was happening in the Middle East. (2) He felt that unless his colleagues in the Cabinet called him back, he should not return. (3) He did not want to give the impression of panic.
58. The following version of Eban's meetings with de Gaulle and Wilson is based mainly on the recollections and reports of the participants: first and foremost, Eban himself, in a series of books, articles, and interviews. See especially Eban, *An Autobiography*, 341–344; St. John, *Eban*, 420–426, which is based upon Eban's

unpublished manuscript on the June-Six-Day War; Eban, *My Country: The Story of Modern Israel* (London and Jerusalem: Weidenfeld and Nicolson, 1973), 175; interview, *Ma'ariv*, 1 December 1967, where he quoted verbatim passages from the discussion; interview, *Ma'ariv*, 2 June 1972; and interview, *Yediot Aharonot*, 22 April 1973. Second, see also Israel, Ministry of Foreign Affairs, Cables and Communications, cited in Michael Brecher, *Decisions in Israel's Foreign Policy* (London: Oxford University, 1974), 381–382. Additional material comes from de Gaulle and de Murville. See de Gaulle's press conference of 27 November 1967, excerpts in the *New York Times*, 28 November 1967; Jabber, ed., *International Documents on Palestine*, 194, 212; Maurice Couve de Murville, *Une Politique Etrangere 1958–1969* (Paris: Plon 1971), 469–471. Third, see Wilson, *The Labour Government*, 396–397, and Michael Brecher and Benjamin Geist, interview with Harold Wilson, 22 December 1972, during which Wilson confirmed the details of his discussion with Eban, as far as he remembered. There are also valuable secondary sources. Gilboa, *Six Years, Six Days*, 136–140, gives a verbatim record of what was said during the meeting. Bar-Zohar, *Embassies in Crisis*, 92–96; Burdett, *Encounter with the Middle East*, 248–249; and Nakdimon, *Toward the Zero Hour*, 65–68, all include verbatim accounts of the contents of these meetings.
59. St. John, *Eban*, 421. All quotations concerning the Eban–de Gaulle meeting, unless otherwise indicated, are from the above. This has been elaborated upon in Eban, *An Autobiography*, 341–344.
60. Eban, interview, *Ma'ariv*, 2 June 1972.
61. Wilson, *The Labour Government*, 397. His speech was a verbatim passage from Great Britain's statement at the UN General Assembly, on 4 March 1957.
62. Eban, interview, *Ma'ariv*, 2 June 1972.
63. At a press conference that Eisenhower held the next day he added that "I can't recall that Egypt ever agreed to this." He urged caution: "None of us should be too hurried about getting into this thing. Any unilateral action by anyone would be a serious mistake" (*New York Times*, 26 May 1967).
64. Dayan, *Story of My Life*, 259.
65. Ariel Sharon, interview, *Yediot Aharonot*, 20 July 1973.

66. Dayan, *Story of My Life*, p. 263.
67. Rabin, "Six Days and Five More Years."
68. Bar-Zohar, *Embassies in Crisis*, 109 (emphasis added).
69. Michael Brecher, interview with Eban, 22 July 1968. This is also discussed in Eban, *An Autobiography*, 349–350.
70. Israel, Ministry of Foreign Affairs, Cables and Communications; Eban, interview, *Ma'ariv*, 2 June 1972; and St. John, *Eban*, 428.
71. Israel, Ministry of Foreign Affairs, Cables and Communications. The Americans did take the Israeli warning seriously, to the extent that the White House directed the State Department to summon the Egyptian Ambassador immediately and hand him a message from the President, which repeated the Israeli warning on Radio Cairo on 28 May 1967, and added: "We have affirmed to them that our information does not confirm theirs in this respect, but we do not want to leave anything to chance. I ask you, on behalf of President Johnson, to inform Cairo immediately that the situation requires self-restraint and abstention from carrying out any offensive military operation that may lead to a large-scale explosion." The Americans also requested the Soviet Union to pass along the warning, informing them of the Israeli message.
72. Israel, Ministry of Foreign Affairs, Cables and Communications. Also partially quoted in Eban, *An Autobiography*, 350.
73. The first illustration is from BBC, 26–27 May 1967; the second, from the *New York Times*, 2 June 1967.
74. See Yigal Allon, *Masakh Shel Hol* [*A Curtain of Sand*], 2nd rev. ed. (Tel Aviv: Hakibbutz Hame'uhad, 1968), 368–372; Gilboa, *Six Years, Six Days*, 180; and Nakdimon, *Toward the Zero Hour*, 98.
75. Israel, Ministry of Foreign Affairs, Cables and Communications.
76. Ibid., based upon Harman's record of the minutes with the President, and Brecher, interview with Ephraim Evron, 3 March 1972. President Johnson (*The Vantage Point*, 293–294) corroborated in general the above account. He stressed his following remark to Eban: "The central point, Mr. Minister, is that your nation not be the one to bear the responsibility of any outbreak of war. Then I said very slowly and positively: Israel will not be alone unless it decides to go alone." Other sources on the Eban–Johnson and Evron–Johnson conversations are: Eban, *An Autobiography*, 353–359; Eban, interview, *Ma'ariv*, 2 June 1972;

Burdett, *Encounter with the Middle East*, 254–256; Draper, *Israel and World Politics*, 90–91; Nakdimon, *Toward the Zero Hour*, 106–108; St. John, *Eban*, 430–434.
77. Israel, Ministry of Foreign Affairs, Cables and Communications.
78. Text of the cable, quoted in Eshkol's answer to a parliamentary question: *Divrei Haknesset*, 53, 9 December 1968, 602–603. The government had in the meantime received Evron's report of his talk with the President. But it was faced with a momentous decision: every word of what the US President had said counted, and it could only rely on a report of a meeting at the level of diplomats. Neither could it know that—substantially—Johnson repeated to Eban what he had said to Evron.
79. United Nations, Report of the Secretary-General of the United Nations, U Thant, to the Security Council, S/7906 (26 May 1967); United States, Senate Documents, Doc. 33, 213 (Washington, DC).
80. All those concerned were playing a very careful game in the Straits. Israel had intended to sail a test ship through the Straits, and for this purpose, an Israeli crew was flown to Massawa on 25 May. But the action was canceled on the Cabinet's orders: there was American pressure to cancel it, but the main reason was military—the action would have announced to Nasser the beginning of hostilities.
81. For details of the meeting, sometimes called the "pajama conference," because Eshkol and Yaffe decided to receive their callers dressed in pajamas, see Yaffe, "The War of Twenty-Seven Days," Burdett, *Encounter with the Middle East*, 262–264. The conversation took place in Russian.
82. *Jerusalem Post*, 4 June 1967.
83. The tone of Kosygin's letters to Eshkol during the 1967 Crisis was qualitatively more moderate than the harsh threats of destruction, put in the form of an ultimatum, in Bulganin's letter to Ben-Gurion on 5 November 1956. See Brecher, *Decisions in Israel's Foreign Policy*, 284.
84. Burdett, *Encounter with the Middle East*, 263.
85. Eshkol, interview, *Yediot Aharonot*, 7 July 1967. The offer to go to Russia, made—as far as can be established—on the spur of the moment, was taken quite seriously in Moscow. Kosygin notified Nasser, indicating that he would be willing to meet Eshkol, but

only if "our Arab friends agree." Nasser, after a meeting with his advisers, in which opinions were divided on the possible effect of such a visit on Egypt's interests, chose a neutral attitude and answered that this concerned the USSR only and depended on her. The Russians finally decided to refuse the offer because it might harm the Soviet Union's position in the Arab world. An early report on these contacts was included in Heikal's weekly article in *Al-Ahram*, 20 October 1967, broadcast over Radio Cairo; BBC, 23 October 1967. A full description is in Heikal, "The 1967 Arab–Israel War."

86. Eshkol's AB. The meeting was considered one of the Labor Alignment Political Committee. Part of the Eshkol method of consultations was to invite military leaders to meetings of this party forum. His predecessor, Ben-Gurion, had always insisted on a clear line of demarcation; his Director of Military Intelligence had never been allowed to appear even before the Foreign Affairs and Security Committee of the *Knesset*.
87. Bar-Zohar, *Embassies in Crisis*, 132.
88. Sources for that Cabinet meeting are: Michael Brecher's interviews with three Cabinet ministers in July–August 1968: Allon, Eban, and Peres; Michael Brecher, interview with Haim-Moshe Shapira, 16 July 1968; Eban, *An Autobiography*, 367–368; Haim Bar-Lev, interview, *Yediot Aharonot*, 5 June 1973; Begin, "A Chapter from a Book to Be Written"; Eshkol, interview by the editors of *Ma'ariv*, 4 October 1967; Nakdimon, *Toward the Zero Hour*, 117–123.
89. Nakdimon, *Toward the Zero Hour*, 119–121; Brecher, interview with Eban, 8 August 1968.
90. Eshkol, interview by the editors of *Ma'ariv*, 4 October 1967.
91. Allon, "The Last Stage of the War of Independence," in *Curtain of Sand*, 373–377; Brecher, interview with Allon, 26 July 1968; Schiff, "The Three Weeks that Preceded the War"; Burdett, *Encounter with the Middle East*, 264–266.
92. Moshe Carmel, "And Yet: We Were Faced with the Danger of Destruction," *Ma'ariv*, 21 April 1972; "Fighting for Survival—Struggling for Peace," *Davar*, 2 June 1972; and interview, *Jerusalem Post*, 2 June 1972.
93. Mordekhai Bentov, "The Truth and Not 'Nightmares' Are of Educational Value," *Al Hamishmar*, 18 May 1972.

94. Eshkol's AB; Brecher, *Decisions in Israel's Foreign Policy*, 398–400.
95. Israel, Ministry of Foreign Affairs, Cables and Communications; and Eban, *An Autobiography*, 370.
96. Bar-Zohar, *Embassies in Crisis*, 140.
97. Israel, Ministry of Foreign Affairs, Cables and Communications.
98. During the day, a small number of key personnel, needed on Israel's economic front, were released.
99. Brecher, interview with Allon; Carmel, "The Danger of Destruction," and "Fighting for Survival."
100. Johnson, *The Vantage Point*, 294.
101. Eshkol, interview by the editors of *Ma'ariv*, 4 October 1967.
102. For other sources on the 28 May Cabinet meeting, see Levi Eshkol, statement in the *Knesset*, 29 May 1967; Burdett, *Encounter with the Middle East*, 266–267; Draper, *Israel and World Politics*, 93–94; Gilboa, *Six Years, Six Days*, 155–157; and Nakdimon, *Toward the Zero Hour*, 128–129.
103. Menachem Begin, interview, *Yediot Aharonot*, 2 June 1967.
104. Israel, Ministry of Foreign Affairs, Cables and Communications.
105. Nakdimon, *Toward the Zero Hour*, 130. The "stammering" incident came after days of mounting tension, with all of Israel—and the world—listening for the authoritative statement of what the Government of Israel intended to do. The mood of Israel's public, under the pressure of virulent assaults by Arab media of communication, was that Israel was faced with the question of survival. The announcement—the first one by Eshkol to the nation—came after days of attacks on him for his "hesitancy" and "indecisiveness" in the nation's hour of crisis. The mode of delivery seemed to underline this and strengthened the hands of the Opposition in their claim that Eshkol was not the right man to lead a nation fighting for its very existence. Many participants in the 1967 decision process testified after the War to the "disastrous" effect of this incident on public morale and as a contributory factor to the ouster of Eshkol from the Ministry of Defense.
106. Practically everybody who took part in that meeting has published—mostly in interview form—his version of what happened. While early descriptions of this meeting as the "Revolt of the Generals" are nonsense, it was traumatic for all concerned, as attested to by most of the accounts. See Eshkol, interview by the editors of *Ma'ariv*; Yaffe, "The War of Twenty-Seven Days"; Bar-

Lev, interview, *Ma'ariv*, 6 May 1973, and interview, *Yediot Aharonot*, 5 June 1973; and Ariel Sharon, interview, *Ma'ariv*, 20 July 1973, and interview, *Yediot Aharonot*, 20 July 1973. Bar-Lev stated in his *Ma'ariv* interview that most of the generals did not listen to Eshkol's radio statement before the meeting but had heard the reactions to it.

107. Bar-Lev, interview, *Yediot Aharonot*, 5 June 1973.
108. Jabber, ed., *International Documents on Palestine*, 328, 549.
109. *Divrei Haknesset*, 49, 2283–2285. The quotation is from Christman, ed., *The State Papers of Levi Eshkol*, 95–104.
110. Jabber, ed., *International Documents on Palestine*, 564.
111. Eshkol's AB shows that of his 19 meetings on that day, 12 were with party leaders and personalities involved in the internal political crisis.
112. Meir Amit, interview by Benjamin Geist, 13 July 1973. Amit was one of Eshkol's closest advisers at the time and one of his main sources of information. Eshkol saw him that day (the 30th) three times. Bitan, in an interview with Brecher on 8 August 1968, added a somewhat different reason for the Amit mission: "There was a search for insight into Johnson's mind. We could not ask Johnson directly; he would have had to say no. But we had to know. The United States and the USSR were in communication, but we were not sure of what they said to each other." Amit's contacts were with Pentagon and CIA circles, whose views were different from White House policy.
113. Israel Government Press Office, 30 May 1967.
114. Israel, Ministry of Foreign Affairs, Cables and Communications.
115. Rabin, "Six Days and Five More Years."
116. Eban, *An Autobiography*, 380; and Brecher, interview with Eban, 8 August 1968.
117. Nakdimon, *Toward the Zero Hour*, 169, 170.
118. The *Jerusalem Post*'s editorial of 1 June was entitled, "Hussein Admits the Wolf"; *Davar*'s editorial of 31 May, entitled "Hussein with Nasser," stated that "there is no doubt that Israel has to consider this development as a strengthening of the threat to its well-being and to take it into account in all its political and military activities." *Ha'aretz* echoed the same theme on 31 May: "Egyptian-Jordanian Defense Pact—A Sign of the Times." And the next day, Schiff, *Ha'aretz*'s military correspondent, wrote

about the "Danger from the East": "Our deterrent power has been undermined not only in the eyes of the Arabs and ourselves, but in the eyes of friends as well, those near and far away."

119. Yeshayahu Gavish stated in an interview by Dov Goldstein in *Yediot Aharonot*, 3 April 1970, that Rabin informed him only at six o'clock the next morning, even then most reluctantly, that he would be replaced by Dayan; and Gavish refused point-blank to serve as Dayan's second-in-command, even when ordered to do so by Rabin. "I told him under no circumstances would I do so. I got up, saluted and left." This was confirmed by Bar-Lev. Rabin's reluctance to accept the suggestion was also mentioned by Matityahu Peled, "The Beauty Is Untouched," *Ma'ariv*, 15 June 1973.

120. Dayan's version is in his *Story of My Life*, 268; and in Israel, Ministry of Foreign Affairs, Cables and Communications. There was, in fact, a substantial difference in the phrase used. The American version, as transmitted by Rusk on 28 May, referred to "every possible effort," while the Eshkol letter, as noted, referred to "any and all measures."

121. *New York Times*, 1 June 1967.

122. Nakdimon, *Toward the Zero Hour*, 202.

123. Israel, Ministry of Foreign Affairs, Cables and Communications. Eban stated in an interview in *Ma'ariv*, 2 June 1972, that Amit, in his preliminary report, also wrote: "There is a growing chance for American political backing if we act on our own."

124. The events of those days made Eshkol bitter toward his colleagues. He felt betrayed by them, that they did not appreciate his role as Defense Minister during the four years he held the post, and that they lost their nerve under pressure. Always a skeptical man, he now trusted no one. For a good summary—pro-Eshkol— see Arie Tzimouki, "Eshkol as I Knew Him," *Yediot Aharonot*, 25 February 1972.

125. Menachem Begin, "The Meeting of 2 June 1967," *Ma'ariv*, 2 June 1972.

126. The role that Dayan played in influencing the outcome of the war was hotly debated in Israel. There is no question that he had a great influence in crystallizing military plans, but what remains controversial is whether or not the same decisions would have been taken anyway.

127. *Encyclopedia Hebraica*, vol. 23, col. 726, s.v. "The Six Day War."
128. See Weizman, interview by Dov Goldstein, 5 June 1973; Gavish, interview by Dov Goldstein, 3 April 1970; and Sharon, interview, *Yediot Aharonot*, 20 July 1973.
129. Dayan, *Story of My Life*, 256–258, 264, 271.
130. Dayan, interview, *Yediot Aharonot*, 16 June 1967, and Begin, "A Chapter from a Book to Be Written."
131. Avigdor Dagan, *Moscow and Jerusalem: Twenty Years of Relations between Israel and the Soviet Union* (London: Abelard-Schuman, 1970), 223–224.
132. Jabber, ed., *International Documents on Palestine*, 49–50.
133. Brecher, interview with Evron, 3 March 1972.
134. Israel, Ministry of Foreign Affairs, Cables and Communications.
135. Israel, Ministry of Foreign Affairs, Cables and Communications confirmed that Israel's decision-makers were by now convinced that the Soviet Union would not intervene directly; this was also confirmed in Brecher's interview with Herzog, Brecher's interview with Allon, and Amit's interview by Geist, 13 July 1973.
136. Laqueur, *The Road to War*, 158.
137. *Jerusalem Post*, 4 June 1967.
138. Schiff, "The Three Weeks that Preceded the War."
139. Eshkol's AB. For details on the 4 June meeting, see Eban, *An Autobiography*, 395–400; Nakdimon, *Toward the Zero Hour*, 276–278; Kimche and Bawly, *The Sandstorm*, 155–156; and Burdett, *Encounter with the Middle East*, 309–316.
140. Carmel stated in an interview in the *Jerusalem Post*, 2 June 1972, that the review of the military situation was the crucial input to the Cabinet's decision: "When on June 4 practically all the ministers, excepting the two from *Mapam*, voted for immediate action ... it was because of the information in our possession of a further build-up on the Egyptian and Syrian fronts and that Iraqi troops were advancing through Jordan to our lines. We felt that the noose was tightening around our necks."
141. Dayan, *Story of My Life*, 275–276.
142. Published by the Government of Israel on the fifth anniversary of the Six-Day War, *Jerusalem Post*, 5 June 1972.
143. Rafael, "May 1967—A Personal Report," 21 April 1972.
144. *New York Times*, 5 June 1967.

145. The title of one of the earliest—and best—accounts of the 1973 October War, by Zeev Schiff (Tel Aviv: University Publishing Projects, 1974).
146. Richard Nixon discerned a Soviet role: "It was hard for me to believe that the Egyptians and Syrians would have moved without the knowledge of the Soviets, if not without their direct encouragement" (*RN: The Memoirs of Richard Nixon* [New York: Grosset and Dunlap, 1978], 921). Sadat confirmed Soviet knowledge by recalling in his autobiography that he told the Soviet Ambassador on 3 October: "I'd like to inform you officially that I and Syria have decided to start military operations against Israel so as to break the present deadlock." Assad conveyed the decision to the Soviet envoy in Damascus the next day. Anwar Sadat clearly implied Soviet discouragement by noting that the sole reply to his query "What will the Soviet attitude be?" was an urgent request on the 4th for permission to land Soviet aircraft to evacuate the families of Soviet civilian advisers in Egypt (*In Search of Identity: An Autobiography* [New York: Harper & Row, 1978], 246, 247, 252). Zeira, then Director of Military Intelligence, was quoted, four years after the events, as having said to Elazar on Friday morning, 5 October: "I think that Israel is not going to war. But the situation today is fraught with more question marks than yesterday" (in Shlomo Nakdimon, "Protocols of Discussions Among the Political and Military Leaders on 5th and 6th October 1973," *Yediot Aharonot*, 21 September 1977). See also Agranat Commission, Partial Report issued by the Committee of Inquiry—Yom Kippur War (Jerusalem: Government Press Office, 3 April 1974); Shlomo Nakdimon, "The Days Before and After the War: New Revelations," *Yediot Aharonot*, 19 July 1974; Aviezer Golan, "Albert," *Yediot Aharonot*, 7 January 1977, excerpt; and Hanoch Bar-Tov, *Dado—48 Years and Another 20 Days* (Tel Aviv: Sifriyat Ma'ariv, 1978), vol. 1, 314–316.
147. Agranat Commission, *Partial Report*.
148. Herzog, *The War of Atonement*, 47.
149. A. Golan, "Albert."
150. Dayan, *Story of My Life*, 386.
151. Gonen, interview, 21 September 1977. Bar-Tov (*Dado*, vol. 1, 315) contends that this was the first time the "C" alert was called since 1967. In view of the many critical situations and repeated

warnings of the possibility of attacks in the past—as noted by Meir, Dayan, Elazar, and others—this is unlikely.

152. The summary paragraph of the AMAN intelligence report released at 13:15 on 5 October read: "In spite of the fact that the ... emergency deployment on the Canal front could, seemingly, be an indicator for offensive intent, nevertheless, in our best judgment, there has been no change in the Egyptian appreciation of the balance between their and *Tzahal's* [IDF's] *forces. Therefore, the likelihood that Egypt intends to renew hostilities is low*" (cited in Agranat Commission, *Partial Report*; see also Golda Meir, *My Life* [Jerusalem and Tel Aviv: Steimatsky's Agency, 1975], 356). Dayan reportedly suggested, at one point in the meeting with Meir, the high probability of an Egyptian crossing of the Canal, but that was not the main thrust of his evaluation. See Nakdimon, "New Revelations."

153. Dayan, *Story of My Life*, 386. According to Bar-Tov (*Dado*, vol. 1, p. 320), this appreciation was voiced at the meeting of the IDF General Staff, immediately following the Cabinet meeting. Bar-Lev, a former IDF Chief of Staff, revealed soon after the October-Yom-Kippur War that he learned of the seriousness of the situation for the first time at the 5 October Cabinet meeting (interview, *Ma'ariv*, 9 November 1973).

The highest level of US decision-makers, too, did not anticipate war. According to Nixon: "The news of the imminent attack on Israel took us completely by surprise." Moreover, "I was disappointed by our own intelligence shortcomings, and I was stunned by the failure of Israeli intelligence. They were among the best in the world, and they, too, had been caught off guard" (*Memoirs*, 920).

154. Agranat Commission, *Partial Report*; Bar-Tov, *Dado*, vol. 1, 320. The Agranat Commission added that these "further indicators" were supposed to arrive within hours, but in fact arrived only the next morning.

155. Golda Meir, interview, *Ma'ariv*, 16 September 1974.

156. Yisrael Galili, interview by Y. Ben-Porath, *Yediot Aharonot*, 27 October 1978.

157. Ray Cline's testimony before the US House of Representatives, Subcommittee on Intelligence, September 1975; Brecher, interview with Eban, 15 July 1974; Eban, *An Autobiography* 500,

501; Bernard Kalb and Marvin Kalb, *Kissinger* (Boston and Toronto: Little, Brown, 1974), 458–459; Matti Golan, *The Secret Conversations of Henry Kissinger: Step-by-Step Diplomacy in the Middle East* (New York: Bantam Books, 1976), 37–39.
158. A. Golan, "Albert"; Herzog, *The War of Atonement*, 45.
159. Dayan recalls 04:00 (*Story of My Life*, 375); Meir mentions 03:30 (interview, *Ma'ariv*, 16 September 1974).
160. "Near-certainty" because there were still some doubts. For example, Pinhas Sapir emphasized that Dayan was skeptical about the outbreak of war until the last minute. He left the Cabinet session at 13:00 "for lunch," signaling his reservations about the thrust of the discussion (Brecher, interview with Pinhas Sapir, 25 June 1974). Moreover, Dayan's actions during the next few days, notably his offer to resign as Defense Minister on 7 October and his morbid assessment to Israel's editors on the 9th testify to the trauma he experienced with the outbreak of war and the IDF's initial setbacks—and his surprise that war occurred at all.
161. US pressure on Israel in 1967 was documented at length in the preceding chapter. There remains a crucial, unresolved controversy about the extent and intensity of US pressure on Israel in 1973, with significant implications for Israel's autonomy of decision about preemption on the eve of the October-Yom-Kippur War. According to the Kalbs, Kissinger had warned Israeli Ambassador Dinitz and Minister Shalev in previous months—repeatedly and in the strongest terms—not to preempt. "'Don't ever start the war,' Kissinger would admonish them. 'Don't ever pre-empt!' He would then forecast absolute disaster if Israel ignored his counsel. 'If you fire the first shot, you won't have a dogcatcher in this country supporting you. You won't have presidential support. You'll be alone, all alone.'" Moreover, according to the Kalbs, the Secretary of State, in a phone conversation with Eban shortly after 06:00 New York time, 6 October, that is, shortly after 12:00 noon, Israeli time, which means almost three hours after the decision was taken, and after Keating's report of the decision reached him, "[added] the extra warning: 'Don't preempt!'" (Kalb and Kalb, *Kissinger*, 459,460). William B. Quandt went further: "In the less than two hours that remained before the war began, Kissinger took charge, calling the Israelis to warn against preemption." (*Decade of Decisions: American Policy toward*

the Arab–Israel Conflict, 1967–1976 [Berkeley, Los Angeles, and London: University of California Press, 1977], 166; see also 169–170). No corroborating evidence appeared, except for Dayan's ambiguous remark in his memoirs that, on the morning of the 6th, "Americans warned us not to take any provocative action" (*Story of My Life*, 379). The Kalbs's contention is highly improbable because of the time sequence noted above; that is, the decision on preemption was taken by Israel's decision-makers without US pressure.

In that context, Eban (*An Autobiography*, 502) recalled that telephone conversation as follows: "He had been studying a report of our Prime Minister's talk with Ambassador Keating. He noted the Israeli decision to abstain from pre-emptive action. He wanted to put on record with me that this was an Israeli decision conveyed to the United States after it had been taken. He personally believed it to be the right decision, but the United States had no need to give advice on an issue which Israel had already determined for herself." The then Israel Foreign Minister also recreated the hectic, tense flow of events in New York during the two hours before the war. He received a cable from Galili shortly before 06:00, New York time, about the anticipated Egypt–Syria attack later in the day and the Prime Minister's assurance to the US Ambassador that Israel would not preempt. According to Mordekhai Gazit, "There were no hints of any kind that I am aware of, from any source in the United States to any source in Israel, not to pre-empt. The only exception was at the meeting with Ambassador Keating where, after Mrs. Meir told him so, he remarked that it was important that we were certain that, in fact, we would not pre-empt. But nobody put pressure or suggested to Israel that she should not pre-empt in this situation" (Brecher, interview with Gazit, 27 July 1974). Ten minutes later, Eban informed Kissinger (who in the meantime had received Keating's report on his talk with Meir). During the next two hours of frantic activity, the Secretary of State informed President Nixon, Soviet Ambassador Dobrynin, UN Secretary-General Waldheim, and the Ambassadors of Egypt and Saudi Arabia, urging restraint upon the latter. Eban was on the phone with the Prime Minister and with the Director-General of Israel's Foreign Ministry, inquiring about Egypt's charge that Israel's navy had initiated the

attack when the latter notified him that war had just broken out (Brecher, interview with Gazit; see also Eban, *An Autobiography*, 501–503; and Nakdimon, "New Revelations").
162. The Chief of Staff did not call for general mobilization but for units totaling 100,000–120,000 men; this was far less than Israel's entire reserves; Bar-Tov, *Dado*, vol. 2, 20–23.
163. Meir, *My Life*, 359.
164. Dayan, *Story of My Life*, 375–376.
165. Memorandum to the Cabinet in May 1975, published in *Ma'ariv*, 20 April 1976.
166. Janice Gross Stein and Raymond Tanter, *Rational Decision-Making: Israel's Security Choices, 1967* (Columbus: Ohio State University Press, 1980).
167. Meir, *My Life*, 358. For Dayan, it was a typical move of "sharing responsibility"; he did so several times in similar circumstances.
168. Ibid., 359.
169. Golda Meir, interview, *Ma'ariv*, 16 September 1974. Much insight into Meir's calculus in choosing not to preempt was provided by Mordekhai Gazit, a senior Israel Foreign Ministry official, who worked closely with her for many years in both the Foreign Ministry and the Prime Minister's Office: "Golda would tell you that she was afraid that this time she could not count on US support. That is to say, she was concerned with the image of the United States and the possible loss of US diplomatic and military support. Secondly, Golda had great confidence in the IDF's ability to win. She felt that in 1967 we were so successful that now, years later, with the large strides made in armament and, particularly, in view of the fact that neither Dayan nor Dado [Elazar] showed any apprehension or made a recommendation for a pre-emptive strike as a necessity, why should she then order it. And in that context, Dado said that a preventive strike would make things easier but he never said it would be essential. If Dayan and/or Dado would have said that a strike was essential, there is no doubt in my mind that Golda would have decided in favor of such a step" (Brecher, interview with Gazit, 27 July 1974).
170. Meir, interview, *Ma'ariv*, 16 September 1974.
171. Elazar asserted in his 1975 Memorandum to the Cabinet (published in *Ma'ariv*, 20 April 1976) that the Prime Minister

approved the limited call-up of reserves "within minutes" of the beginning of the discussion, and the large-scale call-up within 20 minutes. Moreover, the delay arose from the Dayan–Elazar disagreement before the 08:00 meeting.

172. Meir, *My Life*, 359.
173. Brecher, interview with Keating, 30 July 1974.
174. Kalb and Kalb, *Kissinger*, 456–460. Nixon, however, reveals no uncertainty on this point, with his reference to "the news of the imminent attack on Israel" (*Memoirs*, 920).
175. Meir, *My Life*, 359.
176. Brecher, interview with Gazit, 27 July 1974.
177. Dayan, *Story of My Life*, 379.
178. Nakdimon, "The Events that Preceded the War," a series of articles (hereafter "Prewar Events"), *Yediot Aharonot*, 14 December 1973; Schiff, *October Earthquake*, 68–69. Schiff noted (101) that the IDF had held a war game in 1969 which showed the advantages to Egypt of an attack between 14:00 and 15:00. That lesson was forgotten. The error was apparently due to the ambiguous phrase in the Intelligence report, "before sunset." "One of the great puzzles that no one could explain," remarked Meir a year later, "was that it was stated that war would break out at 6 in the evening and nobody knows why, on what basis. The supposition is that, in the information received, the time of sunset was mentioned and somebody concluded that this meant six in the evening" (interview, *Ma'ariv*, 16 September 1974).
179. The Air Force Commander was notified by Elazar at 12:30 that his proposal for an aerial strike had been rejected by the Cabinet. However, Peled, who shared the skepticism of experienced former military commanders about the expected hour of attack, 18:00, ordered patrols into the air at 13:30. Two planes on patrol from Sharm-e-Sheikh were immediately attacked by 12 Egyptian MiGs, and in the engagement, seven MiGs were shot down. Thus, strictly speaking, hostilities began at 13:30 (Herzog, *The War of Atonement*, 255–256). For details on the planned preemptive air strike, see Peled as quoted in Arieh Avnery, *Shamayim Adoumim* [*Red Sky*] (Tel Aviv: Sifriyat Madim, 1975), 106–107.

A provocative thesis about the basic cause of the 1973 October War was recently presented by an Israeli historian: it was the failure of the two dominant Israeli decision-makers in 1973 to recognize that President Sadat was prepared to make considerable concessions to achieve his primary goal, the restoration of Egypt's sovereignty over the Sinai Desert, captured by Israel in the June-Six-Day War in 1967. The most basic flaw in this interpretation is the inability or unwillingness to recognize that protracted conflicts, such as that between Israel and the Arab world, are most likely to be resolved when a qualitative change occurs in the relationship between the principal adversaries. The 1973 October War, objectively, served the crucial purpose of enabling both Egypt and Israel—neither of whom experienced a disastrous defeat or a total victory in 1973, with heavy casualties on both sides—to make the qualitative shift from permanent hostility to a minimal mutual accommodation in a peace agreement. See Yigal Kipnis, *1973: The Road to War* (Charlottesville, VA: Just World Books, 2013), especially Chaps. 7 and 8.

180. Meir, interview, *Ma'ariv*, 16 September 1974; and interviews with Meir aides during the 1973 crisis-war by Brecher and Geist, 16 and 18 August 1977.
181. The *Knesset*, which had been formally dissolved because of impending elections, met only in special plenary sessions during the high-stress war period, on 16 and 23–25 October. At the 16 October meeting, the Prime Minister reported on the situation and indicated that the IDF had crossed the Canal. The tenor of Opposition speeches was that, while many questions had to be answered by the government, this was not the appropriate time to raise them (*Divrei Haknesset*, 68, 4474–4495).
182. Dayan, *Story of My Life*, 388; confirmed in Brecher, interview with Gazit.
183. Dayan, *Story of My Life*, 390–391. For Sadat's vivid account of the first day's fighting, see his *In Search of Identity*, 248–252.
184. Brecher, interviews with Gazit, Yariv, and Peres, 27 July, 7 August, and 11 August 1974, respectively; and with senior officials of the US Embassy, Tel Aviv, 12 August 1974.
185. Brecher, interview with Gazit; see also Quandt, *Decade of Decisions*, 171–172.
186. Brecher, interview with Eban, 15 July 1974. The contention that Israel asked for a cease-fire in place on 6 October was categorically denied in Brecher's interviews with Gazit and Eban, as noted, and with Yariv, Keating, and other US Embassy officials.

Nixon (*Memoirs*, 921) wrote that, on that day, neither side wanted a cease-fire and that he saw no point in trying to impose one: "It would be better to wait until the war had reached the point at which neither side had a decisive military advantage." On the Arab side, there appear to have been differences over a cease-fire at the outset. According to Sadat, the Soviet Ambassador informed him on 6 October that Assad asked Moscow on the 4th to work for a cease-fire no more than 48 hours from the planned attack on the 6th. Assad reportedly denied this to Sadat, on the 7th. Brezhnev, in pressing Sadat to accept a cease-fire in the early days, told Tito that Syria had submitted three requests for a cease-fire. Egypt's President, by contrast, recalled that he had categorically rejected pressure for a cease-fire: on the 6th, from the Soviets; on the 13th, from Kissinger, via British Prime Minister Heath and the British Ambassador in Cairo; and from 16 to 19 October, from Kosygin (Sadat, *In Search of Identity*, 252–254, 256–258, and 258–259). See also Quandt, *Decade of Decisions*, 171–172.

187. Reports of UNTSO observers, confirming the Egypt–Syria attack, are in UN document S/7930/ADD, 2142. Eban spoke at both the General Assembly and Security Council meetings.
188. Dayan, *Story of My Life*, 406–407; Meir, *My Life*, 360–361; Herzog, *The War of Atonement*, 183; Bar-Tov, *Dado*, vol. 2, 63–73. In several Brecher–Geist 1977 interviews with Meir's 1973 aides, the profound effect of Dayan's pessimistic evaluation on Meir during that 7 October meeting was vividly recalled and emphasized, as it also was by Yisrael Galili in an interview by Y. Ben-Porath in *Yediot Aharonot*, 27 October 1978. Dayan's assessment was offset by Elazar and, later, by Bar-Lev, who stayed on the northern front for 24 hours. Bar-Lev's view was that there was no reason to make territorial concessions. He reported to the Prime Minister on the 8th that "the situation is difficult but not lost" (Bar-Lev, interview by Uri Millstein, 26 June 1974).
189. Israel's request for arms was transmitted through three parallel channels: the Defense Ministry to the US Embassy in Tel Aviv; Ambassador to the United States, Dinitz, to Kissinger; and the Israeli Military Attaché in Washington, General Mordechai Gur, to the Pentagon. Requests started on the second day of the war. Dinitz, during his first meeting with Kissinger on Sunday, 7

October, submitted a "modest" list of needed supplies (Kalb and Kalb, *Kissinger*, 464). From that day onward, in the words of the US Chief of Naval Operations in 1973, "almost every day during the war's first week the Israeli Ambassador handed a new and larger shopping list to Henry Kissinger." (Elmo R. Zumwalt, *On Watch, A Memoir* [New York: Quadrangle/*The New York Times*, 1976], 433).

190. Agranat Commission, *Third and Final Report*, press release issued by the Commission of Inquiry—Yom Kippur War (Agranat Commission) (Jerusalem: Government Press Office, 30 January 1975). See also articles by Zeev Schiff, "The 8th of October: The Most Important Day of the War," *Ha'aretz*, 25 and 30 September 1974.

191. For the deliberations in and around the Security Council, see Theodore Draper, "The Road to Geneva," *Commentary* 57, no. 2 (February 1974): 23–39. Eban (*An Autobiography*, 510–511) recalled receiving a cable from Meir on the 8th in the evening, advising him that "we could not possibly conceive of carrying out a cease-fire resolution so long as the enemy forces had not been repelled." See also M. Golan, *The Secret Conversations of Henry Kissinger*, 63.

192. Quandt, *Decade of Decisions*, 176–177.

193. Quandt reported that on both 6 and 7 October Moscow suggested to Sadat that he accept a simple cease-fire at an early date—and that Kissinger was aware of this (Ibid., 174, no. 19).

194. Galia Golan, *Yom Kippur and After: The Soviet Union and the Middle East Crisis* (Cambridge, England: Cambridge University Press, 1977), 85–86.

195. The verbatim text was published in *Ha'aretz*, 15 February 1974.

196. Brecher, interview with Aharon Yariv; and Schiff, *October Earthquake*, 112. Syria fired 14 Frog missiles at an Israeli military airport during the first three days of the war. They caused little damage, but the qualitative escalation of weapons was perceived—by Allon and Dayan, among others—as necessitating a commensurate response. See also Moshe Dayan, Confidential Briefing to Israeli Newspaper Editors, *Ha'aretz*, 15 February 1974.

197. Lebanon had secretly notified Israel that it would stay strictly neutral in fact, if not in word (Dayan, Confidential Briefing, 15 February 1974). However, a Lebanese radar station at El-Barik,

halfway between Damascus and Beirut, kept the Syrians continuously informed of the movement of Israeli aircraft, until it was bombed on 9 October. On the Jordan dimension, Quandt wrote: "As the Syrian front began to weaken, King Hussein of Jordan came under great pressure to enter the war, if not by opening a new front, then at least by sending some of his troops to Syria. Israel conveyed an extremely harsh message to Hussein on October 9, warning of the consequences of opening a front along the Jordan River. Kissinger also urged Hussein to stay out of the fighting, stressing that a diplomatic effort was under way that, it was hoped, would succeed in ending the war in a few days" (*Decade of Decisions*, 177).

198. Brecher, interview with Keating, 30 July 1974.
199. Nixon, *Memoirs*, 922. Later, during her visit to Washington at the beginning of November, Meir reportedly said to Nixon: "There were days and hours when we needed a friend, and you came right in. You don't know what your airlift means to us" (Nixon, *Memoirs*, 942–943). See also Meir, *My Life*, 362; Dayan, *Story of My Life*, 411–412; and Schiff, *October Earthquake*, 150. Nixon also recalled conveying his decision to Kissinger on the 9th (*Memoirs*, 922).
200. Schiff, *October Earthquake*, 148.
201. Herzog, *The War of Atonement*, 199; and, more generally, Chap. 14; see also Dayan, *Story of My Life*, Chaps. 31 and 32.
202. Dayan, *Story of My Life*, 425–426.
203. Ibid., 426–427; see also Quandt, *Decade of Decisions*, 177–178.
204. See Herzog, *The War of Atonement*; Schiff, *October Earthquake*; and Meir, Speech to the Knesset, 16 October 1973, *Divrei Haknesset*, 68, 4474.
205. Herzog, *The War of Atonement*, Chap. 10.
206. G. Golan, *Yom Kippur and After*, Chap. 3.
207. Bar-Tov, *Dado*, vol. 2, 180–193; Herzog, *The War of Atonement*, 202. According to Schiff, *October Earthquake*, 190–192, Dayan's outburst on military versus political decisions was directed at Bar-Lev, not Elazar. Bar-Lev stated that, at his request, the plan for a crossing was prepared on the 11th. He accepted it and submitted the plan to GHQ and then to the Prime Minister. During the meeting, news arrived that the Egyptians would attack on the 13th and 14th. He then suggested that the crossing be postponed

until the IDF "had succeeded in breaking what could be broken.... There was no argument about this" (interview by Millstein, 31 January 1974; confirmed in Brecher, interview with Bar-Lev, 29 July 1974). Dayan, so explicit on so many other points, was silent on the decision process about the crossing, stating only: "After a thorough review, we decided on a Canal crossing" (*Story of My Life*, 429).
208. From the verbatim text of Nixon's television interview with David Frost, 12 May 1977. On the Kissinger–Schlesinger controversy over the delay of US arms deliveries to Israel in 1973, see also Edward N. Luttwak and Walter Laqueur, "Kissinger and the Yom Kippur War," *Commentary* 58, no. 3 (September 1974): 33–40. Admiral Zumwalt, no friend of Kissinger, wrote: "It was Henry himself who stalled the airlift. I do not mean to imply that he wanted Israel to lose the national war. He simply did not want Israel to win decisively." The policy of the United States, Secretary of Defense Schlesinger told Zumwalt, was to "maintain a low profile and avoid visible involvement" (Zumwalt, *On Watch*, 433–435). Nixon, in his *Memoirs* (927), unreservedly supported Kissinger's version. He recalled his reaction, on 12 October, to the Pentagon's continued hesitation about which planes to use for the airlift: "I became totally exasperated. I said to Kissinger, 'Goddamn it, use every one we have. Tell them to send everything that can fly.'" Earlier that day he had told Schlesinger: "Whichever way we have to do it, get them in the air, now." For a detailed description of the US decision process, as well as an assessment of American interests, see Quandt, *Decade of Decisions*, 176–183.
209. According to M. Golan, *The Secret Conversations of Henry Kissinger*, 65–83, Meir decided on acceptance in consultation with Dayan and Elazar. Israel's gains on the Syrian front were cited as the principal stimulus to Meir's decision. See Insight team of *The Sunday Times*, *The Yom Kippur War*, 279. This was also noted by Quandt, *Decade of Decisions*, 180 and no. 35, referring to "a highly-placed Israeli source."
210. Brecher, interview with Eban, 15 July 1974; see also Eban's *An Autobiography*, 514–515, and his "Kissinger Told Me that He Went to Sleep Quietly After He Received the Israeli Intelligence

Appreciation on the Eve of October 5," *Ma'ariv*, 21 September 1977.
211. Quandt, *Decade of Decisions*, 181–182.
212. Ido Disentshik, "You Don't Ask for a Cease-Fire with Your Back to the Wall," *Ma'ariv*, 21 September 1977.
213. Sadat's account, with the clear message, "Please tell Kissinger.... I haven't agreed to a cease-fire proposed by the Soviet Union or any other party," is contained in his *In Search of Identity*, 256–258.
214. M. Golan, *The Secret Conversations of Henry Kissinger*, 96.
215. Nixon recalled with pride that there were more than 550 American missions during the next few weeks, "an operation bigger than the Berlin airlift of 1948–49" (*Memoirs*, 927–928). For an informative discussion of the details of the US airlift, see Quandt, *Decade of Decisions*, 183–185. He adds that its impact on Israel's military decisions during the October-Yom-Kippur War was minimal.
216. Dayan, *Story of My Life*, 428–429; G. Golan, *Yom Kippur and After*, 90–95; Schiff, *October Earthquake*, 196.
217. Schiff, *October Earthquake*, 196–199; Zumwalt, *On Watch*, 436–437; G. Golan, *Yom Kippur and After*, 108–109.
218. The Druze are an Arabic-speaking ethnic and religious minority of several millions who live in Syria, Lebanon, Jordan, and Israel. Israel's Druze minority is accepted as loyal, and Druze serve in the IDF. Druze living in Arab states serve in their armies, though in Syria there is some resentment toward them. Schiff notes that Dayan opposed the idea of Druze serving in the army "as an unnecessary burden on the IDF; anyway, he isn't at all certain that the Druze are really interested" (*October Earthquake*, 200).
219. Ibid., 215; Herzog, *The War of Atonement*, 208–209; Bar-Lev, interview by Millstein, 26 June 1974.
220. Schiff, *October Earthquake*, 238.
221. *Divrei Haknesset* 68, 4474–4476.
222. See G. Golan, *Yom Kippur and After*, 107–108; Schiff, *October Earthquake*, 240, 250; Herzog, *The War of Atonement*, 232.
223. Heikal, *The Road to Ramadan*, 235–236.
224. For Nixon's negative response to the Soviet proposal, see his *Memoirs*, 930–931.
225. Brecher, interview with Eban, 15 July 1974.
226. Dayan, *Story of My Life*, 439.

227. Richard Nixon, interview by David Frost, and his *Memoirs*, 931; Quandt, *Decade of Decisions*, 188. The way the amount of $2.2 billion of US assistance was arrived at highlights the effect of time pressure on US decision-making: "It was an interaction process. The Israelis made it clear from the outset that they really did not have the resources to pay for this. The U.S. Embassy [in Tel Aviv] made it clear to Washington that the cost would have a very adverse effect on the Israeli economy. They urged Washington very strongly to make the first billion dollars—which was the estimate of what was needed at first—a straight grant and worry about what was coming later. It was a fight for survival. As to how the sum was arrived at: It was clear to everybody that the minimal figure for the airlift was one billion. It was also clear that the airlift would go on and that they would need much more in the later stages of the war. Nobody knew what the figure was. The Israelis calculated at some stage 3.5 billion; some put it even higher. We knew that this was an exaggeration, but we did not know what the correct figure ... was. It was probably a compromise between the figure the Israelis said they needed and what Washington calculated they needed" (Brecher, interview with US Embassy officials, 12 August 1974).
228. An American intelligence memorandum quoted in Zumwalt, *On Watch*, 439, noted: "If the Soviets were going to introduce troops, they would want their own people doing reconnaissance in advance."
229. Kalb and Kalb, *Kissinger*, 483; this is also discussed in Eban, *An Autobiography*, 524–525.
230. Kissinger repeated on several occasions that one of the reasons he agreed to go to Moscow was that it gave Israel another 96 hours to improve her military position; see, for example, his talk with American Jewish intellectuals, as reported in *Yediot Aharonot*, 15 February 1974. Quandt, by contrast, indicated as the primary goal, "to obtain Soviet and Arab agreement to a cease-fire resolution that could serve as the basis for a subsequent diplomatic effort" (*Decade of Decisions*, 191).
231. Nixon, *Memoirs*, 936; G. Golan, *Yom Kippur and After*, 112–118; Meir's speech to the *Knesset*, 23 October 1973, *Divrei Haknesset*, 68, 4507–4510.

232. Nixon tried to assuage Meir's hurt feelings by sending her a letter, while Kissinger was en route to Israel, "expressing my regret that there had not been more time for consultation" (*Memoirs*, 936).
233. Schiff, *October Earthquake*, 267–270.
234. Dayan, *Story of My Life*, 411; Yeshayahu Ben-Porath et al., *Hamechdal* [*The Fiasco*] (Tel Aviv: Hotza'a Meyuhedet, 1973), 220–222. The message was transmitted, simultaneously, through Dinitz and Keating. It reached Israel while Eban was briefing the *Knesset* Foreign Affairs and Security Committee, which was suspended immediately. Yariv stated that the Cabinet erred in interpreting Nixon's message as straight pressure; it contained no appeal, but also no threats. Israel should have insisted on another 12 hours (Brecher, interview with Yariv). The scene was repeated in Cairo. At exactly the same time, Sadat received through Ambassador Vinogradov a message from Brezhnev, urging him to accept the agreed proposal for a cease-fire in place. But Brezhnev's message also contained assurances that the Soviet Union would enforce the cease-fire, if necessary, on its own. See Heikal, *The Road to Ramadan*, 238–240; G. Golan, *Yom Kippur and After*, 115.
235. Israel, *Divrei Haknesset*, 68, 4507–4508.
236. Dayan, *Story of My Life*, 443–444.
237. Brecher, interview with Bar-Lev and Bar-Lev, interview by Millstein. Bar-Lev indicated that Israel needed another day to place the IDF in a strong advantageous position. A message to Nixon from Brezhnev on the "hotline" at 11:00 A.M. (New York time), 23 October, charged the Israelis with rupturing the cease-fire: "I sent a reply that, according to our information, Egypt was the first party to violate the cease-fire" (Nixon, *Memoirs*, 936).
238. Ben-Porath et al., *Hamechdal*, 220; Quandt, *Decade of Decisions*, 194.
239. The Resolution was passed by 14 to 0; China did not participate in the vote. Within 12 hours, UN observers dispatched from Cyprus, Cairo, and Jerusalem were on the scene.
240. Sadat's version of the renewed fighting from 22 to 24 October, markedly at variance with all others, is in his *In Search of Identity*, 265–267.
241. Kalb and Kalb, *Kissinger*, 490.

242. Richard Nixon, interview by David Frost. Nixon's perception of the danger of a nuclear confrontation with Moscow and his decision to order a nuclear alert, including the text of his messages on the 24th to Brezhnev and to Sadat, explaining US opposition to superpower forces in the Middle East, are recalled vividly in his *Memoirs*, 937–941.
243. Zumwalt, *On Watch*, 443–448; Kalb and Kalb, *Kissinger*, 493–494; Nixon, interview by David Frost, 12 May 1977; Foy D. Kohler, Leo Gouré, and Mose L. Harvey, *The Soviet Union and the October 1973 Middle East War: The Implications for Detente* (Miami: Monographs in International Affairs, Center for Advanced International Studies, University of Miami, 1974), 65.
244. The full text of Resolution 340, passed on 25 October by a vote of 14 to 0 (with China not participating) is:

The Security Council,
Recalling its Resolutions 338 (1973) of 22 October and 339 (1973) of 23 October 1973,
Noting with regret the reported repeated violations of the cease-fire in noncompliance with Resolutions 338 (1973) and 339 (1973),
Noting with concern from the Secretary-General's report that the United Nations military observers have not yet been enabled to place themselves on both sides of the cease-fire line,
1. Demands that immediate and complete cease-fire be observed and that the parties return to the positions occupied by them at 16:50 hours GMT on 22 October 1973;
2. Requests the Secretary-General, as an immediate step, to increase the number of United Nations military observers on both sides;
3. Decides to set up immediately under its authority a United Nations Emergency Force to be composed of personnel drawn from State/Members of the United Nations except the permanent members of the Security Council and requests the Secretary-General to report within 24 hours on the steps taken to this effect;
4. Requests the Secretary-General to report to the Council on an urgent and continuing basis on the state of implementation of the present resolution, as well as Resolutions 338 (1973) and 339 (1973);
5. Requests all Member States to extend their full cooperation to the United Nations in the implementation of the present resolution, as well as Resolutions 338 (1973) and 339 (1973).

On the behind-the-scenes maneuvering at the UN, see Draper, "The Road to Geneva."
245. Brecher, interview with US Embassy officials, 12 August 1974.
246. Dayan, *Story of My Life*, 447–448. See also Quandt, *Decade of Decisions*, 198 and no. 71 and Bar-Tov, *Dado*, vol. 2, 339–341.
247. Michael Brecher, interview with Eban, 15 July 1974. Also noted in Eban, *An Autobiography*, 528–530.
248. The list of equipment lost by the armies of Egypt and Syria during the war is given in Table 10.5.

CHAPTER 11

Evidence on Conflict Resolution: Partial Agreements and Overall Failed Attempts, 1937–2014

The *scope* and *frequency* of attempts to *resolve* the *Arab–Israel* PC are more complex than, and as voluminous as, but qualitatively *less successful* than, the *record of conflict management* of specific Arab–Israel *crises* since the onset of this PC in 1948. I turn now to a survey of the essentials of the most important attempts to resolve the Arab–Israel PC, in chronological sequence.

PEEL COMMISSION REPORT (7 JULY 1937)

The first substantial effort to resolve the pre-state conflict between the Jewish and Arab communities in Palestine since the implementation of the British Mandate over Palestine on 29 September 1923—the draft of the Mandate had been confirmed by the League of Nations Council on 24 July 1922—was the recommendations of the Peel Commission on 7 July 1937. Its point of departure was a judgment that the Mandate was unworkable and should be replaced by a *partition* of the Mandate territory into *two independent states, Jewish and Arab Palestinian*. In preparation for that solution, the Peel Commission recommended that Jewish immigration should be limited to 12,000 each year, for five years, after which partition should be implemented. Moreover, citing the 1923 Greece–Turkey agreement to resolve their intercommunal conflict over western Anatolia, the Peel Commission recommended a Jewish–Palestinian exchange of land and population, the latter to be compulsory, if necessary.

The reaction of the principal adversaries and the Mandatory power was mixed. Both institutional expressions of Palestinian opinion, the Husseini-led Arab Higher Committee and the Nashashibi-led National Defense Party, rejected categorically the Peel partition plan (or any plan calling for a Jewish state). The Zionist Congress, at the behest of its two most prominent leaders, Weizmann and Ben-Gurion, accepted the Peel proposal, without enthusiasm, "as a basis for negotiation." The UK government was initially well disposed. However, on the basis of the recommendation of the 1938 Woodhead Commission, appointed to inquire about the feasibility of the Peel Commission Report, the British Cabinet rejected the partition plan.

UN GENERAL ASSEMBLY PARTITON RESOLUTION (29 NOVEMBER 1947)

The significance of the Peel Commission's effort at conflict resolution lay in its role as a precedent for the majority partition plan of the UN Special Committee on Palestine (UNSCOP), which became the basis of UN General Assembly Resolution 181, approved on 29 November 1947. The importance of this resolution, one among hundreds adopted by a UN body during the past 69 years, derived from the fact that it became the global organization's *imprimatur* for the proclamation of Israel's independence on 14–15 May 1948. That momentous political act, in turn, along with the immediate rejection of the General Assembly Resolution by the Arab League and the launching of the First Arab–Israel War on 15 May by the "frontline" Arab states, Egypt, Iraq, Jordan, Lebanon, and Syria, triggered the Arab–Israel *interstate* PC. Unlike the October-Yom-Kippur War in 1973, which led to formal resolution of the Egypt–Israel segment of the *Arab–Israel* PC in 1979, the UN Partition Resolution, a political act that, for some, promised a termination of incipient violence, contributed to both the onset of this interstate PC and the outbreak of full-scale war.

UN CONCILIATION COMMISSION FOR PALESTINE (UNCCP) (BETTER KNOWN AS THE PALESTINE CONCILIATION COMMISSION [PCC]), LAUSANNE CONFERENCE (27 APRIL–12 SEPTEMBER 1949)

This Commission was created by the UN General Assembly in December 1948 (during the First Arab–Israel War) as part of Resolution 194, with the goal of mediating disputed issues between the conflicting parties arising from the First Arab–Israel War, mainly related to refugees. The unchanged text of that resolution, an integral part of UN-created international law, enshrined the "Right of Return" to their homes by all Palestinian refugees willing to live at peace with Israel. This right has been reaffirmed continuously as the foundation of the Palestinian attitude to any proposed plan for resolution of the Israel–Palestine conflict. Equally, Resolution 194 and the provisions dealing with refugees in the UN General Assembly's Partition Resolution 181, 29 November 1947, have been rejected by Israel throughout the conflict as a basis of any formula for resolution of the *Arab–Israel* PC. Nonetheless, the Arab Higher Committee, representing the Palestinians, and Israel accepted the invitation to attend the PCC Lausanne Conference, along with Egypt, Jordan, Lebanon, and Syria, and some refugee organizations.

Many issues were discussed at this first "peace conference," aimed at achieving resolution of the Arab–Israel conflict, including *borders*, *Jerusalem*, and many secondary aspects related to *Palestinian refugees*, such as the *absentee property left in Israel by refugees* and the fate of their *bank accounts in Israel*; all are still unresolved and the first two are among the most contentious issues in this PC. The only items discussed at Lausanne that are recalled as exhibiting a *very slight* glimmer of hope for progress were Israel's *Gaza Plan* and its "100,000 refugee offer." On the former, Israel conveyed a willingness to accept all Arab *inhabitants* and *refugees* in Gaza, estimated then at 70,000 and 230,000, respectively, as citizens of Israel—in exchange for two conditions: *Israel's annexation of the Gaza Strip* and the *international community's agreement to cover the entire costs of refugee resettlement*; the Arab delegations rejected the first condition, and the international community did not respond to the second. As for the 100,000 refugee offer by Israel, made under US pressure, there were also two Israel conditions. One was an agreement by the Arab states to a *comprehensive peace with Israel*, based on the borders existing at the time of the Armistice Agreements in 1949, which reflected Israel's victories during the 1948 war, rather than the map accompanying the UN Partition Resolution in November 1947, preferred by the Arab states. The other condition was resettlement of the Arab refugees in Israel subject to its security and developmental needs, *not* their return to their homes before the 1948 war. The Arab delegations rejected both of these conditions, and the PCC sponsor of the Lausanne Conference termed Israel's proposal "unsatisfactory."

In sum, the Lausanne Conference was the first of many failed attempts to *resolve* the total *Arab–Israel* PC. The basic cleavage on the refugee dimension of their conflict reflected a fundamental *policy* difference: the Arab delegations at the Lausanne Conference insisted that the refugee issue be resolved *separately* from the conflict with Israel as a whole, while Israel insisted that this core issue be solved as an *integral part* of the entire Arab–Israel conflict. Moreover, that conference became linked with another disputed issue between the Arab–Israel adversaries: on 11 May 1949, one day before Israel signed the Lausanne Protocol, a symbolic but substantively insignificant formal document expressing the Parties' support, in principle, of their peace process, the UN General Assembly formally approved Israel's admission to membership of the global organization, by a vote of 37 to 12, a decision that Israel eagerly sought and the Arab UN members strongly opposed.

UN Security Council Resolution 242 (22 November 1967)

Among the most enduring and crucial UN resolutions adopted by the Security Council on the *Arab–Israel* PC, this Resolution was approved *unanimously* by the 15 members, all of whose representatives were present for the vote, along with most of the principal adversaries—Egypt, Israel, Jordan, and Lebanon. There were two dissenters, initially: Syria, which was bitterly critical when the Resolution was adopted, and on 15 October 1968, by the Palestine Liberation Organization (PLO), then acknowledged, informally, as the most representative organization of the Palestinian nation.

Although five principles of a peaceful resolution of this conflict were enunciated in Resolution 242, its essence was contained in the first two principles, an explicit trade-off of obligations by the principal adversaries. The first principle, exhibiting very careful drafting, called for "the withdrawal of Israel armed forces from territories occupied in the recent conflict"; this phrasing did not specify "all" or "the" territories, indicating less than total withdrawal from the territories occupied by Israel during the June-Six-Day War in 1967. The Palestinians and their Arab and other supporters chose the French translation, "de territoires," implying "from the," that is, "from all" the territories; however, since the resolution was drafted and submitted in English, the English version has always been the primary source. The second principle called for "the termination of all claims or states of belligerence ... and the acknowledgment of sovereignty, territorial integrity and political independence of every state in the area and the right to live in peace within secure and recognized boundaries." *In sum*, the "trade-off" was Israel's *withdrawal* from some of the territories conquered during the 1967 War, in exchange for Arab *recognition*, or, as the drafters of "242" intended, an "exchange of land for peace."

Over time, dissent by Syria and the PLO changed to acquiescence, though without enthusiasm. Syria accepted "242" conditionally in 1972, and indirectly in 1973, after the October-Yom-Kippur War, when it accepted Security Council Resolution 338, which incorporated Resolution 242. Negotiations between Israel and Syria came much later, initially between senior diplomats in the early mid-1990s, and at the Head of State level, between Assad and Clinton in 2000. The PLO accepted Resolutions 242 and 338 as the basis for negotiations with Israel in 1993, when Arafat signed the Declaration of Principles (DOP), the core document of the Israel–Palestine Oslo Accord. Moreover, Resolution 242 is among the most durable Arab–Israel agreements: it formed the basis of negotiations leading to the Egypt–Israel and Israel–Jordan peace agreements, in 1979 and 1994, as well as the Oslo Accords I and II in 1993 and 1995, respectively. And it remains the committed principles of the unfinished peace process between Israel and the Palestinian Authority (PA) 49 years after its adoption by the Security Council. The other three principles, specified in Resolution 242 but not acted upon, are: freedom of navigation, "a just settlement of the refugee problem," and security measures.

JARRING MEDIATION (23 NOVEMBER 1967–MARCH 1971)

In accordance with a provision in Resolution 242, UN Secretary-General U Thant appointed Gunnar Jarring on 23 November 1967 as his Special Envoy to mediate the implementation of this Resolution. Egypt, Israel, Jordan, and Lebanon agreed to participate in his shuttle diplomacy— Jarring was then, and simultaneously throughout his Mission, Sweden's Ambassador to the USSR. Syria, as noted above, denounced Resolution 242 because it did not call for Israel's "total withdrawal" from all the territories conquered during the June-Six-Day War in 1967. Jarring presented his peace plan to all the adversaries in February 1971: its most controversial provisions were the restoration of Egypt's sovereignty over all of Sinai and the withdrawal of Israel's forces to the pre-4 June 1967 lines.

Egypt, Jordan, and Lebanon accepted the Jarring plan. Although talks with Jarring continued until 1973, the failure of his attempt to resolve the Arab–Israel PC was evident by February 1971, when Israel rejected his peace plan, declaring that it would not revert to the pre-1967 War *de facto* borders. A fundamental obstacle to a successful Jarring Mission was the adversaries' basic disagreement on *the timing of territorial changes and direct peace talks*. Israel insisted on the primacy of direct peace negotiations by the adversaries and a clear linkage between any territorial concessions and a commitment by the Arab states to a formal peace agreement. The Arab states insisted on the reversal of the sequence—an Israel commitment to total withdrawal of Israeli forces as a precondition of direct talks.

CAMP DAVID SUMMIT I AND EGYPT–ISRAEL PEACE AGREEMENT (5 SEPTEMBER 1978–26 MARCH 1979)

The initiative for this breakthrough achievement of conflict resolution—for the Egypt–Israel segment of the *Arab–Israel* PC—was an announcement by President Sadat to Egypt's parliament on 9 November 1977 of his intention to go to Jerusalem to address Israel's *Knesset*; this was a surprise follow-up of his informal remark several months earlier that he would go "anywhere," specifically mentioning Jerusalem, to regain the territory lost by Egypt in the 1967 War. Moreover, his formal announcement followed secret talks in Morocco during the summer of 1977 between his Deputy Prime Minister, Hassan Tohami, and Israel's then Foreign Minister, Moshe Dayan, Chief of Staff of the IDF in the 1956 Suez War and Israel's Defense Minister in the June-Six-Day War in 1967 and the October-Yom-Kippur War in 1973, setting out the terms deemed essential by both adversaries for an agreement between the leaders of Egypt and Israel. Sadat came to Jerusalem ten days after his announcement (19–22 November), addressed the *Knesset*, and engaged Prime Minister Begin in the first round of Talks.

The crucial negotiations, at Camp David from 5 to 17 September 1978, were initiated—and mediated—by President Carter. The successful outcome was expressed in two "Framework" agreements, "for the Conclusion of a Peace Treaty between Egypt and Israel" and "for

Peace in the Middle East." It was clear—to the political leaders and all commentators then and later—that the Camp David Talks had produced: (1) a *plan for peace between two adversary states*, not a general peace agreement between all Arab states and Israel; and (2) the first of several stages that, hopefully, would culminate in a peace agreement between Israel and the Palestinian nation, a goal that remains elusive 39 years later.

The Egypt–Israel "Framework" agreement provided for: the withdrawal of Israel's armed forces and the 4500 Israeli civilians residing in Sinai from Egypt, the establishment of normal diplomatic relations between Egypt and Israel, Egypt's guarantee of freedom of passage for Israeli ships through the Suez Canal and the Strait of Tiran, a reduction in the size of Egyptian armed forces in Sinai, and Israel's return of the Abu Rodeis oil fields in Sinai to Egypt. The peace treaty was signed on 26 March 1979, but only after a crucial shuttle by President Carter between Cairo and Jerusalem to resolve remaining disagreements over the implementation of their agreements.

The "agreed basis" of the "Framework" agreement "for Peace in the Middle East" was explicitly identified as UN Resolution 242. However, the agreement focused exclusively on the Palestinian–Israeli dimension of the *Arab–Israel* PC, that is, on future governance of the West Bank and Gaza Strip. (There was no mention of disputed issues between Israel and Syria, notably the Golan Heights, or those between Israel and Jordan or issues between Israel and Lebanon.) *Part A* called for the establishment of an autonomous "self-governing authority," with "full autonomy," to be implemented within five years. Moreover, Israel armed forces in the West Bank and Gaza were to be withdrawn after the election of a "self-governing authority" to replace Israel's military government in the West Bank and Gaza. *Part B* applied to Egypt–Israel relations, which were specified in the Egypt–Israel "Framework" agreement. And *Part C* was a *pro forma* indication of principles to apply to relations between Israel and its Arab neighbors, with an emphasis, as noted, on Resolution 242 as the "agreed basis" for those relations. Only Part A had any operational meaning. Critics, including most Palestinians, noted the absence of any reference in the "Framework Agreement for Peace in the Middle East" to the vexed, unresolved issues of *Jerusalem* or the Palestinian claim of the *Right of Return* of Palestinian refugees since 1948.

These 1979 agreements between Egypt and Israel were buttressed by pledges of substantial US financial aid—1.3 billion dollars in military aid to Egypt, annually, and 3 billion dollars annually to Israel, which have been implemented during the past 38 years. For several years after the signing of these agreements, the Egypt–Israel relationship appeared to improve, substantially, as evident in a very large increase of Israeli tourists visiting Egypt, though not reciprocated by Egypt. This tapered off, and the overall relationship between the two nations and states since 1979 has been correctly termed as "Cold Peace."

Israel–Lebanon Abortive Agreement (17 May 1983)

In the aftermath of the first Lebanon War (5 June–1 September 1982), Israel and Lebanon negotiated a peace agreement, largely under US and Israeli pressure. The draft agreement, signed on 17 May 1983, provided for the termination of their "state of war," and the phased withdrawal of Israeli forces from Lebanon, with the Lebanon army taking over IDF positions. There were also two concessions to Israel, the victor in that war. One was the establishment of a "security zone" in South Lebanon by Lebanon's army. The other, a closely related provision, called for "security cooperation" between Israel and Lebanon, aimed at preventing PLO infiltration of the border area between the two signatories.

The agreement was not ratified by Lebanon's government because of several reinforcing reasons. One was strong opposition by Lebanon's Muslim community and the Arab states (except Egypt) to peace and *rapprochement* with Israel. Moreover, Lebanon's army, crucial for the implementation of the agreement, collapsed in February 1984. The most decisive factor was Syria's refusal to remove its military forces from Lebanon, the ultimate source of Syria's domination of Lebanon throughout its civil war (1975–90). Under these combined pressures, Lebanon's government repudiated the peace agreement with Israel on 5 March 1984. By then, Israel had established its "security zone" in South Lebanon, a spillover from its 1982 invasion, with the assistance of a proxy, the South Lebanon Army: Israel's occupation lasted until its unilateral withdrawal from Lebanon in 2000. There has been no further evidence of progress toward conflict resolution between Israel and Lebanon, especially because of the emergence of the most powerful militant Shiite community in Lebanon, *Hezbollah*, which was intensely opposed to peace and accommodation with the "Zionist Enemy."

Arafat Statement at Stockholm News Conference and Address to UN General Assembly (8 and 13 December 1988)

After a two-day meeting between a PLO delegation led by Yasser Arafat and five American Jews in Stockholm, the PLO leader reportedly stated on 8 December that the Palestinian parliament, at its November meeting in Algiers, had "accepted the existence of Israel as a state in the region" and "declared its rejection and condemnation of terrorism in all its forms." Moreover, at a news conference the same day, he reportedly declared: "We accept two states, the Palestine state and the Jewish state of Israel," adding that this statement was an important clarification of the declaration issued by the Palestine National Council in November (Steve Lohr, *New York Times*, 8 December 1988, A10). Israeli and US governmental leaders were not persuaded. US Secretary of State Shultz reportedly said, "so far as it's been reported to me, they haven't met these conditions [which the US government had set for formal interaction with the PLO]." Both Prime Minister Shamir and Foreign Minister Peres dismissed Arafat's initiative; the latter, who became an Israeli high-profile supporter of conciliatory relations with the PLO in the early 1990s regarding the first Oslo Accord (see below), reportedly termed Arafat's public statements "a cunning exercise in public relations" (Ibid.).

On 13 December, in a lengthy speech to the UN General Assembly in Geneva, replete with multiple harsh criticisms of Israel and US behavior toward the Palestinians, Arafat reiterated the Palestinian recognition of Israel as a state. In fact, he went much further: as if anticipating the insistence by Israel's Prime Minister Netanyahu 25 years later that Palestinian recognition of Israel as a Jewish state was a precondition for peace, he specifically acknowledged Israel as a Jewish state: "the only birth certificate for the establishment of the state of Israel is international Resolution 181, which was issued by the UN General Assembly on 29th November 1947. It stipulates the establishment of two states in Palestine—a Palestinian Arab state and a Jewish state." There is no evidence that any Israeli or US political leaders altered their dismissal of Arafat's words of recognition in 1988, dooming another attempt at conflict resolution.

Madrid Peace Conference (30 October–1 November 1991)

This three-day conference brought together all of the *Arab–Israel* PC principal adversaries, except Egypt, which had signed a peace treaty with Israel in 1979, that is, Israel, Jordan, Lebanon, Syria, and a non-PLO Palestinian group that was, formally, part of Jordan's delegation (because of Israel's refusal, then, to negotiate with the PLO). Although the conference and the peace process that it initiated was, officially, co-sponsored by the United States and the USSR, it emerged as a byproduct of the US-created Iraq War coalition, including two Arab states, Egypt, and Syria, formed in 1990 to achieve "regime change" in Iraq by overthrowing its Saddam Hussein–dominated Ba'ath Party government. The road to Madrid was paved by the first Bush president's Secretary of State, James Baker, during eight months of shuttle diplomacy among the "frontline" Arab states and Israel immediately after Gulf War I in February–early March 1991. The key goals enunciated by the US President at the opening session were peace agreements; diplomatic, economic, and cultural relations; and economic development and tourism—peace to be achieved through direct negotiations, based on mutual compromise.

None of these objectives was achieved. However, in perspective, the conference broke fresh ground in the elusive peace process. It was the first forum for *direct, face-to-face negotiations* among the principal adversaries that had not yet achieved peace, other than for cease-fire agreements during a war. Moreover, the Palestinians received an incipient, indirect recognition as a legitimate participant in the Arab–Israel peace process, although muted. And the "spirit of Madrid" was sustained for several years by two parallel tracks of negotiations. The bilateral track aimed at peace treaties between the four pairs of adversaries. The negotiations continued through 12 meetings in Washington from November 1991 until January 1994 (see below). Although the post–Madrid Conference "peace process" did not contribute directly to the Oslo Accord—in fact, it was an alternative path, aimed at all-encompassing peace between the Arab world and Israel—it created a precedent for direct negotiations and sustained a growing acceptance by the adversaries of its legitimacy and a modest optimism about its potential success as a "road map" or model for future negotiations. Moreover, the "Preamble" to the Oslo II Accord (1995) acknowledged its roots in UN Security Council Resolutions 242 (1967) and 338 (1973), and in the deliberations at the 1991 Madrid Conference: certainly, the atmosphere generated by the Madrid Conference and the follow-up bilateral track of peace negotiations contributed to both the initial Israel–Palestine agreements, the Oslo Accords in 1993 and 1995, though their promise was not fulfilled, and the Israel–Jordan peace agreement in 1994.

OSLO I ACCORD (20 AUGUST AND 13 SEPTEMBER 1993)

After lengthy, atypically successful secret negotiations in 1993 between PLO representatives and two Israeli academics, actively supported from the outset by Israel's Deputy Foreign Minister Yossi Beilin and, later, by Israel's then Foreign Minister Shimon Peres, a "back-channel" agreement, facilitated by the Foreign Minister of Norway, produced the *Declaration of Principles on Interim Self-Government Arrangements*, known as the *Declaration of Principles* (*DOP*), or the *Oslo I Accord*, approved by a senior official of the PLO and Peres, who was visiting Norway, on 20 August 1993. The agreement then emerged into the public domain at a high-profile ceremony on the White House Lawn on 13 September 1993, signed by PLO Leader Arafat, Israel Foreign Minister Perez, US Secretary of State, and Russia's Foreign Minster in the presence of President Clinton.

The first directly negotiated substantive agreement between these two principal adversaries in the *Arab–Israel* PC was, like all subsequent agreements, a dense, extremely detailed document, containing 17 articles and 4 annexes. In essence, the DOP (Oslo I Accord) comprised substantive concessions by the occupying power in two domains. One was *the transfer of governing authority*: the Palestinians were granted *limited self-government over parts of the territory of the West Bank and the Gaza Strip*. These territories, not specified in the Oslo I Accord, were to be administered by an elected Interim Palestine Authority for a transitional *five-year period*, to *begin* after the formation of the PA, no later than May 1996. The scope of the interim self-government would be granted in phases: the PA's initial jurisdiction comprised education and culture, health, social welfare, tourism, and direct taxation. The second domain of substantive concessions to the Palestinians, closely related, was the provision that *Israel's military government and the IDF* were *to be redeployed, that is, withdrawn* from territories transferred to the PA. To fill that security void, the PA was also granted authority to establish a police force for the territories to be transferred to its jurisdiction; external security was to remain under Israel's control.

It is noteworthy—and was noted by critics of the Oslo I Accord—that none of the most contested issues in this PC was addressed in the DOP. Rather, it was specified that *Jerusalem, Palestinian refugees, Israeli settlements, security arrangements*, and *border* would be the focus of "permanent status negotiations" that would begin as soon as possible. Nonetheless, optimists and well-wishers among Israelis and Palestinians, and foreign supporters of conflict resolution and reconciliation of the principal adversaries in the *Arab–Israel* PC welcomed the Oslo I Accord as the most promising development ever, especially the stated aim of the DOP, namely, that the five-year transition period would lead to a peace agreement, based on UN Security Council Resolutions 242 (1967) and 338 (1973). The optimistic expectations were also reinforced by the letters of mutual recognition in the exchange between Arafat and Israeli Prime Minister Rabin that accompanied the signing of the DOP: Israel's government recognized the PLO as the legitimate representative of the Palestinian nation, and the PLO recognized the right of Israel to exist, as well as pledged to renounce terrorism. Notwithstanding these conciliatory pledges and the progress implicit in the Oslo II Accord (see below), the promise of conflict resolution and reconciliation remains unfulfilled.

During the six years following the Oslo I Accord (1993), there were five supplementary agreements in the continuing, frequently affirmed, quest for resolution of the core Israel–Palestine segment of the *Arab–Israel* PC. None broke fresh ground: thus they will be noted briefly here, except for the Oslo II Accord (1995).

Gaza–Jericho Agreement (Also Known as the 1994 Cairo Agreement) (4 May 1994)

In this Agreement, Israel translated its Oslo I intention to begin the "redeployment" of its military forces in Jericho and the Gaza Strip by promising to withdraw the IDF, partly, from these two occupied areas within three weeks from the signing of the Cairo Agreement. Moreover, it implemented another statement of intent in Oslo I, namely, the creation of the Palestinian Authority (PA), with Yasser Arafat named as President on 5 July 1994. There was also a Protocol on Economic Relations between

Israel and the PA, essentially integrating the two economies, and the activation of another intention indicated in Oslo I—to create the Palestinian Civil Police Force. These pledges and acts were incorporated into the next agreement, the Oslo II Accord, in 1995.

OSLO II ACCORD (28 SEPTEMBER 1995)

Like Oslo I, this was a high-profile agreement, signed by Israel Prime Minister Rabin and PLO Chairman Arafat in Washington on 28 September 1995, witnessed by President Clinton and representatives of Egypt, Jordan, Norway, and Russia, and the European Union. Moreover, the Oslo II Accord was an extraordinarily complex and, in many places, obtuse legal document, seemingly designed by its Israeli drafters to yield minimal, highly restricted governing powers to the PA and very limited "redeployment," that is, withdrawal, of the IDF from occupied territories in the West Bank and Gaza.

The Oslo II Accord, formally known as the Interim Agreement on the West Bank and the Gaza Strip, contained a Preamble, 5 chapters, and 31 articles, along with 7 annexes and 9 maps, running to more than 300 pages! However, it too merely amplified the intention of the adversaries, as spelled out in Oslo Accord 1; and it absorbed the content of agreements since Oslo I, notably the Cairo Agreement on 4 May 1994 and a 27 August 1995 Protocol on Further Transfer of Powers and Responsibilities to the Palestinian Authority. The major substantive provision of Oslo II was the creation of three Areas in the West Bank. Limited powers and responsibilities were granted to the PA in Areas A and B, notably Palestinian self-rule in six West Bank cities, Bethlehem, Hebron, Jenin, Nablus, Qalqilya, and Ramallah, and 450 Palestinian Arab villages, along with a signal that these might be enlarged in "final status negotiations" for a peace settlement, repeated *ad nauseam*, based upon UN Security Council Resolutions 242 and 338. Area C was to remain under Israel's exclusive jurisdiction. The *Interim Agreement* was to last for a transition period of no more than five years. And negotiations on the highly contested "permanent status" issues in this PC were to begin no later than 4 May 1996.

In reality, those elusive "permanent status" issues in the Israel–Palestine conflict, noted earlier, were first given high-level attention in the first decade-plus of the twenty-first century: at the Clinton-initiated

Second Camp David Talks with Arafat and Prime Minister Barak in 2000; at the Clinton-initiated Taba Talks in 2001; the 2008 secret negotiations between Prime Minister Olmert and Mahmoud Abbas, the successor to Arafat as President of the PA, and the 2013–14 prolonged (9 months) secret negotiations between senior Israel and Palestinian officials, actively mediated by US Secretary of State Kerry and a team of US assistants. During this phase of high-profile attempts to resolve the "permanent status" issues, the Oslo Accords had run their course and were replaced by another major power-initiated mediation effort, the 2002 "road map" (see below for these five most recent failed attempts at resolution.

HEBRON AGREEMENT (17 JANUARY 1997)

This Israel–PA agreement, also known as the Hebron Protocol, focused on "redeployment" (withdrawal) of the IDF from the highly contested city of Hebron in the West Bank. Tension between its overwhelming Palestinian population and a Jewish settler community in the city (the Kiryat Arba Settlement), which, since 1968, had grown steadily, reinforced by the experience of a 1929 Palestinian massacre of Jews in Hebron. The Hebron Agreement divided the city into two Areas: H-1, with approximately 80 percent of the population, would come under Palestinian control; and Area H-2 would remain under Israel's control: IDF forces would withdraw from the H-1 territory within ten days, but the entire Hebron area would remain under Israel's military control. The "final status" negotiations on Hebron would begin within two months, to be completed by 4 May 1999. The Prime Minister justified the time frame as follows, in a 16 January 1997 statement to the *Knesset* on Israel's goals that illuminates the rationale for all policy by the Netanyahu governments regarding the West Bank and Gaza to the present: "our goals [are] to maintain the unity of Jerusalem, to ensure the security depth necessary for the defense of the State, to insist on the right of Jews to settle in their land, and to propose to the Palestinians a suitable arrangement for self-rule but without the sovereign Powers which pose a threat to the State of Israel." Two weeks later, the Jewish settlements in Hebron were granted special government funding for their expansion and the building of new settlements.

WYE RIVER MEMORANDUM (23 OCTOBER 1998)

After an eight-day Summit meeting in the United States, this agreement focused on technical security issues—further modest "redeployments" of Israel military forces among West Bank territories, in three stages extending over three months (November 1998–January 1999): the total withdrawals would be 13 percent in Area C (reducing the IDF presence in the area under exclusive Israel control), from 74 percent to 61 percent; an increase in Area A of 7 percent; and an increase of 5 percent in Area B. In fact, this marginal transfer of Israeli forces in the West Bank was not implemented.

SHARM EL-SHEIKH MEMORANDUM (4 SEPTEMBER 1999)

This agreement set forth an accelerated timetable for "permanent status" negotiations, which had been delayed since their inclusion in the Oslo I Accord in 1993: they were to begin nine days later, with the goal of a comprehensive permanent status agreement between Israel and the PLO within one year. There was also a provision for further IDF redeployments. This timetable, too, was a casualty of a peace process that had gone awry during the six years since the Oslo I Accord. Only the release of 350 Palestinian prisoners, stipulated in the Memorandum, was implemented in 1999.

CAMP DAVID SUMMIT II (11–25 JULY 2000)

This conference was similar to the 1978 Camp David Summit I in several respects. The two principal adversaries, Israel and the PLO, were represented by their most senior political leader, Arafat, as at Camp David I, and Israel's Prime Minister Ehud Barak. The initiator of both Camp David conferences was the US President, President Carter of Camp David Summit I and President Clinton of Camp David Summit II. The objective of both Summit conferences was identical—formal resolution of the Israel–Palestine conflict. However, the outcome of these conferences was fundamentally different—success in 1978, culminating in the Egypt–Israel Peace Agreement in March 1979, failure in 2000 regarding the Israel–Palestine conflict.

The adversaries disagreed on every issue, though with flexibility on some. Moreover, the PLO leader, throughout the conference, did not convey clear Palestinian proposals aimed at resolution of the conflict: this role was performed by lesser Palestinian officials. Rather, Arafat's behavior seemed to reflect his unconcealed discomfort at the need to attend a conference that he regarded as premature. This will be evident from the following brief discussion of incompatible positions on core issues that had been in contention for decades.

Territory

The Palestinians claimed *unqualified sovereignty over the West Bank and Gaza Strip*, with flexibility on one aspect, a willingness to consider an absolutely equal exchange of some territory, a "land swap," that is, Palestinian acceptance of the transfer of the territory of Israeli "settlement blocs" in the West Bank to Israel in exchange for the transfer of an equal size of territory in Israel to Palestine. Israel offered to transfer 73 percent of the West Bank territory, along with 100 percent of the Gaza Strip, to an independent Palestine, along with a willingness to accept a further transfer of an additional 19 percent of the West Bank, thus expanded to 92 percent of the West Bank territory, in 10–25 years, with one exception—Israel would retain the settlement of Kiryat Arba, adjacent to Hebron, a holy city for Jews, as an Israeli enclave within a Palestine state, and Israel would control Palestinian airspace. The Palestinian demand for complete sovereignty over the West Bank, except for a possible land swap, was not accepted by Barak, and the Barak offer was not accepted by Arafat. The Palestinians perceived Israel's annexation proposal as leading to the "cantonization" of the territory of Palestine.

East Jerusalem

This was among the most contentious issues at the Camp David II conference, as in all attempts to resolve the Israel–Palestine conflict. The Palestinians claimed *sovereignty* over all of East Jerusalem and the Holy Places, notably the Al-Aqsa Mosque and the Dome of the Rock, within the Temple Mount, along with the dismantling of Israeli neighborhoods located beyond the Green Line; the one exception was a Palestinian offer to place the Jewish Quarter in the Old City and the Western Wall under Israeli *authority*, but not sovereignty. Barak's offer comprised the PA as *custodian*, but not sovereign, of the Temple Mount (*Haram al-Sharif*), along with Palestinian *administrative control* of the Muslim and Christian

Quarters of the Old City, Muslim and Christian Holy Places, and Arab neighborhoods; Israel would retain control over the Jewish and Armenian Quarters, and Jewish neighborhoods in East Jerusalem and sovereignty *over all of Jerusalem*. The gap in claims to Jerusalem, too, was unbridgeable.

Palestinian Refugees

The Palestinians reaffirmed their demand since the onset of this PC—the implementation of the Palestinian *Right of Return*, as enshrined in UN General Assembly Resolution 194 in 1948. This was accompanied by an offer to implement this right by a mechanism agreed to by both adversaries and a pledge to attempt to persuade a majority of Palestinian refugees to seek a destination other than Israel. Israel denied responsibility for creating the Palestinian refugee problem but offered to accept a return of a maximum of 100,000 refugees and a financial contribution to an international fund of 30 billion dollars to provide compensation for property lost by Palestinians and expropriated by Israel. Here too the outcome of negotiations was deadlock.

Security

The gap between the adversaries on this issue, too, was glaring. Israel made a series of demands designed to enhance its security: the right to use Palestine's airspace at will; deployment of troops in Palestinian territory in case of emergency; the long-term presence of an international force in the Jordan Valley; a permanent Israeli security presence along the Palestine–Jordan border; most important, the demilitarization of Palestine, except for its police force; a Palestine commitment not to form an alliance without Israel's approval; a Palestine commitment not to allow the introduction of foreign forces west of the Jordan River; and Israeli management of shared water resources in the West Bank. It also insisted that Palestine formally declare the end of the conflict with Israel, foregoing any further demands in the future. The Palestinians at the Summit regarded these demands as a gross infringement on Palestine's sovereignty, though they seemed prepared to undertake a commitment to long-term, even permanent, demilitarization of their state.

The reality of near-total deadlock was evident in a *trilateral statement* issued by the three leaders at the end of their two-week Summit conference. The dismal outcome was evident in a meaningless, if polite, expression of an intention "to continue their efforts to conclude an agreement on all permanent status issues as soon as possible."

CLINTON PARAMETERS (23–27 DECEMBER 2000)

Following the Israel–PLO deadlock at the Camp David Summit II conference in July 2000 and in its brief resumed form at the US Air Force Base in Washington (19–21 December 2000), President Clinton made a final attempt to generate a viable solution to the Israel–Palestinian conflict with a set of "parameters" for a negotiated agreement on the elusive "permanent status" issues. The terms, framed by Dennis Ross, head of a five-person group of advisors to Clinton on the Israel–Palestine conflict, reflected an involved, empathetic, official US view of an equitable compromise on all the major components of a viable four-day "take-it-or-leave it" proposal to terminate the conflict (23–27 December), less than a month before the end of the Clinton presidency.

Territory

The Parameters proposed the creation of a Palestinian state, comprising 94–96 percent of the West Bank and all of the Gaza Strip. Israel was to annex the remaining territory in "land swaps" with Palestine that would transfer to Israel existing "settlement blocs" containing 80 percent of the Israeli settlers in the West Bank, in exchange for an identical size (1–3 percent) of Israeli territory to be granted to the new, contiguous Palestinian state.

Jerusalem

Israel would be granted sovereignty over Jewry's most hallowed shrine, the Western ("Wailing") Wall; Palestine would receive sovereignty, with Israel acquiring "symbolic ownership," over the rest of the Temple Mount. East Jerusalem and the Old City would be divided along ethnic lines—sovereignty for Israel over Jewish-majority districts, and sovereignty for Palestine over Arab-majority districts.

Palestinian Refugees

The new state of Palestine would waive its long-standing claim to an unqualified "Right of Return" to territory that has been part of Israel since 1948. Israel would acknowledge "the moral and material suffering caused to the Palestinian people by the 1948 war and the need to assist the international community [financially] in addressing the problem." The new state of Palestine would accept all refugees willing to settle there. All refugees who did not choose Palestine would be resettled in their existing host countries or exercise the right to immigrate to third countries. A limited number could resettle in Israel if granted entry by Israel. All aspects of the rehabilitation of refugees would be implemented by an international commission. Both Israel and Palestine would acknowledge, in their peace agreement, that these provisions constituted the implementation of the 1948 UN General Assembly Resolution 194 that embodied the Right of Return.

Security

The Parameters provided for the withdrawal of Israel's armed forces from most of the West Bank and Gaza during three years after a peace agreement, to be replaced by an international force; a small IDF unit would remain in the Jordan Valley under the authority of the international force for an additional three years. Moreover, Israel would retain three early-warning stations in the West Bank indefinitely: their continued presence would be subject to review every decade, with a change in status requiring agreement by both states. Palestine would be granted sovereignty over its airspace, with Israel granted a role in training and providing operational assistance. Palestine would be designated a "nonmilitarized state," that is, permanent demilitarization, but would have the right to create and maintain a strong police force and to have an international force for border security. Israel would be granted the right to deploy military forces in select, agreed-upon areas, in cases of a military threat to Israel's security requiring a state of emergency.

End of the Conflict

According to the Clinton Parameters, Israel and Palestine would formally agree to end their conflict and forego any future claims from the adversary on any former contested issue. Conflict termination could take the form of a UN Security Council Resolution certifying that its Resolutions 242, in 1967, and 338, in 1973, had been implemented, the perennial requirement of the vast majority of attempts to resolve this PC.

Unsurprisingly, in light of their response to many earlier proposals for resolution of their PC, the leaders of the two principal adversaries, Israel's Prime Minister Barak and Palestine's President Arafat, accepted the Clinton Parameters *with reservations*. Israel focused on two highly controversial provisions in the Clinton Parameters: Barak declared in a very long letter to Clinton that "he would not sign any document that transfers sovereignty on the Temple Mount to the Palestinians"; further, that "no Israeli prime minister will accept even one refugee on the basis of the right of return" (Ehud Barak, "Continuation of Eyes Wide Shut," interview by Ari Shavit, *Ha'aretz*, 4 September 2002). Similarly, the Palestinian Negotiating Team rejected the *territorial* provisions of the Clinton Parameters, on the ground that the Palestinian state would be divided into separate cantons and unconnected islands, and it opposed Israel's annexation of any settlement blocs in the West Bank and East Jerusalem. Moreover, it dismissed the provision in the Parameters calling on the Palestinians to waive the Right of Return (Clayton E. Swisher, *The Truth about Camp David: The Untold Story about the Collapse of the Middle East Peace Process* [New York: Nation Books, 2004]; MEMRI, *Arafat's Letter of Reservations to President Clinton*, 11 January 2001). It should have been evident to the drafters of the Clinton Parameters that, notwithstanding the imprimatur of the US President, they, the Parameters, were a nonstarter as an attempt to achieve mutually acceptable conflict resolution: this PC was clearly not yet ripe for fundamental concessions by the principal adversaries, the crucial precondition for conflict resolution.

TABA TALKS (21–27 JANUARY 2001)

This final attempt by the Clinton presidency to achieve a mutually agreed basis for Israel–Palestine conflict termination seemed to be much more promising than the Clinton Parameters. Negotiators from both adversaries moved considerably from their *opening positions*. For Israel, there were three nonnegotiable points: categorical denial of the *Right of Return* by Palestinian refugees *to their 1948 homes and properties within Israel's territory in 2001*; rejection of the *Palestinian claim to sovereignty* over the holiest of the holy sites for both adversaries in the Old City of Jerusalem, the Temple Mount (*Haram al-Sharif*); and the transfer to *Israel's sovereignty* of *settlement blocs*, in which 80 percent of Jewish residents in the West Bank lived at that time. For the PLO, the obverse of Israel's nonnegotiable posture applied to these three opening positions: an *unqualified Right of Return by Palestinian refugees* to their 1948 homes and properties in Israel; acknowledgment of Palestine's sovereignty over the entire *Haram al-Sharif*; and the categorical denial of Israel's claim to the transfer of territory occupied by Israeli settlers—settlement blocs in the West Bank and East Jerusalem.

During six days of intense negotiations in Taba, the adversaries had communicated wide-ranging compromise positions on most of the issues on which contention had been the norm since the onset of their conflict in 1947, extending to the period prior to the implementation of the UK Mandate over Palestine in September 1923. *These changes* were noted in a January 2001 report on the outcome of the Taba Talks by the EU Representative to the Middle East Process, Miguel Moratinos, in what became known as "the Moratinos nonpaper," the published contents of which were not challenged by either adversary.

Significantly, *both sides at Taba reportedly accepted the 4 June 1967*, pre–June-Six-Day War in 1967 *de facto* border as *the basis* for *the future border between Israel and a Palestinian state.*

The parties disagreed about *Israel's annexation of "settlement blocs"*: Israel noted that the Clinton Parameters provided for such annexation, as part of a "land swap" between Israel and Palestine; the PLO team denied that the 2000 Clinton proposal included such annexation and rejected the proposal by Israeli negotiators.

As for *Gaza*, no maps were presented, but the negotiators *implied agreement that all of Gaza would be part of a sovereign Palestine state*, with a "safe passage" between Gaza and Hebron in the West Bank. Moreover, all Israeli settlements in Gaza would be evacuated, though there was disagreement on the time frame—no more than six months, claimed the Palestinian team, a longer period proposed by the Israeli team.

There was a considerable "meeting of minds" on *Jerusalem-related issues.* Both favored an *"open city."* Both accepted the Clinton proposal of Israel's sovereignty over Jewish neighborhoods and Palestine's sovereignty over Arab neighborhoods, as noted above. The *Israeli team accepted that Jerusalem would be the capital of both states.* The *Palestinian team accepted Israel's sovereignty over the Western Wall,* though with some disagreement on the area covered by the Wall and the nearby space sacred to Judaism. Both accepted the principle of each party's control of its holy sites; however, they *disagreed about sovereignty over the Temple Mount (Haran-al-Sharif).*

On the vexed issue of *Palestinian refugees*, there was an agreement in principle that any solution, in accordance with a Security Council Resolution, must lead to implementation of Resolution 194, the UN's "Right of Return" resolution. While a specific solution was not reached, the Israeli team showed understanding that the wish to return would be implemented with one of the following frameworks: *return and repatriation*—to Israel, to Israel-swapped territory, or to the Palestine state; or *rehabilitation* in the refugee's host country; or *relocation* to a third country.

As for *security*, the Israeli team indicated a wish for *three early-warning stations on Palestine territory*. More significant, Israel conveyed its wish that Palestine be "nonmilitarized," that is, accept the status of a *demilitarized state*; the Palestinian team accepted the idea of a general, but unspecified, limitation on its acquisition of arms. It was agreed that Palestine would have sovereignty over its airspace; Israel, while accepting all Palestinian civil aviation rights specified by international regulations, requested a unified air control system under Israel's control, along with access to Palestinian airspace for military operations and training. Israel agreed to withdrawal of its forces from the West Bank within three years, along with an additional three years for withdrawal from the Jordan Valley; Palestine urged a shorter time frame. Israel requested five *emergency locations on Palestinian territory*; Palestine agreed to two locations, with a specified time limit for termination.

Overall, the Taba Talks indicated a potentially significant step in the direction of an Israel–Palestine peace agreement. While recognizing that "it proved impossible to reach understandings on all issues, despite the substantial progress that was achieved," the negotiating teams of the two adversaries added, in a joint statement: "The Taba Talks conclude ... with a sense of having succeeded in rebuilding trust between the sides .... The sides declare that they have never been closer to reaching an agreement" and expressed "our shared belief that the remaining gaps could be bridged with the resumption of negotiations following the Israeli elections." Participants in the Taba Talks echoed these sentiments: Professor Shlomo Ben-Ami, Israel's Foreign Minister, declared: "We made progress, substantial progress. We are closer than ever to the possibility of striking a final deal." And Saeb Erekat, the long-time senior negotiator for the PLO and then the PA, exclaimed: "My heart aches because I know we were so close. We need six more weeks to conclude the drafting of the agreement."

The negotiations were not resumed, however, terminating what seemed a hopeful indicator of *a rarely evident willingness of both adversaries to compromise on some crucial issues of discord*. The basic reason was *a conjunction of adverse political circumstances*. Ten days after the winding down of the Taba Talks, on 6 February 2001, Prime Minister Barak was defeated in Israel's elections by Ariel Sharon, who quickly announced that he would not pursue the Taba track. Moreover, the patron of the 2000–early 2001 quest for an Israel–Palestine peace agreement, President Clinton, gave way to the incoming President Bush, who showed no interest in echoing his predecessor's policies on the Israel–Palestine conflict—or on any other issue. In light of the long-standing failure of all attempts to achieve resolution of the Israel–Palestine segment of the Arab–Israel conflict, it is possible, perhaps likely, that, even if the Taba Talks had been resumed and an agreement achieved, political leaders of one or both of the adversaries may have declined to accept or to implement one or more of the controversial concessions by their negotiators at Taba or, as evident in Sharon's reaction, rejection of the entire Taba path.

Arab Peace Initiative (27 March 2002)

The Arab world's attitude, policy, and behavior toward Israel since the end of the June-Six-Day War in 1967 were shaped and sustained by a decision on the "three No's," adopted by the League of Arab States (LAS or the Arab League) at its Khartoum Conference on 1 September 1967—"No Negotiations, No Recognition, and No Peace"; (Israel's best-known military leader in three early Arab–Israel wars, 1956, 1967 and 1973–74, Moshe Dayan, added a fourth dimension, "No Concession on the issue of Palestinian National Rights") (*Story of My Life*, 1976, 362). The "No" era changed dramatically 35 years later, when the Arab League Council, at its Beirut Summit on 28 March 2002, adopted the Arab Peace Initiative (API), proposed by Saudi Arabia's Crown Prince, later King, Abdullah.

The essence of the API resolution, which was reaffirmed by the Arab League in 2007 and was adopted by the Islamic Conference and the Gulf Cooperation Council, is contained in the first three of its seven clauses:

> Emanating from the conviction of the Arab countries that a military solution to the conflict will not achieve peace or provide security for the parties, the council

1. Requests Israel to reconsider its policies and declare that a just peace is its strategic option as well.
2. Further calls upon Israel to affirm:

   (a) Full Israeli withdrawal from all the territories occupied since 1967, including the Syrian Golan Heights, to the lines of June 4, 1967 as well as the remaining occupied Lebanese territories in the south of Lebanon.
   (b) Achievement of a just solution to the Palestinian Refugee problem to be agreed upon in accordance with UN General Assembly Resolution 194.
   (c) The acceptance of the establishment of a Sovereign Independent Palestinian State on the Palestinian territories occupied since the 4th of June 1967 in the West Bank and Gaza Strip, with East Jerusalem as its capital.

3. Consequently, the Arab Countries affirm the following:

   (a) Consider the Arab–Israel conflict ended, and enter into a peace agreement with Israel, and provide security for all the states of the region.
   (b) Establish normal relations with Israel in the context of this comprehensive peace. (*Agence France-Presse*, 28 March 2002)

The initiator of the API Resolution, Crown Prince Abdullah, summarized the initiative at the 2002 Summit, as follows: "I propose that the Arab summit put forward a clear and unanimous initiative addressed to the United Nations Security Council based on two basic issues: normal relations and security for Israel in exchange for full withdrawal from all occupied Arab territories, recognition of an independent Palestinian state with al-Quds al-Sharif as its capital, and the return of refugees" (*New York Times*, 27 March 2002).

Formally, the Saudi-inspired API was adopted unanimously by the 10 (of the 22) attending Arab League members at the Beirut Summit meeting on 27 March 2002. However, there was some dissent in the discussion preceding the vote. Syria was the most vocal opponent, insisting that the Palestinians be supported by the Arab League in their armed resistance and asserting that "normal" relations with Israel would be premature. Lebanon expressed concern that its large Palestinian refugee community dating to 1970 would remain and continue to contribute to Lebanon's domestic instability. The strongest opposition to the API was conveyed by the military wing of *Hamas*, which committed a suicide bombing at the

Park Hotel in Netanya the same day as the announcement of the Saudi peace initiative.

Thirty Israelis celebrating the Passover service in Netanya were killed, with 170 injured by the "Passover Massacre," four years before *Hamas* attained power in the Gaza Strip. Israel's government rejected the API on the grounds that a large inflow of Palestinian refugees and two generations of their descendants would transform Israel into an Arab state. Moreover, Jerusalem was not negotiable, and the return to the 4 June 1967 borders would render Israel more vulnerable to attack. The API was reaffirmed by 21 of the 22 Arab League members at the Riyadh Summit in March 2007 and was endorsed by every Arab League Summit until 2014, as well as by the Organization of Islamic Cooperation and the Gulf Cooperation Council. In 2007, the Israeli response was less negative: "Israel has no interest in stagnation and unfortunately, if the Arab initiative is 'take it or leave it,' that will be a recipe for stagnation" (Foreign Ministry spokesman, *USA Today*, 20 May 2007). Several public opinion polls in 2008 revealed a range of support for the API by Israelis from 36 to 39 percent, and 67 percent of Palestinians.

The API has been dormant since 2009, though there have been occasional attempts to revive it, including a strong endorsement by Saudi Prince Turki Al Feisal, Head of Saudi Arabia's General Intelligence Agency for 24 years (1977–2001) and Ambassador to the United Kingdom and the United States (2002–05 and 2005–06), in a passionate article in the Israeli newspaper, *Ha'aretz*, 7 July 2014. Portraying an idyllic era of cooperation that would follow an Arab world–Israel peace agreement, he exuded confidence in the future: "Just imagine too how commerce, medicine, science, art, and culture between our two peoples will develop …. The alternative, I fear, is continued conflict, with the realities on the ground … pushing us closer and closer to the day when the issue will … be … whether conflict and bloodshed will continue to be the norm."

ROAD MAP FOR PEACE (24 JUNE 2002)

A few months after the API was launched, in March 2002, US President Bush initiated another peace plan for the Israeli–Palestinian segment of the multistate Arab–Israel PC. The essence of the plan, formally presented to the two principal adversaries by the recently formed Middle East Quartet (the European Union, Russia, the UN, and the United States) on 30 April 2003, was a three-year "performance-based and goal-driven" road map for the achievement of a peace agreement between Israel and Palestine in three phases by the end of 2005.

Stage I called for: *mutual recognition* by the two principal adversaries; an *immediate and unconditional cease-fire*; *Palestinian elections and reform of its political structure*; the *withdrawal of Israeli forces to positions held by the IDF on 28 September 2000*, the beginning of the second Palestinian Intifada; the *cessation of Israeli deportations of Palestinians and destruction of Palestinian property in the West Bank and Gaza*; the *reopening of Palestinian institutions in East Jerusalem*; and, most important, the *dismantling of Israeli settlement outposts built since 2001*; all of these goals were to be accomplished in less than one year, by May 2003. In May 2003, Israel's Prime Minister Sharon declared a settlement freeze "impossible."

Stage II was even more ambitious. It called for: *international support for Palestinian economic recovery*; the *establishment of an independent Palestinian state with provisional borders*; the *beginning of a multilateral involvement in the quest for solutions to long-standing complex regional issues*—distribution of water resources, economic development, refugees, and arms control; and the *restoration of pre*-Intifada *links by some Arab states with Israel.*

Stage III set as the goals within one or two years: an *Israeli–Palestinian agreement on all "permanent status issues"*—sovereignty and administrative control over Jerusalem, final borders, Israeli settlements in the West Bank and Gaza, and Palestinian refugees, on all of which no progress had been made throughout the PC.

The PA and several Arab states, Egypt, Jordan, and Saudi Arabia, accepted the road map. Israel approved the road map, but with 14 substantive reservations. Suffice it to note some of these. One was the fulfillment of several conditions by the Palestinians in Stage I as necessary before the beginning of Stage II: the dismantling of the PA's security organizations, the cessation of violence and terror, and the dismantling of *Hamas* and other Palestinian militant groups, along with the destruction of their weapons. Other conditions were the replacement of the leadership of the PA, including the ouster of Arafat; the need to negotiate the powers of a provisional Palestinian state, with "certain aspects of sovereignty"; the PA's abandonment of any claim to a "Right of Return"; a declaration of Israel's right to exist as a Jewish state; and discussions in Stages I and II were to be confined to illegal outposts and a Settlement freeze. Since the road map did not provide for changes, and Israel declared that its reservations must be implemented as an integral part of the road map, which the Palestinian leader, Mahmoud Abbas declared "not acceptable to the Palestinians," the prospects for achievement of the benchmarks laid out in the road map's three stages were discouraging, despite President Bush's visit to the region and discussions with Arab and Israeli leaders in June 2003, a short-lived cease-fire that month, and UN Security Council Resolution 1515 in November 2003, calling for an end to violence and terror. However, it was evident by the end of 2003 that neither Israel nor the PA had fulfilled the obligations of the road map during Phase I. The road map lingered, formally, until 2005, but it remained a shell: the peace process never advanced to Stage II, let alone to the achievement of the crucial goals of Stage III, notably an agreement on all the contested "final status issues," the creation of an independent Palestinian state, and a peace agreement between Israel and Palestine. Another attempt by one or more of the major powers to resolve this PC had failed.

OLMERT PEACE PLAN (SEPTEMBER 2008)

Among the myriad of attempts to resolve the Israel–Palestine core of the Arab–Israel PC, one of the most imaginative was a proposal made by Prime Minister Ehud Olmert in September 2008. In essence, his peace plan focused on the disputed issue of *territory* between Israel and the PA, which had been created by the Oslo II Accord in 1995, summarized above. As such, the *Olmert Peace Plan* was, formally, narrower in scope than the Clinton-initiated multi-issue *Taba Talks* in 2001, discussed above, and the Kerry-initiated *Israel–Palestine Peace Talks* in 2013–14, which attempted to construct a "package deal" embracing all the disputed issues between the Israelis and the Palestinians, to be summarized below.

The implicit assumption underlying the Olmert Plan was that mutually accepted changes in the territorial map of the West Bank and adjacent Israeli territory would catalyze changes in the other disputed issues and thereby facilitate an overall agreement between Israel and an emerging state of Palestine. The proposal envisaged an estimated equal exchange of territory, with the following components: eight pieces of land, ranging from 151 square kilometers in the Judean Desert and 100 square kilometers near the Gaza Strip to 3.2 square kilometers in the Shomeriya area and 0.5 kilometers in the Mevo Betar area, totaling 5.8 percent of Israeli territory, supplemented by the construction of a "safe passage" route between Hebron and Gaza, linking the Gaza Strip physically to the West Bank, the route remaining under Israeli sovereignty but without any Israeli presence; this was calculated as a total of 6.3 percent of Israel's territory, to be transferred to Palestine; and 6.3 percent of the West Bank territory, comprising "settlement blocs" created by Israel in the West Bank since 1968, notably Ma'aleh Adumim, the Gush Etzion settlements, Ariel, and settlements near Jerusalem, in which 75 percent of Israeli settlers were currently resident, would be annexed by Israel. Ironically, this exchange, a transfer of Israeli land to Palestine bordering the Gaza Strip and from the Judean Desert Nature Preserve, in exchange for settlement blocs in the West Bank, would implement the concept of "land for peace" supported by the UN and many member states since 1967, but long rejected by previous governments of Israel.

Olmert presented his peace plan to the president of the PA at a meeting in Jerusalem on 16 September 2008, in the form of a large map that was based upon dozens of conversation with Abbas: the map specified all the proposed territorial changes by the two leaders. However, Olmert insisted on Abbas initialing the map, to indicate his consent to the map as a final and complete agreement. Abbas declined to sign the map before submitting it to his PA colleagues. Olmert withheld the map. Abbas, on returning to Ramallah, produced a hand-drawn sketch of the map, from memory! No formal decision was made by the Palestinian leadership. Olmert pressed his successor as Prime Minister, Netanyahu, to demand a formal response from Abbas to Olmert's proposal. His successor declined, and Olmert did not present the detailed map to Netanyahu. Another attempt to resolve the Israel–Palestine PC failed. (Accounts of the Olmert Plan are to be found in Aluf Benn, "Olmert's Plan for Peace with the Palestinians," *Ha'aretz*, 17 December 2009, 1–3, reprint, *Ha'aretz*, 16 April 2016; Stuart Winer, "Hand-Drawn Map Shows What Olmert Offered for Peace," *The Times of Israel*, 23 May 2013, 1–3, reprint, *The Times of Israel*, 28 July 2014; Avi Isacheroff, "Revealed: Olmert's 2008 Peace Offer to Palestinians," *Jerusalem Post*, 24 May 2013, 1–3, reprint, *Jerusalem Post*, 27 July 2014.)

There were, as often, several reported, unsubstantiated causes of this failure. One was that Abbas was ready to initial Olmert's map on the day it was presented to him, 16 September 2008. However, on that day, he was advised—and decided—to seek the approval of Jordan and Egypt to accept Olmert's proposal, which was not forthcoming. Olmert was reported to have blamed Foreign Minister Livni and Defense Minister Barak for the breakdown of negotiations. Olmert was also reported to have attributed the collapse to Abbas's view that, with the impending end of the Bush presidency, the Palestinians would benefit from the change in the presidency and decided to wait. However, these are mere speculations. The cause of failure remains unknown.

Israel–Palestine Peace Talks—Kerry Mediation (29 July 2013–29 April 14)

The most recent, high-profile attempt to resolve the Israel–Palestine segment of the Arab–Israel PC was the US Secretary of State John Kerry-initiated negotiations between Israel and the PA. Although it lacked the visible presence of Heads of Government, in the direct Egypt–Israel negotiations (1977–79), leading to their 1979 peace agreement—President Sadat, President Carter, and PLO Chairman Arafat, the most senior Israeli and PLO leaders were actively engaged in the negotiations with the Secretary of State and his appointees during the nine months assigned to this attempt at conflict resolution, 29 July 1913–29 April 1914; this was evident in the frequency of meetings between Kerry and Palestinian President Abbas, reportedly 34 sessions, and between Kerry and Israeli Prime Minister Netanyahu, approximately twice as often (Jodi Rudoren and Isabel Kerschner, "How Nine Months of Mideast Talks Ended in Disarray," *New York Times*, 28 April 2014).

The detailed negotiations were conducted by Israel's Minister of Justice Tzipi Livny and Netanyahu aide Yitzhak Molcho, and by Saeb Erekat and Muhammed Shtayyeh, for the Palestinians, all experienced negotiators for the adversaries, with Martin Indyk and Frank Lowenstein as Kerry-appointed US mediators.

Apart from modest, symbolic, mutual concessions before the talks began—the PLO's offer to delay its application to international organizations for recognition of Palestinian statehood, and Israel's offer to release 104 Palestinian prisoners, the latter a repetition of an Israeli offer almost a decade earlier, but never implemented—the negotiations exhibited no reported meaningful compromises by either adversary. Both parties reaffirmed long-established rigid positions on every issue.

On *territory*: The Palestinians reiterated their commitment to the territorial configuration of the entire disputed territory, the West Bank, Jerusalem, and Gaza, as of 4 June 1967; Israel categorically rejected that demand except for an offer of Palestinian *custodianship*, but not sovereignty, over the *Haram-al-Sharif* (Temple Mount, including the Al-Aqsa Mosque).

On *Jerusalem*: Israel restated its insistence on a united Jerusalem as an integral part of Israel; the Palestinians reaffirmed the demand for Palestine's sovereignty over all of East Jerusalem, designated as its capital, except for Israel's custodianship, but not sovereignty, over the Western Wall.

On *Palestinian refugees*: The Palestinians reaffirmed a commitment to UN General Assembly Resolution 194 in 1948, with an unrestricted "Right of Return" by all Palestinian refugees to their former homes and properties in Israel; the Israel negotiators, like their predecessors, categorically denied a Right of Return, though acknowledging the right of return to the territory of the Palestinian state or to migrate to a third state.

On *Israeli Settlements* in the West Bank: The Palestinians renewed their demand that all Israeli Settlements be disbanded and all Israeli Settlers return to Israel beyond the 4 June 1967 border; they also insisted on Israel's commitments to no further settlements in the West Bank; Israel rejected all Palestinian demands regarding Settlements in their peace treaty.

On *security issues*: Israel renewed its long-standing insistence that Palestine become a permanently demilitarized state, except for a police force to cope with internal threats to security; further, that it would not possess the authority to form alliances with any state without Israel's approval and would not permit the entry of any foreign forces into its territory. Moreover, Israel would control Palestinian airspace and would be granted long-term rights to station the IDF in the Jordan Valley, bordering on Jordan. On all of these issues, the Palestinians rejected Israeli demands except for *de facto* demilitarized status of the new Palestine state.

In sum, the Kerry-initiated peace talks in 2013–14 were a fiasco; there was no agreement by the Israeli and Palestinian negotiators, on any disputed issue, a notable failure in negotiations compared with the reported compromise by both principal adversaries on several basic issues, during the Taba Talks initiated by President Clinton in January 2001, noted above.

CAUSES OF ISRAEL–PALESTINE AND OVERALL ARAB–ISRAEL DEADLOCK IN QUEST OF CONFLICT RESOLUTION

What explains the modest achievements of the *quest for conflict resolution* of the *Arab–Israel* PC—two "cold" peace agreements, Egypt–Israel and Israel–Jordan, with limited agreements far short of conflict resolution of the core Israel–Palestine segment of this PC? At the most general level, the central obstacle has been—and continues to be—the *extraordinary complexity* of these conflicts.

One dimension of this complexity is the *multiple pairs of hostile political entities* serving as both independent and interdependent principal adversaries—Egypt–Israel, Israel–Jordan, Israel–Lebanon, Israel–Palestine, and Israel–Syria—and the general conflict between the steadily growing membership of the Arab League, 6 at the onset of this PC, increasing over the decades to 22, versus Israel since 1948.

Another dimension of this complexity is the very *wide range of actors*, in addition to the principal adversaries, many of whom played *active roles* in this quest for conflict resolution, not always in harmony with other participants. One high-profile actor was the *UN*, operating through several of its (sometimes competing) constituent agencies—the *Secretary-General*, his *Special Representative* for this PC, the *Security Council*, and the *General Assembly*, along with several UN specialized agencies, an involvement that was more far-reaching in the Arab–Israel PC than in any of the other 32 active PCs since the end of World War I. One or more *principal adversaries* were often initiators of policies and acts directed to conflict resolution, in different time frames: Israel and Egypt in the late 1970s; Israel and the PLO (Palestine) since 1988–89; Israel and Jordan since 1947, especially after the Egypt–Israel Peace Agreement in 1979; Israel and Lebanon since 1980; Israel and Syria since the early 1990s. One *regional organization*, the Arab League, formally the League of Arab States (LAS), was often a verbal participant. Both *superpowers* were actively engaged: the *United States* since 1967, the USSR much later and much less frequently. *Other states* played a crucial role on specific occasions, notably Norway, a key interlocutor in the back-channel discussions between Israeli academics, and later, officials, and representatives of the PLO, which culminated in one of the most promising achievements of a perennial peace process, the 1993 Oslo Accord I.

The third, most persistent, contributor to this complexity, as obstacles to successful conflict resolution, were/are *contested issues*: together, they have constituted the core of the PC and have been constant, even before the emergence of an *interstate* PC since 1948. One issue is the conflicting attitudes to the *legitimacy* of one of the PC's principal adversaries, Israel, especially its claim to rightful statehood in the Middle East. This claim was, and continues to be, rejected by all the Arab adversaries since 1948, with three notable exceptions: direct negotiations and the signing of formal peace agreements by Egypt and Israel in 1978–79 and between Israel and Jordan in 1994, along with the Palestinian (PLO) public recognition of Israel's existence as a state in 1988, the last accompanied by

Israel's formal acknowledgment of a Palestinian Nation in 1993, to be noted below. A second issue is *territory*, especially the West Bank: this was a contested issue between Israel and Jordan from 1948 to 1967 and between Israel and Palestine since 1967, along with Gaza between Israel and Palestine until 2005, when Israel implemented a decision of total unilateral withdrawal. The other sources of discord over territory were the Sinai Desert between Egypt and Israel from 1967 to 1983, the Golan Heights between Israel and Syria since 1967, and Israel's self-created "security zone" in South Lebanon between Israel and Lebanon from 1982 to 2000. More generally, this issue has been—and continues to be—focused on *borders* between Israel and a future state of Palestine.

One of the most contentious issues is the unresolved struggle over *Jerusalem* since 1948. So too with the issue of *security*, emphasized by Israel, and the legacy of the *Palestinian refugees*, from both the 1948–49 and 1967 Arab–Israel wars, an issue emphasized by negotiators for Palestine.

This combination of *multiple pairs/clusters of adversaries, multiple participants* in the quest for conflict resolution, and most important, *multiple issues in dispute* among the adversaries, along with *competing interests of major powers* in the Middle East region, has contributed to the *complexity* of the quest for conflict resolution and its *limited success* since the onset of this intrastate PC 68 years ago.

ARAB–ISRAEL PC: CAUSES OF CONFLICT RESOLUTION

In addition to the *multiple dimensions of complexity* in the Arab–Israel conflict, a *model of PC resolution* was designed to serve as a theoretical guide to a universal question about state behavior in a protracted interstate conflict: *what are the conditions most likely to generate PC termination?* A priori, the presence of six conditions shaping the behavior of one or more principal adversaries in a PC was postulated as most likely to lead to resolution of an *interstate* PC. These conditions were designated as: physical and/or psychological *exhaustion* of their decision-making élites, attentive public, and mass public; *changes in the balance of military and/or economic capability* between the principal adversaries; *external pressures* by major powers and international institutions on one or more PC adversaries; *domestic pressures* emanating from diverse individual, group, and institutional sources of power in the shaping of foreign policy by PC adversaries; *reduction in discordance among basic objectives* by conflicting adversaries, and

EVIDENCE ON CONFLICT RESOLUTION: PARTIAL AGREEMENTS... 309

decline in the volume and intensity of conflict-sustaining acts by PC adversaries. A Conflict Resolution model, specifying, *a priori*, and elaborating the intellectual rationale for designating these six *most likely conditions* of PC termination was presented and tested elsewhere against the evidence from 33 PCs that were active during all, most, or part of the last century, including the Arab–Israel PC (Michael Brecher, *The World of Protracted Conflicts* [Lanham, MD: Rowman & Littlefield/Lexington Books, 2016], Chaps. 12 and 13).

Exhaustion

From the evidence on crisis management and attempts at conflict resolution presented above, notably the 30 international crises and 9 wars that occurred during the *Arab–Israel* PC from 1948 to 2016, it would be highly plausible, perhaps compelling, to infer collective exhaustion among the élites and population of both the Israelis and the Palestinians, the most enduring of the principal adversaries in this PC. While the Egypt–Israel conflict dyad formally ended with the signing of their peace agreement in March 1979, certainly by April 1982, when the withdrawal of the IDF and Israeli settlers in Sinai was completed, and the Israel–Jordan conflict dyad ended with their peace agreement in 1994, the Israeli–Palestinian conflict dyad persists unabated since its Onset in 1948, in fact, much earlier. Casualties on both sides have been very high: to cite but one illustration on each side—6500 killed, that is, 1 percent of the Jewish population of Israel during the 1948 War, 2200+ Palestinians killed in Gaza in the much shorter (one month) war between *Hamas* and Israel in 2014.

While hard data on *collective exhaustion* is not available, the human and material cost for Israelis and Palestinians since 1948 has been very high. However, there is no reliable evidence that *either adversary* experienced collective exhaustion—not Israel after 1948 or after the 1973 October War, a second case of high casualties, or the Palestinians, during 1948–49, the initial period of a large number of Palestinian refugees or, in the most recent case of heavy Palestinian casualties and material damage, the 2014 Gaza crisis-war—2200 killed and war damage, estimated from 42,000 to 96,000 homes destroyed or damaged. Neither adversary has ever regarded these human and material costs as *intolerable*; neither adversary has perceived these losses as requiring a change in fundamental "national interests" and goals that would lead to concessions to facilitate a peace agreement. Thus, collective exhaustion is deemed *absent* as a condition that would facilitate, on either side in this PC, a change in *perceptions* and *attitudes* toward "the enemy," sufficient to warrant a change in *policy* from conflict persistence to conflict termination.

Balance of Capability

During the first phase of this PC (1948–56), the balance of power within the *Arab–Israel* PC favored the Arabs, but the disparity was not decisive, that is, sufficient to generate an Arab, essentially an Egypt, disposition to peace with an adversary, whose legitimacy was rejected. And while Israel, in this phase, indicated an interest in peace, far-reaching concessions were not accepted as necessary or even possible. The balance of power began to change after the 1956–57 Suez crisis-war, but the qualitative change in the power balance occurred only as a result of Israel's decisive victory in the June-Six-Day War in 1967. It was only after the change in the capability balance for both Egypt and Israel in the October-Yom-Kippur War in 1973, which Egypt perceived as a victory, that both adversaries were receptive to a compromise peace agreement. Egypt realized that a decisive triumph in war against Israel in the foreseeable future was most unlikely and that Egypt's primary objective, regaining control of Egypt's territories lost in war, could be attained in a peace agreement. Israel realized that Egypt's departure from the status of war leader against Israel would drastically reduce the prospects of another Arab–Israel war. The prospect for mutual benefits made their conflict "ripe for peace" in 1979.

It was always understood that Jordan could and would be the second Arab state to make peace with Israel, and this occurred in 1994, without complications. The decade-long negotiations for peace between Israel and Syria in the 1990s merely demonstrated that, for the Israel–Syria pair of adversaries, the conditions for peace were not yet ripe. By contrast, they seemed ripe in the Israeli–Palestinian segment of the *Arab–Israel* PC, once PLO leader Arafat realized that a Palestinian state would not be attained by war or *Intifada*. Thus, changes in the balance of capability, adverse for the Arab participants in this PC, was a *positive condition* for conflict resolution in most of the active pairs of adversaries within this PC: Egypt–Israel (1979 peace treaty), Israel–Jordan (1994 peace treaty), and Israel–Palestine (1993 Oslo Accord). This condition also facilitated the Israel–Syria negotiations in the 1990s, but a peace agreement was premature.

External Pressures

The *abundance of foreign efforts*—by the UN and individual states, notably the United States—to generate a mutually acceptable resolution of the *Arab–Israel* PC or a segment of that conflict—is evident in the discussion of attempts at conflict resolution above, from the UN Conciliation Commission for Palestine, Lausanne Conference in April–May 1949 to the Israel–PA negotiations under US auspices (Secretary of State Kerry Mission) from the end of July 2013 to the end of April 2014. UN Security Council and General Assembly resolutions have been legion, many successful, some ending in failure, but there is no doubt of their high-profile active *presence* as mediators, especially in the Israel–Palestine dimension of the Arab–Israel PC.

Domestic Pressures

The presence of individuals and groups advocating accommodation and peace with "the other" emerged slowly in the Arab–Israel conflict. There is no evidence of their existence until soon after the October-Yom-Kippur War in 1973. This sentiment was first expressed in Israel by a small group of half-a-dozen persons that included two senior- and middle-ranking IDF officers, Hebrew University of Jerusalem professors, and an active journalist, Uri Avnery, who produced a peace manifesto of their creation, the Israel Council for an Israeli–Palestinian Peace, advocating a "two-state solution." It was followed by the Peace Now organization and Avnery's Peace Bloc created in 1993, both still functioning in 2016, and others, but the "peace movement" in Israel was a marginal interest group, with little impact on Israeli public opinion and none on Israeli policy. Much later, after two Palestinian *Intifadas* (Uprisings) (1987–93 and 2001–06), despite the growth of influence of hard-line nationalists in Israeli politics, in the governing *Likud* Party and others after 2000, Israeli voices for peace with the Palestinians became more visible and audible, as evident in a manifesto signed by 196 former general-rank officers in the IDF and other national security agencies, in 2014, calling upon Israel's right-wing government to adopt a more accommodationist posture toward the Palestinians, including a willingness to consider the 2002 Saudi Arabia Peace Initiative, renewed in 2007 and 2014, as a basis for a peace initiative acceptable to Israel. Within the Israel political community, there are several supporters of an Israel peace initiative, including the Labor

Party, *Meretz* and *Hadash*, academics, journalists, and others. However, together, advocates of an Israel-Palestinian peace, in 2016, represent a distinct minority of the Israel public. Overall, domestic pressure for mutually agreed conflict resolution has been *marginal*.

Within the Arab world, evidence of domestic pressure on governments to adopt a policy directed to Arab–Israel peace seems to be even more marginal, perhaps because of the authoritarian character of political systems in the Arab world. Even in Lebanon, the most democratic polity among "frontline" Arab states, domestic pressure on governmental policy toward Israel has been hawkish, ever since the emergence of *Hezbollah*, the most prominent and effective Shiite political and military force in Lebanon, officially in 1985; *Hezbollah* was an offshoot of the mainstream Shiite movement, *Amal*, formed Islamic *Amal*, and was an active anti-Israel militia during and after the 1982 invasion and 18-year occupation of part of South Lebanon (1982–2000). To the extent that pressure for accommodation with Israel exists, and it is more marginal in Arab polities than in Israel, its primary source is political leaders, as with Sadat in Egypt and King Hussein in Jordan, in the mid-late 1970s and 1980s, respectively, and Saudi Arabia's Crown Prince, later King, Abdullah in 2000 and beyond. Overall, domestic pressures for Arab–Israel peace have been sparse in the Arab world and modest in Israel; they must be regarded as *absent* among the conditions favorable to conflict resolution.

Reduction of Discordance Among Basic Objectives

Assessing the presence or absence of discordance among basic objectives from the onset of the *Arab–Israel* PC to the year 2000, the evidence clearly indicates its belated *presence*. During the first three decades (1948–77), there was *no* change in the objective of the Palestinians and the Arab states: they were committed to the eradication of Israel as a state, an objective that was captured at the end of the 1967 War in paragraph 3 of the Khartoum Declaration, the "three No's," to which the Arab League and its members, except Egypt from 1979 onward, were committed to the guidelines "no peace with Israel, no recognition of Israel, no negotiations with it." The first change came in 1977–79, with Egypt's President Sadat's visit to Jerusalem, the negotiations from 1977 to 1979, and the signing of a peace agreement, leading to the complete Israel withdrawal of its military forces and civilians from the Sinai Peninsula in April 1982. Then, in 1988, Arafat, Chairman of the PLO, publicly recognized Israel's existence as a state. Five years later, Arafat and Israel's Prime Minister Rabin exchanged letters of mutual recognition, transforming their relationship from mutual nonrecognition to mutual recognition. Even though the Oslo Accord of 1993 did not develop into a formal peace agreement between Israel and Palestine and became moribund, the concept of a "two-state solution" remains in 2016, but no longer reflects a majority in either adversary.

Hostile words between the leaders of Israel and Palestine and frequent incidents of enmity and distrust exhibited by the mass public of both adversaries have continued, most recently in the autumn and winter of 2015–16. More basic, their long-standing basic discordance over the future status of the West Bank—territorial foundation of an independent Palestinian state, genuine autonomy within a continued Israel-dominated territory, or continued *de facto* status as an Israel colony—remains a fundamental obstacle to conflict resolution, despite occasional expressions of verbal support by leaders of both principal adversaries for a long-term *sustained basic reduction in discordance among basic objectives* between Israel and Palestine.

Decline in Conflict-Sustaining Acts

The reality of conflict-sustaining acts in this PC is mixed. These acts have ceased in two conflict pairs, Egypt–Israel since 1979 and Israel–Jordan since 1994. The Arab boycott of Israel remains in place formally. And most important, the conflict relationship between the two principal adversaries, Israel and Palestine, has persisted, with frequent escalation, especially since the *Hamas* movement expelled the PLO from Gaza and achieved total power in Gaza in 2007. Moreover, there have been three violent encounters between the IDF and Palestinian forces in Gaza since 2007—in 2009, 2012 and 2014, noted earlier. The first and third of these, *Gaza I* and *Gaza III* were full-scale wars, with heavy Palestinian casualties and massive material damage in Gaza, as noted above. Moreover, the West Bank–Israel relationship has experienced two Palestinian *Intifadas* in 1987–93 and 2001–05, and a continuing, informal uprising, mostly in Israel-occupied East Jerusalem, since October 2015. Thus, the overall evidence indicates the *absence* of a decline in conflict-sustaining acts in this unresolved PC.

In sum, two of the six conditions postulated, *a priori*, as likely to contribute to conflict resolution have been *present* in the Arab–Israel PC—*changes in the balance of capability* and *external pressures*. The other four conditions—*exhaustion, domestic pressures, reduction in discordance among basic objectives* by the adversaries, and *decline in conflict-sustaining acts*—were absent or manifested a marginal presence. This PC remains largely unresolved. The most important reasons would seem to be the absence of exhaustion, the absence of domestic pressures for peace in both of the principal adversaries, and the absence of a decline, that is, the persistence of discordant objectives, and continuing frequent conflict-sustaining acts, along with the multidimensional complexity of this PC.

CHAPTER 12

Assessments of the Way Out

On the Arab–Israel conflict and the path to conflict resolution, my analyses have been consistent over the decades. My first overall assessment, based on more than a decade of intensive research on the Arab–Israel conflict and Israel's foreign policy, refers to the period 1948–70:

> The conceptual point of departure was a conviction that an analyst bears a responsibility beyond the description, explanation and attempted prediction of state behavior: it is to lay bare an evaluation of the record, in this case, of Israel's performance in the vital field of foreign policy. There have been notable achievements and notable failures; and the latter are too important to be explained solely in terms of the disharmony between Reality and Perceptions.
>
> There were six major achievements in Israel's foreign policy during its first 22 years:
>
> 1. *Instant diplomatic recognition and support by the U.S. and soon after by the other superpower*, the USSR, during Israel's critical formative phase, 1948;
> 2. *Early admission of Israel to the United Nations*, 1949, that is, global system legitimacy, at a time when many states, old and new, were excluded or their admission delayed;
> 3. *Diplomatic relations with the vast majority of Western and Communist states*; the major exceptions were China, India, and Arab and Muslim states—there were very few independent African states until a decade after Israel's independence;

4. *A positive image and an established presence in post-colonial Africa* from 1957 until 1972 [severed in 1972 but restored in the 1990s];
5. *Crucial military and diplomatic support from France* in the form of a *de facto* alliance from 1955 to 1966; and
6. *Massive U.S. political-diplomatic support, and economic and military assistance*, the latter especially after the June 1967 War.

These were considerable achievements. Yet there were countervailing failures, including *the still-elusive goal of peace with most of the Arab and Muslim worlds.*

The *grand gesture by Israel to break the total impasse in the summer of 1967 was not forthcoming*, perhaps because it was not politically feasible in the euphoria of total victory. Never, under pain of ostracism from Israel's political and military establishments, was the word "withdrawal" from occupied Palestinian territory used. It was a curious lapse from logic and consistency, for Israel had accepted, from the outset, the November 1967 Security Council Resolution 242, which explicitly referred to "withdrawal from territories occupied in the recent conflict" (the 1967 War).

The mantra of "united Jerusalem," that is, after the 1967 Israeli annexation of overwhelmingly Arab East Jerusalem, as the "eternal capital" of Israel did not absolve Israeli decision-makers from the responsibility to acknowledge the legitimate Arab claim to a formal political presence in Jerusalem.

The bankruptcy of this policy was revealed in August 1970, when Israel accepted the US (Rogers) "peace initiative": in so doing, it abandoned the commitment to exclusive "direct negotiations" with the Arabs, broke the spell surrounding the word "withdrawal," and reaffirmed its acceptance of the November 1967 UN Security Council "land for peace" Resolution 242.

It is true that, in the last analysis, Israel's ability to survive depends on self-help, that is, on the strength of the IDF and the morale of its people, though military capability was heavily dependent on external aid for most of its years of independence. The reality of Arab hostility was compounded by an Israeli policy response which did not recognize *change in:*

- *the balance of military power* between Israel and the Arab states *in favor of Israel*, especially after the 1967 War and, therefore, the doubtful wisdom of behaving—always—as if Israel were—and destined to be always—the weaker party in the conflict;

- *the political system of Egypt created by the coming to power of Nasser*, and the possibility, never *fully exploited*, of achieving accommodation of vital interests between Israel and Egypt;
- *the character of "Palestine," that is, the crystallization of a genuine Palestine Arab nationalist movement, especially after the June-Six-Day War in 1967* (indeed, one of the byproducts of that traumatic event); and
- *the character of political forces in the Arab–Israel confrontation*, that is, the fact that, whatever arrangements may be reached with Egypt, Jordan, and even Syria and Iraq, *Palestine Arab nationalism will have to be recognized, and Israel and Arab Palestine will have to live side by side as independent states in the historic boundaries of the Land of Israel*, that is, post-1967 Israel and Jordan.

What has been absent in *Israeli decision-makers' images of the Arab–Israel conflict* is the kind of historical vision that made the State of Israel become a reality; only in the case of Ben-Gurion did this vision, at times (and Sharett and Eban always), extend to coexistence and accommodation with "the Arabs." Even the proponents of caution (Israeli doves) have not displayed imaginative ideas in an attempt to achieve the goal they recognize to be an historic necessity. (The result is that, in 2016, accommodation, let alone peace between Israel and the Arab world, except with Egypt and Jordan, especially with the Palestinians, remains elusive and remote.)

In sum, during its first two decades, in fact, during its first near-seven decades, Israel made massive progress in military and economic capability. Moreover, it mastered many of the problems of nation-building. Throughout, its political system has been an island of democracy in a sea of authoritarianism. But these achievements have not been matched in the sphere of the core issue in its foreign policy. The *supreme goal of peace has been thwarted, in part by the failure of the basic foreign policy decisions that Israel made* toward its premier neighbor, shaped by its most influential leaders' unchanging perception of "the enemy." The qualitative jump in their psychological environment, particularly their perceptions of the Arabs, notably the Palestinians, and the prospects of, and path to, peace remains a historic task only partly fulfilled. In a reassessment during the 68th year of Israel's independence, my assessment did not change (see Chap. 13).

1972: Brecher, *The Foreign Policy System of Israel*, pp. 562–565

It would be inaccurate to make Israel and her foreign policy primarily responsible for the protracted war with her Arab neighbors. ... The relevant question in this context is whether Israeli policy contributed to an easing of that psychological block. The evidence points strongly to a negative reply. It is this shortcoming which causes the most disquiet, for relations with the Arabs constitute the core issue-area of Israeli foreign policy. ...

There can be no doubt that Israel as a nation passionately desires peace and accommodation, and, even more, reconciliation and co-operation with her Arab neighbors: anyone who has lived in Israel is persuaded of the genuineness of this objective. Yet those who make and enunciate her foreign policy have not shown originality in moving beyond declarations of intent to concrete proposals for peace. ...

At no time has the paucity of imagination been so striking as in the period since the Six Day War. ... Ironically, it was Ben Gurion, the only high-policy decision-maker with historical vision, who publicly advocated withdrawal, as early as June 1967 and consistently thereafter, from all occupied territories except Jerusalem and the Golan Heights. But that display of imagination occurred after he had resigned from the summit of power. His successors followed the path of Ben Gurionism, not the views of Ben Gurion in his twilight years. Nor has there been evidence of imaginative formulae to deal with complex specific issues. ...

Israel was more isolated diplomatically than ever before in her history. ... It is ... true that persecution and anti-Semitism have been central to Jewish history. But that reality does not relieve—or excuse—the analyst and the policy-maker from asking whether Israel's behavior did or did not contribute to this diplomatic dead end.

Decision-makers do not appear to have posed this question: this is one conclusion to be reached from our inquiry. They have thereby failed to perform a vital task of leadership—self-analysis free of clichés. ...

[One of the reasons for this failure was] an inflexible adherence to the Ben Gurionist image of "the Arabs" as Israel's implacable enemies, "who understand only the language of force."

That image of "the Arabs" contained a large element of truth; but it suffered from constancy in a world of change. ... [As noted,] [w]hat has been absent in Israeli decision-makers' images of the Arab–Israel conflict have been the kind of historical vision that made the State of Israel become a reality.

These words were written 47 years ago. Yet, they resonate in 2017: little progress has been made in the *total* achievement of Arab–Israel peace.

1975: Dialogue in Cairo

These views on the conflict and the way out of the impasse were stated by me with utmost candor to a group of Egyptian scholar-researchers associated with the Al-Ahram Institute of Political and Strategic Studies in Cairo in June 1975:

> If the path to a solution is now possible it is by no means certain of success. And the gap between possibility and certainty is strewn with land mines. Moreover, those land mines, I think, are not only in the minds of men; they lie, too, in the capacity of leadership, in this country [Egypt] and obviously on the other side [Israel] as well, to make a "great leap forward," to admit that "we cannot expect all and yield nothing." We must understand that the psychology of insecurity is legitimate: it is inevitable; it is deeply rooted; it is genuine, it is not a function of verbal sparring and public relations to the outer world.
>
> I am not suggesting that there are no rights of the Palestinians. Rather, the failure ever to define those rights is equated automatically [in Israel] with the goal of the destruction of Israel. I think you have to understand that equation. It is genuine and deeply rooted in the mentality of those who make decisions on the other side.
>
> We are confronted with the most extraordinary syndrome that I am aware of in modern international relations; it is what I called the case of the two non-recognitions. The Palestinians do not recognize that Israel exists, but more important, that the Jewish nation-state has a legitimate right to exist. The Israelis thus far have not recognized that there is, legitimately, a Palestinian national entity that is different from the larger Arab People. One of the tasks in the movement towards accommodation is to transform mutual non-recognition into mutual recognition. We must move, initially at least, from total conflict to the absence of unlimited hostility.
>
> It is true that the term, "total withdrawal," has never been used by Israeli leaders. I think I must be perfectly frank and say that, as I understand it, as of today [1975], total withdrawal is an unacceptable concept to Israel's

decision makers. But there is an abundance of evidence in signals, which should be read correctly, that refer to "very substantial," "nearly all" or "almost everything." They are conveying the signal of "total withdrawal minus one." [This was most evident in 2006, in the coalition program of the newly formed Olmert government and Olmert's negotiations with Palestinian President Abbas in 2008, noted above.]

I am convinced that *the negotiation process is important* for two reasons. *No conflict*—no matter where or when it is—*can ever be resolved without a process of direct interaction between the parties. An imposed solution is bound to be a disaster.* Moreover, I think this is true of the Rhodes armistice talks in 1949, that the very process of negotiation and interaction creates a change in the attitudes of the participants. The term, "total withdrawal," will never be used by Israel *before* the negotiations for three reasons. First, the Israeli interpretation of UN Resolution 242 is the English version, which does not say, "total withdrawal" or "withdrawal from *all the territories.*" I won't go into that any more, except to note that the principal drafter of the resolution was the UK delegate, Lord Caradon. Second, the Israelis are not prepared for *total* withdrawal—for reasons which I indicated. And third, to say anything more than they have said, which is "almost all," or "virtually everything," would be to rob the negotiations of any meaning.

I think that we must recognize the need for several stages from past hostilities to future accommodation. The first task is to move from open *war* to what I call *hostile coexistence*, and then gradually towards *peaceful coexistence*, and finally, *cooperation*. What the time span between each of these stages will be cannot be determined precisely because it is difficult to know what the behavior of the parties will be, once the formal piece of paper is signed. I am not prepared here to try to set down a scenario with great precision. But I am concerned to convey to you the sense that the issue of peace is not simply, or even primarily, a piece of paper. A piece of paper is a formal symbol of something that must be substantive and meaningful. And if peace is defined merely as a formal agreement of recognition, to be followed by the continuation, after a generation, of war or a chasm between the parties—that is not a settlement which augers well for the future. I am not suggesting that you can have a total transformation overnight. But equally, I am expressing the concern of many people on the other side that we see a peace agreement as an intermediate stage on the road to the kind of accommodation which we saw between France and Germany after eight centuries of conflict. We hope that it won't take eight centuries to achieve it here. (Personal tape recording of the 1975 dialogue in Cairo)

1975: ISRAEL COUNCIL FOR AN ISRAELI–PALESTINIAN PEACE

Although my primary interest has always been in the intellectual domain of world politics, I was not immune from involvement in politics. One such foray was a modest role in the quest for peace in the Middle East. I translated the sentiments expressed in Cairo into (an early exercise in) political activity in the autumn of 1975—helping to draft the manifesto of the Israel Council for an Israeli–Palestinian Peace, along with then leaders of the Israeli peace movement: Uri Avneri, then editor of a controversial magazine, *Ha-Olam Hazeh* (*This World*), later a member of the *Knesset*, and for many years, an outspoken peace activist, including leadership of the *Gush Shalom*, (the *Peace Bloc*); Arye (Lova) Eliav, then a dynamic, younger leader of the mainstream *Mapai* (Israel Labor Party), which he served as Secretary-General and, later, an Israel Prize laureate for his many contributions to Israeli society; Colonel Meir Pa'il, a noted military historian; and Major-General Matityahu Peled, a prominent member of the IDF's General Staff in the June-Six-Day War in 1967.

We were among the earliest in Israel *to advocate a two-state solution to the already-then protracted Israeli–Palestinian conflict.* And we called on Israel, as the much-stronger party, to take the initiative by declaring its agreement in principle to a Palestinian state living side by side with Israel, as the only viable solution, that is, Partition, along with a Palestinian (PLO) formal recognition of Israel's right to exist as a Jewish state in (part of) its historic homeland. Few listened at the time. However, this message became the core strategic objective of the peace movement, in particular, the *Peace Now* organization, for the last four decades. Over time, this virtually "unthinkable" idea in 1975 penetrated into broader sections of the political, intellectual, and media élites and, eventually, to the attentive and mass publics of Israel. Even segments of the largest party on the Right, the *Likud*, including Prime Minister Sharon, and his successor as leader of the newly created *Kadima* Party since 2006, Prime Minister Olmert, accepted the principle of a two-state solution to the conflict. (It may, in the future, be recalled as a "preface to peace" when the Israeli–Palestinian conflict becomes "ripe for resolution.")

1977: Lessons from the Begin–Sadat Jerusalem Encounter

Two years later, in November 1977, while I was present at a conference in Tel Aviv of academics and activists on the elusive Arab–Israel peace process, it was announced that President Sadat would meet with Prime Minister Begin and other Israeli officials in Israel, with the highlight of an exchange of views between Egyptian and Israeli leaders beamed to the world via television. In the perspective of time, this dramatic encounter was a turning point in the Arab–Israel conflict and the Arab–Israel peace process. While the road to a peace agreement between Egypt and Israel was strewn with ideological and verbal land mines, despite the transformed atmosphere initiated by the Begin–Sadat meeting in November 1977, it was clear then, that, despite the enormous obstacles, this first direct meeting between the leaders of the principal antagonists in the conflict was certain to be crowned with success.

The reason was that the Begin–Sadat prenegotiation meeting was the expression of a *fundamental change in their attitude to war and peace*. Both leaders had come to a crucial realization and a mutual recognition by the summer of 1977—when preliminary discussions by their aides in Morocco paved the way for the historic meeting in Jerusalem—that the war path had failed for 30 years to achieve the basic goal of both states. For Egypt, five wars from 1948 to 1973 had failed to realize the long-standing core aim of the Arab states, the destruction of the State of Israel. For Sadat, the compelling trigger to a transformation of his attitude was the failure, in the October-Yom-Kippur War in 1973, despite Egypt's gratifying performance on the battlefield, to regain the "lost territory," the Sinai Peninsula, which Israel had conquered in the June-Six-Day War in 1967. Since this was the primary Egyptian objective in the conflict since 1967, and Sadat realized that the path of war had failed, he arrived at the conclusion that Egypt must attempt to regain its lost territory by the path of peace. Similarly, Israel had triumphed on the battlefield in all Arab–Israel wars, except for the stalemate in 1973, but the cherished goal of peace remained elusive, indeed distant. For Begin, too, this reality led him inexorably to the path of peace—when Sadat's initiative was accepted as genuine.

There were other stimuli to this change in policy, for both leaders. It was evident then, at the time of their Jerusalem conference, that, although only a dramatic preliminary conciliatory act, the peace process was dramatically energized. This occurred because of the extraordinary confluence of mutual recognition by Begin and Sadat, in their own interest, that negotiation and peace now held the key to the achievement of their core objective: for Egypt, the restoration of its lost territory, the Sinai Peninsula; and for Israel, the establishment of peace with the largest, most powerful, and most influential Arab state.

The basic lesson from that process is that a successful peace process between Israel and its three remaining hostile neighbors, the Palestinians, Syria, and Lebanon, will occur only when each of the three pairs of antagonists experience a similar confluence of mutual recognition that the path of violence has failed and will fail—to achieve a viable Palestinian state, Syria's restored sovereignty over the Golan Heights, occupied by Israel since 1967, and Lebanon, its remaining territorial grievance, in exchange for a meaningful peace agreement by all three Arab entities with Israel.

To attempt to predict a date for this outcome would be foolhardy, I was convinced four decades ago. The key is captured by the term "ripe for resolution"; that is, a protracted conflict (PC) ends when it is "ripe for resolution." This may seem like a tautology. Not so, for "ripeness" can be viewed as the logical outcome of a process of mutual recognition that the war path, at least in the Arab–Israel conflict, is fraught with failure. The key to this simultaneous mutual recognition that a change in strategy is imperative is a situation in which pain, collective pain, in particular, by the attentive and mass publics of both antagonists, becomes unbearable. There have been several occasions, especially the second Palestinian *Intifada*, from 2000 to 2005, the second Lebanon War in 2006, and Gaza War II, 2014, when collective pain on both sides of the conflict seemed very high. Certainly, the human and material costs, for the Palestinians and the Lebanese, and for the Israelis, seemed to approach intolerability. However, the necessary condition for "ripeness," mutual recognition that the path of violence has failed to achieve the basic objectives of the adversaries, has not yet occurred for these adversarial pairs in the Arab–Israel conflict. Primary reliance on violence during an extended period and conflict resolution is an oxymoron!

2001, 2016: Principles and Proposals for Negotiating Peace and Conflict Resolution

A carefully considered nonofficial attempt to frame a viable peace project for the Israelis and the Palestinians was presented soon after the turn of the millennium, in a joint article with Irving Brecher, an Emeritus Professor of Economics at McGill. The essence of our analysis and proposed concrete solution was set out in "Israelis versus Palestinians: Is There a Way Out?" (*International Journal* 56, no. 3 [Summer 2001]: 519–526).

We began with the dismal state of the conflict at the time of the second Palestinian *Intifada* in 2000. "It is easy to despair at the turn of events the Israeli/Palestinian conflict has taken since late September 2000, the outbreak of the second Palestinian *Intifada*: persistent violence; wanton killing and maiming by both sides, mostly of civilians—men and women, children and the elderly; escalating anger and hostility; and an increasingly rigid mind-set on the part of leaders on both sides, which makes compromise and concessions even more difficult than usual. The most tragic and disquieting result of *Intifada* II is the shattering of trust—a fragile, carefully nurtured, intangible gift of the Oslo Accord in September 1993" (alas, that dismal state is even more apparent in 2016, during a third, informal replica of another *Intifada*):

> The issue of blame in the Arab/Israel conflict has been debated for more than half a century, certainly since the 1937 British-appointed Peel Commission and the 1947 Special United Nations General Assembly: both called for two independent states in the British-mandated territory of Palestine. The "blame game" has never been helpful, except for those engaged in scoring debating points and seeking support from the major powers. For us, the truth about this endless controversy was captured by Chaim Weizmann, the long-time leader of world Zionism and first president of Israel, who declared: "The conflict between Jews and Arabs is not a conflict between Right and Wrong but rather between two Rights." We would add—a conflict between two Wrongs as well.

> Both parties have committed gross violations of individual and collective human rights in the course of this bitter conflict, especially during the current upheaval. Israelis are responsible for: the imposition of a siege around many Palestinian towns and cities in the West Bank as the most visible expression of collective punishment; the widespread destruction of Palestinian homes; and the assassination of suspected Palestinian militants. The responsibilities on the Palestinian side include: indiscriminate killing, even lynching, of Israeli soldiers; *carte blanche*—in some cases, active encouragement—by the Palestinian (PA) leadership, including Arafat, to the most extreme organizations in the West Bank and Gaza to commit heinous acts of terror against civilians wherever they can be found; and inflammatory rhetoric calculated to accentuate hatred of "the enemy." The record is abysmal on both sides.

"It may well be that the vicious spiral of escalation of violence and hostility cannot, in the short run, be reversed," we noted 15 years ago. From that perspective, one could adopt a "plague on both their houses" approach: let the Israelis and Palestinians continue their low-intensity war until they both reach the threshold of individual and collective pain that would make their conflict "ripe for resolution." It is difficult to know precisely what that threshold is—perhaps 5000 Palestinians and 1000 Israelis killed. On the Palestinian side, massive unemployment, even larger than at present, with the majority living below the poverty line, and the consequent decline of the PA's capacity to govern and provide basic needs for its children might be enough. For the Israelis, apart from ten times the number of fatalities to date, it might be a universal sense of personal insecurity that transforms a free, open, risk-prone, willingness-to-experiment lifestyle into a rigid, obsessively insecure "stockade mentality" (this appears to have happened on both sides since 2006—the global isolation of the Palestinians under the Islamist *Hamas* regime, and the Israeli Wall separating the two nations, even more so 10 years later):

> There has to be a better way. In our view, the better way is a rational program of action that may, in the end, lead both parties away from a nightmare scenario and towards mutual accommodation. But such a program is only the first step towards more enduring conflict resolution.

"Final status" negotiations—and anything less is doomed—must, in our view, be based upon the following principles:

1. The creation—and recognition by Israel—of *an independent state of Palestine* in the West Bank and Gaza, based upon the 4 June 1967 line, with any territorial changes subject to mutual agreement.
2. Palestine's *recognition of Israel's right to national security* after half a century during which most of the Arab world has not recognized Israel's right to exist as an independent state in the Middle East. Such recognition would embrace the demilitarization of Palestine beyond a lightly armed police force and a Palestinian waiver of the right to introduce any non-Palestinian forces into the West Bank and Gaza for an extended period.
3. Israel's *recognition, in principle, of the right of return of Palestinian refugees*, in accord with United Nations Resolution 194 of 1948, with several options offered to the refugees. The Palestine Authority (PA), Israel, the United States, the European Union, and the United Nations should

actively encourage refugees to choose either to remain in the lands in which they have lived during the past half-century—Jordan, Syria, and Lebanon, with equal rights of all other Arab citizens—or return to the territory of the new state of Palestine. Israel would contribute to a global compensation fund. The number of refugees allowed to return to Israel would be subject to approval by both sides to ensure Israel's survival as a viable, predominantly Jewish state.

4. There are three *Jerusalems*: overwhelmingly Jewish West Jerusalem, an integral part of the State of Israel; overwhelmingly Palestinian East Jerusalem, that is, the villages east of the Old City; and the Old City itself with its four quarters—Armenian, Christian, Jewish, and Muslim. In our view, any enduring solution must acknowledge *Israel's sovereignty over West Jerusalem, Palestine's sovereignty over East Jerusalem, and a special approach to the Old City*. Ideally, it should be proclaimed an "International City," but earlier experience, notably with Danzig during the inter-World War period, demonstrates that this is unworkable in the long run. Therefore, we propose the following: *Israel's sovereignty over the Jewish Quarter; Palestine's sovereignty over the Muslim Quarter; a referendum in the Armenian and Christian Quarters to discover their preference in terms of association with Israel or Palestine; and "God's sovereignty" over the Temple Mount/*Haram-al-Sharif, *governed by an international régime appointed by—and responsible to—the secretary-general of the United Nations*. This is not an ideal solution but it is eminently workable.

At this point, too, one could fairly ask: what if Israelis and Palestinians agree to these principles of negotiation and then one side, or both, begin(s) to show signs of failure to put them into practice? The skeptics could be forgiven for going no further. Once again, though, we believe that there is a better way.

We propose the creation of an international monitoring body of experts that would report to the United Nations secretary-general at regular intervals. Consistent findings of good-faith negotiations would send a message that the international community should play a more active role in terms of diplomatic and financial support for the peace process. By the same token, consistent findings of less-than-genuine good faith in negotiations would signal, to one or both parties, that they cannot count on strong support from the international community.

We are not at all unmindful of the heavy risks attached to any set of proposals for a breakthrough in the seemingly intractable Israeli/Palestinian conflict. There is simply no guarantee that negotiations would proceed along the lines that we propose—even in the "monitoring" context that we have provided.

We remain hopeful. Who would have predicted the destruction of the Berlin Wall, or the collapse of Soviet communism, or the rapidly expanding democratization of Eastern Europe? An Israel-Palestinian peace? A positive peace between two democratic states co-operating for the development of the region's water and agricultural resources, and the economy in general? We cannot answer "yes." But 50+ [now, 68] years of killing are enough. We are, therefore, content with "maybe."

These ideas and proposals for a path to peace between the Israelis and the Palestinians could set in motion a new era in the tortured relations between two nations destined to share both the benefits and trials of mutual accommodation and, ultimately, cooperation. Resolution of this bitter conflict would also have a major additional benefit of facilitating termination of the much larger conflict of which it has been the core for more than a century, the Arab–Israel PC as a whole.

CHAPTER 13

Israel at 68: Beneath the Glitter

TRIBUTES

The State of Israel, during its first 68 years, has become a modern, industrialized, high-tech society, whose *material achievements* are recognized worldwide. In this context, two rave reviews of its accomplishments appeared during the past decade. The first was an ode to Israel's 57th birthday, in 2005:

> The cell phone was developed by Israelis working in the Israeli branch of Motorola, which has its largest development center in Israel.
> Most of the Windows NT and XP operating systems were developed by Microsoft-Israel.
> The Pentium MMX Chip technology was designed in Israel at Intel.
> Both the Pentium-4 microprocessor and the Centrino processor were entirely designed, developed and produced in Israel.
> Voice mail technology was developed in Israel. Both Microsoft and Cisco built their only R&D facilities outside the U.S. in Israel.
> Israel has the fourth largest air force in the world (after the U.S., Russia and China). In addition to a large variety of other aircraft, Israel's air force had an aerial arsenal of over 250 F-16's, the largest fleet of F-16 aircraft outside of the U.S.
> Israel's $100 billion economy is larger than all of its immediate neighbors combined.
> Israel has the highest percentage in the world of home computers per capita.

According to industry officials, Israel designed the airline industry's most impenetrable flight security.

Israel has the highest ratio of university degrees to the population in the world.

Israel produces more scientific papers per capita than any other nation by a large margin—109 per 10,000 people.

With more than 3,000 high-tech companies and start-ups, Israel has the highest concentration of hi-tech companies in the world—apart from the Silicon Valley.

Israel has the highest average living standards in the Middle East. The per capita income in 2000 was over $17,500, exceeding that of the U.K.

Twenty-four percent of Israel's workforce holds university degrees, ranking third in the industrialized world, after the United States and Holland, and 12 % hold advanced degrees.

Israel is the only liberal democracy in the Middle East.

Relative to its population, Israel is the largest immigrant-absorbing nation on earth.

Israel has the world's second highest per capita of new books.

Israel has more museums per capita than any other country.

Israel leads the world in the number of scientists and technicians in the workforce, with 145 per 10,000, as opposed to 85 in the U.S., over 70 in Japan, and less than 60 in Germany.[1]

The second, even more adulatory tribute, on Israel's 68th birthday, in May 2016, cited 68 reasons "to respect, if not love, Israel." An illustrative selection of 14 reasons is noted here:

Israel has more museums per capita than any other country, including the world's only one underwater.

Relative to its population, Israel has absorbed more immigrants than any other country, with newcomers from more than 100 countries.

Life expectancy in Israel is among the highest in the world, at 82 years.

On a per capita basis, Israel tops the list of countries when it comes to the annual production of scientific papers.

More than 90% of Israeli homes use solar power to heat their water.

Israel has the highest proportion of water used for irrigation that comes from recycled wastewater.

Security measures (much of them unseen) at Ben Gurion Airport are the best in the world.

An Israeli start-up invented a non-touch, radiation-free device, Babysense, that prevents crib death by monitoring a baby's breathing and movement during sleep.

Israel has the world's highest rate of university degrees on a per capita basis.

Israel developed the technology that allowed for the original cell phone.

An Israeli company developed the first ingestible video camera that helps doctors diagnose cancer and digestive disorders.

Israeli engineers invented a new form of drip irrigation that minimizes the amount of water needed to grow crops.

A Jerusalem high-tech company specializing in artificial vision has invented a tiny camera to help drivers navigate more safely. The device, called Mobile Eye, is being built into many new cars around the world.

The popular mobile mapping program, Waze, was developed in Israel. Google purchased the GPS-based navigation app in 2013 for a reported $1.3 billion.[2]

Some of the claims, in both tributes, are exaggerated; others are open to question. However, these are impressive portraits. Yet, as if anticipating skepticism from knowledgeable readers, the author of the recent tribute correctly noted Israel's grave imperfections:

> Like other countries, Israel is a work in progress. Blemishes abound and Israelis are the first to criticize and question their own shortcomings: political corruption, a dysfunctional electoral system, the extortion and blackmail of the ultra-Orthodox parties, the rampant economic iniquities, the status of Israeli Arabs, the treatment of Ethiopian immigrants, the situation of Palestinians in the West Bank, the plight of African refugees. The problems are longstanding and a searing indictment of Israeli leadership.[3]

State of the Economy

Overall, the macro-level evidence is positive. Early in the twenty-first century, before the "Great Recession" of 2008–09, Israel's economy was booming, with a gross domestic product (GDP) growth of 6.6 percent in the first quarter of 2006, much higher than the Israel Finance Ministry forecast of 4.1 percent, and the International Monetary Fund (IMF) forecast of 4.2 percent, for all of 2006; and this growth continued throughout 2006—the economy grew by almost 8 percent in the last quarter of 2006. This boom extended into the first quarter of 2007 with an annualized growth rate of 6.3 percent, and the Israel Finance Ministry forecast a 4.2 percent growth rate in 2008. However, the GDP growth rate has declined to 2–4 percent since 2011, with a rate of 2.3 percent in 2015.

Other economic indicators also revealed impressive progress in the early years of the twenty-first century. Foreign direct investment in 2006 reached the enormous figure of 13.4 billion dollars. The stock exchange continued to reach new heights in 2007. Israel's currency, the New Israel Shekel (NIS), was strong. Inflation and interest rates were low. The balance of payments was favorable; that is, Israel was approaching economic independence before it reached the age of 60. The standard of living rose by 11.8 percent, as measured by private consumption, and unemployment dropped to 7.7 percent.

Many of these economic trends continued to 2015, after setbacks generated by the deep global recession in 2008 and 2009. In 2012, Israel received 3 billion dollars in foreign direct investment, the fourth highest level of foreign direct investment in a member of the OECD for that year, though 60 percent, 1.8 billion dollars, came from the United States. The net balance of payments remained positive in 2015. Israel's unemployment rate continued to drop from 2007 and was low compared to other OECD countries, standing at 5.4 percent in 2015. In 2016, inflation rates remain relatively low, projected at 0.6 percent.[4]

Israel's economic achievements, however, were accompanied by a grave disquieting state of its society. Several indicators are noteworthy.

Poverty

The first is the level of poverty in Israel, in absolute terms and relative to the other members of the club of economically developed states, the OECD. Along with the evidence of a flourishing high-tech economy is the stark reality of Israel's highest overall poverty level among the 34 members of the OECD: using the "conventional approach ... for measuring poverty, based on the disposable money income households have for consumption and saving," 22 percent of Israelis lived below the poverty line in 2011, especially among the Orthodox Jews (*Haredim*), a gross monthly household income of NIS 3804, and Arab Israelis, NIS 4247, with non-Orthodox Jewish households, NIS 9692. Moreover, during this year, there was a "substantial gap between total household income and total expenditures among Israeli households, showing that, on average, all population groups in Israel consistently find themselves with a deficit at the end of the month, with their income unable to cover their expenses." The gaps vary among segments of Israel's population: Israeli Christians, a deficit of NIS 671 per month, the smallest gap; non-Orthodox Jews, NIS

864; Israeli Muslims (Palestinians) and Druze, approximately NIS 2000; and Orthodox Jews, NIS 3209. "Soaring housing prices and increased indebtedness due to housing are key factors causing Israeli families to struggle to make ends meet." Using the OECD method of calculating poverty based on disposable income, the proportion of Israeli households whose head was 59 or less in age, below the poverty line in 2011, was: Orthodox Jews, 49 percent; Arab Israelis, 44 percent; non-Orthodox Jews, 11 percent, and total population, 18 percent, the last compared with 13 percent on average for all other OECD members. As for individuals living below the poverty line, based upon disposable income, the difference is considerable for the age group 59 or less: 21 percent in Israel, 10 percent among all other OECD members.[5]

Another disquieting socioeconomic indicator of poverty was the increase in the proportion of Israelis living in poverty during the last 17 years: 22 percent of its population and 35 percent of Israeli children from all communities were living below the official poverty line in 2015, compared to 17 percent and 23 percent in 1998, respectively. Among the Arabs in Israel and the ultra-Orthodox Jews, child poverty exceeded 50 percent. Moreover, "when it is measured by disposable income, about one-fifth of individuals in Israel are below the [poverty] line, a rate almost double the average in other developed countries."[6]

As for the possible role of employment in reducing the burden of poverty, while overall *unemployment* declined from 10.9 percent in 2004 to 7.6 percent at the end of 2006, the employment conditions were worse. The number of subcontract workers and part-time workers had increased. Further, in 2007, 36 percent of workers earned low wages, that is, 60 percent of the average wage or NIS 2550, or 600 dollars per month. And in Arab Israeli towns, the unemployment rate ranged from 10 to 15 percent.[7]

In that context, an uninformed, well-intentioned Nobel Prize Laureate in Economics, Robert Solow, from the Massachusetts Institute of Technology (MIT), during a visit to Israel in June 2006, was reportedly "shocked to learn the nature and extent of poverty in Israel."[8] Moreover, a Hebrew University professor of political science and communications, Gadi Wolfsfeld, reported that Israel's four largest circulation newspapers devoted only 0.3 percent of their coverage—articles and op-ed pieces—to the poverty issue during the period April 2005–March 2006. And in the enormous compensation paid to its corporate CEOs, Israel had gone the US way.

This dismal reality can be credited to the Thatcherite policies applied with relentless determination by Benyamin Netanyahu, during his tenure as Finance Minister from February 2003 to August 2005 and, later, as Prime Minister. The statistics on the pervasiveness of poverty in Israel reflected, empirically, an economic and social conception that was captured by the following words, attributed to the then Finance Minister:

> The most vital element in a society that aspires to life is the working person, the productive person, the person who earns and the person who earns even more. People who are weak, ill, dependent and non-productive are a human blight that is liable to bring down society. Therefore, the former should be encouraged and nurtured like costly diamonds, and, as for the others, minimal support systems should be created, which will enable them to survive.[9]

Mrs. Thatcher, the advocates of rampant capitalism in the United States, Britain, China, Russia, India, Japan, and much of the world, could not have expressed this socioeconomic model more bluntly. However, few, including Netanyahu and his followers, would dare to state in public their crass advice to "the others," that is, for the "nonproducers," who constitute a large segment of any modern society: "if you are poor, weak, sick or old, go away and die." Israel's political leadership in the early twenty-first century, even earlier, had completely subscribed to this model.

INEQUALITY

As *The Economist* reported in the summer of 2007, in a typical understatement: "The country [Israel] is ... becoming more unequal"[7] (28 July 2007, 46–47). The most dramatic evidence of this growing *inequality* was the revelation of the *Concentration Index*: 19 Israeli families were reputed to control one-third of the entire Israel economy in 2006. The top five families controlled 61 percent of the income of the 19 families, an increase from 54 percent a year earlier. The total income of the 19 families was NIS 248 billion in 2006 (approximately 63 billion dollars), about one-third of the revenues of the 500 leading Israeli companies. The income of the 19 families in 2006 was equal to 88 percent of the state budget.[10] And in the enormous compensation paid to its corporate CEOs, Israel had gone the US way.

Income inequality in Israel was reinforced by a substantial reduction in income taxes between 2003 and 2011. "The main findings point to a reduction in the direct and indirect tax burden borne by all Israeli households. However, this reduction was not uniform, and it primarily benefited households in the lowest decile and in the highest three deciles." The financial benefits "rose substantially along with household wealth. Households belonging to the first six deciles 'earned' NIS 130 to NIS 500 per month from the tax rate change ...; households in Decile 8—NIS 800; households in Decile 9 saved over NIS 1200 per month; and households in the highest decile saved more than NIS 2,500 per month thanks to the decline in the tax burden." Thus, "one may confidently conclude that Israeli tax policy during the period 2003–2011 mainly benefited the three highest deciles, contributing to wider net income disparities and to a sense that Israel is experiencing an erosion of its middle class."

This process of steadily growing inequality in the distribution of income was further exacerbated by increases in Israel's value added tax (VAT), from 16 percent in 2011 to 17 percent in 2012 to 18 percent in 2013. "Given the fact that, the poorer the household, the greater the share of VAT in the indirect taxes that it pays (due to the higher consumption rate), this change was more harmful to households in the lower part of the income distribution."[11]

The findings on inequality in Israel reinforce those on poverty: for "market income inequality ... over two decades for a sample of 21 countries ... among working-age households," age 59 or less, "Israel has been at the top of the rankings since the 1990s .... In 2006, the rise in inequality in Israel stopped and after that there was even a decline, although the level of inequality remains high compared to other developed countries surveyed."

The most illuminating indicator of this process of growing inequality in the distribution of Israel's wealth was the staggering figures on accumulated wealth of individuals, in US dollars. In 2006, there were 5 billionaires, 87 multi-millionaires, and 7000+ millionaires in a population of seven million. By 2015, these figures revealed an astonishing increase: 17 billionaires and 88,231 millionaires living in Israel, most with a net worth of 1–5 million dollars, in a population of less than eight million.[12]

Finally, in a "comparison of inequality among different households in Israel with inequality in OECD countries ... using disposable income (after transfer payments and taxes), Israel ranked fourth in income inequality in

2011 among all other developed countries," after Turkey, Chile, and the United States.[13]

ISRAEL'S SENIOR CITIZENS

Seemingly in accord with the spirit of Netanyahu's reputed ode to "the productive person, the person who earns and the person who earns even more" and his reputed disparagement of "[p]eople who are weak, ill, dependent and non-productive ... [as] a human blight that is liable to bring down society," cited above, the poor elderly segment of Israel's population suffers from acute material deprivation in the Israel of 2016: this is the central finding from a representative sample survey of 400 Israeli senior citizens aged 65 and older, conducted by the International Fellowship of Christians and Jews: 18 percent of Israel's elderly lack home heating and 20 percent forsake basic goods in order to pay for heating, 12 percent cannot afford hot water for at least half of each week, 12 percent experience lack of medications or medical care, and 15 percent sacrifice food for financial reasons. The founder and president of this social welfare organization, Rabbi Yechiel Eckstein, declared in a statement: "The immense need of the elderly in Israel is a social catastrophe which we must treat like any other emergency situation. For the elderly, giving up food, medications, or heating can sometimes be a death sentence."[14]

As noted in the *State of the Nation Report* for 2015 by the Taub Center for Social Policy Studies in Israel, "the public funding component is dominant in the income of the elderly in most [OECD] countries, and comprises an average of about 59 percent of total income. In contrast, in Israel, the proportion of total income for the elderly from a public source is only 34 percent." In answer to the question, "to what extent does overall expenditure on the elderly (public and private) compensate for the loss of income from work after retirement," Israel's spending on public social expenditure "is about 8.8 percent of GDP, in contrast to an average of about 12.5 percent of GDP in the OECD." As evident in Figure 13 of this Taub Report, Israel ranks 7th for the lowest proportion of cash benefits for the elderly among 34 OECD members, with cash benefits as 6.8 percent of GDP: Italy and France provided the highest percentage, 19.1 percent each. Ranking below Israel in this service for the elderly were Australia, Turkey, Iceland, Chile, Korea, and Mexico, the last at 2.7 percent of GDP. Moreover, "in terms of disposable income, about one fifth of Israeli citizens aged 66 and over are below the poverty line," compared with 12 or 9 percent of OECD citizens, depending on the basis of calculation.[15]

The most comprehensive, nongovernmental, in-depth analysis of Israel's society and social policy, the respected annual Taub *State of the Nation Report*, concludes its most recent (December 2015) report with the following thought-provoking general observations on *poverty, inequality in the distribution of income*, and *material conditions of the elderly* in Israel:

1. Among the population group of those [whose head was] aged 59 and under [the OECD definition of the working segment of its members' societies], the findings point to poverty and inequality rates that are among the highest in the Western world in both market and disposable income.
2. Even after some improvement over the decade [2002–2011], there is still a gap of about 10 percentage points to Israel's disadvantage in the share of households within the total group that have at least two income earners – 65 percent in Israel, compared with 75 percent on average in the OECD.
3. [There has been] an increase in employment rates among all population groups, along with a significant and real increase in market income, primarily among Arab Israelis and Haredim …. This increase has helped to reduce the levels of market income inequality in recent years, although… there was no accompanying significant decrease in poverty rates. That is, the new entrants to the labor market earn low wages and although their position has improved somewhat, they remain below the poverty line in market income.
4. In Israel, the percentage of per capita GDP dedicated to cash benefits to individuals is lower than the OECD average. In addition, the impact of these payments on reducing disparities could be even more limited in light of the fact that households in Israel are larger on average than in the OECD.
5. Among the population over age 66 in Israel, too, the rate of disposable income poverty is among the highest in the Western world, [along with] high levels of inequality within this population.[16]

Education

One of the most disquieting features of Israeli society at 68 was the *state of education* at the *elementary and secondary levels* for the nation which, like Jewish communities everywhere, had long prided itself as "the People of the Book."

In a 2007 OECD study of the *status and salaries of teachers* in 28 member states, Israel ranked from low to average in almost all categories:

- 27th in the overall status enjoyed by school teachers;
- 15th in elementary education and 19th in secondary teaching, in expenditure on students; from 1995 to 2003 the expenditure on Israeli primary and secondary school students grew by 2 percent, compared to an increase of average expenditure on these two levels of students among the OECD members of 33 percent;
- Close to the OECD average in its student-teacher ratio for elementary students and slightly above the average for secondary school students.
- Close to the average of working days per year, 180 days, but more hours in the classroom than the average for OECD teachers; and 24th in annual wages for teachers with 15 years of experience.
- Finally, official Israel Finance Ministry data revealed the lowest wages for teachers among all college graduates.[17]

In 2014, according to an OECD study, expenditures on students remained dismally low: Israel ranked 29th of 36 OECD members in pre-primary education, 24th out of 38 in primary education, 27th out of 38 in secondary education, and 18th of 38[18] in tertiary education, despite 7.3 percent of its GDP in 2011 spent on educational institutions, ranking 6th among OECD members[19]:

- Israel remains close to the average number of working days per year, but with significant improvements in the index of change in statutory teachers' salaries for teachers with 15 years of experience, ranking 1st in pre-primary, 3rd in lower secondary, and 3rd in upper secondary education respectively.[20]
- The student-teacher ratio has been decidedly mixed since 2011, with Israel ranking 1st in pre-primary education, but 21st and 22nd in secondary and tertiary education.[21]
- In 2012, wages for teachers among all college graduates have improved to encompass the OECD average, an increase from the 2007 OECD statistics.[22]

This abundance of official OECD data indicates that Israeli governments placed a low value on education at the elementary and secondary school levels. This was noteworthy when Netanyahu was Finance Minister (2003–05) and beyond. According to the Chair of the *Knesset* Education Committee at that time, Michael Melchior, former Chief Rabbi of Norway, "there were 16 budget cuts in education and higher education, something that deepened the gap between us and countries we aspire to be like, as far as education is concerned. Today, we are a Third World country in terms of education."[23]

Another noteworthy trend in Israeli education, for those of a secular persuasion, was the steadily increasing *proportion of ultra-orthodox and religious students in the elementary school system*.[24] Israel's Central Bureau of Statistics projected that, from 1992 to 2012, the secular schools would lose 10 percent of their pupils, the state religious schools would experience a 3.7 percent increase, and the ultra-orthodox schools would see a 196 percent growth in their number of pupils. By 2012, secular schools would decline to barely half of the total (50.9 percent) of the elementary school students, the ultra-orthodox schools, 30.9 percent, and state religious schools, 18.2 percent. This seemed to some an irreversible trend for the future of Israeli schools. What made this trend more notable was the fact that, according to a 2007 law, all ultra-orthodox students would be exempt from the "core program," that is, from studying science, English, and civics! As the late Yossi Sarid, a trenchant critic from the secular Left, remarked, "They are being returned to the Ashkenazi's ghetto or the Moroccan Melah, which they will not be able to leave for the rest of their life. These children are lost. And the ultra-Orthodox parties will ensure their Knesset seats for a long time."[25]

There have continued to be significant changes in the demographic makeup of Israel's education system in the years since 2010, but also accompanying shifts in the curriculum and the influence of ultra-Orthodox Jews in the workforce. The percentage of students in the religious school system, out of the total first-grade student body, grew from 18.9 percent in 2007–08 to 19.6 percent in 2009–10. However, the percentage of students in the secular public education system also grew, but minimally, from 55.6 percent in 2008–09 to 55.7 percent in 2009–10, indicating a further demographic shift to more religious youth.[26]

In marked contrast with the trend in primary and secondary education, there was a noteworthy expansion of *higher education* in Israel during the past two decades, the most visible arena of social policy leading to a basic change in the direction of greater equality among Israelis.

This transformation was noted by the Taub researchers in the following summation:

> In the last two decades [1995–2011], there has been an increase in the share of young adults continuing on to Higher education …. There has also been a substantial rise in the share of students and academic Degree holders among the younger population. Relative to the past, the share of students rose in all of the age groups, especially among ages 23–30, where the share of students almost doubled between 1995 and 2011 …. In the 23–26-year-old age group—which has the largest share of students—the figure almost doubled: 28 percent attended institutions of higher education in 2011 … as opposed to 16 percent in 1995 …. The share of those studying in this age group in 2011 is even higher, reaching 35 percent, if students at nonacademic institutions are also taken into account.

Moreover, "generally women are better educated than men, with a higher percentage of female students than male students. This phenomenon is even more striking among the Arab Israeli population."[27]

This expansion of Israel's higher education student population was made possible by a vast expansion of its university and college facilities—from six academic colleges in 1990 to 36 in 2014, with 96,000 students. This was accompanied by a decline in the number of university students since 2005, lower than the number of students in academic colleges since 2008.[28]

OTHER SOCIETAL CHANGES

The *quality of political leadership* in Israel has deteriorated steadily over the past 40 years. There was not a single politician with the vision of Ben-Gurion, the nobility of Sharett, the innate honesty and common sense of Eshkol, the ability to make difficult decisions in crises like Golda Meir, and the superior talents of the second generation—Allon and Dayan, as warriors and politicians; Eban as the supreme advocate and diplomat; and Peres in his younger days, as a superior technocrat, with major contributions to Israel's national security.[29]

The political leaders of Israel since the founders and the second-generation leaders have been mediocre, except for Ehud Barak, who, like many Israeli generals, moved to the political arena: he behaved like a transient meteor in Israel's political system, serving as Prime Minister from 1999 to 2001, returning as Defense Minister in 2007 until 2013. Although forgotten, the commanding figure of the Zionist movement for decades in the pre-state period and the first President of Israel, Chaim Weizmann, remarked: "the governors have not yet learned how *to govern* effectively."

Civility is conspicuous by its absence in a rabble-rousing parliament. *Debates in the Knesset* have been and are often more in the nature of shouting matches than civilized discussions. Moreover, according to a public opinion poll in May 2006, 74 percent of Israelis believed that members of the *Knesset* (MKs) act mainly in their own interest. Trust in public officials and institutions in 2016 remains low; a poll reveals that 76 percent of Israelis believe MKs care more about themselves than about the public, and following a similar trajectory, 84 percent of Israelis feel that the *Knesset* does not represent them or their values.[30] The *misuse of public funds*—undisguised bribery—to form inevitable coalition governments in a faction-ridden polity, especially but not exclusively by ultra-orthodox and less orthodox parties, is common.

CORRUPTION

Corruption is rampant, along with an array of acts verging on, and sometimes crossing the boundary of, criminal behavior. According to the same 2006 poll, 82 percent of Israel's public believed that Israel had become a corrupt state, and 75 percent believed that one cannot win a public tender without "connections," that is, *protectzia*. *Bureaucratic inefficiency* and *malpractice*, including nepotism and jobbery—appointment to positions in the public service unrelated to merit—were rampant.

Similar results on corruption among Israelis have been found in the most recent years: According to the 2013 Transparency International's Global Corruption Barometer, Israel slid from 30th in 2007 to 39th in 2012 in a survey of 1004 online respondents, making it one of the most corrupt state members of the OECD. Moreover, over 80 percent of Israelis believe that personal contacts are important or very important for getting policies enacted in the public sector, behind only Lebanon, Ukraine, and Russia. Israel ranked second to Greece among OECD members on the perception that government is beholden to special interest groups. Sadly, 12 percent of Israelis reported paying bribes, akin to Argentina, the Philippines, and Rwanda.[31] Additionally, in April 2016, a Panels Research poll broadcast on the Knesset Channel found that "83 percent of Israelis believe their politicians are corrupt."[32]

Supporting evidence of these *malpractices in government administration*, evident in Israeli polls, was reinforced by a World Bank report on Governance Indicators of 212 countries from 1996 through 2006. While Israel (and the United Arab Emirates [UAE]) led Middle East states in the fight against corruption, Israel's 79.6 percent score for corruption control ranked below 20 percent of the countries assessed, notably, Australia, Canada, Germany, France and the United States, all above 90 percent. On the *good governance* scale, Israel ranked much higher than almost all Middle East states but conspicuously below most Western states. And, on the indicator of political stability, Israel ranked with several African states such as Kenya and Liberia. Finally, the World Bank rated Israel in 2005 as one of the riskiest states in the Western world, with an unstable, inefficient, and irresponsible government and a high level of corruption compared to economically underdeveloped states.[33]

The World Bank report on Governance Indicators of 212 countries in 2014 reveals similar results over the last decade. In terms of *corruption control*, Israel had a 76 percent score, well below most modern industrialized states, including Canada, France and the United States. On *governance effectiveness*, Israel remains well above all the Middle Eastern states, but still below most Western countries. Last, on the *political stability and absence of violence/terrorism* scale, Israel ranks among many African nations currently embroiled in conflict, far below all Western states, with a rating of 13 percent.[34]

CENSORSHIP

For most of its history, Israel was correctly perceived as a state in which freedom of speech was entrenched in its society, a "beacon light" in a geographic region where this right was generally curtailed, often trampled, by authoritarian political regimes. Israelis are known as argumentative, to the point of intense verbal conflict, but the right to free speech was a near-universal norm in society and politics. The only important exception was the area of military security; respect for curtailment of free speech, that is, censorship, on matters that relate to the military domain was a norm for Israeli verbal behavior. Violations of this norm were generally punished by authority as legally unacceptable. This restriction did not, generally, extend to the Arts, though disagreements about the quality of works of

Art abound, as everywhere However, concern has been expressed by some members of the community of fine Arts about the impartiality of governmental authority in the use of public funds to support art forms pleasing to those wielding political power, and especially "power of the purse," in their allocation of funds for the fine Arts.

Those concerns were expressed recently in a candid report in May 2016 on the funding of Arts projects by cultural affairs ministers in the Netanyahu government. The critique was expressed in a report "Censorship in Israel" by a curator in the Israel fine Arts community:

> Over the past two years, the Arts in Israel have been increasingly threatened by censorship and draconian government funding proposals. Some see this as the beginning of a culture war ... The metanarrative in Israel is one of continuous existential fear and victimization, which leads to the increased justification of insularity and nationalism, and the silencing of opposition ....
>
> The calls for and instances of censorship over the past two years have been both top-down (from government officials) and grassroots (by private citizens calling for the removal of artworks). Some individuals have taken matters into their own hands and established paramilitary organizations that spy on human rights activists and organizations, most notably the extrapolitical group *Im Tirtzu*, which recently published a blacklist of "moles"— cultural producers of all stripes who support leftist organizations that Im Tirtzu perceive as anti-Zionist.
>
> The bullying of human rights organizers and prominent cultural personalities, as well as incidents of grassroots censorship, began during the war with Gaza ... in the summer of 2014. Not only did antiwar demonstrators face violence from counter-demonstrators, but people who expressed any opinion other than support for the offensive on Gaza risked trolling, workplace conflict, and even dismissal. ... Artist-choreographer Arkadi Zaides was criticized for a video and dance work incorporating footage from B'Tselem's Camera Project (through which cameras are given to Palestinians to document conflicts with the army and neighboring settlers). The Museum of Petach Tikva, which presented the work, was asked by the municipality to close the exhibition early following pressure from a "concerned citizen," while the Ministry of Culture withdrew its funding from the show. ...
>
> Elections in May 2015 ... installed two eager ministers in top positions to influence the Arts. Minister of Education Naftali Bennett and Minister of Culture and Sport Miri Regev have been responsible for a string of incidents of, or attempts at, censorship, ranging from the banning of books and plays to a withdrawal of state funding from Jaffa's Elmina Theater unless its director, Norman Issa, reversed his refusal to perform in a settlement in the West

Bank. ... Her recent Loyalty in Culture Bill proposed legislation that would authorize her ministry to cut funding to institutions that attack Israel and its symbols ...
Herein lies the crux of contemporary censorship: public funding is being manipulated to become a mechanism of censorship. The use of defunding as a form of censorship should come as no surprise in a world where money talks. ... If in a democracy, the government serves the people and must demonstrate its loyalty to them; in fascism, individual citizens must demonstrate allegiance to their government, and nowhere is that more easily done than through the platform that art provides.[35]

The concern expressed in this and other critical reports on government funding for the Arts was proved to be well-founded; in mid-June 2016, it was reported that "Israel's culture minister [Miri Regev] is collecting information about which theater and dance troupes perform in Jewish settlements in the West Bank. ... [T]he [culture] ministry will cut by 33 percent government funding for institutions that do not perform in West Bank settlements, the Negev or the Galilee."[36] The Minister of Culture confirmed the report in order to lead a "revolution" against the boycotts.[37]

MALPRACTICE OF POLITICIANS

The most disquieting evidence of these public service ills that pervaded Israel's polity long before it reached its 68th year were the *police investigations, indictments,* and *potential punishments for alleged criminal acts* among a considerable number of the then-holders of the most senior governmental and some civil service positions.

President Moshe Katzav was cited for an array of grave crimes, in a draft indictment issued by Israel's Attorney-General, Menachem Mazuz, in January 2007: two counts of rape, two counts of forcible sexual assault, sexual intercourse in violation of superior–subservient status at the workplace, and of fraud, breach of trust, and bribery—during his tenure as President (2000–07) and, earlier, as Minister of Transport in the 1990s. In a highly controversial case, that created a storm in the Israeli media and public opinion, as well as among jurists and legal experts, the charges were drastically reduced at the end of June 2007 to charges of sexual harassment, harassment of a witness, and indecent assault, for which he has been serving a moderate term in prison. In March 2011, Katzav was sentenced to seven years in prison.

Prime Minister Ehud Olmert, who succeeded Ariel Sharon after Sharon's grave illness in January 2006, was accused of several indictable offenses: corruption related to his sale and purchase of homes in the Old Katamon and German Colony residential areas of Jerusalem; attempting, while Prime Minister, to influence the sale of controlling shares in Israel's second largest bank, Bank Leumi, to a friend in Australia; granting favors and promotions to 115 political activists in governmental bodies he controlled during his earlier tenure as Industry and Trade Minister (2001–05)—the ministry's Investment Center, the Israel Small and Medium Enterprises Authority, and the Employment Bureau and Foreign Workers unit, and members of the *Likud* Central Committee— he was a member of the Right-wing *Likud* Party and its forerunners during his entire political life, until he switched to Sharon's new *Kadima* Party in late 1995, and so on. And in May 2008, it was disclosed that a police investigation had uncovered the transfer of large sums—tens of thousands of US dollars, perhaps more—to Olmert since the early 1990s, from an American backer, for purposes and uses not yet clarified. Olmert was convicted of breach of trust in July 2012 following a lengthy court process, in addition to bribery in March 2015. In May 2015, Olmert was sentenced to 6 years in prison; however, his sentence was reduced to 18 months in December 2015, for which he is currently serving in an Israeli prison.

Finance Minister Abraham Hirchson was under police investigation in 2007 for several alleged finance-related crimes—fraudulent acquisition under aggravated circumstances, breach of public trust, theft by a director and fraudulent registration of corporate documents; specifically, misuse of some of the NIS 5.65 million, allegedly embezzled from Nili, a nonprofit association associated with the National Workers Organization, while Hirchson headed the organization, to finance political activity in the *Likud* Party and for personal gain: between January 1999 and December 2002, NIS 585,755 in cash and NIS 1,634,740 in checks and bank transfers were reportedly deposited in Hirchson's bank account in Tel Aviv.[38] The Finance Minister suspended himself from his ministerial portfolio for three months, in April 2007, due to the ongoing police investigation of his alleged corruption. And, at the end of June, he resigned as Finance Minister. In 2009, Hirchson was convicted of stealing up to NIS 2 million from the National Workers Labor Federation (NWLF) while he was acting chairman of the union. Hirchson was eventually sentenced to five years and five months in prison, along with a fine of NIS 450,000.

Former Justice Minister Haim Ramon was convicted in March 2007 of indecent assault—forcibly kissing a female soldier at an office party. He was sentenced to 120 hours of community service and ordered to pay the victim a modest financial compensation. However, the Tel Aviv Magistrate Court ruled that his act, although "in poor taste and callous," did not constitute "moral turpitude," thereby clearing the way for his return to political life. A coalition of nine prominent women's organizations criticized the court for yielding to pressure "to save Ramon's career." In June 2007, he was appointed Vice-Premier, succeeding Shimon Peres, who had just been elected President of Israel by the *Knesset*; and Ramon immediately resumed his position as one of the most influential colleagues of Prime Minister Olmert.

Former Minister of Internal Security, Tzachi Hanegbi, was charged with "political" appointments in his ministry, without regard to merit or qualifications, in flagrant violation of rules specified by the Civil Service Commission.

Former Minister of Labor and Welfare, Shlomo Benizri, was accused of bribery and mishandling of funds, especially in connection with arranging (illegal) work permits for foreign workers.

Director of Israel's Tax Authority, Jacky Matza, resigned in February 2007, two months after being arrested on suspicion of having ties to corruption within the tax system.

The Chief of Staff of the IDF, Lieutenant-General Dan Halutz, resigned in February 2007, in the aftermath of the inconclusive Second Lebanon War. He was not accused of any illegal or criminal act, only of failure in time of war. However, his behavior was viewed by many as less than moral when it was revealed that, hours after the kidnapping of IDF soldiers by the *Hezbollah*, on 12 July 2006, before Israel's decision to respond massively against *Hezbollah* forces in South Lebanon, Halutz instructed his bank to sell a block of shares in his name worth NIS 160,000 (40,000 US dollars)! Adding insult to this extraordinary behavior, he reportedly demanded compensation from Bank Leumi for leaking the sale of this part of his investment portfolio(!).[39]

Israel's Police Commissioner, Moshe Karadi, resigned in February 2007 after an investigative committee criticized his failure to pursue an investigation in 1999 into alleged close ties between police and a crime family in Israel's southern police district, of which he was then head; he was also accused of promoting a police commander in the south who was suspected of concealing a case for the benefit of this crime family, who had hired a policman to kill a rival gang leader then in hospital!

This political episode became more complicated when the then Minister of Public Security, Avi Dichter, a rising star in Israeli politics, nominated Yaakov Granot, Commissioner of the Prisons Service, to succeed Karadi as Police Commissioner. In 1994, while serving as a district commander in the police, Granot was convicted by a lower court for bribery, fraud, and breach of trust. The Supreme Court overturned his conviction in 1996, but severely reprimanded him for his behavior; he was suspended from the police force for three years, and he admitted to disciplinary offenses. Moreover, he was criticized for his performance as head of the Immigration Administration and for inflating the number of migrant workers expelled from Israel. In March 2007, following widespread criticism of his suitability for the position of Police Commissioner by civil society organizations in Israel, Granot withdrew his candidacy.

In March 2007, too, the Israeli police recommended that Yisrael Katz, Minister of Agriculture from 2003 to 2006, be indicted for fraud and breach of trust arising from alleged political appointments at the ministry during his tenure.

To this growing list of tainted public figures, one must add that four Israel Prime Ministers—Netanyahu (1996–99, 2008–present), Barak (1999–2001), Sharon (2001–05), and Olmert (2006–08)—were investigated for alleged improprieties, extending, in some cases, to charges of criminal acts (Sharon and Olmert); one of Sharon's sons was given a prison sentence for acts done in collusion with and at the behest of his father, and Olmert began a sentence to prison in 2016. (Netanyahu was criticized again in May 2016, by the State Controller, the Israel government's "watchdog" on expenditures by public officials, in a report that declared: "The trips by Netanyahu and his family [more than a decade ago] that were funded by external sources when he was Finance Minister, deviated from the rules, and could give the impression of receiving a gift or of a conflict of interest." Moreover, his failure to provide a government committee with full details of funding for his family's trips abroad gave "rubber stamp approval" of their travel on official business. The Prime Minister's lawyers denied any wrongdoing.) (*Reuters*, 24 May 2016, reported in *Ha'aretz* on the same date.)

An increasing number of Israeli officials, government ministers, and important IDF and police figures have been accused, are under investigation, or have been convicted of sexual harassment against female cohorts. In November 2015, Jewish Home MK Yinon Magal resigned over accusations of sexual harassment against two women at Walla!News, leading him to resign from the *Knesset*.[40]

On 24 March 2014, Silvan Shalom, a *Likud* MK and former Minister of Science and Interior Minister, was accused by a woman who complained that Shalom sexually harassed her at work. By late 2015, new allegations of sexual harassment were made by 11 women, triggering Shalom's announcement on 21 December 2015 that he was resigning from the *Knesset* and removing himself from public life.[41]

In March 2016, deputy commissioner of the Israeli Police, Hagai Dotan, was charged with six counts of conduct unbecoming of an officer over accusations of sexual harassment.[42]

Ilan Mor, a commander of the police's traffic division, was found guilty in May 2016 of sexually harassing two female subordinates as he was being promoted to be the Israeli Police forces representative in the United States.[43]

There were two polar opposites in the response of Israeli self-styled "public intellectuals" to this catalog of immoral, in some cases, criminal behavior. An optimistic view was reportedly expressed by a prominent novelist: "I have not spoken out about the corruption, and one of the reasons is that I am in less of a panic about it than most people. I think that things stink to high heaven not when the sewage drain is blocked but when it is being cleaned out. The stench is sky-high, but ... it is a sign that all the gutters are being opened ... and in the future people will be afraid to commit acts of corruption." So much for wishful thinking! At the other extreme of reactions, a prominent journalist expressed the anguish of many: "Why do we deserve this? Why are we doomed to be managed by a chain of command, whose reputation and personal conduct have been so heavily compromised? These men appear to be incapable of controlling their desires – greed or other cravings." The future will uncover which of these reactions is more insightful.

Treatment of Arab Israelis

The most disturbing aspect of Israel's record at home, with serious implications for the Arab–Israel conflict, is the persistent rampant *discrimination against its Arab minority*, 20 percent of Israel's citizens—in elementary and secondary school educational facilities—in the allocation of funds for roads, housing, medical facilities, and so on, and employment in the public service.

The most controversial Israeli act *vis-à-vis* the Palestinian Arabs in East Jerusalem and the occupied West Bank since the outbreak of *Intifada II*, in 2000, was the *Wall* that Israel constructed along, and sometimes beyond, the entire north–south boundary between pre-4 June 1967 Israel and the West Bank. The rationale for the *Fence*, the Israeli term for the physical barrier between the two conflicting nations, is that it is necessary to eliminate or drastically reduce the flow of Palestinian suicide bombers, who have created havoc in Israeli towns and cities.

An interim assessment of the Fence-Wall until 2016 was partial success: the number of successful suicide bombings and Israeli casualties has been drastically reduced, though acts of violence and casualties have increased in East Jerusalem since October 2015. However, the consequences of the Wall, along with the roadblocks and enforced closure of towns and villages for the Palestinians, have been near-catastrophic: children unable, or able only with great difficulty, to attend schools on the other side of the Wall; farmers unable to tend to their fields; pregnant women unable to get to nearby hospitals easily; family members in different towns and villages virtually unable to reunite because of the Wall. A leading Israeli commentator, Danny Rubinstein, on the impact of the Wall and, generally, on the Palestinians, referred to:

> the hallucinatory world that the fences and walls have created around Jerusalem .... It is a known truth that Israel's security considerations in determining the route of the fence have been joined by many other considerations—the good of Jewish settlements in the West Bank, for example .... The consideration is a political consideration of annexing territory, even at the price of abandoning security .... At least in the Jerusalem area, it can be said with certainty that the fences and walls are creating an impossible reality.[44]

An Israeli *Peace Now* official declared that "the planning, construction and location of the separation fence are clearly an unadulterated expression of

Israel's unilateral policy ... Thus, the fence project is a faithful successor to Israel's settlement activities in the West Bank."[45] Israel's High Court of Justice occasionally mitigates the negative effects of the Wall by ruling in favor of petitions—there have been a large number—against one or another section of the Fence, for example, on 15 June 2006, when it demanded that the government dismantle the present section in the Tzofin area—because the route of the existing Wall annexed lands for the purpose of expanding that settlement: Supreme Court President Aharon Barak administered a stern rebuke: "The information provided to the court did not reflect all the considerations before the decision-makers .... We hope this will not be repeated."[46]

In fact, persistent inquiries by several human rights organizations—Ha-Moked Center for the Defense of the Individual, *B'Tselem*, the Council for Peace and Security, and *Bimkom*, Planners for Planning Rights—revealed more than ten other cases in which the route of the Wall accommodated settlement expansion at the expense of the Fence's efficacy, as well as at the expense of Palestinian residents of the area. Government of Israel leaders, too, occasionally exhibited concern about the everyday needs of the Palestinian population, but were also recommending revising the Fence route in the Jerusalem area so as to reduce the number of Palestinians, some 200,000, on the western (Israel) side of the Wall. (*B'Tselem* and *Bimkom*, "Under the Guise of Security: Routing the Separation Barrier to Enable Israeli Settlement Expansion in the West Bank," December 2005.)

In terms of Jewish values, the Wall is an abomination. As an instrument of national security, the record is mixed—some suicide bombers have continued to penetrate the Wall, and Qassam rockets from Gaza are not deterred by the Wall, as evident in their resumption in May 2007 and during the three Gaza military crises and Wars, in 2008–09, 2012, and 2014, thousands in the most recent war. As a long-term, permanent solution of the Israeli–Palestinian conflict, the Wall is fundamentally flawed. As a visible expression of Israel's image in the world, it is a disaster: few outside of Israel defend the Wall, although Israel's sole patron, the United States, tolerates its construction, but only on the condition that it is a temporary instrument to enhance Israel's physical security, not a permanent border demarcation. And, as a consequence for Israel's self-image, the Wall recalls the classic period of the ghetto: in the eighteenth and nineteenth centuries, the Jewish ghetto in Eastern Europe was a type of self-generated isolation of the Jews from their neighbors. In the early twenty-first century, the Wall, if perpetuated, will have the effect of transforming the entire state of Israel into a small Middle East ghetto state, not likely to be a source of great pride among the Israeli youth of the coming generations.

The Israeli record on discrimination against its large Arab minority and its construction of the Wall are dismal and indefensible. A May 2006 public opinion poll that reported 62 percent of Israel's Jewish population in favor of encouraging the emigration of Israeli Arabs reinforces the external negative image of Israel's policies.[47] Moreover, a report at the 2006 annual Caesarea Conference on economic, social, and political dimensions of life in Israel revealed that discrimination against Arabs, in education, industry, investment aid, and wages, has led to poverty among Israel Arabs three times as much as that of Israeli Jews.

Despite a slight decline in anti-Arab sentiment in Israel, additional polls in March 2016 reveal that 48 percent of Israelis support the expulsion or transfer of Israeli Arabs out of Israel, according to a Pew survey.[48] Moreover, a 2010 survey indicated that 86 percent of Israeli Jews believe that any *Knesset* decision regarding the country's future political arrangement or foreign policy must be approved by a Jewish majority, according to the Israel Democracy Institute.[49]

These findings from two respected opinion surveys of attitudes of Israeli Jews toward the desired future status and role of Israeli Arabs in shaping future Israeli policy reflect and were exacerbated by punitive collective measures by Israel's government—a myriad of check points throughout the West Bank and, until the withdrawal of the IDF from Gaza in 2005, in that depressed part of the occupied Palestinian territories as well, and severe restrictions on Palestinian movement. In May 2007, the World Bank criticized Israel for undermining Palestinian freedom of movement in their own territories, including denial of access to 50 percent of the territory of the West Bank and more than 40 percent of its highways, while lavishing Israeli settlers with a myriad of material benefits. Most recently, a new wave of unorganized individual Palestinian attacks on Israelis, especially in the persistently contested area of East Jerusalem, since October 2015, has led to a renewal of Israel's pop-up checkpoints and road closings.[50] Palestinian officials condemned the continuing road closings as collective punishment, with resulting escalation of tension.[51] The result has been to retard economic development in the occupied territories. In human terms, such measures adversely affect adults from commuting to and from work and getting health care, and children from getting to school and back home at the end of a school day; normal life and the prospects for economic growth are both gravely undermined. Another illustration was the IDF's distorted implementation of a directive from Israel's Defense Minister to terminate the ban on Palestinians entering the Jordan Valley; instead, Palestinian nonresidents of this area were allowed to pass through the checkpoints but only on foot.[52] No wonder that Palestinian commentators, Israeli civil rights activists, and representatives of international organizations refer to life in the West Bank as having assumed the character of Palestinian imprisonment in the occupied territories.

Two other types of outright discrimination surfaced in June 2007. First, the number of East Jerusalem (Arab) residents whose permanent residency status had been revoked increased by more than 600 percent in one year, from 222 in 2005 to 1363 in 2006, the largest number of revoked permanent residency permits since the policy was introduced in 1995: residence can be revoked for acquiring a residence in the West Bank or abroad. And this "emigration" arose primarily from a policy by the Jerusalem District of Israel's Interior Ministry of making it more difficult for East Jerusalem residents to acquire construction permits in the city, creating a serious housing shortage for Jerusalem Arabs; *ergo*, the need to seek housing elsewhere.[53]

Another Israeli report revealed that 25 percent of illegal structures constructed by Israeli Jews in Area C of the West Bank, which had been placed under exclusive Israeli control by an Israeli–Palestinian agreement implementing the Oslo Accord of 1993, were built on private Arab land, compared to 0.5 percent of these structures constructed on land owned by Jews. Moreover, the number of enforced demolition of illegal Arab structures in Area C was three times larger than demolished Jewish structures—1968 illegal Arab structures, 660 Israeli Jewish structures—even though the Jewish population in this area was four times the size of the Arab population, according to a report by Israel's Civil Administration in that territory.[54]

The one notable positive development in the social condition of Palestinian citizens of Israel is evident in their proportion of students in Israel's higher education institutions: in 2013, they constituted 35.2 percent of students at academic colleges and 24.6 percent at teacher training colleges, both higher than their approximately 20 percent proportion of Israel's citizens. However, their proportion of students at Israel's highest education level, universities, is only 13.4 percent. Like Israeli Jewish students, their current choice of subjects has changed from the humanities and education to a greater emphasis on business administration and management, as well as on engineering.[55]

Most recently, several 2016 reports conveyed mixed evidence of discriminatory and accommodative attitudes and behavior of institutions and individuals of Israel's predominant Jewish majority toward the Palestinian Arab minority. A survey among 505 Hebrew-speaking respondents, conducted on 7 April 2016, noted: "While most Israelis oppose separation of Jews and Arabs in hospitals ..., some 49 percent of Israeli Jews [reportedly] told Israel's [widely viewed] TV Channel 2 that they would not live in the same building as Arab families." Nonetheless, 82 percent indicated a willingness to be treated by an Arab doctor, and 34 percent said that they supported segregation between Jewish and Arab women in hospital maternity wards; 61 percent opposed segregation.[56]

Another report indicated that only two of seven Israeli hospitals responded to a Health and Science reporter that they refused to segregate Arab and Jewish patients, though separation is forbidden by Israel's Ministry of Health regulations and violates the official policy of the hospitals: one hospital nurse reportedly responded, "We try to separate [Jews and Arabs] anyway. We always do it, even without being asked," and when asked whether this was hospital policy, she replied, "of course, especially at the maternity ward."[57] A news report about segregation in Israel's maternity wards had appeared in 2006 in *Ha'aretz*, and the issue was discussed by a *Knesset* committee in 2012, with a report that the Ministry of Health is trying, in 2016, to terminate the practice of separation.[58]

The most recent incident of (thinly concealed) discrimination by Israeli officials against Palestinian citizens of Israel was a ruling by an Israeli judge on 24 April 2016 disallowing tenders won by Arab families to build 47 houses in the northern Israeli city of Afula. This judicial ruling, justified on the grounds that the Arab families had organized their bids, rather than competing with each other, and that their coordination "seriously harmed the principle of equality ..., a principle that is at the foundation of tender law," overruled the approval of the Arabs' bids by the Israel Land Authority![59]

A month later, "Israeli police officers in civilian clothes savagely assaulted an Arab supermarket worker in central Tel Aviv ... after he refused to identify himself because he didn't know who they were, according to eye witnesses." Moreover, the Jewish owner of the supermarket, where this violent incident occurred, was reported as telling *Walla!News*,

"He was beaten only because he's a Muslim. His only crime was that he is not Jewish." The head of the Israel Police media department denied the reports, claiming that the Arab worker assaulted the police officers first; and he urged a boycott of the grocery chain where the reported incident occurred.[60]

A trenchant recent critique of Israel's current descent into undisguised Far-Right extremism, highlighted by its multiple incidents of discrimination against Israel's Arab minority and human rights organizations, is evident in a review article of six books by and about Palestinians and Israeli defenders of civil rights, by a renowned Israeli professor of the Humanities at the Hebrew University in Jerusalem:

> Israeli human rights activists and what is left of Israeli peace groups, including joint Israeli-Palestinian peace organizations, are under attack. In a sense, this is nothing very new; organizations such as *B'Tselem*, the most prominent and effective in the area of human rights, and *Breaking the Silence*, which specializes in soldiers' firsthand testimony about what they have seen and done in the occupied territories and in Gaza, have always been anathema to the Israeli right, which regards them as treasonous. But open attacks on the Israeli left have now assumed a far more sinister and ruthless character; some of them are being played out in the interrogation rooms of Israeli prisons. Clearly, there is an ongoing coordinated campaign involving the government, members of the Knesset, the police, various semi-autonomous Right-wing groups, and the public media. Politically driven harassment, including violent and illegal arrest, interrogation, denial of legal support, virulent incitement, smear campaigns, even death threats issued by proxy—all this has become part of the reservoir of the far right, which dominate the present government and sets the tone for its policies.
>
> There is now a palpable sense of danger, and also an accelerating decline into a situation of incipient everyday state terror. Palestinians have lived with the reality of state terror for decades ... it has now seeped into the texture of life inside the Green Line. ... We are witnessing a brutal wave of accelerated demolitions in the West Bank: in the first six weeks of 2016 alone, 293 homes were destroyed by the army. The goal, in a word, is a form of ethnic cleansing. Israel wants these Palestinians who inhabit what is called Area C, the zone of intense Israeli settlement (some 60 percent of the West Bank) to disappear. ... [However], it is important to note that some parts of the democratic apparatus of the state still function ... So far, one can still speak and write more or less freely, although new moves to censor social media have been announced.[61]

By contrast, "the Israeli government unanimously adopted a five-year plan (2016–2020) for the Arab population, estimated at approximately NIS 15 billion."[62] If this decision were fully implemented, it would represent a major shift in Israel government policy and behavior toward its Palestinian population; the overwhelming evidence of Israel's treatment of its Arab population raises profound doubts that such an ambitious, conciliatory decision would in fact become a reality.

Renewal of Turmoil, 2015–16

Politics and interethnic tension in Israel and the occupied West Bank are rarely tranquil. However, domestic turmoil escalated during the nine months preceding and one month after Israel's 68th birthday on 14–15 May 2016. It began on 13 September 2015, in the form of spasmodic, seemingly unorganized knife attacks on individual Israeli Jews by Palestinians, mostly in the Jerusalem area, with spillover to highly contested towns in the West Bank, notably Hebron. After waning for several months, two violent incidents occurred in the West Bank on 30 June and 1 July 2016—the stabbing to death of a 13-year-old Israeli girl in her West Bank home by a Palestinian teen-ager, and the firing on an Israeli couple, with two children, driving near Hebron, killing the father and seriously wounding the mother. These atrocities led to severe reprisals by Israel: restrictions on Hebron and surrounding towns and villages, designed to prevent all movement of Palestinians except for urgent humanitarian aid, affecting many thousands of Palestinians, including those with permits to work in Israel. Moreover, an unspecified amount from the 130 million dollars transferred monthly by the Government of Israel to the Palestinian Authority was withheld. These acts of collective punishment were the harshest Israel governmental measures imposed on Palestinians since the kidnapping–murder of three Israeli teenagers in June 2014, which precipitated the very high Palestinian casualties in Gaza War II in July–August 2014.

Compounding the interethnic turmoil was a report by the *Quartet* (the European Union, Russia, the United States, and the United Nations [UN]), prepared by the UN representative to Israel and PA, blaming both of the principal adversaries in this protracted conflict (PC) for not returning to negotiations and engaging in hostile acts against each other. The report directed blunt criticism of Israeli settlements in the West Bank, reportedly double the number since 1993, with few approved applications for Palestinian housing construction during this period and none in 2015. Further, the report said that "[the settlements] raises legitimate questions about Israel's long-term intentions," and, as often in UN reports, urged: "Israel should cease the policy of settlement construction and expansion, designating land for exclusive Israel use, and denying Palestinian development." The report also sharply criticized the Palestinians "for glorifying individuals who carry out deadly attacks." As usual, the Israeli Prime Minister responded that the UN report "perpetuates the myth that Israeli construction in the West Bank is an obstacle to peace," even though the report blamed *Hamas* for glorifying terrorism, openly calling for violent attacks against Jews and issuing instructions on how to carry out stabbings.[63]

The scale of this renewal of ethnic violence, measured in terms of scope and number of casualties (estimated at 34 Israelis killed and 466 wounded, and 218 Palestinians killed, 15,620 injured, and over 2400 detained as of the end of June 2016), was incorrectly dubbed by the Israeli media as the third Palestinian *Intifada* (also identified as the Silent *Intifada* or the Stabbing *Intifada*). The two full-scale *Intifadas*, discussed earlier in this chapter, lasted several years, with much larger casualties. However, the consequence of the 2015–16 acts of violence was a widespread increase in personal insecurity in parts of Israel and the Israel-occupied West Bank during the past half century, comparable to the pattern of events that led to the Gaza War II in July–August 2014, with enormous Palestinian casualties and material damage.

An indicator of the emotional impact in Israel of the most recent specific phase of ethnic violence was the intense debate evoked by a single act of an Israeli soldier, who fired at and killed a wounded Arab assailant in the West Bank town of Hebron, who lay helpless on the ground after a knifing raid. The IDF charged the offending soldier with manslaughter, creating a passionate debate—between Right-wing political leaders and segments of the attentive and mass publics, opposed to a Palestinian state and Palestinians *en bloc*, and Center-Left-wing political leaders and their followers, who condemned the act as unworthy of Israel's soldiers. The political upheaval was intensified when the IDF Deputy Chief Staff, in a clear reference to the Hebron incident, supported the Military's decision to try the soldier with a charge of manslaughter, decrying the "aberrant use of weapons," and adding that the IDF was committed "to investigate difficult issues impartially." The then Defense Minister, General Moshe Yaalon, a prominent figure in the ruling *Likud* Party, concurred with the IDF decision, to the chagrin of party colleagues. Prime Minister

Netanyahu initially supported the IDF decision, but then yielded to the vocal opposition, among politicians and members of the Israeli public who hailed the accused soldier as a "national hero."

A more dramatic source of intense political turmoil in Israel was a remarkable statement by the IDF Deputy Chief of Staff, Major-General Yair Golan, in a speech marking a revered Israeli national day of mourning, Holocaust Day, on 4 May 2016. Urging Israelis to honor the annual Remembrance Day by deep soul-searching about "how we, here and now, treat the stranger [clearly, Palestinians]", he uttered words which had never been heard on Holocaust Day or any of the other national mourning days in Israel: "If there is something that frightens me about Holocaust Remembrance, it's the recognition of the revolting processes that occurred in Europe in general, and particularly in Germany, back then –70, 80 and 90 years ago—and finding signs of them here among us today in 2016." Although his statement triggered condemnation from two Right-wing Cabinet ministers the next day and led to an IDF—not a General Golan—retraction of the emotive words the same day, his words were not forgotten. Moreover, Defense Minister Moshe Yaalon issued a statement expressing his "complete faith" in General Golan, with the following words: "The role of every IDF commander … does not end just with leading soldiers into battle, but also obligates him to set out a path and values for them, using both compass and conscience." Yaalon also defended the IDF decision to try the Israeli soldier for killing a wounded, helpless Palestinian in March.[64] For several reasons, including his reaction to both incidents, Defense Minister Yaalon was sacked by the Prime Minister a few weeks later.[64]

Not surprisingly, the Israeli media mistakenly referred to these incidents, in March and May, the latter only days before the state's 68th anniversary, as "the revolt of the generals." Nonetheless, the incidents triggered a sharp escalation of the intense turmoil in Israeli politics a few weeks later. The peak of this most recent episode of domestic political turmoil took the form of blunt verbal assaults on the skills and behavior of the Netanyahu government, including the Prime Minister, at the high-profile annual Herzliya Conference, where political and military leaders address the nation on major issues of public policy, including Israel's perennial security preoccupations, notably National Security. Four of the six living former leaders of Israel's Military Establishment declared political war on the current Israel government, two of them in very strong critical language.

Ehud Barak, a former IDF Chief of Staff, Defense Minister in Netanyahu's coalition governments from 2009 to 2013, and Prime Minister in 1999–2001, accused Netanyahu of fostering "incipient fascism" through anti-democratic legislation and of leading Israel toward possible "apartheid." He also called upon the public to "bring down the government by taking to the streets if necessary."[65] The same day, Moshe Yaalon, who was sacked from the Defense Ministry during this upsurge of turmoil, declared in a speech at the Herzliya Conference that Israel's current leadership had "ceased to function." Moreover, he accused the Netanyahu government of "clinging to power by tactics of 'scare and rule,' and dividing Israelis, pitting Jews against Arabs and Right against Left"; and Yaalon announced plans to contest for the prime ministership in the next general election, scheduled for 2019. Moreover, three of the four former military leaders declared, in sharp conflict with Netanyahu's frequent warning that Iran's nuclear energy program posed a grave threat to Israel, that Israel was not confronted with an existential threat at present or in the foreseeable future. The profound cleavage between Netanyahu and the Military-cum-Intelligence leadership in Israel was of long standing, with no end in sight. Thus far, there is no threat to the survival of the most extreme Right-wing government in independent Israel's history; nor is it likely to be threatened before the 2019 general election, since it derived substantial electoral benefit from the adherence of the Far-Right-wing party headed by Lieberman to the Netanyahu government, in exchange for the crucial Defense portfolio in May 2016, a majority of 14 in the 120-member *Knesset*, compared to Netanyahu's majority of one during the year since the 2015 general election.

Disenchantment

The ubiquity of these and other similar developments in Israeli perceptions of, and behavior toward, their Arab minority and critics on the Center-Left—for some Israelis, progress, for others, a counterrevolution—is starkly evident in a comparison between the predominant Israeli values in 2016, especially the dramatic evidence of poverty and inequality, and those that pervaded the pre-state Jewish community in Palestine and the early years of Israel's independence. "Socialism with a human face," in Israel, 1949–52, which I had the good fortune of experiencing (it continued until 1977), was epitomized by the cooperative values of the *kibbutz*, the reservoir of the elites in Israel's political, military, and civil service, for decades. However, over the years, especially after the 1967 crisis-war, the *kibbutz* values gradually gave way to American-style consumerism, individual gain as the driving force in human behavior, and the consequent growing gap between rich and poor—and the conflict between Israel and the Palestinians over their competing claims seemed eternally irresolvable.

Many *kibbutzim* succumbed to the lure of privatization. The model in this regard was *Kibbutz* Degania A, the widely recognized "mother of all *kibbutzim*," then almost a century old. In February 2007, a large majority of its members voted to change their cooperative way of life to an individual set of values. Most of the services that had been communal were henceforth privatized: the main change was less equality and privatization of personal income, which undermined the values underlying the traditional *kibbutz*.

In sum, Israeli society at 68 contrasts sharply with the highly developed sense of community and social conscience that pervaded the new state, in the city and the *kibbutz*, from 1948 to 1967. There was a bond, a sense of sharing in the awesome challenge of surviving and building what so many believed would be a new, model society. Orthodox Jews, like all members of the Jewish society, were accorded respect and equal rights, but no more. Since then, *Israel as a state* has flourished materially and technologically, as noted. However, the values that pervaded the first two decades began to erode in the aftermath of Israel's greatest military triumph in the June-Six-Day War in 1967. Since then, the promise of *Zionism*, its *ideological underpinning*, has steadily lost its luster. Indeed, it has become for some, perhaps many, another "God that failed," a metaphor designed by half-a-dozen prominent European and American intellectuals—Louis Fischer (the United States), André Gide (France), Arthur Koestler (Germany), Ignazio Silone (Italy), Stephen Spender (England), and Richard Wright (the United States)—who were drawn to the ideals of Communism in earlier years, to convey their disillusionment more than three decades after the Bolshevik Revolution (1949).[66]

NOTES

1. Pamela Geller, "Happy 57th Birthday to Israel! A Few Israeli Accomplishments," *Atlas Shrugged* (blog), 12 May 2005.
2. Robert Sarner, "68 Reasons to Respect, If Not Love, Israel on Its 68th Birthday," *Forward*, 14 May 2016.
3. Ibid.

4. The data on several macro-level dimensions of Israel's economy in 2006, 2007, 2012, and 2015 are derived from the following sources: Eran Azran, "Israeli Economy Grew 2.3% in 2015, Its Slowest Pace since 2009," *Ha'aretz*, 1 January 2016; Niv Elis, "OECD: Israel Fourth in Foreign Direct Investment," *Jerusalem Post*, 20 August, 2014; Bank of Israel, Data and Statistics, "Net Balance of Payments (Credits Less Debits) – Goods and Services Account and Unilateral Transfers," 10 March 2016.
5. Taub Center for Social Policy Studies in Israel, *State of the Nation Report: Society, Economy and Policy in Israel 2015*, December 2015 [hereinafter referred to as the Taub Report, December 2015], 2–3, 363, and Figure 3, "Gross Monthly Household Income, Ages 59 or Under, 2002 and 2011"; 364 and Figure 4A, "Share of Households Below the Poverty Line, Ages 59 and Under, by Population Group, 2002–2011"; and 365.
6. Ibid., 355, 359, 361.
7. Ruth Sinai, *Ha'aretz*, 1 March 2007, 1.
8. *Ha'aretz*, 30 June 2006, A7.
9. Daniel Ben Simon, *Ha'aretz*, 23 February 2007, B3.
10. Ora Cohen, "Economic Concentration Keeps on Growing," and The Marker, *Ha'aretz*, 20 July 2007.
11. Taub Report, December 2015, 347, 349, 348, and Figure 12, "Overall Decrease in Tax Burden, from 2003 to 2011, by Household Income Decile, Monthly in Shekels, 2011 Prices."
12. Roee Bergman, "Israel in 2015: 17 Billionaires, Over 88,000 Millionaires," *Ynet News*, 14 October 2015.
13. Taub Report, December 2015, 354, and Figure 1A.
14. *Forward*, 27 January, 2016.
15. Taub Report, December 2015, 381, 384, Figure 13, "Public Social Expenditure, 2011: Cash Benefits, as Percent of GDP in OECD Countries," and p. 379.
16. Taub Report, December 2015, 390–391.
17. *Ha'aretz*, 20 March 2007, 1.
18. OECD, "Education at a Glance 2014: Israel," 2014.
19. Lidar Grave-Lazi, "OECD Report: Israel Has Large Expenditure on Education but Lower Spending per Student," *Jerusalem Post*, 9 September 2014.
20. OECD. "Education at a Glance 2014: Israel."
21. Ibid.

22. Ibid.
23. Michael Melchior, interview, *Ha'aretz*, 12 March 2007, 7.
24. Ha'aretz, 8 July 2007, 3.
25. Ha'aretz, 12 July 2007, 5.
26. Yaakov Faitelson, "Demographic Trends and their Influence on Israeli Education," The Institute for Zionist Strategies.
27. Taub Report, December 2015, 143–144 and Figure 1, "Share of Students Pursuing an Academic Degree, 1995–2011."
28. Ibid., 146 and Figure 3, "Number of Students, 1990–2014," 147.
29. The perceptions and roles of most first- and second-generation political leaders of Israel (1948–74) were explored in my *Political Leadership and Charisma—Nehru, Ben Gurion, and Other 20th Century Political Leaders: Intellectual Odyssey I* (New York: Palgrave Macmillan, 2016).

    The only two leaders of stature in Israel's first quarter-century whom I did not encounter were Menachem Begin, the Revisionist leader, who, after 29 years in the political Opposition, served as Prime Minister from 1977 to 1983, and an architect, with Egypt's President Sadat, of the Egypt–Israel Peace Agreement in 1979; and Yitzhak Rabin, the Labor Prime Minister from 1974 to 1977 and from 1992 to 1996, who, in collaboration with Yossi Beilin and Peres, facilitated mutual recognition between Israel and the PLO and the Oslo Accords in 1993, and the 1994 peace agreement with Jordan.
30. Raphael Poch, "In New Poll, Public Casts No Confidence Vote against Knesset," *Arutz Sheva* [TV], 19 January, 2016.
31. Joshua Lipson, "Israel Among Most Corrupt of OECD Countries," *Jerusalem Post*, 9 July 2013.
32. Ben Hartman and Gil Hoffman, "Interior Minister Deri's Brother Questioned for Third Straight Day in Corruption Probe," *Jerusalem Post*, 14 April 2016.
33. The Marker and Reuters, *Ha'aretz*, 12 July 2007.
34. World Bank, Worldwide Governance Indicators 2015.
35. Chen Tamir, "Censorship in Israel," *Perspective* (blog), *Guggenheim Museum*, 20 May 2016.
36. Julie Wiener, "Israel Imposes Penalties on Cultural Groups That Shun West Bank Settlements," *Forward*, 16 June 2016.
37. Ibid.
38. *Ha'aretz*, 29 March 2007, 1 and 30 March 2007.

39. *Ha'aretz*, 22 February 2007, 10.
40. "Magal Resigns Knesset amid Sexual Harassment Scandal," *Times of Israel*, 30 November 2015.
41. Mati Tuchfeld et al., "Interior Minister Resigns amid Sexual Misconduct Allegations," *Israel Hayom*, 21 December 2015.
42. "Ex-Senior Cop Indicted on Sexual Harassment Charges," *Times of Israel*, 22 March 2016.
43. "Cop Found Guilty of Sexual Harassment to Be Promoted," *Times of Israel*, 8 May 2016.
44. *Ha'aretz*, 19 June 2006, 5.
45. *Ha'aretz*, 25 June 2006, 5.
46. Aviram Zino, "High Court: Dismantle Part of Fence," *Yedioth Ahronoth*, 15 June 2006.
47. Israel Democracy Institute, May 2006.
48. Naomi Zeveloff, "48% of Israeli Jews Back 'Expulsion' or 'Transfer' of Arabs, New Pew Survey Says," *Forward*, 8 March 2016.
49. "Poll: Most Israeli Jews Believe Arab Citizens Should Have No Say in Foreign Policy," *Ha'aretz*, 30 November 2010.
50. Diaa Hadid, "In West Bank, Israel Imposes Pop-Up Checkpoints and Road Closings," *New York Times*, 13 April 2016.
51. *Ha'aretz*, 9 May 2007, 1.
52. *Ha'aretz*, 8 June 2007, A3.
53. Ilan Shahar, *Ha'aretz*, 24 June 2007, 2.
54. Uri Blau, *Ha'aretz*, 5 June 2007, 3.
55. Central Bureau of Statistics, as reported in Taub Report, 146–147.
56. Jewish Telegraph Agency (JTA), reported in *Forward*, New York, 11 April 2016.
57. Naomi Darom, "Maternity Ward Segregation Just Tip of the Iceberg in Israel," *Forward*, 12 April 2016.
58. Ibid.
59. Naomi Zeveloff, "Israeli Judge Says No to Arabs Building in Jewish Town—Cites Bidding Woes," *Forward*, 26 April 2016.
60. "Israeli Police Caught on Tape Brutally Beating Arab Supermarket Worker," *Ha'aretz*, 23 May 2016, reported in *Forward*, the same date; and Yaniv Kubovich, "Israel Police Commander Pushes Boycott of Supermarket Where Cops Brutally Beat Arab Worker," *Ha'aretz*, 25 May 2016, reported in *Forward*, the same date.
61. David Shulman, "Israel: The Broken Silence," *New York Review of Books*, 7 April, 2016.

62. Meir Elran, Eran Yashiv, and Mohammed Abo Nasra. "The Five-Year Plan to Integrate the Arab Population in Israel: A Quantum Leap Forward?," *Institute for National Security Studies*, no. 792, 2 February 2016.
63. Diaa Hadid and Somini Sengupta, "Israel Imposes Restrictions on Palestinians in West Bank After Attacks," *Forward*, 2 July 2016, and *New York Times*, 2 July 2016; and Somini Sengupta, "Faulting Both Israelis and Palestinians, Report Aims to Revive Peace Talks," *New York Times*, 2 July 2016.
64. Jeffrey Heller, "Israeli General Warns of Nazi-Like Jewish Extremists in Holocaust Remembrance Speech," *Forward*, 5 May 2016.
65. J. J. Goldberg, "4 Men Who Want to Bring Down Benjamin Netanyahu—and the Tragic Reasons They Won't," *Forward*, 22 June 2016.
66. Arthur Koestler et al., *The God That Failed*, ed. Richard Crossman (New York: Harper & Row, 1963).

BIBLIOGRAPHY

All items in Israeli Hebrew-language newspapers (*Davar*, *Ha'aretz*, *Ma'ariv*, *Yediot Aharanot*, etc.) were in Hebrew.

GENERAL

Interviews

A. *Select list of interviews by Michael Brecher*
Al-Baz, Mahmoud. May 1975.
Allon, Yigal. 1960, 1965–66, 1968, 1973–74, 1977–78.
Eytan, Walter. 1956.
Avner, Gershon. July 1968.
Bar-Lev, Haim. July 1974.
Bar-On, Hanan. August 1968.
Ben-Gurion, David. June 1966, May 1971.
Bitan, Moshe. August 1968.
Boutros-Ghali, Boutros. May 1975.
Dayan, Moshe. May 1969.
Eban, Abba. 1948, 1965–66, 1968 July 1968, 1973–74, 1977–78, 1995.
Evron, Ephraim. March 1972.
Eshkol, Levi. April 1966.
Gazit, Mordekhai. July 1968, July 1974.
Herzog, Ya'acov. April 1966, August 1968.
Joseph, Dov. July 1960, June 1971.
Keating, Kenneth. July 1974, August 1974.

Meir, Golda. August 1966, June 1968.
Mohammed Sayeed Ahmad. May 1975, June 1975.
Navon, Yitzhak. 1965–66.
Peres, Shimon. 1960, 1965–66, 1968, 1973–74, 1977–78.
Rafael, Gideon. August 1968.
Rosen, Pinchas. February 1971.
Sapir, Pinhas. August 1974.
Shapira, Haim M. July 1968.
Sharett, Moshe. July 1960.
Sharif, Zehev. March 1966.
Wilson, Harold. December 1972.
Yariv, Aharon. August 1974.

B. Other Interviews

Barak, Ehud. "Continuation of Eyes Wide Shut." Interview by Ari Shavit, *Ha'aretz*, 4 September 2002.
Melchior, Michael. Interview, *Ha'aretz*, 12 March 2007, 7.

Other Sources

Azran, Eran. 2016. Israeli Economy Grew 2.3% in 2015, Its Slowest Pace since 2009. *Ha'aretz*, 1 January 2016.
Bank of Israel, Data and Statistics. 2016. Net Balance of Payments (Credits Less Debits)—Goods and Services Account and Unilateral Transfers. 10 March 2016.
Benn, Aluf. 2016. Olmert's Plan for Peace with the Palestinians. *Ha'aretz*, 17 December 2009, 1–3. Reprint, *Ha'aretz*, 16 April 2016.
Bergman, Roee. 2015. Israel in 2015: 17 Billionaires, Over 88,000 Millionaires. *Ynet News*, 14 October 2015.
Brecher, Michael. 2016a. *Political Leadership and Charisma—Nehru, Ben Gurion, and Other 20th Century Political Leaders: Intellectual Odyssey I*. New York: Palgrave Macmillan.
———. 2016b. *The World of Protracted Conflicts*. Lanham: Rowman & Littlefield/Lexington Books.
Brecher, Michael, and Irving Brecher. 2001. Israelis versus Palestinians: Is There a Way Out? *International Journal* 56(3): 519–526.
Cohen, Ora. 2007. Economic Concentration Keeps on Growing. *Ha'aretz*, 20 July 2007.
Elis, Niv. 2014. OECD: Israel Fourth in Foreign Direct Investment. *Jerusalem Post*, 20 August, 2014.

Elran, Meir, Eran Yashiv, and Mohammed Abo Nasra. 2016. The Five-Year Plan to Integrate the Arab Population in Israel: A Quantum Leap Forward? *Institute for National Security Studies* 792: 2 February 2016.
"Ex-Senior Cop Indicted on Sexual Harassment Charges." *Times of Israel*, 22 March 2016.
Faitelson, Yaakov. 2011. *Demographic Trends and their Influence on Israeli Education*. Jerusalem: The Institute for Zionist Strategies.
Geller, Pamela. 2005. Happy 57th Birthday to Israel! A Few Israeli Accomplishments. *Atlas Shrugged* (blog), 12 May 2005.
Goldberg, J. J. 2016. 4 Men Who Want to Bring Down Benjamin Netanyahu—and the Tragic Reasons They Won't. *The Forward*, 22 June 2016.
Grave-Lazi, Lidar. 2014. OECD Report: Israel Has Large Expenditure on Education but Lower Spending per Student. *Jerusalem Post*, 9 September 2014.
Hadid, Diaa. 2016. In West Bank, Israel Imposes Pop-Up Checkpoints and Road Closings. *New York Times*, 13 April 2016.
Hadid, Diaa and Somini Sengupta. 2016. Israel Imposes Restrictions on Palestinians in West Bank After Attacks. *Forward*, 2 July 2016.
Halpern, Ben. 1969. *The Idea of the Jewish State*. Cambridge, MA: Harvard University Press.
Hartman, Ben and Gil Hoffman. 2016. Interior Minister Deri's Brother Questioned for Third Straight Day in Corruption Probe. *Jerusalem Post*, 14 April 2016.
Heller, Jeffrey. 2016. Israeli General Warns of Nazi-Like Jewish Extremists in Holocaust Remembrance Speech. *Forward*, 5 May 2016.
Isacheroff, Avi. 2014. Revealed: Olmert's 2008 Peace Offer to Palestinians. *Jerusalem Post*, 24 May 2013, 1–3. Reprint, *Jerusalem Post*, 27 July 2014.
"Israeli Police Caught on Tape Brutally Beating Arab Supermarket Worker." *Ha'aretz*, 23 May 2016, reported in *Forward*, the same date.
Joseph, Dov. 1960. *The Faithful City: The Siege of Jerusalem, 1948*. New York: Simon and Schuster.
Koestler, Arthur, et al. 1963. In *The God That Failed*, ed. Richard Crossman. New York: Harper & Row.
Kubovich, Yaniv. 2016. Israel Police Commander Pushes Boycott of Supermarket Where Cops Brutally Beat Arab Worker. *Ha'aretz*, 25 May 2016, reported in *Forward*, the same date.
Lipson, Joshua. 2013. Israel among Most Corrupt of OECD Countries. *Jerusalem Post*, 9 July 2013.
"Magal Resigns Knesset amid Sexual Harassment Scandal." *Times of Israel*, 30 November 2015.
Ma'oz, Moshe. 1995. *Syria and Israel: From War to Peacemaking*. New York: Oxford University Press.

Mohn, Paul. 1950. Jerusalem and the United Nations. *International Conciliation*, no. 464.
Organization for Economic Co-operation and Development (OECD). 2014. Education at a Glance 2014: Israel.
Poch, Raphael. 2016. In New Poll, Public Casts No Confidence Vote against Knesset. *Arutz Sheva* [TV], 19 January, 2016.
Rabinovich, Itamar. 1998. *The Brink of Peace: The Israeli-Syrian Negotiations.* Princeton: Princeton University Press.
Rudoren, Jodi and Isabel Kerschner. 2014. How Nine Months of Mideast Talks Ended in Disarray. *New York Times*, 28 April 2014.
Sarner, Robert. 2016. 68 Reasons to Respect, If Not Love, Israel On Its 68th Birthday. *Forward*, 14 May 2016.
Sengupta, Somini. 2016. Faulting Both Israelis and Palestinians, Report Aims to Revive Peace Talks. *New York Times*, 2 July 2016.
Sharef, Zeev. 1962. *Three Days.* New York: Doubleday.
Shulman, David. 2016. Israel: The Broken Silence. *New York Review of Books*, 7 April, 2016.
Swisher, Clayton E. 2004. *The Truth about Camp David: The Untold Story about the Collapse of the Middle East Peace Process.* New York: Nation Books.
Tamir, Chen. 2016. Censorship in Israel. *Perspective* (blog), *Guggenheim Museum*, 20 May 2016.
Taub Center for Social Policy Studies in Israel. 2015. *State of the Nation Report: Society, Economy and Policy in Israel 2015.* December 2015.
Tuchfeld, Mati et al. 2015. Interior Minister Resigns amid Sexual Misconduct Allegations. *Israel Hayom*, 21 December 2015.
United Nations (UN). 1947. UN General Assembly. Resolution 181 (II). Future Government of Palestine. 29 November 1947.
Wiener, Julie. 2016. Israel Imposes Penalties on Cultural Groups that Shun West Bank Settlements. *Forward*, 16 June 2016.
Winer, Stuart. 2014. Hand-Drawn Map Shows what Olmert Offered for Peace. *The Times of Israel*, 23 May 2013, 1–3. Reprint, *The Times of Israel*, 28 July 2014.
World Bank. Worldwide Governance Indicators 2015.
Zeveloff, Naomi. 2016a. 48% of Israeli Jews Back 'Expulsion' or 'Transfer' of Arabs, New Pew Survey Says. *Forward*, 8 March 2016.
———. 2016b. Israeli Judge Says No to Arabs Building in Jewish Town—Cites Bidding Woes. *Forward*, 26 April 2016.
Zino, Aviram. 2006. High Court: Dismantle Part of Fence. *Yediot Ahronoth*, 15 June 2006.

The 1967 Crisis-War

Interviews

A. Interviews by Michael Brecher
Allon, Yigal. 26 July 1968.
Avner, Gershon, 24 July 1968.
Bar-On, Hanan, 6 August 1968.
Ben Gurion, David, May 1971.
Bitan, Moshe, 8 August 1968.
Eban, Abba, 22 July and 8 August 1968.
Evron, Ephraim, 3 March 1972.
Gazit, Mordekhai, 15 July 1968.
Herzog, Ya'acov, 10 August 1968.
Meir, Golda, June 1968.
Peres, Shimon, 15 July 1968
Rafael, Gideon, 12 August 1968.
Shapira, Haim M., 16 July 1968.
Wilson, Harold, 22 December 1972 (interview also conducted by Benjamin Geist)

B. Other Interviews
Allon, Yigal. Interviews, *Lamerhav*, 14 May and 4 June 1967.
Amit, Meir. Interview by Benjamin Geist, 13 July 1973.
Avner, Gershon. Interview by Benjamin Geist, 25 February 1973.
Bar-Lev, Haim. Interview, *Ma'ariv*, 18 April 1972.
Bar-Lev, Haim. Interview, *Ma'ariv*, 6 May 1973.
———. Interview, *Ma'ariv*, 16 May 1973.
Bar-Lev, Haim. Interview, *Yediot Aharonot*, 5 June 1973.
Begin, Menachem. Interview, *Yediot Aharonot*, 2 June 1967.
Ben Gurion, David. Interview, *Ma'ariv*, 13 November 1970.
Carmel, Moshe. Interview, *Jerusalem Post*, 2 June 1972
Dayan, Moshe. Interview, *Ma'ariv*, 13 June 1967.
Dayan, Moshe. Interviews, *Yediot Aharonot*, 13 and 16 June 1967.
Eban, Abba. Interview, *Ha'aretz*, 5 June 1970.
Eban, Abba. Interviews, *Ma'ariv*, 1 December 1967 and 2 June 1972.
Eban, Abba. Interview, *Yediot Aharonot*, 22 April 1973.
Elazar, David. Interview, *Yediot Aharonot*, 9 June 1972.
Eshkol, Levi. Interview, *U.S. News and World Report*, 17 April 1967.
Eshkol, Levi. Interviews, *Yediot Aharonot*, 7 July and 18 October 1967.
Eshkol, Levi. Interview by the editors, *Ma'ariv*, 4 October 1967.

Gavish, Yeshayahu. Interview by Dov Goldstein, *Yediot Aharonot*, 3 April 1970.
Meir, Golda. Interview, *Jerusalem Post*, 16 June 1972.
Narkiss, Uzi. Interview, *Davar*, 1 June 1973.
Narkiss, Uzi. Interview, *Ma'ariv*, 8 June 1972.
Narkiss, Uzi. Interview with five generals, including Uri Narkiss, *Ma'ariv*, 4 June 1971.
Nasser, Abdel. Interview, *Newsweek*, 10 February 1969.
Rabin, Yitzhak. Interview, *Ma'ariv*, 4 October 1967.
Rafael, Gideon. Interview, *Ma'ariv*, 4 August 1967.
Rafael, Gideon. Interview, *Yediot Aharonot*, 4 June 1971.
Serlin, Joseph. Interviews, *Yediot Aharonot*, 26 May and 5 June 1972.
Serlin, Joseph. Interview, *Yediot Aharonot*, 5 June 1972.
Sharon, Ariel. Interview, *Ma'ariv*, 20 July 1973.
Sharon, Ariel. Interview, *Yediot Aharonot*, 20 July 1973.
Sneh, Moshe. Interview, *Yediot Aharonot*, 16 June 1967.
Weizman, Ezer. Interview by Dov Goldstein, *Ma'ariv*, 5 June 1973.

Other Sources

Allon, Yigal. 1967a. 'Active Defense': A Guarantee for Our Existence. *OT*, November 1967, 5–13.

———. 1967b. Speech in Tel Aviv, 2 June 1967. English Summary issued by the State of Israel, *Government Press Office*, Press Bulletin, 3 June 1967.

———. 1968. *Masakh Shel Hol [A Curtain of Sand]*. 2nd rev ed. Tel Aviv: Hakibbutz Hame'uhad.

———. 1970. *The Making of Israel's Army*. London: Vallentine, Mitchell.

Bar-Zohar, Michael. 1968. *The Longest Month*. Tel Aviv: Levin-Epstein.

———. 1970. *Embassies in Crisis: Diplomats and Demagogues Behind the Six Day War*. Englewood Cliffs: Prentice-Hall.

Begin, Menachem. 1971. A Chapter from a Book to Be Written. *Ma'ariv*, 18 June and 2 July 1971.

———. 1972a. Eulogy for Ya'acov Herzog, March 1972.

———. 1972b. The Meeting of 2 June 1967. *Ma'ariv*, 2 June 1972.

Benkler, R. 1971. General Rikhye's Truth. *Al Hamishmar*, 13 August 1971.

Ben-Porath, Yehoshua, and U. Dan. 1967. *Mirage Contre MiG*. Paris: R. Laffont.

Bentov, Mordekhai. 1972. The Truth and Not 'Nightmares' Are of Educational Value. *Al Hamishmar*, 18 May 1972.

Blechman, Barry M. 1972. The Impact of Israel's Reprisals on Behavior of the Bordering Arab Nations Directed at Israel. *Journal of Conflict Resolution* 16: 155–181.

Brecher, Michael. 1972. *The Foreign Policy System of Israel: Setting, Images, Process*. London: Oxford University Press; and New Haven: Yale University Press, 1972.

———. 1974. *Decisions in Israel's Foreign Policy*. London: Oxford University Press; and New Haven: Yale University Press, 1975.
British Broadcasting Corporation. 1967. *Summary of World Broadcasts, Part 4, The Middle East and Africa, Second Series (BBC)*. Monitoring Service of the British Broadcasting Corporation, Caversham Park, Reading, England, April–June 1967.
British Parliamentary Debates. 1967. Hansard, House of Commons, 2nd Session, 27th Parliament, I, 8 May–5 June 1967.
Bull, Odd. 1976. *War and Peace in the Middle East*. London: Leo Cooper.
Bunche, Ralph. 1967. Letter to the editor, *New York Times*, June 11, 1967.
Burdett, Winston. 1970. *Encounter with the Middle East: An Intimate Report of What Lies Behind the Arab-Israeli Conflict*. London: Andre Deutsch.
Canadian Parliament, House of Commons. *Debates*. 27th Parliament, 2nd session, vol. 1, 8 May–5 June 1967.
Carmel, Moshe. 1972a. Fighting for Survival—Struggling for Peace. *Davar*, 2 June 1972.
———. 1972b. And Yet: We Were Faced with the Danger of Destruction. *Ma'ariv*, 21 April 1972.
Christman, Henry M., ed. 1969. *The State Papers of Levi Eshkol*. New York: Funk & Wagnalls.
Churchill, Randolph S., and Winston S. Churchill. 1967. *The Six Day War*. London: Heinemann.
Dagan, Avigdor. 1970. *Moscow and Jerusalem: Twenty Years of Relations between Israel and the Soviet Union*. London: Abelard-Schuman.
Darom, Naomi. 2016. Maternity Ward Segregation Just Tip of the Iceberg in Israel. *Forward*, 12 April 2016.
Dayan, Moshe. 1967a. Broadcast to *Tzahal*, 5 June 1967, State of Israel, Government Press Office.
———. 1967b. Press Conference, 13 June 1967, State of Israel, Government Press Office.
———. 1976. *Story of My Life*. Jerusalem/Tel Aviv: Steimatzky's Agency.
———. 1969. *Mapa Hadasha—Yachasim Aherim [New Map—Other Relations]*. Tel Aviv/Haifa: Sifriyat Ma'ariv-Shikmona.
De Gaulle, Charles. 1967. Press Conference, 27 November 1967. Excerpts in *New York Times*, 28 November 1967.
De Murville, Maurice Couve. 1971. *Une Politique Etrangere 1958–1969*. Paris: Plon.
Dishon, Daniel, ed. 1971. *Middle East Record: 1967*. Vol. 3. Tel Aviv: Israel Universities Press.
Draper, Theodore. 1968. *Israel and World Politics: Roots of the Third Arab-Israeli War*. New York: Viking Press.
Eban, Abba. 1967a. Address to the UN Security Council, 6 June 1967, *Israel Information Services*. New York: June 1967.

———. 1967b. Press Conference in Jerusalem, 30 May 1967. English text issued by State of Israel, *Government Press Office*.
———. 1967c. Press Conference in Tel Aviv, 5 June 1967. English text issued by State of Israel, *Government Press Office*.
———. 1967d. Speech in Rehovot, 17 May 1967. Reported in *Ma'ariv*, 18 May 1967.
———. 1968. *To Live or Perish* [unpublished manuscript], 1968.
———. 1969. *Voice of Israel*. New York: Horizon Press.
———. 1973a. *My Country: The Story of Modern Israel*. London/Jerusalem: Weidenfeld and Nicolson.
———. 1973b. Revelations from the Waiting Period. *Ma'ariv*, 6 May 1973.
———. 1977. *An Autobiography*. Jerusalem/Tel Aviv: Steimatsky's Agency.
Encyclopedia Hebraica 23, cols. 722–750, s.v. The Six Day War. (in Hebrew).
Eshkol, Levi. 1967a. Appointment Book (AB) as Prime Minister for 14 May to 10 June 1967.
———. 1967b. Broadcast to the Nation, 28 May 1967. English version in *BBC, Summary of World Broadcasts, Part 4, The Middle East and Africa, Second Series (BBC)*. Monitoring Service of the British Broadcasting Corporation, Caversham Park, Reading, England, April-June 1967, 30 May 1967.
———. 1967c. Letter to USSR Premier Kosygin on 1 June 1967. English version in *Jerusalem Post*, 4 June 1967.
———. 1968. Answer to Question in Knesset, 9 December 1968. *Divrei Haknesset* 53, 602–603.
———. 1969a. Address to the Chief Rabbis and Spiritual leaders of all of Israel's Communities, 7 June 1967. English version. In *The State Papers of Levi Eshkol*, ed. H. M. Christman, 114. New York: Funk & Wagnalls, 1969.
———. 1969b. Broadcast to the Nation, 5 June 1967. English version. In *The State Papers of Levi Eshkol*, ed. H. M. Christman, 107–110. New York: Funk & Wagnalls.
———. 1969c. Statement in the Knesset, 22 May 1967. *Divrei Haknesset* 49, 2225–2227. English version. In *The State Papers of Levi Eshkol*, ed. H. M. Christman, 95–104. New York: Funk & Wagnalls.
———. 1969d. Statement in the Knesset, 29 May 1967. *Divrei Haknesset* 49, 2283–2285. English version. In *The State Papers of Levi Eshkol*, ed. H. M. Christman, 95–104. New York: Funk & Wagnalls.
———. 1969e. Statement in the Knesset, 12 June 1967. *Divrei Haknesset* 49, 2327–2331. English version. In *The State Papers of Levi Eshkol*, ed. H. M. Christman, 113–134. New York: Funk & Wagnalls.
———. 1972. Letter to Harold Wilson, 5 June 1967. In *Eban*, ed. Robert St. John, 452. Garden City: Doubleday.
Geist, Benjamin. 1974. The Six Day War: A Study in the Setting and Process of Foreign Policy Decision-Making Under Crisis Conditions. Ph.D. dissertation, The Hebrew University of Jerusalem, Jerusalem, 1974.

Gilboa, Moshe. 1969. *Shesh Shanim, Shisha Yamim [Six Years, Six Days: Origins and History of the Six Day War]*. Tel Aviv: Am Oved.
———. 1973. The Crisis that Reached the Top. *OT*, 31 May 1973.
Harif, Yosef. 1974. In the Argument around the 'Separation of Forces' on the Syrian Frontier, Washington Bases Itself on an Israeli Document of 19 June 1967. *Ma'ariv*, 22 March 1974.
Heikal, Mohamed. 1972. *Nasser: The Cairo Documents*. London: New English Library.
———. 1973. The 1967 Arab-Israeli War. *Sunday Telegraph*, 21 and 28 October 1973. Translated in *Ma'ariv*, 9 November 1973.
Higgins, Rosalyn. 1969. *United Nations Peacekeeping, 1946–1967: Documents and Commentary, vol. 1, The Middle East*. London: Oxford University Press.
Hussein, Ibn Talal, King of Jordan. 1969. *My "War" with Israel*. As told to and with additional material by Vick Vance and Pierre Lauer. New York: William Morrow, 1969.
International Institute for Strategic Studies, London. 1966. *The Military Balance, 1966–67*. London: International Institute for Strategic Studies.
———. 1967. *The Military Balance, 1967–68*. London: International Institute for Strategic Studies.
Israel, Knesset. 1948–1976. *Divrei Haknesset [Parliamentary Proceedings]*. Jerusalem/Tel Aviv: Government Printer.
Israel, Ministry of Defense. 1969. *The War of Four Days, the Southern Command, 5 June–9 June 1967*. Jerusalem, June 1969.
Israel, Ministry of Foreign Affairs. 1967. Cables and Communications, Jerusalem, 1967.
Israel Information Services. 1967. *The Record of Aggression 1958–1967*. New York, 1967.
Jabber, Fuad A., ed. 1970. *International Documents on Palestine 1967*. Beirut: The Institute for Palestine Studies.
Johnson, Lyndon B. 1971. *The Vantage Point: Perspectives of the Presidency, 1963–1969*. New York: Holt, Rinehart and Winston.
Kimche, David, and Dan Bawly. 1968. *The Sandstorm; The Arab-Israeli War of June 1967: Prelude and Aftermath*. London: Secker & Warburg.
Kollek, Teddy. 1978. *For Jerusalem*. Jerusalem/Tel Aviv: Steimatsky's Agency.
Laffin, John. 1973. *Fedayeen: The Arab-Israeli Dilemma*. London: Cassell.
Lall, Arthur. 1970. *The United Nations and the Middle East Crisis, 1967*. 2nd ed. New York: Columbia University Press.
Laqueur, Walter Z. 1968. *The Road to War 1967: The Origins of the Arab-Israel Conflict*. London: Weidenfeld and Nicolson.
Lau-Lavie, Naftalie. 1968. *Moshe Dayan, A Biography*. London: Vallentine, Mitchell.

Legler, A., and W. Liebisch. 1967. Militärische, Ereijuisse im Nahen Osten, June 1967, Eine Documentation. In *Bibliothek fur Zeitgeschichte Jahres-Bibliographie*. Stuttgart: 1967.
Levi, Eliyahu S., ed. 1967. *This Was Goliath: Facts and Figurers [sic] on Arab Military Strength in the Six Day War*. Tel Aviv: IDF Information Office.
Nakdimon, Shlomo. 1968. *Likrat Sha'at Haefes [Toward the Zero Hour: The Drama that Preceded the Six Day War]*. Tel Aviv: Ramdor.
———. 1971. The Moves that Preceded the Occupation of the Old City. *Yediot Aharonot*, 4 June 1971.
O'Ballance, Edgar. 1972. *The Third Arab-Israeli War*. London: Faber and Faber.
Peled, Matityahu. 1972. The Character of Danger. *Ma'ariv*, 24 March 1972.
———. 1973. The Beauty Is Untouched. *Ma'ariv*, 15 June 1973.
Rabin, Yitzhak. 1972. Six Days and Five More Years," *Ma'ariv*, 2 June 1972.
Rafael, Gideon. 1972. May 1967—A Personal Report. *Ma'ariv*, 18 and 21 April 1972.
Rodinson, Maxime. 1968. *Israel and the Arabs*. London: Penguin Books.
Safran, Nadav. 1969. *From War to War: The Arab-Israeli Confrontation, 1948-1967: A Study of the Conflict from the Perspective of Coercion in the Context of Inter-Arab and Big Power Relations*. New York: Pegasus.
Schiff, Zeev. 1967a. Three Days of the Campaign. *Ha'aretz*, 9 June 1967.
———. 1967b. The Three Weeks that Preceded the War. *Ha'aretz*, 4 October 1967.
St. John, Robert. 1972. *Eban*. Garden City: Doubleday.
Tzimouki, Arie. 1967. "The Longest Month" [a résumé of crisis events]. *Yediot Aharonot*, 16, 21, and 25 June 1967.
———. 1972. Eshkol as I Knew Him. *Yediot Aharonot*, 25 February 1972.
Ulam, Adam B. 1968. *Expansion and Coexistence: The History of Soviet Foreign Policy, 1917–67*. New York: Praeger.
United Nations (UN). 1967a. UN Document, 8/7953, 8 June 1967.
———. 1967b. Report of the Secretary-General of the United Nations, U Thant, to the Security Council, S/7896 (19 May 1967).
———. 1967c. Report of the Secretary-General of the United Nations, U Thant, to the Security Council, S/7906 (26 May 1967).
———. 1967d. Report on the Withdrawal of the United Nations Emergency Force, by U Thant, Secretary-General of the United Nations, 26 June 1967. *UN Monthly Chronicle* 4(7): 135–161.
Veli, Lester. 1969. *Countdown in the Holy Land*. New York: Funk & Wagnalls.
Weizman, Ezer. 1973a. A Chapter from My Memoirs. *Ma'ariv*, 26 September 1973.
———. 1973b. Text of Speech before Herut Center, 14 January 1973, *Yediot Aharonot*, 19 January 1973.
Wilson, Harold. 1971. *The Labour Government 1965–1970: A Personal Record*. London: Weidenfeld and Nicolson.

Yaffe, Aviad. 1967. The War of Twenty-Seven Days. *Nitzoz*, September 1967.
Yonah, Major. 1968. The Background of the Six Day War in the Eyes of the Arabs: Egypt and Her Entry Into the War. *Ma'arakhot* 191-192: 37-40, 73-103.
Yost, Charles W. 1968. The Arab-Israeli War: How It Began. *Foreign Affairs* 46(2): 304-320.

THE 1973 CRISIS-WAR

Interviews

A. Interviews by Michael Brecher
Bar-Lev, Haim, 29 July 1974.
Eban, Abba, 15 July 1974.
Gazit, Mordekhai, 27 July 1974.
Keating, Kenneth and other U.S. Embassy officials, 30 July and 12 August 1974.
Meir, Golda aides, 16 and 18 August 1977 (interviews also conducted by Benjamin Geist).
Peres, Shimon, 11 August 1974.
Sapir, Pinhas, 25 August 1974.
Yariv, Aharon, 7 August 1974.

B. Other Interviews
Bar-Lev, Haim. Interviews, *Ma'ariv*, 9 November 1973 and 21 September 1977.
Bar-Lev, Haim. Interviews by Uri Millstein, 24 and 31 January, and 26 June 1974.
Dayan, Moshe. Interview, *Time*, 30 July 1973.
Dayan, Moshe. "Interview on Israeli Television, 14 October 1973." In special issue, *Ma'arakhot* (November 1973): 232-233.
Dayan, Moshe. Interview on U.S. Telvision, CBS, "Face the Nation," 9 December 1973.
Eban, Abba. Interview, *Davar*, 28 December 1973.
Eban, Abba. Interview, *Ha'aretz*, 4 October 1974.
Eban, Abba. Interview on United Kingdom Television, "Panorama," 30 October 1973.
Hafez, Ismail. Interview with Mohamed Heikal in *Al-Ahram* (Cairo), 18 November 1973. In Avi Shay, "Egypt before the Yom Kippur War: War Aims and Plan of Attack," *Ma'arakhot* 250 (July 1976): 18.
Meir, Golda. Interview, *Ma'ariv*, 16 September 1974.
Sadat, Anwar. "The October War: As Seen Through the Eyes of Anwar Sadat." Interviews by Mussa Sabri, *Akhbar el-Yom*, 10 September 1974. In *Ma'ariv*, 13 September 1974.
Tal, Y. Interview, *Yediot Aharonot*, 21 September 1977.

Other Sources

Agranat Commission. 1974. *Partial Report* issued by the Committee of Inquiry—Yom Kippur War. Jerusalem: Government Press Office, 3 April 1974.
———. 1975. *Third and Final Report*, press release issued by the Commission of Inquiry—Yom Kippur War (Agranat Commission). Jerusalem: Government Press Office, 30 January 1975.
Al-Haytham al-Ayoubi. 1975. The Strategies of the Fourth Campaign. In *Middle East Crucible: Studies on the Arab-Israeli War of October 1973*, ed. Naseer H. Aruri, 65–96. Wilmette: Medina University Press International.
Allon, Yigal. 1973a. Address at the Van Leer Jerusalem Foundation, 3 June 1973.
———. 1973b. Address at the Van Leer Jerusalem Foundation, 26 November 1973.
Aruri, Naseer H., ed. 1975. *Middle East Crucible: Studies on the Arab-Israeli War of October 1973*. Wilmette: Medina University Press International.
Avnery, Arieh. 1975. *Shamayim Adoumim [Red Sky]*. Tel Aviv: Sifriyat Madim.
Bar-Lev, Haim. 1975. We Knew Where the Egyptians Would Attack and How—But We Made a Mistake about the Timing. *Ma'ariv*, 1 August 1975.
Bar-Tov, Hanoch. 1978. *Dado—48 Years and Another 20 Days*. 2 vols. Sifriyat Ma'ariv: Tel Aviv.
Begin, Menachem. 1973. Statement in the Knesset, 16 October 1973. *Divrei Haknesset* 68, 4476–4479.
Ben-Porath, Yeshayahu, et al. 1973. *Hamechdal [The Fiasco]*. Tel Aviv: Hotza'a Meyuhedet.
Brecher, Michael. 1974. *Decisions in Israel's Foreign Policy*. London: Oxford University Press; and New Haven: Yale University Press, 1975.
Dayan, Moshe. 1973. Speech to the *Knesset*, 30 October 1973. *Divrei Haknesset* 68, 4585–4587.
———. 1974. Confidential Briefing to Israeli Newspaper Editors, 9 October 1973. *Ha'aretz*, 15 February 1974.
———. 1976. *Story of My Life*. Jerusalem/Tel Aviv: Steimatzky's Agency.
Disentshik, Ido. 1977. You Don't Ask for a Cease-Fire with Your Back to the Wall. *Ma'ariv*, 21 September 1977.
Draper, Theodore. 1974. The Road to Geneva. *Commentary* 57(2): 23–39.
Eban, Abba. 1973. Press Conference with UN Correspondents Association, 17 October 1973; reported in *New York Times*, 18 October 1973.
———. 1977a. *An Autobiography*. Jerusalem/Tel Aviv: Steimatsky's Agency.
———. 1977b. Kissinger Told Me that He Went to Sleep Quietly after He Received the Israeli Intelligence Appreciation on the Eve of October 5. *Ma'ariv*, 21 September 1977.
Elazar, David. 1975. The Yom Kippur War: Military Lessons. In *Military Aspects of the Israeli-Arab Conflict: Proceedings of an International Symposium Held in*

Jerusalem, 12–17 October 1975, 245–250. Tel Aviv: University Publishing Projects.
———. 1976. Memorandum submitted to the Cabinet in May 1975 in response to the Agranat Commission's findings. *Ma'ariv*, 20 April 1976.
Gazit, Shlomo. 1975. Arab Forces Two Years after the Yom Kippur War. In *Military Aspects of the Israeli-Arab Conflict: Proceedings of the International Symposium Held in Jerusalem, 12–17 October 1975*, 188–195. Tel Aviv: University Publishing Projects.
Golan, Matti. 1976. *The Secret Conversations of Henry Kissinger: Step-by-Step Diplomacy in the Middle East*. New York: Bantam Books.
Golan, Galia. 1977. *Yom Kippur and After: The Soviet Union and the Middle East Crisis*. Cambridge: Cambridge University Press.
Gonen, Shmuel. 1977. Interview with Major-General Gonen on the Fourth Anniversary of the Yom Kippur War (Hebrew Calendar). *Yediot Aharonot*, 21 September 1977.
Government of Jordan Communiqué, 13 October 1973, published in *New York Times*, 14 October 1973.
Handel, Michael I. 1976. Perception, Deception and Surprise: The Case of the Yom Kippur War. *Jerusalem Papers on Peace Problems* 19. Jerusalem: Leonard Davis Institute of International Relations, Hebrew University of Jerusalem, 1976.
Haselkorn, Avigdor. 1964. Israeli Intelligence Performance in the Yom Kippur War. Discussion Paper, Hudson Institute, 17 July 1964.
Heikal, Mohamed. 1975. *The Road to Ramadan*. London: Collins.
Herzog, Chaim. 1975. *The War of Atonement, October 1973*. Jerusalem/Tel Aviv: Steimatsky's Agency.
Hussein, Ibn Talal, King of Jordan. 1973. Statement in the Jordanian Cabinet, broadcast over Radio Amman, 7 October 1973; text in *Ma'arakhot*, special edition (November 1973): 232–233.
Insight Team of *the Sunday Times*. 1974. *The Yom Kippur War*. London: Andre Deutsch.
International Institute for Strategic Studies, London. 1973. *The Military Balance 1973–74*. London: International Institute for Strategic Studies.
Khalidi, Ahmed S. 1975. The Military Balance 1967–73. In *Middle East Crucible: Studies on the Arab-Israeli War of October 1973*, ed. Naseer H. Aruri, 21–63. Wilmette: Medina University Press International.
Kipnis, Yigal. 2013. *1973: The Road to War*. Charlottesville: Just World Books.
Kissinger, Henry. 1973. Press Conference, 25 October 1973. Reported in *New York Times*, 26 October 1973.
Luttwak, Edward N., and Walter Laqueur. 1974. Kissinger and the Yom Kippur War. *Commentary* 58(3): 33–40.

Medzini, Meron, ed. 1976. *Israel's Foreign Relations, Selected Documents, 1947–1974.* Jerusalem: Ministry of Foreign Affairs.
Meir, Golda. 1973a. Address to the Nation on Television, 10 October 1973.
———. 1973b. Press Conference, 3 November 1973; reported in *New York Times,* 4 November 1973.
———. 1973c. Speech to the Knesset, 16 October 1973. In Israel, *Divrei Haknesset,* 68, 4459–4474.
———. 1974. Statement to the Knesset, 22 January 1974. In Israel, *Divrei Haknesset* 69, 10–12.
———. 1975. *My Life.* Jerusalem/Tel Aviv: Steimatsky's Agency.
Monroe, Elizabeth, and Anthony Farrar-Hockley. 1974. *The Arab-Israel War, October 1973: Background and Events.* London: The International Institute for Strategic Studies, 1974. Adelphi Paper No. 111.
Nakdimon, Shlomo. 1973. The Events that Preceded the War. *Yediot Aharonot* [series of articles], 23, 30 November; and 7, 14 December 1973.
———. 1974. Protocols of Discussions among the Political and Military Leaders on the 5th and 6th October 1973. *Yediot Aharonot* [series of articles], 12, 19, 26 July; and 2, 9, 16 August 1974.
Peled, Binyamin. 1975. The Air Force in the Yom Kippur War. In *Military Aspects of the Israeli-Arab Conflict: Proceedings of the International Symposium Held in Jerusalem, 12–17 October 1975,* 228–245. Tel Aviv: University Publishing Projects.
Quandt, William B. 1977. *Decade of Decisions: American Policy Toward the Arab-Israeli Conflict, 1967–1976.* Berkeley/Los Angeles/London: University of California Press.
Sadat, Anwar. 1978. *In Search of Identity: An Autobiography.* New York: Harper & Row.
Schiff, Zeev. 1974a. The 8th of October: The Most Important Day of the War. *Ha'aretz,* 25 and 30 September 1974.
———. 1974b. *October Earthquake, Yom Kippur 1973.* Tel Aviv: University Publishing Projects.
———. 1975. The Full Story of the Encirclement that Ended the Yom Kippur War. *Ha'aretz,* 14 September 1975.
Shay, Avi. 1976. Egypt before the Yom Kippur War: War Aims and Plan of Attack. *Ma'arakhot* 250: 15–38.
Shlaim, Avi. 1976. Failures in National Intelligence Estimates: The Case of the Yom Kippur War. *World Politics* 28: 348–380.
Text of Agreement on Disengagement between Israel and Syrian Forces, signed on 31 May 1974. *New York Times,* 30 May 1974.
United Nations (UN). 1973. UN Security Council. Resolution 340. UN Emergency Force for Middle East. 25 October 1973.

Van Creveld, Martin. 1975. *Military Lessons of the Yom Kippur War: Historical Perspectives*. The Center for Strategic and International Studies, Georgetown University, Washington, D.C., The Washington Papers, vol. 3. London/Beverly Hills: SAGE.
Williams, Louis. 1975. *Military Aspects of the Israeli-Arab Conflict: Proceedings of the International Symposium Held in Jerusalem, 12–17 October 1975*. Tel Aviv: University Publishing Projects.
Yariv, Aharon. 1974. Israeli Intelligence Believed Already in the Summery of 1972 that Egypt Would Be Ready for War in May 1973. *Ma'ariv*, 18 July 1974.
Zumwalt, Elmo R. 1976. *On Watch, A Memoir*. New York: Quadrangle/The New York Times Book Co.

WORKS CONSULTED

Arab/Israel: General

Bar-Siman-Tov, Yaacov. 1994. *Israel and the Peace Process 1977–1982*. Albany: State University of New York Press.
Ben-Yehuda, Hemda, and Shmuel Sandler. 2002. *The Arab-Israeli Conflict Transformed: Fifty Years of Interstate and Ethnic Crises*. Albany: State University of New York Press.
Brecher, Michael. 1972. *The Foreign Policy System of Israel: Setting, Images, Process*. London: Oxford University Press.
———. 1974. *Decisions in Israel's Foreign Policy*. New Haven: Yale University Press.
Brecher, Michael, and Benjamin Geist. 1980. *Decisions in Crisis: Israel, 1967 and 1973*. Berkeley: University of California Press.
Brecher, Michael, and Jonathan Wilkenfeld. 1997. *A Study of Crisis*, 268–300. Ann Arbor: University of Michigan Press.
Eisenberg, Laura Zittrain, and Neil Caplan. 2010. *Negotiating Arab-Israeli Peace: Patterns, Problems, Possibilities*. 2nd ed. Bloomington: Indiana University Press.
Fraser, T.G. 2004. *The Arab-Israeli Conflict*. New York: Palgrave Macmillan.
Frisch, Hillel. 2004. Perceptions of Israel in the Armies of Syria, Egypt, and Jordan. *Political Studies* 52(3): 395–412.
Hermann, Tamar S. 2009. *The Israeli Peace Movement: A Shattered Dream*. New York: Cambridge University Press.
Herzog, Chaim, and Shlomo Gazit. 2004. *The Arab–Israeli Wars*. New York: Vintage Books.
Jones, Clive. 2002. The Foreign Policy of Israel. In *The Foreign Policies of Middle East States*, ed. Raymond A. Hinnebusch and Anoushiravan Ehteshami, 115–141. Boulder: Lynne Rienner.

Karsh, Efraim. 2002. *The Arab-Israeli Conflict: The Palestine War 1948*. Toronto: Osprey Publishing.
Khalidi, Rashid. 2013. *Brokers of Deceit: How the Us Has Undermined Peace in the Middle East*. Boston: Beacon Press.
Khouri, Fred J. 1985. *The Arab-Israeli Dilemma*. Syracuse: Syracuse University Press.
Kissinger, Henry. 2003. *Crisis: The Anatomy of Two Major Foreign Policy Crises*. New York: Simon & Schuster.
Lukacs, Yehuda, ed. 1992. *The Israeli–Palestinian Conflict: A Documentary Record 1967–1990*. Cambridge: Cambridge University Press.
Mahler, Gregory S., and Alden R.W. Mahler. 2010. *The Arab-Israeli Conflict: An Introduction and Documentary Reader*. London: Routledge.
Ma'oz, Moshe. 1999. From Conflict to Peace? Israel's Relations with Syria and the Palestinians. *Middle East Journal* 53(3): 393–416.
Maoz, Zeev. 2006. *Defending the Holy Land: A Critical Analysis of Israel's Security & Foreign Policy*. Ann Arbor: University of Michigan Press.
Morris, Benny. 2001. *Righteous Victims: A History of the Zionist Arab Conflict, 1881–2001*. New York: Knopf.
———. 2008. *1948: A History of the First Arab-Israeli War*. New Haven: Yale University Press.
Oren, Michael B. 2002. *Six Days of War: June 1967 and the Making of the Modern Middle East*. New York: Presidio Press.
Quandt, William B. 2005. *Peace Process: American Diplomacy and the Arab–Israeli Conflict since 1967*. 3rd ed. Washington, DC: Brookings.
Rabinovich, Itamar. 1991. *The Road Not Taken: Early Arab–Israeli Negotiations*. New York: Oxford University Press.
———. 2011. *The Lingering Conflict: Israel, the Arabs and the Middle East 1948–2011*. Washington, DC: Brookings.
Ross, Dennis. 2004. *The Missing Peace*. New York: Farrar, Straus and Giroux.
Safran, Nadav. 1969. *From War to War: The Arab–Israel Confrontation 1948–1967*. New York: Pegasus.

Arab/Israel Protracted Conflict (2)

Shlaim, Avi. 2000. *The Iron Wall: Israel and the Arab World*. London: Allen Lane/Penguin.
———. 2005. *The Camp David Summit – What Went Wrong?: Americans, Israelis, and Palestinians Analyze the Failure of the Boldest Attempt Ever to Resolve the Palestinian-Israeli Conflict*. Brighton: Sussex Academic Press.
Stein, Janice G., and Raymond Tanter. 1980. *Rational Decision–Making: Israel's Security Choices, 1967*. Columbus: Ohio State University Press.

Tucker, Spencer, and Priscilla M. Roberts. 2008. *The Encyclopedia of the Arab-Israeli Conflict: A Political, Social, and Military History*. Santa Barbara: ABC-CLIO.

EGYPT/ISRAEL

Barnett, Michael N. 1992. *Confronting the Costs of War: Military Power, State, and Society in Egypt and Israel*. Princeton: Princeton University Press.
Boutros-Ghali, B. 1997. *Egypt's road to Jerusalem*. New York: Random House.
Hinnebusch, Raymond A. 2002. The Foreign Policy of Egypt. In *The Foreign Policy of Middle East States*, ed. Raymond Hinnebusch and Anoushiravan Ehteshami, 91–115. Boulder: Lynne Rienner.

ISRAEL/PALESTINE

Caplan, Neil. 2010. *The Israel-Palestine Conflict: Contested Histories*. Malden/Oxford: Wiley-Blackwell.
Ciment, James. 1997. *Palestine/Israel: The Long Conflict*. New York: Facts on File.
Dowty, Alan. 2012. *Israel/Palestine*. 3rd ed. Cambridge: Polity.
Farsoun, Samih K., and Naseer H. Aruri. 2006. *Palestine and the Palestinians: A Social and Political History*. 2nd ed. Boulder: Westview Press.
Flapan, Simha. 1979. *Zionism and the Palestinians*. London: Croom-Helm.
Ġānim, As'ad. 2001. *The Palestinian-Arab Minority in Israel, 1948–2000: A Political Study*. Albany: State University of New York Press.
Gelvin, James L. 2007. *The Israel–Palestine Conflict: One Hundred Years of War*. 2nd ed. New York: Cambridge University Press.
Golan, Galia. 2007. *Israel and Palestine: Peace Plans from Oslo to Disengagement*. Princeton: Markus Wiener Publishers.
Harms, Gregory, and Todd M. Ferry. 2005. *The Palestine–Israel Conflict: A Basic Introduction*. Ann Arbor: Pluto Press.
Hassassian, Manuel S. 1997. Policy and Attitude Changes in the Palestine Liberation Organization, 1965–1994: A Democracy in the Making. Chap. 5. In *The PLO and Israel: From Armed Conflict to Political Solution, 1964–1994*, ed. Avraham Sela and Moshe Ma'oz, 73–94. New York: St. Martin's Press.
International Court of Justice. 2004. Request for an Advisory Opinion. Legal Consequences of the Construction of a Wall in the Occupied Palestinian Territory. Written Statement submitted by Palestine. 30 January 2004.
Khalidi, Rashid. 1997. *Palestinian Identity: The Construction of Modern National Consciousness*. New York: Columbia University Press.
———. 2006. *The Iron Cage: The Story of the Palestinian Struggle for Statehood*. Boston: Beacon Press.

Kimmerling, Baruch, and Joel S. Migdal. 2003. *The Palestinian People: A History.* Cambridge, MA: Harvard University Press.
Lesch, Ann M., and Mark A. Tessler. 1989. *Israel, Egypt, and the Palestinians: From Camp David to Intifada.* Bloomington: Indiana University Press.
Makovsky, David. 1996. *Making Peace with the PLO: The Rabin Government's Road to the Olso Accord.* Boulder: Westview Press.

Arab/Israel Protracted Conflict (3)

Menachem, K. 2010. *The Shift: Israel-Palestine from Border Struggle to Ethnic Conflict.* New York: Columbia University Press.
Milton-Edwards, B. 2009. *The Israeli-Palestinian Conflict: A People's War.* New York: Routledge.
Morris, Benny. 1990. *1948 and After: Israel and the Palestinians.* New York: Oxford University Press.
———. 1988. *The Birth of the Palestinian Refugee Problem, 1947–1949.* Cambridge: Cambridge University Press.
———. 2009. *One State, Two States: Resolving the Israel/Palestine Conflict.* New Haven: Yale University Press.
Nisan, Mordechai. 1978. *Israel and the Territories: A Study in Control, 1967–1977.* Ramat Gan/Israel: Turtledove.
O'Neill, Bard E. 1978. *Armed Struggle in Palestine: A Political–Military Analysis.* Boulder: Westview Press.
Pappé, Ilan. 1986. Moshe Sharett, David Ben-Gurion and the 'Palestine Option,' 1948–1956. *Studies in Zionism* 7(1): 77–96.
Pearlman, Wendy. 2011. *Violence, Nonviolence, and the Palestinian National Movement.* Cambridge: Cambridge University Press.
Rolef, Susan H. 1997. Israel's Policy Toward the PLO: From Rejection to Recognition. Chap. 14. In *The PLO and Israel: From Armed Conflict to Political Solution, 1964–1994,* ed. Avraham Sela and Moshe Ma'oz, 253–272. New York: St. Martin's Press.
Rubin, Barry M. 1994. *Revolution Until Victory?: The Politics and History of the PLO.* Cambridge, MA: Harvard University Press.
Said, Edward. 1979. *The Question of Palestine.* New York: Times Books.
Ṣāyigh, Yazīd. 1997a. The Armed Struggle and Palestinian Nationalism. Chap. 2. In *The PLO and Israel: From Armed Conflict to Political Solution, 1964–1994,* ed. Avraham Sela and Moshe Ma'oz, 23–35. New York: St. Martin's Press.
———. 1997b. *Armed Struggle and the Search for State: The Palestinian National Movement, 1949–1993.* Oxford: Clarendon Press.
Schanzer, Jonathan. 2008. *Hamas vs. Fatah: The Struggle for Palestine.* New York: Palegravwe Macmillan.
Sela, Avraham, and Moshe Ma'oz, ed. 1997. *The PLO and Israel: From Armed Conflict to Political Solution, 1964–1994.* New York: St. Martin's Press.

Shlaim, Avi. 1994. Prelude to the Accord: Likud, Labor, and the Palestinians. *Journal of Palestine Studies* 23(2): 5–19.
Smith, Charles D. 2004. *Palestine and the Arab–Israeli Conflict: A History with Documents*. 5th ed. Boston: Bedford/St. Martin's Press.
Telhami, Shibley. 1999. From Camp David to Wye: Changing Assumptions in Arab–Israeli Negotiations. *Middle East Journal* 53(3): 379–392.
Tessler, Mark A. 2009. *A History of the Israeli–Palestinian Conflict*. 2nd ed. Bloomington: Indiana University Press.
Wasserstein, Bernard. 2008. *Divided Jerusalem: The Struggle for the Holy City*. 3rd ed. New Haven: Yale University Press.

ISRAEL/SYRIA

Cobban, Helena. 1991. *The Superpowers and the Syrian–Israeli Conflict: Beyond Crisis Management?* New York: Praeger.
———. 1999. *The Israeli–Syrian Peace Talks: 1991–96 and Beyond*. Washington, DC: United States Institute for Peace.
Drysdale, Alasdair, and Raymond Hinnebusch. 1991. *Syria and the Middle East Peace Process*. New York: Council on Foreign Relations Press.
Hinnebusch, Raymond A. 1996. Does Syria Want Peace? Syrian Policy in the Syrian–Israeli Peace Negotiations. *Journal of Palestine Studies* 26(1): 42–57.
———. 2002. The Foreign Policy of Syria. In *The Foreign Policies of Middle East States*, ed. Raymond A. Hinnebusch and Anoushiravan Ehteshami, 141–167. Boulder: Lynne Rienner.

ARAB/ISRAEL PROTRACTED CONFLICT (4)

Kessler, Martha. 2000. Syria, Israel, and the Middle East Peace Process: Past Successes and Final Challenges. *Middle East Policy* 7(2): 68–89.
Khouri, Fred J. 1963. Friction and Conflict on the Israeli–Syrian Front. *Middle East Journal* 17(1): 14–34.
Lawson, Fred H. 1996. *Why Syria Goes to War: Thirty Years of Confrontation*. Ithaca: Cornell University Press.
Ma'oz, Moshe. 1994. Syria, Israel, and the Peace Process. In *From War to Peace: Arab–Israeli Relations, 1973–1993*, ed. Barry Rubin, Joseph Ginat, and Moshe Ma'oz, 157–181. New York: New York University Press.
———. 1995. *Syria and Israel: From War to Peacemaking*. Oxford: Clarendon Press.
Muslih, Muhammad. 1993. The Golan: Israel, Syria, and Strategic Calculations. *Middle East Journal* 47(4): 611–632.
Neff, Donald. 1994. Israel–Syria: Conflict at the Jordan River, 1949–1967. *Journal of Palestine Studies* 23(4): 26–40.

Rabinovich, Itamar. 1998. *The Brink of Peace: The Israeli–Syrian Negotiations*. Princeton: Princeton University Press.
Seale, Patrick. 2000. The Israel–Syria Negotiations: Who is Telling the Truth? *Journal of Palestine Studies* 29(2): 65–77.
Shaaban, Bouthaina. 2013. *Damascus Diary: An Inside Account of Hafez Al-Assad's Peace Diplomacy, 1990–2000*. Boulder: Lynne Rienner Publishers.
Siegman, H. 2000. Being Hafiz Al-Assad: Syria's Chilly but Consistent Peace Strategy. *Foreign Affairs* 79(3): 2–7.
Slater, Jerome. 2002. Lost Opportunities for Peace in the Arab–Israeli Conflict: Israel and Syria, 1948–2001. *International Security* 27(1): 79–106.

ARAB/ISRAEL WARS

Aruni, N.H. 1975. *Middle East Crucible: Studies on the Arab-Israeli War of October 1973*. Wilmette: Medina University Press.
Bar-Zohar, Michael. 1970. *Embassies in Crisis; Diplomats and Demagogues behind the Six-Day War*. Englewood cliffs: Prentice-Hall.
Chuchill, Randolph Spencer, and Winston Spencer Churchill. 1967. *The Six-Day War*. London: Heinemann.
Daigle, C., and N. Howland. 2011. *Foreign Relations of the United States (FRUS), 1969-1976*, Arab-Israeli Crisis and War, 1973. Vol. XXV. Washington: United States Government Printing Office, Office of the Historian Bureau of Public Affairs.
Eden, Sir Anthony. 1960. *Full Circle*. London: Cassell, Book Three, Suez.
Ferris, Jesse. 2013. *Nasser's Gamble: How Intervention in Yemen Caused the Six-Day war and the Decline of Egyptian Power*. Princeton: Princeton University Press.
Segev, Tom. 2007. *1967: Israel, the War, and the Year That Transformed the Middle East*. New York: Metropolitan.
Sobel, L. 1974. *Israel & the Arabs: The October 1973 War*. New York: Facts on File, Inc.
Wagner, Abraham R. 1974. *Crisis Decision-making: Israel's Experience in 1967 and 1973*. New York: Praeger.

OTHER SOURCES

Avineri, Shlomo. 1981. *The Making of Modern Zionism: The Intellectual Origins of the Jewish State*. New York: Basic Books.
Bar-Tal, Daniel. 2013. *Intractable Conflicts: Socio-psychological Foundations and Dynamics*. Cambridge: Cambridge University Press.
Benvenesti, Meron. 1976. *Jeurusalem: The Torn City*. Jerusalem: Isratypeset Ltd.

Boulding, Kenneth Ewart. 1956. *The Image: Knowledge in Life and Society.* Ann Arbor: University of Michigan Press.
Bull, Hedley. 1966. International Theory: The Case for a Classical Approach. *World Politics* 18(3): 361–377.
Dayan, Moshe. 1966. *Diary of the Sinai Campaign.* New York: Harper & Row.
———. 1976. *Moshe Dayan: Story of My Life.* New York: Morrow.
———. 1981. *Breakthrough: A Personal Account of the Egypt-Israel Peace Negotiations.* New York: Knopf.
de Mesquita, Bruce Bueno. 1985. Reply to Stephen Krasner and Robert Jervis. *International Studies Quarterly* 29(2): 151–154.
Easton, David. 1957. An Approach to the Analysis of Political Systems. *World Politics* 9(3): 383–400.
Elazar, David. 1975. The Yom Kippur War: Military Lessons. In *Military Aspects of the Israeli-Arab Conflict: Proceedings of an International Symposium Held in Jerusalem, 12–17 October 1975.* Tel Aviv: University Publishing Projects.
Halpern, Ben. 1969. *The Idea of the Jewish State.* Cambridge: Harvard University Press.
Harvey, Mose L. 1974. *The Soviet Union and the October 1973 Middle East War: The Implications for Détente.* Miami: Monographs in International Affairs, Center for Advanced International Studies, University of Miami.
Holsti, Oil. 1965. Perceptions of Time and Alternative Factors in Crisis Decision-making. *Peace Research Society Papers* 3: 79–120.
Janis, Irving L. 1972. *Victims of Groupthink: A Psychological Study of Foreign-Policy Decisions and Fiascoes.* Boston: Houghton, Mifflin.
———. 1989. *Crucial Decisions: Leadership in Policymaking and Crisis Management.* New York: Free Press.
Janis, Irving L., and Leon Mann. 1977. *Decision Making: A Psychological Analysis of Conflict, Choice, and Commitment.* New York: Free Press.
Kaplan, Robert B. 1966. Cultural Though Patterns in Inter-Cultural Education. *Language Learning* 16(1–2): 1–20.
Korany, Bahgat, 'Alī -D. Hilāl, and Aḥmad Y. Aḥmad. 1991. *The Foreign Policies of Arab States: The Challenge of Change.* Boulder: Westview Press.
Lehrs, Lior. 2016. Jerusalem on the Negotiating Table: Analyzing the Israeli-Palestinian Peace Talks on Jerusalem (1993–2015). *Israel Studies* 21(3): 179–205.
Leng, Russell J. 1983. When Will They Ever Learn? Coercive Bargaining in Recurrent Crises. *The Journal of Conflict Resolution* 27(3): 379–419.
Neustadt, Richard E., and Ernest R. May. 1986. *Thinking in Time: The Uses of History for Decision-Makers.* New York: Free Press.
North, Robert, Ole Holsti, and Richard Brody. 1968. *Perception and Action in the Study of International Relations: The 1914 Case: Quantitative International Politics: Insights and Evidence.* New York: The Free Press.

Said, Edward W. 1979. *Orientalism*. New York: Vintage Books.
Shlaim, Avi. 2008. *Lion of Jordan: The Life of King Hussein in War and Peace*. New York: Alfred A. Knopf.
Snyder, Richard C., H.W. Bruck, and Burton M. Sapin. 1962. *Foreign Policy Decision-Making; An Approach to the Study of International Politics*. New York: Free Press of Glencoe.
Sprout, Harold, and Margaret Sprout. 1965. *The Ecological Perspective on Human Affairs, with Special Reference to International Politics*. Princeton: Princeton Center of International Studies, Princeton Univ. Press.
Vertzberger, Yaacov. 1990. *The World in their Minds: Information Processing, Cognition, and Perception in Foreign Policy Decision-making*. Stanford: Stanford University Press.

Name Index

A

Abbas, Mahmoud, 120, 287, 290, 303, 304, 305, 320
Abdullah, King, 29, 37, 299, 300, 312
Abu Meizer, Abdul Mouhsen, 53
Ahmad, Mohammed Sayeed, 54–66
al-Assad, Hafiz, 42, 122
Al-Baz, Osama, 7, 54, 66–77
Allenby, Edmund, 10, 290
Allon, Yigal, 48–52, 159, 177, 183, 184, 189, 191, 194, 196, 203, 204, 206, 208, 212, 215, 219, 223, 225, 228, 229, 231, 233, 238, 241, 252n57, 269n196, 340
Almogi, Yoseph, 171
Alphand, Herve, 162
al-Quwwatli, Shukri, 40
Amit, Meir, 158, 161, 162, 173, 199, 202, 206–9, 258n112, 259n123
Anderson, Robert, 45, 203

Arafat, Yassir, 16, 39, 71, 109, 113, 119–22, 285, 288, 289, 290, 291, 292, 296, 302, 305, 310, 312, 313, 324
Aranne, Zalman, 159, 171, 173, 191
Aref, Abdul Rahman, 200, 213
Assad, Hafez al, 261n146, 268n186, 281
Attasi, President Nureddin, 198
Avigur, Shaul, 159
Avnery, Uri, 311, 321

B

Badran, Shamsuddin, 189, 192
Baker, James, 286
Balfour, Lord, 11
Barak, Aharon, 350
Barak, Ehud, 120, 290, 291, 292, 296, 299, 304, 340, 347, 358
Barbour, Walworth, 193

Note: Page numbers with "n" denote notes.

Bar-Lev, Haim, 160, 177, 180, 189, 196, 215, 217, 219, 223, 225, 229, 230, 231, 234, 259n119, 262n152, 268n188, 270n207, 274n237
Bar-Tov, Hanoch, 261n151, 262n152
Barzilai, Yisrael, 159, 191, 211
Basheer, Tahseen, 53
Battle, Lucius, 169, 181
Begin, Menahem, 159, 171, 203, 204, 205, 206, 223, 282, 322–3, 361n29
Beilin, Yossi, 287, 361n29
Ben-Ami, Shlomo, 298
Ben-Eliezer, A., 171
Ben-Gurion, David, 5–6, 17, 20–2, 24, 27–8, 30, 39, 43–5, 48, 108–9, 122, 141, 159, 168, 172, 183, 184, 197, 203, 211, 212, 248n23, 251n47, 255n83, 256n86, 278, 317, 318, 340
Benizri, Shlomo, 346
Bennett, Naftali, 343
Bentov, Mordekhai, 159, 191, 211
Bernadotte, Folke, 27–9
Bitan, Moshe, 160, 161, 250n37, 258n112
Boulding, Kenneth, 2
Boutros-Ghali, Boutros, 7, 53–4, 77–100
Brecher, Irving, 324
Brecher, Michael, 104, 318–19
Brezhnev, Leonid, 226, 227, 236, 240, 268n186, 274n234
Brown, George, 165, 166, 176, 179, 202
Bruck, H.W., 2
Bunche, Ralph, 24, 133, 162, 163, 245–6n9
Burdett, Winston, 248n25
Burg, Yoseph, 159, 191, 220, 229
Bush, George W., 299, 301, 303, 305
Bykov (Soviet diplomat), 188

C
Cannel, M., 191
Caradon, Lord, 204, 320
Carmel, Moshe, 159, 171, 173, 183, 191, 194, 200, 284n140
Carter, President James E., 282, 283, 291, 305
Chuvakhin, Dmitri, 165, 188, 189, 190, 213
Clinton, Bill, 42, 120, 281, 287, 289, 290, 291, 294, 296, 297, 299, 303, 306
Couve de Murville, Maurice, 165, 177
Curzon, Lord, 11

D
Dayan, Moshe, 43, 48–52, 73, 158, 159, 166, 168, 171, 172, 180, 184, 197, 201, 203, 204, 205, 206, 208, 209, 210, 212, 215, 216, 217, 218, 219, 220, 221, 222, 223, 225, 227, 228, 229, 230, 231, 233, 234, 235, 236, 238, 241, 250n41, 259n119, 259n126, 262n151, 262n152, 263n160, 264n161, 265n167, 266n171, 268n188, 269n196, 270n207, 271n207, 271n209, 282, 299, 340
De Gaulle, Charles, 165, 166, 171, 173, 174, 176, 177, 178, 190, 194, 195, 206, 207, 210, 211, 248n23, 251n44, 251n47, 252n58
de Mesquita, Bueno, 4
Dichter, Avi, 347
Dinitz, Simha, 219, 227, 228, 231, 232, 235, 236, 237, 241, 263n161, 268n189, 274n234
Dinstein, Zvi, 159, 189, 208
Dirksen, Everett, 179
Disentshik, Ido, 233

NAME INDEX 389

Dobrynin, Anatoly, 233, 235, 264n161
Dori, Y., 168
Dotan, Hagai, 348
Dulles, John Foster, 179

E
Easton, David, 2
Eban, Abba, 2, 3, 18–19, 24, 30, 32, 47, 51–2, 73, 158, 161, 162, 163, 165, 166, 167, 169, 170, 171, 172, 173, 174, 176, 177, 178, 179, 180, 181, 182, 183, 184, 185, 186, 187, 190, 191, 192, 193, 194, 195, 198, 199, 201, 202, 203, 204, 206, 208, 209, 210, 211, 212, 220, 224, 226, 229, 231, 232, 235, 238, 242, 247n21, 248n28, 251n47, 252n58, 254n76, 255n78, 259n123, 264n161, 267n186, 268n187, 269n191, 274n234, 317, 340
Eckstein, Yechiel, 336
Eisenhower, Dwight D., 45, 179, 253n63
El Khani, Abdullah, 53
El Magd, Kamal Abu, 53
Elazar, David, 142, 151, 212, 215, 217, 218, 219, 220, 221, 222, 223, 225, 226, 227, 229, 231, 234, 237, 243, 261n146, 262n151, 265–6n171, 265n169, 266n179, 268n188, 271n209
Eliav, Arye (Lova), 321
en-Lai, Zhou, 128
Erekat, Saeb, 298, 305
Eshkol, Levi, 17, 47–8, 158, 159, 161, 162, 163, 164, 165, 166, 167, 168, 169, 170, 171, 172, 173, 174, 176, 180, 181, 182, 183, 184, 185, 188, 189, 190, 191,
192, 193, 194, 195, 196, 197, 198, 199, 200, 201, 203, 205, 206, 208, 209, 211, 212, 248n23, 251n47, 255n81, 255n83, 255n85, 256n86, 257n105, 258n106, 258n111, 258n112, 259n120, 259n124, 340
Evatt, Herbert, 29
Evron, Ephraim, 160, 166, 169, 172, 176, 181, 182, 185, 198, 201, 207, 213, 255n78
Eweiss, Yehia, 53
Eytan, Walter, 23, 162, 177, 192, 210, 211

F
Fischer, Louis, 359
Fishman, Rabbi, 19–21

G
Galili, Yisrael, 159, 161, 171, 177, 183, 189, 191, 195, 212, 217, 219, 225, 229, 231, 238, 264n161, 268n188
Gavish, Yeshayahu, 201, 205–6, 259n119
Gazit, Mordekhai, 217, 219, 224, 264n161, 265n169, 267n186
Gazit, Shlomo, 149
Ghanem, Ismail, 53
Gide, André, 359
Golan, Galia, 227
Golan, Matti, 233
Golan, Yair, 357
Goldberg, Arthur, 187, 202, 213, 245n8
Gonen, Shmuel, 219, 226
Granot, Yaakov, 347
Gromyko, Andrei, 176, 179, 207
Gur, Mordekhai, 268n189
Gvati, Haim, 159, 191, 220, 229

H

Habib, Philip, 137
Hacohen, David, 171
Haig, Alexander, 237
Halpern, Ben, 24
Halutz, Dan, 346
Hammarskjold, Dag, 161, 244–5n5, 245n9
Hanegbi, Tzachi, 346
Harkabi, Yehoshafat, 53
Harman, Avraham, 160, 162, 166, 169, 179, 181, 182, 184, 187, 192, 198, 199, 201, 204, 207, 208, 248n28
Hazan, Ya'acov, 184, 211
Hazani, Michael, 200, 217, 229
Heath, Edward, 268n186
Heikal, Mohamed, 154n2, 187, 247n18
Herzl, Theodore, 10
Herzog, Ya'acov, 23, 30, 160, 161, 171, 180, 189, 208, 229, 248n25
Hillel, Shlomo, 217, 229
Hirchson, Abraham, 345–6
Hofi, Yitzhak, 205, 219
Holsti, Ole, 2
Horowitz, David, 23
Humphrey, Hubert H., 175, 203, 204, 213
Hussein, King, 69, 123, 198, 200, 213, 270n196, 312
Hussein, Saddam, 286
Hussein, Sharif, 11
Husseini, Faisal, 120

I

Indyk, Martin, 305
Issa, Mahmoud Khairy, 53
Issa, Norman, 343

J

Janis, Irving L., 7
Jarring, Gunnar, 281–2
Jervis, Robert, 4
Johnson, Lyndon B., 135, 162, 163, 166, 169, 170, 173, 175, 179, 180, 184, 185, 186, 192, 193, 198, 199, 201, 203, 208, 210, 211, 248n28, 254n71, 254n76, 255n78, 258n112
Joseph, Dov, 19, 21–3, 30

K

Kalb, Bernard and Marvin, 236
Kaplan, Eliezer, 20
Karadi, Moshe, 346, 347
Karame, Rashid, 200
Katz, Katriel, 207
Katz, Yisrael, 347
Katzav, Moshe, 344
Keating, Kenneth, 219, 222, 228, 241, 263n161, 264n161, 267n186, 274n234
Kennedy, John F., 248n28
Kerry, John, 290, 303, 305–6
Khaled, King, 113
Kidron, Aharon, 219
Kissinger, Henry, 137, 143, 217, 218, 224, 227, 228, 231, 232, 233, 235, 236, 237, 238, 239, 241, 263n161, 264n161, 268n186, 268n189, 269n189, 269n193, 270n196, 271n208, 273n230, 274n232
Koestler, Arthur, 359
Kol, Moshe, 159, 191
Kollek, Teddy, 53, 250n41
Kony, Mohamed El-, 163

Kosygin, Aleksei, 135, 166, 176, 179, 188, 189, 192, 206, 234, 235, 238, 255n83, 255n85, 268n186
Krasner, Stephen, 4

L
Landau, Haim, 171
Lawson, Edward B., 32
Levavi, Arye, 160, 161, 188, 189, 208
Lieberman, Avigdor, 358
Lior, Yisrael, 219
Livni, Tzipi, 304, 305
Lourie, Arthur, 161
Lowenstein, Frank, 305

M
McMahon, Monsignor, 29
McMahon, Sir Henry, 11
MacMillan, Harold, 170
McNamara, Robert, 184, 213
Magal, Yinon, 348
Maimon, Yehuda Leib (Rabbi Fishman), 19–21
Makhus, Ibrahim, 198
Mann, Leon, 7
Mansfield, Michael, 179, 213
Martin, Paul, 246n15
Matza, Jacky, 346
May, Ernest R., 7
Mazuz, Menachem, 344
Meir, Golda, 17, 23, 48, 121, 152, 159, 165, 171, 173, 189, 217, 219, 222, 223, 224, 225, 228, 229, 231, 232, 233, 234, 235, 236, 237, 238, 239, 241, 242, 262n151, 262n152, 264n161, 265n169, 266n178, 268n188, 270n199, 271n209, 340
Melchior, Michael, 339

Mendler, Avraham, 152, 218
Menon, Krishna, 3
Molcho, Yitzhak, 305
Mor, Ilan, 348
Moratinos, Miguel, 297
Mubarak, Hosni, 54, 66
Muhi-a-Din, Zahariyah, 203

N
Nakdimon, Shlomo, 250n39
Nasser, Gamal Abdel, 44, 47, 59, 109, 133, 141, 154n2, 160, 161, 162, 164, 165, 168, 169, 170, 173, 174, 175, 176, 178, 179, 183, 187, 188, 191, 193, 195, 197, 198, 202, 203, 204, 205, 207, 211, 213, 221, 246n9, 247n18, 247n21, 248n25, 249n33, 255–6n85, 255n80, 317
Navon, Yitzhak, 31
Nehru, Jawaharlal, 3
Netanyahu, Benjamin, 124, 285, 290, 304, 305, 334, 336, 339, 343, 347, 357, 358
Nixon, Richard M., 226, 227, 228, 230, 231, 232, 235, 236, 237, 238, 240, 241, 242, 261n146, 262n152, 264n161, 266n174, 268n186, 270n199, 271n208, 272n215, 274n232, 274n234, 274n237, 275n242
Nutting, Anthony, 213

O
O'Ballance, Edgar, 247n18
Olmert, Ehud, 290, 303, 304, 320, 321, 345, 346, 347
Omar, 9, 13

P

Pa'il, Meir, 321
Pearson, Lester, 168, 204
Peled, Matityahu, 196, 219, 229, 259n119, 266n179, 321
Peres, Shimon, 50–2, 53, 123, 159, 168, 171, 172, 184, 203, 217, 285, 287, 340, 346, 361n29
Pickering, Thomas, 53
Pozhidaev, Dmitri, 249n33

Q

Quandt, William B., 227, 232, 263n161, 269n193, 270n196, 273n230

R

Rabin, Yitzhak, 122, 143, 158, 160, 161, 162, 163, 164, 166, 167, 168, 170, 171, 174, 177, 180, 183, 184, 189, 194, 196, 200, 203, 204, 206, 208, 211, 249n37, 252n48, 259n119, 288, 289, 313, 361n29
Rabinovich, Itamar, 40, 53
Rafael, Gideon, 160, 161, 162, 163, 169, 204, 213, 245n9
Rafei, Abdul Ghani, 53
Ramon, Haim, 346
Regev, Miri, 343, 344
Remez, Aharon, 192
Remez, David, 21
Riad, Mahmoud, 53
Rimalt, E., 171
Robinson, Jacob, 18
Rosen, Pinchas, 28

Ross, Dennis, 294
Rostow, Eugene, 162, 166, 169, 172, 181, 192, 194, 198, 204, 207
Rostow, Walt, 169, 185, 198, 201, 213
Rothschild, Baron, 12
Rubinstein, Danny, 349
Rusk, Dean, 181, 182, 184, 185, 192, 193, 194, 198, 201, 202, 204, 207, 213

S

Sadat, Anwar el-, 7, 53, 54, 66, 85, 102, 115–16, 122, 233, 234, 235, 240, 261n146, 267n179, 268n186, 269n193, 272n213, 274n234, 274n240, 275n242, 282, 305, 312, 322–3, 361n29
Said Aly, Abdel Moneim, 101
St. John, Robert, 251n44
Saphir, Yoseph, 159, 203
Sapin, Burton, 2
Sapir, Pinhas, 159, 171, 172, 183, 191, 229, 263n160
Sarid, Yossi, 339
Sasson, Eliahu, 159, 189, 191
Scali, John, 226
Schiff, Zeev, 228, 266n178
Schlesinger, James, 271n208
Scowcroft, Brent, 218, 235
Serlin, Yoseph, 171
Shalev, Arye, 231, 263n161
Shalom, Silvan, 348
Shamir, Yitzhak, 285
Shapira, Haim Moshe, 23, 159, 167, 173, 191, 211
Shapira, Y.S., 191, 229
Shapiro, Y.E., 159

NAME INDEX 393

Sharef, Ze'ev, 24, 30–1, 159, 183, 191, 220
Sharett, Moshe, 17, 20–2, 24, 34, 43, 46–8, 52, 317, 340
Sharon, Ariel, 119–20, 180, 196, 206, 299, 302, 321, 345, 347
Shazar, Zalman, 164, 168
Shtayyeh, Muhammed, 305
Shukeiry, Ahmed, 183
Shultz, George P., 285
Silone, Ignazio, 359
Silver, Abba Hillel, 22
Sneh, Moshe, 251n46
Snyder, Richard C., 2
Sokolow, Nahum, 12
Solow, Robert, 333
Spender, Stephen, 359

T
Tabor, Hans, 204
Tal, Yisrael, 180, 219, 229
Tekoah, Yoseph, 161, 213
Thant, U, 160, 162, 163, 164, 166, 167, 169, 174, 176, 184, 187, 188, 210, 244n5, 245n8, 245n9, 248n28, 281
Thatcher, Margaret, 334
Thomson, George, 176, 179
Tohami, Hassan, 282
Turki Al Feisal, Prince, 301

V
Veliotis, Nicholas, 219, 228, 241
Vertzberger, Y., 7
Vinogradov, Vladimir, 274n234

W
Waldheim, Kurt, 264n161

Warhaftig, Zerah, 159, 171, 183, 191, 220, 229
Weizman, Ezer, 160, 161, 171, 174, 177, 189, 205, 250n37, 252n48, 278
Weizmann, Chaim, 12, 324
Wheeler, Earl, 182, 184, 185, 210
Wilson, Harold, 166, 170, 176, 178, 179, 190, 192, 202, 204, 207, 210, 213, 251n44, 251n47, 252n58
Wolfsfeld, Gadi, 333
Wright, Richard, 359

Y
Ya'acobi, Gad, 229
Yaalon, Moshe, 356, 357, 358
Ya'ari, Meir, 184, 211
Yadin, Yigael, 159, 208
Yaffe, Aviad, 160, 161, 171, 172, 188, 255n81
Yaffe, Avraham, 196
Yariv, Aharon, 160, 161, 162, 171, 180, 183, 189, 190, 204, 208, 244n2, 267n186, 274n234
Yassin, Al-Sayed, 101
Yeshayahu, Yisrael, 159, 191

Z
Zadok, Haim, 229
Zaides, Arkadi, 343
Zeira, Eliahu, 216, 217, 219, 229, 261n146
Zubi, Mohammed, 198
Zumwalt, Elmo, 271n208
Zur, Tzvi, 168, 219

Subject Index

A

absence of collective exhaustion by either of the principal adversaries, 314

Abu Rodeis, Egypt, 227, 229

Agranat Commission, 221
  criticism of IDF by, 226
  on delay in 1973 mobilization, 222

Agudat Yisrael Party, 19, 195, 229, 262n156, 268n188, 347

Ahdut Ha'avoda party, in National Unity Government, 157, 183

Al-Ahram intellectuals: view, 100–15

Al-Biqa Missiles I crisis (28 April–24 July 1981), 130–1

Al-Biqa Missiles II crisis (19 November 1985–15 January 1986), 131

Alexandria, Egypt
  military action contemplated against, 213
  Soviet nuclear weapons in, 241, 244

Aliya, 47–8

Allon, Yigal
  in 1967 crisis, 191; decision-making and consulting role, 183–4, 189, 194, 196, 204, 206, 208, 212; military strategy suggested by, 183–4, 191, 194, 196; in National Unity Government, 159, 203; visit to Soviet Union, 177
  in 1973 crisis; advocated establishment of Druze state, 233; decision-making and consulting role, 215, 219, 223, 225, 229, 231; negotiation with U.S. by, 228, 238, 241
  perceptions, 48–51

AMAN (IDF military intelligence), 216–17, 262n152
  information processing by, 216
  probability of war perceived by, 217, 262n152

Note: Page numbers with "n" denote notes.

American Professors for Peace in the Middle East, 53, 101
Amit, Meir, General
  in 1967 crisis; decision-making and consulting role, 162, 173, 208–9; probability of war perceived by, 161; U.S. mission of, 158, 199, 200, 202–3, 207
Aqaba, Gulf of, freedom of access to, 170, 188
  French position on, 195
  Great Britain's position on, 176
  U.S. position on, 174–6, 186–7, 208
Arab/Israel PC: causes of deadlock in quest for conflict resolution, 308–14
  absence of collective exhaustion by either of the principal adversaries, 309–10
  continuance of unequal capability, 310
  increase in conflict-sustaining acts, 313–14
  lack of domestic pressures for conflict termination, 311–12
  persistence of discordance in basic objectives, 312–13
Arab/Israel wars and UN resolution, 19, 120–1, 141, 142, 299, 308, 322
  "land for peace," 3
Arab League, 16, 53, 66, 97, 124–5, 128, 278, 299–301, 307, 312
Arab Peace Initiative (27 March 2002), 299–301
Arab Socialist Union, 168
Arab Workers Conference, 187
Arafat statement of recognition of Israel's existence at Stockholm News Conference and address to UN General Assembly (8, 13 December 1988), 285

arms embargo, French declaration of, 1967, 207, 211
Assad, Hafez al
  and cease-fire terms, 1973, 268n186
  on Soviet withdrawal of advisers, 261n146
attitudinal prism
  Israel, 21–4, 36–41
  Palestine, 36–9
  Syria, 39–41
Australia, 207

B
Bar-Lev, Haim
  in 1967 crisis decision-making and consulting role, 160, 177, 180, 189, 196
  in 1973 crisis; and crossing Suez Canal, 231, 234; decision-making and consulting role, 217, 219, 223; heads IDF Southern Command, 215; military assessments by, 225, 229, 230, 268n188
Bar-Lev Line, 135, 152
Begin, Menahem
  decision-making and consulting role, 159, 171, 203
  on delay of Eshkol Government pre-emptive attack decision, 194
  in National Unity Government, 159, 171, 203, 206
  proposes political truce, 1973, 223
  behavior towards Arab Israelis, 349–55
Beirut Airport crisis (28 December 1968–January 1969), 142
Ben-Gurion, David
  acknowledgment of human emotion in crisis decision-making, 5–6

SUBJECT INDEX   397

decision-making and consulting
  role, 159, 168, 197, 212,
  256n86
de Gaulle's commitment to, 248n23
influence on and support for Eban,
  172
perceptions, 43–7
views of, 183, 184, 212
Ben-Gurion complex, 211
Ben-Gurionism, 318
Bir Gafgafa airbase (Sinai), Nasser
  speech on nationalization of Suez
  Canal at, 170, 188
B'not Ya'akov Bridge, Syrian threat to,
  226
Boutros-Ghali, Boutros, views,
  77–100
Brezhnev, Leonid, 236, 240,
  268n186
exchange of messages with Nixon,
  226
Brown, George, 165
and British retreat from maritime
  force idea, 202
Moscow visit of, 176, 179
bureaucratic élite, decision-making and
  consulting role in 1967 crisis
crisis period, 160

C
Cabinet, Israel
  in 1967 crisis; consulting role, 161,
    167, 189–90, 192, 193–5, 201;
    as decisional forum, 157,
    192–5, 210–12; decides to go
    to war, 158, 193–5, 210–12;
    expansion of, 203
  in 1973 crisis; and cease-fire
    acceptance, 233, 238, 242;
    changes in and structure of,
    229; consulting role, 217, 218,
    220, 222–5, 227–30, 234; as

decisional forum, 208–9, 217,
  227–8
Camp David Summit I and Egypt–
  Israel Peace Agreement (5
  September 1978–26 March
  1979), 282–4
Camp David Summit II (11–25 July
  2000), 291–4
Canada, in 1967 crisis
calls for convening of Security
  Council, 174, 179
and maritime force, 192, 193, 199,
  204
Shazar visit, 164, 168
and UNEF withdrawal, 163, 164
Carmel, Moshe
consulting role of, 171, 173, 183,
  191, 194
in National Unity Government, 159
suggests enlargement of
  government, 200
case studies of perceptions and
  decisions, 4–5
causes of Israel/Palestine and overall
  Arab/Israel deadlock in quest for
  conflict resolution, 306–8
cease-fire agreements, 1973
discussion and acceptance of, 224,
  232–3
Meir's premature acceptance of, 234
negotiation of, 239–42
UN and superpower pressure for,
  230, 232–9
Chuvakhin, Dmitri (Soviet
  ambassador, Israel), 213
discussions with Eban and Eshkol,
  165, 188–90
civil defense, Israeli precautions taken,
  163
clash of belief systems, 9–10
Clinton Parameters (23–27 December
  2000), 294–6
Communist Party, Israeli (*Maki*), 174

conflict resolution, 3, 277–315, 323–7
continuance of unequal capability,
    334–6
core questions on Arab/Israel conflict,
    4
corruption in the public services,
    341–2
Crete, Sea of, 201
crises that escalated to full-scale war
    (9 cases), 133–41
crisis actor, 133, 136–7
crisis periods
    in 1967 crisis, decisions and
        decision-makers, 157–60
    in 1973 crisis; decision process,
        214–44; decisions and decision-
        makers, 214

D
Damascus, Israeli bombing of, 1973,
    215, 228, 229–31
Dardanelles, 178, 201
Davar (newspaper), advocates
    expansion of Israel's government
    in 1967, 197
Dayan, Moshe
    in 1967 crisis, 166, 172, 209;
        becomes defense minister, 158,
        159, 197, 201–3, 204–6;
        decision-making and consulting
        role, 168, 171, 184, 204–5,
        208–9, 212; and Israeli military
        strategy, 158, 211–12
    in 1973 crisis; decision-making and
        consulting role, 215, 217–24;
        information processing by,
        241–2; and Israeli military
        strategy, 215, 219–22, 225,
        227–9, 231, 234–5, 262n152
    perceptions, 48–51; of threat and
        probability of war, 263n160
    role in negotiations with U.S.,
        Arabs, 238

debates on methodology in
    International relations, 3–4
decision process, in crisis periods,
    214–44
decisions and decision-makers, in crisis
    periods, 157–60, 173, 214,
    217–22, 228–9, 232–4, 238–9
Defense Committee (Israel's
    Ministerial Committee of
    Defense), in 1967 crisis
    decision-making and consulting
        role, 161, 183, 204–5, 210
    response to closing Straits, 171–3
De Gaulle, Charles
    Eban correspondence and meeting
        with, 165, 166, 174, 176–8,
        190
    Eshkol correspondence with, 194–5,
        206–7
    Eytan meets with, 210, 211
    Israeli image of, 173
Denmark, 174, 179, 199
Dimona, Israel, Egyptian overflight of,
    160
Dinitz, Simha, 219, 263n161
    arms aid requested by, 1973, 227,
        228, 231–2, 268n189
    conducts cease-fire negotiations with
        U.S., 232, 235–7, 241
Dinstein, Zvi
    decision-making and consulting
        role, 159, 189, 208
discordant UK pledges, 11–12
discovery of Egypt's readiness for
    peace with Israel, 6–7
Druze, Mount (Syria), 233

E
Eban, Abba
    in 1967 crisis; communications with
        Eshkol, 180–2, 184–7, 195,
        209; decision-making and
        consulting role, 159, 161–3,

170–3, 190–1, 202–5, 206, 208–12; discussions with Chuvakhin, 165, 171; and Israeli military policy, 202; pre-war diplomatic offensive by, 158, 167, 170–3, 177–82, 184–7, 190–1, 199–201; as recipient and source of information, 170–3, 190–1, 210–11
in 1973 crisis, arms soliciting and peace negotiating in U.S. by, 229, 231–2, 238
in cease-fire discussions, 224, 231–2, 235, 242
decision-making and consulting role, 224, 235, 242, 263–4n161, 274n34
perceptions, 51
role in U.N., 226
economic boycott, 124–5
Egypt, 3, 11, 35, 44, 53, 117, 127, 145, 160, 278, 317, 361n29
in 1967 crisis; bellicose aims of, 182–3; demands withdrawal of UNEF and closes Straits, 160–4, 187, 197; military accords with Syria, Jordan, 198, 200–2, 210, 212; military buildup, 164, 171–4, 180, 199, 210; relations with U.S., 175
in 1973 crisis; cease-fire negotiations with, 239; consequences of October-Yom-Kippur War for, 242; military offensive of, 218–20, 229; Third Army encirclement, 241–2
Egypt–Israel Armistice Agreement, 169
Eilat (Elath), Israel
blockade of, 167
Eban demands access to, 178
Nasser denies Israeli right to, 174

Elazar, David, 212
in cease-fire talks and postwar negotiations, 237
decision-making and consulting role, 215, 217–20
military preparations and assessment by, 218–23, 225–7, 231, 234, 237, 261n146
perception of probability of war by, 217
and pre-emptive strike question, 1973, 219
El Samu crisis (12–15 November 1966), 129
Entebbe Raid crisis (27 June–4 July 1976), 142–3
Eshkol, Levi
communications with U.S. during 1967 crisis, 199, 208, 211
decision-making and consulting role, 157, 161–3, 166–7, 170, 173–4, 177, 183–4, 190–1, 193–5, 201, 204–6, 208–9, 212
enlarges government, names Dayan as defense minister, 158–9, 168, 197, 199–203
evaluates decision to go to war, 180–1, 185, 188–90, 194–203, 205–6, 212
leadership and consultative style, 255–6n85, 256n86
perceptions, 47–8
reaction to closing of Straits, 170–4, 177
Evron, Ephraim
contacts with Rostow, 1967 crisis, 166, 169, 181, 182, 201, 213
decision-making and consulting role, 160
used as channel of communication by U.S., 172, 175–6, 181, 182, 185–6, 198, 207

F
four levels of Arab/Israel conflict, 9–12
France
  arms embargo of Israel declared, 207, 211
  effect on Israeli decision-making, 207
  disavows Tripartite Declaration 1950, rejects maritime force, 169, 213
  Israeli negotiations with, 165–7, 177–8
  reaction to closing Straits, 176, 195, 198, 200

G
Gahal party, 157, 159, 171, 203, 250n39
Galili, Yisrael
  in 1967 crisis; decision-making and consulting role, 159, 161, 171, 177, 189, 191, 212; and Eshkol speech, May 28, 1967, 195; military initiative suggested by, 183
  in 1973 crisis; decision-making and consulting role, 217–19, 229, 231; evaluation of military situation by, 225
Gaza, 6, 36, 41, 47, 50, 63, 68–70, 74, 82, 106, 118–19, 123, 125–6, 128–9, 139–41, 147, 164, 171, 175, 177, 192, 205–6, 245n9, 279, 283, 287–90, 292, 294–5, 297, 300–5, 308–9, 313, 323–5, 343, 350–1, 354–6
Gaza–Jericho Agreement (4 May 1994), 288–9
Gaza Raid/Czechoslovak Arms crisis (28 February 1955–23 June 1956), 128–9

Gaza Strip
  in 1967 war, 164, 175
  role in Israeli strategic plans, 171, 205, 206
Gaza War I (Operation Cast Lead; Palestinian designation, *Arab Massacre*) (27 December 2008–18 January 2009), 139
Gaza War II (Operation Protective Edge) (8 July–26 August 2014), 139–41
Gazit, Mordekhai
  in cease-fire discussions, 224
  decision-making and consulting role, 217, 219
  and pre-emptive strike question, 1973, 264n161, 265n169
General Staff (IDF), 148, 171, 177, 196, 212, 262n153, 321
  decision-making and consulting role, 158, 161, 214–17, 219
Germany, Federal Republic of, 12, 32, 38, 86, 109, 132, 163, 198, 320, 330, 342, 357, 359
Golan Heights, 40, 42, 45, 49, 71, 74, 107–8, 124, 126, 135, 137, 151, 220, 226, 230–1, 233, 283, 300, 308, 318, 323
Goldberg, Arthur, 245n8
  communications with Israeli spokesmen, 187, 213
  states U.S. goals in Security Council, 202
Great Britain, 163, 213, 232–3, 268n186
  and closing of Straits, 174, 176, 192, 193, 200, 202, 213
  Eban's diplomatic initiatives to, 165, 178–9
  Tripartite Declaration disavowed by, 169
  U.N. in strategy of, 179
Gromyko, Andrei

SUBJECT INDEX 401

George Brown's visit to, 176, 179
warnings to Israel, 207
growth of censorship in Israel, 342–8
growth of inequality in Israel society, 334–6

H
Haifa Suicide Bombing crisis (4 October–2 December 2003), 132
Hamas, 36, 39, 41, 117–19, 126, 132, 139–40, 300–2, 309, 313, 325, 356
Harman, Avraham
attempts to get U.S. commitments, 166, 169, 179, 182, 184, 187, 192, 204
decision-making and consulting role, 160, 207, 208
information transmittal role, 187, 198, 199, 201
U.S. urges restraint through, 162, 198, 199
Hebron Agreement (17 January 1997), 290
Hermon, Mount, 231, 236
Herut Party, 19–20
Herzog, Ya'acov
decision-making and consulting role, 160, 161, 171, 180, 189, 208
on Egyptian military preparations 1967, 229
Hezbollah, 37, 41, 117–18, 121, 131–2, 138, 284, 312, 346
Hofi, Yitzhak, 219
military plans by, 205
Homs, Syria, decision to bomb, 215
Hula Drainage crisis (12 February–15 May 1951), 128
Huleh Valley, threat to Israel settlements in, 226
Hussein, King, 213
Israeli warnings to, 228

military cooperation with Arab states, 198, 200

I
IDF (Israel Defense Forces)
in 1967 crisis, decision-making and consulting role, 160, 174, 196
increase in conflict-sustaining acts, 117–26
increase in poverty in Israel, 332–4
Independent Liberals, 157, 159
initial contact with Arab/Israel Conflict 1948–1952, 2
inter-communal rivalry, 10–11
Iraq, 232
joins Arab military pact, 210, 213
sends troops to Jordan, 168, 200, 208, 210
Iraq Nuclear Reactor (January–19 June 1981), 130
Israel Council for an Israel–Palestine peace agreement, 298–9
cofounder of, 321
Israel decision-makers on Jerusalem issue, 19–20
attitudinal prism, 21–4
Ben-Gurion, 17, 20–2, 24, 27–31; perception of Jerusalem issue 1949, 20–2
Eban, 18, 19, 24, 30, 32
Eshkol, 17
Eytan, Walter, 23
Fishman, Rabbi, 19, 20, 21
Herzog, Ya'acov, 19, 23, 30
Joseph, Dov, 19–23, 27, 28, 30
Meir, Golda, 17, 23
Navon, Yitzhak, 31
perceptions, 21–4
Rosen, Pinchas, 28
Shapiro, H.M., 23
Sharef, Ze'ev, 22, 24, 30, 31
Sharett, 17, 20–2, 24, 28, 29, 31

Israel decisions on Jerusalem issue, 17–20
Israel strategic decision 11 December 1949, 17, 18, 20, 25, 28, 32
process, 24–31; role of domestic interest groups, 19; implementation of Israel, 31–2
Israel–Egypt Peace Treaty, 122–3, 282–3, 310
Israeli vulnerability, 74, 301
Israel leaders' perceptions, 43–52
Israel–Lebanon Abortive Agreement (17 May 1983), 284
Israel Mobilization crisis (10 April–late June 1973), 142
Israel officials' reaction to M.B. findings on Egypt's readiness to make peace (1975), 115
Israel/Palestine Peace Talks—Kerry Mediation (29 July 2013–29 April 2014), 305–6
Israel settlements in East Jerusalem and West Bank, 123–4, 302, 306, 350
Italy, refuses to sign maritime declaration 1967 crisis, 213

J
Japan
effect of oil embargo on, 235
refuses to join maritime force, 213
Jarring Mediation (23 November 1967–March 1971), 281–2
Jerusalem, 9–10, 13, 39, 45, 47, 49, 51, 53, 74, 100, 107–8, 115–16, 119–20, 123, 137, 147, 154n5, 155n6–7, 155n9, 162, 169n190, 173, 182, 186, 208, 213, 220, 236, 241, 247n20, 248n31, 250n41, 251n43, 253n58, 261n46, 262n152, 274n239, 282–3, 290, 292–4, 296–7, 300–2, 304–6, 308, 311–13, 316, 318, 322–3, 326, 331, 345, 349–52, 354–5
issue, 15–33
Jewish–Arab, Israel–Palestine struggle for control, 15–33
Jewry, world
support sought, 184, 194
Johnson, Lyndon B.
communications with Eshkol, 168–9, 194, 199, 208
Eban's talks with, 180, 182, 184–7, 201
Eban's views of, 210–11
exchange of views with Wilson, 201, 207
guarantees made to Israel in 1964, 163
importance of views to Israeli decision-makers, 184
and Straits closure, 166, 175
urges restraint on Israel, 162–3, 172, 192–3
Jordan–Egypt Military Pact, 146, 154n2, 201
Jordan joins defense pact and enters June-Six-Day War, 198, 200, 201, 208, 210
Jordan role in October-Yom-Kippur War, 228, 232
Jordan Waters crisis (11 December 1963–5 May 1964), 141–2
June-Six-Day War (17 May–11 June 1967), 66, 134–5, 145–213

K
Karameh crisis (18–22 March 1968), 129
Keating, Kenneth

SUBJECT INDEX 403

and cease-fire negotiations 1973, 241, 267n186, 274n234
dissuades Meir from pre-emptive strike, 219, 222, 263–4n161
Israeli arms requests to, 228
"Kedem" group, 220
Kissinger, Henry
  cease-fire arrangements 1973 war by, 235, 238–9, 241, 268n186
  communicates with Israeli government, 238–9, 263–4n161
  Israeli arms requests to, 227, 228, 231–2, 268–9n189
  talks with Brezhnev, other Soviet officials, 233, 236
Kitchen Cabinet, 214–15, 219–20, 231, 233
  and crossing Suez Canal, 231
  decision-making and consulting role, 214–15, 219, 229
Knesset, 6–7, 19, 21–2, 29, 47, 115, 154n6, 161, 167, 169, 171, 173–4, 184, 189, 190, 191, 194, 197, 200, 223, 234, 238, 248n30, 256n86, 257n102, 267n181, 270n204, 273n231, 274n234, 282, 290, 321, 339, 341–2, 346, 348, 351, 353–4, 358, 361n30, 362n40
  in 1967 crisis, 161, 169, 173–4, 184, 189, 191, 194, 200, 256n86; in 1973 crisis, 223, 238
  debate on Straits closure, 173–4
  Eshkol's speeches, April–June 1967, 167, 169
  meetings during October-Yom-Kippur War, 267n181
  Meir's speeches to, 234, 238

knowledge gap between scholars and diplomacy practitioners, 1, 3, 6–7
Kosygin, Aleksei, 166
  communications with Israel, 188, 192, 206, 255n85
  George Brown's talks with, 176, 179
  visits Egypt, 1973, 234, 238

L
Labor Party, 229
Labor-*Mapam* Alignment, 171
lack of domestic pressures for conflict termination, 311–12
"land for peace," 3, 115, 281, 304, 316
Latakia, Syria, IDF attack on, 215, 233
Lebanon, 35, 37, 40–1, 79, 80–4, 95–6, 98, 99, 110, 116, 117–18, 120–4, 126, 130–3, 137–9, 141–3, 154n2, 200, 228, 269n197, 272n218, 278–9, 281–4, 286, 300, 307–8, 312, 323, 326n3, 341, 346
  remains out of 1973 war, 228
  role in 1967 war, 168
  study of decision-making during civil war in, xv
Lebanon War II (12 July–8 September 2006), 138–9
Levavi, Arye
  decision-making and consulting role, 160, 161, 189, 190, 208
  in talks with Chuvakhin, 188
Libyan Plane (21 February 1973), 129–30
Litani Operation crisis (14 March–13 June 1978), 130

M

Madrid Peace Conference (30 October–1 November 1991), 286–7
Mafdal (National Religious Party; NRP), 220
  role in Eshkol government, 157, 159, 194, 229
Maki (Israel Communist Party), 19, 174, 251n46
malpractice of politicians, 344–8
Mandelbaum Gate, Jerusalem, 213
Mapai party, 19–21, 28, 159, 191, 203, 321
Mapam party, 19, 159, 184, 191, 194, 200, 211–12, 260n140
  in 1967 government, 157, 159, 184, 191, 194, 211–12
maritime force, plans for, 1967, 192–4, 200–1, 203, 204, 213
material achievements, Israel, 329–31
McNamara, Robert
  Eban's talks with, 184
  before Senate Foreign Relations Committee, 213
Meir, Golda
  in 1967 crisis; decision-making and consulting role, 159, 171, 173, 189; statement on passage through Straits, 165
  in 1973 crisis; cease-fire negotiations, and premature acceptance of cease-fire, 231–3, 235, 238, 241–2; communications with and visit to Nixon, 228; decision-making and consulting role, 215–17, 219–25, 228–9, 231, 234; discussion and rejection of pre-emptive strike, 219–23; information processing by, 217; and military conduct of October-Yom-Kippur War, 223–5, 228–9, 231, 234; war probability and threat perceived by, 219
Meir perceptions, 48
methodological pluralism. *See* paths to knowledge
methodology. *See* paths to knowledge
Michael Brecher views, 53–116
Michael Brecher views on Israeli perceptions, 43–52
military élite
  in 1967 crisis; decision-making and consulting role, 160; pressure for war from, 180, 196
  in 1973 crisis; decision-making and consulting role, 215, 231
military lineup (1967)
  Arab forces, 145–6
  Israel forces, 146
  forces committed on 5 June 1967, 146–8
  qualitative balance, 148
military lineup (1973)
  Arab forces, 149–51
  Israel forces, 152
  qualitative balance, 152–3
military strategy, Israeli
  in 1967 crisis, 204–6, 209, 212
  in 1973 crisis, 218, 227–31, 236; Israeli military intelligence findings as trigger for crisis period, 261n146
Mizrahi Party, 19
mobilization, Israeli
  in 1967, 164, 194
  in 1973, 215, 218–22
Mohammed Sayeed Ahmad: views, 54–66
Morocco, SDW participation of, 200
Mossad, 206

SUBJECT INDEX 405

N

Nasser, Gamal Abdel
 demands UNEF withdrawal and closes Straits, 161–2, 168–70, 174
 Israeli images of, 164, 193
 negotiations of, prior to SDW, 176, 187, 203
 Soviet encouragement of provocation by, 170
 statements of aims, 197, 198, 213
national goals, 10
National Unity Government
 decision-making and consulting role, 157, 159
 formation of, June 1967, 197, 200, 203
NATO alert, May 1967, 197
NATO treaty, comparison of Eban's requested U.S. policy commitment to, 182
needs of senior citizens, 336–7
Netherlands, and maritime force plan, 192, 193
Nixon, Richard M.
 communications with Meir, other Israeli leaders, 228, 241
 decides resupply of arms to Israel, 231, 235
 perception of threat by, 262n153
 and pre-emptive strike question, 264n161
 Soviet contacts with, and cease-fire, 226, 230, 232, 235, 236, 240–2
 on Soviet role in starting before October-Yom-Kippur War, 261n146
non-violent crises (6 cases), 141–3
Norway, and maritime force plan, 199

O

October-Yom-Kippur War (5 October 1973–31 May 1974), 136–7, 214–44
 Commission of Inquiry into (Agranat Commission), 222, 226
 as dominant event in 1973 crisis period, 214
 military losses in, 243
 oil embargo, 235
 declaration of, 235
Olmert Peace Plan (September 2008), 303–5
onset phase, 4, 15–17
Operation Accountability crisis (10–31 July 1993), 131–2
Operation Dovecote, 218
Operation Grapes of Wrath/"April War" (11–27 April 1996), 132
Organization of Arab Petroleum Exporting Countries (OAPEC), 213, 235
Osama Al-Baz: views, 66–77
Oslo I Accord (20 August and 13 September 1993), 287–8, 291
Oslo II Accord (28 September 1995), 286, 288–90, 303

P

Palestine, and Palestinians
 Nasser assertion of rights of, 198
Palestine Liberation Army (PLA), 164
Palestine Partition/Israel crisis Independence (29 November 1947–20 July 1949), 133
Palestinian *Intifadas*, 302, 311, 313, 323–4, 356
 Intifada 1, 119, 121, 125
 Intifada 2, 119–20, 121, 125
paths to knowledge, 1–8

Peel Commission Report (7 July 1937), 26, 277–8
Peled, Binyamin
  decision-making and consulting role, 219, 229, 266n179
  opposes Eshkol "waiting" policy, 196
  and pre-emptive strike, 1973, 219
perceptions, 2, 4–6, 21–4, 35–52, 54, 87–8, 101–2, 126, 127, 143, 199, 214, 245n9, 275n242, 310, 315, 317, 341, 358, 361n29
  of national identity; Israel, 35–6; Palestine, 35–6
Peres perceptions, 51–2
Peres, Shimon, 172
  decision-making and consulting role, 159, 171, 184, 217
  role in cabinet reorganization, 1967, 168, 203
persistence of discordance in basic objectives, 312–14
personal disenchantment, 358–9
political hostility, 4, 117, 120–4, 126, 143
political parties
  government consultation with opposition during crises, 161, 170–1, 200, 223, 250n39
  in government crisis and formation of National Unity Government, 161, 197–203, 250n39
pre-emptive strike
  in 1967 crisis; Allon's thinking on, 191; British concern about, 176; decision for, 164; Johnson warns against, 192–3
  in 1973 crisis; decision against, 215, 218–22; informational inputs into decision, 218–19
Prime Minister, decision-making and consulting role, 215–16

Q
Qalqilya crisis (13 September–15 October 1956), 129
Qibya crisis (14 October 1953–faded), 128

R
Rabin, Yitzhak
  in 1967 crisis; decision-making and consulting role, 158, 160–4, 166–7, 170–1, 174, 177, 189, 204, 206, 208, 211; and Eshkol-military élite confrontation, 168, 196, 200, 201, 206, 208; illness of May 1967, 177, 252n48; military preparations by, 158, 167, 180, 183, 200, 201
Rabinovitch, Iamar, 53
Rafael, Gideon
  decision-making and consulting role, 160
  on Straits question in U.N., 161–2, 163, 169, 204
  U.S. communications through, 213
Rafi party
  decision-making and consulting role, 159, 171, 250n39
  in National Unity Government, 157, 159, 203
renewal of turmoil in 2015–16 Israel/Palestinian relations, 355–8
Road Map for Peace (24 June 2002), 301–3
role of domestic interest groups, 311–12
role of interviews in IR Research, 5–6, 54
Rostow, Eugene
  Eban meets with, 181
  Israeli overtures to, 166, 169, 192, 198, 207

urges restraint on Israel, 162, 172
Rottem (15 February–8 March 1960), 141
Rusk, Dean
  Israeli communications with, 181, 184, 192, 207
  and maritime force, 198
  states U.S. policy on Straits, 201–2, 204, 213

S
Sadat, Anwar al-, 53, 54, 60, 85, 100, 102, 106, 109, 110, 115–16
  in 1973 crisis; cease-fire question, 233, 234, 240, 268n186, 274n234; plans war, 261n145
Sapir, Pinhas
  appeal to world Jewry by, 194, 229
  decision-making and consulting role, 159, 171, 172, 191
  mobilization plans of, 183
  perception of probability of war by, 263n160
Saudi Arabia, 164, 200, 232
scholars' contribution to foreign policy process, 7
Shapira, Haim Moshe
  decision-making and consulting role, 173, 191
  in National Unity Government, 159, 167, 211
Sharett perceptions, 43–7
Sharm-el-Sheikh, 165, 171
  occupation of by IDF, 204–6
  UNEF leaves, 165
  U.S. policy on U.N. presence in, 175
Sharm el-Sheikh Memorandum (4 September 1999), 107, 110, 113, 120, 291
shuttle diplomacy, 137, 281, 286

Sinai, Egyptian massing of forces in, 160, 164
Sinai Incursion crisis (25 December 1948–10 January 1949), 127
South Asia field research in 1950s, 1960s, 1
Soviet Union, 29, 47, 59–61, 63, 64, 134–6, 165, 167, 169, 176–8, 186, 188, 192, 207–9, 211, 212n213, 216–17, 223, 225, 230, 233–5, 237–41, 243–4, 252n57, 254n71, 256n85, 260n135, 274n234
Straits of Tiran, 125, 134, 161, 165–6, 170, 175, 179, 185, 187, 198, 201, 209
Suez Canal, Israeli crossing of, 1973, 235
Suez Nationalization Crisis-War (26 July 1956–12 March 1957), 133–4
superpowers
  French desire for solution through, 1967, 195, 198
  involvement of in October-Yom-Kippur War, 233, 234
Syria, 6, 11, 35, 49, 53, 117, 128, 145, 162, 278, 317
  in 1967 crisis, 174, 175, 198; improves relations with Arab neighbors, 168, 200; Israeli images of, 162; military preparation of, 164, 210; shelling from Golan, and air battle in April, 162
  in 1973 crisis; Allon suggests creation of Druze state in, 233; cease-fire talks with, 238, 268n186; preparations and participation in October-Yom-Kippur War, 215, 218–20, 226, 227, 230–1

Syria Mobilization crisis (21 November–13 December 1976), 143
Syria perceptions of balance of military capability, 41–2

T
Taba Talks (21–27 January 2001), 289–90, 296–9, 303, 306
Tal, Yisrael
  decision-making and consulting role, 180, 219, 229
terrorism, 175
Thant, U, 210, 244n5
  criticized by Eban, 199
  responds to Egyptian demand to withdraw UNEF, 160
  visit to Mideast, 162, 166, 167, 176, 184, 187–8
time pressure, constraints of in 1973 crisis, 218, 219, 230–1
Tiran, Straits of, closing of, 164, 167–70
  Assad's pressure on Nasser for, 168
  effect on Israeli attitudinal prism, 161
  French position on, 165, 207
  Israeli consideration of response, 158, 165, 170–97, 198, 199, 205–6, 255n80
  maritime force plan, 192–4, 200–1, 202, 204, 213
  seen as *casus belli* by Israel, 185
  U.S. position on, 181–2
Transformative event–UN Partition Resolution 187 in 1947, 13–14
trigger mechanisms, in international crises, 160, 214, 216, 261n146
Tripartite Declaration (1950), 169, 248n23
two-state solution
  consistent advocacy of, 318–19
  co-author, peace plan for, 323–7

U
U.A.R.-Arab States Defense Pact, 198, 200–2, 210, 213
UN Conciliation Commission for Palestine (UNCCP), Lausanne Conference (27 April-12 September 1949), 278–80, 311
UN General Assembly resolutions on territorial internationalization of Jerusalem 1947, 1948, 1949, 15, 18–21, 30
  Israel leaders' perceptions, 15
  attitudes of Israel political parties–Herut, Mapai. Mapam, Maki, Mizrachi, Agudat Yisrael, 19–20
Union of Soviet Socialist Republics
  in 1967 crisis, 178, 198
  in 1973 crisis; and cease-fire negotiations, 230–2, 234, 237, 240, 242, 268n186; military threats from, 243–4; resupply of Egypt and Syria by, 227; U.S. restraint on, 233; withdrawal of advisers and families from Egypt, Syria, 261n146
  and cease-fire negotiations; Israeli images of, 211; role in provoking crisis, 165, 167, 169, 170; sends ships to Mediterranean, 200–1; threats to Israel from, 188–9; Tiran Straits closing blamed on Israel, 176
United Nations, in 1967 crisis
  attempts to defuse crisis by resort to, 161, 204

SUBJECT INDEX   409

blamed for Tiran crisis, 167–8
Charter, Israel invokes Article 51,
  165
Israeli images of, 194, 199
Jerusalem headquarters, Jordanian
  shelling of; role in 1967 crisis,
  163
Security Council; convening of, after
  closing of Straits, 164, 174,
  176, 179, 198, 200, 202, 204;
  Resolution 248, 235; U.S.
  policy toward intervention of,
  176, 181, 202
United Nations Emergency Force
  (UNEF); Egypt demands
  withdrawal of, 160–3, 165;
  Israel rejects transfer of to its
  territory, 166; U Thant
  convenes Advisory Committee,
  164
United Nations Truce Supervisory
  Organization (UNTSO),
  168
U.S. view of, 186–7, 204
United Nations, in 1973 crisis
  discussion of aggression charges,
  224
  and negotiation of cease-fire and
  Disengagement Agreements,
  239–41
  Security Council, 226, 227;
  Resolutions 344, 345, and 346;
  237, 239–40, 275n244
  United Nations Emergency Force,
  role of in Disengagement
  Agreements, 240–1
United States
  in 1967 crisis; Congressional and
  public opinion as influence on
  policy, 179, 182, 186, 201,
  204, 213; differences in
  intelligence estimates between

  agencies, 258n112; invokes
  U.N. role, 176; Israeli
  overtures to, in pre-crisis
  period, 167–9, 181–2, 184–7;
  Israeli perception of policies,
  190, 208–9, 210–11; maritime
  plan forwarded by, 192, 193,
  198, 200–1, 202–3, 208;
  Nasser challenge to, 197;
  response to closing of Straits,
  163, 166, 174–6, 184–7, 192,
  248n31; restraints on Israel,
  and withdrawal of, 194; Sixth
  Fleet movements, effect of,
  183, 213
  in 1973 crisis; cease-fire negotiation
  role, 226, 227, 230, 236,
  240–2, 267–8n186; dealings
  with Soviet Union on cease-fire
  proposals, 230, 234–5, 237;
  intelligence assessments of
  Mid-east military situation,
  217, 226–7; Israeli requests of
  aid from, 181, 225–8, 231–2,
  233, 273n27; response to
  Soviet intervention threats,
  233, 242
United States role in Arab-Israel PC,
  225
UN Partition Resolution 187 (29
  November 1947), 13–14, 278
UN Security Council Resolution 248
  (22 November 1967), 280–1

V
verbal hostility–propaganda, 117,
  126
violence in nine Arab/Israel Wars
  1948–2014, 117–21
violent crises (less than full-scale war
  (15 cases)), 127–32

W

war, 198
war aims, Israeli
 in 1973 crisis, 243–4
Warhaftig, Zerah, 159, 220
 decision-making and consulting role, 171, 191, 229
 "dove" view represented by, 183
war in Lebanon (5 June 1982–17 May 1983), 137–8
War of Attrition (8 March 1969–7 August 1970), 135–6
war, probability of
 perception of; in 1967 crisis, 161, 162, 207; in 1973 crisis, 214–18; in 1973 crisis, IDF view of, 214–18
Weizman, Ezer
 acting Chief of Staff Israel Defense Forces during Rabin's illness, 174, 177
 decision-making and consulting role, 160, 161, 171, 189, 205
West Bank, 3, 16, 25, 36, 49, 63, 68–70, 74, 82, 106–7, 113, 119–20, 123–6, 140, 219, 231, 236, 283, 287, 289–98, 300, 302–6, 308, 313, 324–5, 331, 344, 349–52, 354–6, 361n36, 362n50, 363n63
Wilson, Harold
 Israeli communications with British Prime Minister, 166, 176, 178–9, 190, 192, 193
 position on Straits, 166, 202, 204
 Washington visit of, June 1967, 207, 210, 213
Wye River Memorandum (23 October 1998), 291

Y

Yaffe, Aviad
 arranges Eshkol–Chuvakhin talks, 188
 decision-making and consulting role, 160, 161, 171, 172
Yariv, Aharon
 in 1967 crisis; decision-making and consulting role, 160–2, 171, 189, 190, 196, 208; presents intelligence briefings, 180, 183, 204; on trigger incident of crisis period, 244n2
 in 1973 crisis, on cease-fire talks, 267n186, 274n234
Yehoshafat Harkabi, 53
Yemen, 145, 147, 164, 247n18

Z

Zeira, Eliahu
 decision-making and consulting role, 217, 219, 229
 presents intelligence briefing to government, 216

GPSR Compliance
The European Union's (EU) General Product Safety Regulation (GPSR) is a set of rules that requires consumer products to be safe and our obligations to ensure this.

If you have any concerns about our products, you can contact us on

ProductSafety@springernature.com

In case Publisher is established outside the EU, the EU authorized representative is:

Springer Nature Customer Service Center GmbH
Europaplatz 3
69115 Heidelberg, Germany

www.ingramcontent.com/pod-product-compliance
Lightning Source LLC
LaVergne TN
LVHW020339260326
834688LV00045B/1445